Nahuatl Nations

Nahuatl Nations

Language Revitalization and Semiotic Sovereignty in Indigenous Mexico

Magnus Pharao Hansen

OXFORD
UNIVERSITY PRESS

Oxford University Press is a department of the University of Oxford. It furthers
the University's objective of excellence in research, scholarship, and education
by publishing worldwide. Oxford is a registered trade mark of Oxford University
Press in the UK and certain other countries.

Published in the United States of America by Oxford University Press
198 Madison Avenue, New York, NY 10016, United States of America.

© Oxford University Press 2024

All rights reserved. No part of this publication may be reproduced, stored in
a retrieval system, or transmitted, in any form or by any means, without the
prior permission in writing of Oxford University Press, or as expressly permitted
by law, by license, or under terms agreed with the appropriate reproduction
rights organization. Inquiries concerning reproduction outside the scope of the
above should be sent to the Rights Department, Oxford University Press, at the
address above.

You must not circulate this work in any other form
and you must impose this same condition on any acquirer.

CIP data is on file at the Library of Congress
ISBN 978–0–19–774616–5 (pbk.)
ISBN 978–0–19–774615–8 (hbk.)

DOI: 10.1093/oso/9780197746158.001.0001

Paperback printed by Marquis Book Printing, Canada
Hardback printed by Bridgeport National Bindery, Inc., United States of America

Contents

Acknowledgments	ix
1. Introduction: Nahuatl Revitalization in the Mexican Nation	**1**
Nahuatl: A Language in the Plural	5
Semiotic Ideologies: Valorizing Languages	11
Nationalisms: Nations with and without States	18
Communities: Of Nations and Publics	25
Communality and the Sphere of Indigenous Politics	28
The Altepetl as the Indigenous Public	30
Language as the Medium of Political Community	32
Revitalization: State-Sponsored Languages, Semiotic Sovereignty, and Emergent Vitalities	34
National Language Revitalization in Ireland	35
National Language Revitalization in Bolivia	36
The Decolonial Critique of the "Reversing Language Shift" Paradigm	37
Language Activism as a Communal Practice	40
Semiotic Sovereignty	42
Chapter Road Map	43
Methods: Interscalar, Transtemporal, and Translingual Ethnography	44
Positionalities	46
Translation Practices	48
1b. Interlude: On Transcription	**51**
Ideologies of Nahuatl Writing	51
The Sounds of Nahuatl	54
Linguistic, Historical, and Intuitive Orthography	56
Comparison of Different Conventions	66
Orthographic Relativism	67
2. From Indian Republics to Covert Publics: Colony to Nation	**68**
Colonial Language Policy in Theory and Practice	72
The Three-Stage Model of Colonial Language Change	76
Nahuatl and *Criollo* Nationalism	80
Independence: Nahuas and the Nation	82
The Cargo System as Indigenous Mutualism	85
Nahuatl Text Production in the 19th Century	86
Rebellions and Revolutions as Signs of Covert Publics	90
Nahua Publics during the Reform Wars	92
Nahua Publics in the Mexican Revolution	96
Nationalizing Nahuatl Publics	101

Lázaro Cárdenas and the Indigenous Constituency 103
Modernity and the Decline of the Nahuatl Public Spheres 111
Indigenous Activism and the Seeds of the Current Resurgence 112

3. **Nahuatl Is Very Fashionable Now: Nation Branding and Cultural Expropriation** 119
   When the State Speaks Nahuatl 123
   The Constitution in Nahuatl 124
   INALI: Standardization and Translation 126
   Nahuatl Belletrism and the Indigenous Heritage of the Nation 131
   Fashionable Nahuatl: National Expropriations of Indigenous Culture 133
   Indigenous Signs as Nation Branding 136
   Fashion as Nation Branding 138
   The Semiotic Economy of National Nativism 140
   Anti-Indigenous Backlash and Mock Nahuatl Online 142
   National Promotion of Indigenous Languages: A Critical Evaluation 146

4. **Language, Autonomy, and Indigenous Politics in Hueyapan, Morelos** 151
   Hueyapan's Municipal Independence 155
      Tlalolintle: The Earthquake 155
      Independence 156
   Friedlander's Hueyapan 157
   Another History of Hueyapan in the 20th Century: What Caused the Decline of Nahuatl? 160
      Tetela and Hueyapan: The Story of a Rivalry 160
      Traditionalist Farmers and Progressive Teachers 162
   Political Resurgence of Hueyapan in the 21st Century 164
   Multicultural Governance in Morelos 166
   Chimalnahuatlajtole: Ethnic and Linguistic Revival and Independence in Hueyapan 168
   Migration and Local Identity 170
   The Nahuatl Course 173
   Engaging Government through Cultural Politics 176
   Conclusion: From Outlaw Public to Indigenous Pride 180

5. **Land, Language, and Higher Learning in the Zongolica Highlands** 187
   The Man Who Visited Tlalokan 187
   Regions of Refuge: The Zongolica Highlands 190
   Indigenous Education as Development in the Zongolica Region 193
   A Region of Covert Abundance: An Indigenous Conceptualization of the Highlands 196
   Interculturality and the UVI 200
   Indigenous Languages in Intercultural Education 204
   A Space of Possibilities: What Grows at the UVI 209
      Community-Grounded Research 209
      Intercambio de Semillas 211

La Escuelita "*Nikan Tipowih*"	212
Indigenous Theorization	212
Monolingual Nahuatl-Language MA Program	214
Activism and Counter-Publics at the UVI	214
Knowledge, Self-Knowledge, and Territory	218

6. Nahuatl across Borders: Mexican Transnationalism in the United States — 221

Nahuatl and the Mexicayotl Movement in the United States	224
Aztlán: A Brief History of Nahuatl and Mexican Nationalism in the US Southwest	228
Nahuatl in the Genes: Race and Ancestry and Mexicayotl	232
Ancestry and Language on Facebook, March 2014	233
Mexicayotl Nahuatl Purism and Educational Practice	236
Nahuatl on the Inside: Chicano Gang Culture	240
Politics of Nahuatl in the Mexicayotl Movement	245
"Natives Against Aztlán"	247
The River and the Wall	252

7. Conclusions: The Current State of Nahuatl — 257

Communities and Language: Theorizing the Dynamics of Revitalization	260
The State of the Nation: Indigenous Mexico Now	264
Scales and Publics: Experienced and Imagined Communities	269
Semiotic Sovereignties	273
Nahuatl Futurity	274

Works Cited	277
Index	301

Acknowledgments

Being the result of some 20 years of experience and work with Nahuatl speakers and scholars, there is no way for me to extend individual thanks to everyone who has helped and supported me through the process. As does any text worth writing or reading, it stands on a foundation of intellectual and social input and support of many kinds. Some of these sources of thought, ideas, and intellectual nurture are located in the bibliography, but many others cannot be so easily listed or cited in the text.

Of most crucial importance for being able to carry out the research that led to this book have been the people in the communities in Mexico who have welcomed me into their homes, shared with me their knowledge, food, and care. Any attempt to name and enumerate them all is doomed to be absurdly deficient. But I should not fail to mention all my friends, family members, and collaborators in Hueyapan, Morelos, or the support I have received in the communities of Tequila, Tlaquilpa, Zaragoza, Cuacuila, Huauchinango, and Tancanhuitz.

From the University of Copenhagen, Brown University, the center for US–Mexican Studies at UC San Diego, the Spencer Foundation and the American Academy of Education, the Danish Independent Research Foundation, and at the Intercultural University of Veracruz and at the UNAM, I have received institutional and/or economic support at various moments during the process. At Brown I benefited from an academic life-support system: Yana Stainova, Rama Srinivasan, Bhawani Buswala, Yunus Rafiq, Susan Ellison, Josh McLeod, Yağmur Nuhrat, and Kate Blankenship, and at a distance, Jena Barchas-Liechtenstein.

I also thank my doctoral adviser, Paja Faudree, for her unwavering support and gentle attentions. She has been a truly amazing adviser, inspiring many of the core theoretical ideas of this work—often in ways so gentle that I haven't realized her contributions to my thinking, until her next article came out covering topics and solving questions that I was only then myself beginning to think about. My other committee members also provided wonderful support and intellectual stimulus: Michael Silverstein, Jessaca Leinaweaver, Stephen Houston, Kay Warren. And I have also received foundational mentorship from Una Canger, Nancy Dorian, Shirley Brice Heath, and Paul Kockelman. Several scholars have read part of the work as it was being written and helped me with their comments, which I have incorporated into the work: Judith Friedlander, Günther Dietz, Carlos Octavio Sandoval, Eric van Young, and Margarita Hidalgo. In Oaxaca, Michael Swanton was enormously generous in reading the entire book manuscript, giving highly useful and incisive comments, and then taking the time to talk me through my thoughts about how to approach his suggestions. Liv Green also read the manuscript and supplied useful editing suggestions. I have also been fortunate to participate at many of the yearly meetings of the Northwestern Nahuatl scholars, where many colleagues have contributed to my thinking, among them: Frances Karttunen, R. Joe Campbell, Kelly McDonough, Victoriano de la Cruz, Gordon Whittaker, Stephanie Wood, Ben Leeming, John Sullivan, Justyna Olko, and many others, all of whom have provided intellectual input and inspiration along the way. In Mexico, another group of scholars has helped me with their perspectives and practical support: particularly my interactions with Karen Dakin, Rafael Nava Vite, Sylvia Schmelkes, Günther Dietz, Malaquias and Adán Sánchez Rosales, Gaby Citlahua, Fortino Ramírez, Guillermo Garrido Cruz, Carlos Octavio Sandoval, and Félix Antonio Jaurégui have been important for my thinking about Indigenous education, Nahuatl, and Nahua people past and present. Diego Mendoza and Joe Roe made the useful maps, and Alicia Smith generously made a truly meaningful piece of art for the cover.

Nimechtlasohkamachilia!/Nanmechtlasohkamachilia!

I dedicate this book to the three people whose lives have been affected the most by my life as a nomadic academic, and whose constant love and support have provided the stable ground on which it was built:

Claudia:
Nomatlagech/my wandering staff

Nellike & Rosalee:
Notlasohketzalwan/my precious green feathers.

Magnus Pharao Hansen, Spring 2024

1
Introduction

Nahuatl Revitalization in the Mexican Nation

Nahuatl is one of the names of the most widely spoken Indigenous language in Mexico; somewhere between one and two million Mexicans speak one of the many different varieties of Nahuatl. The rest of the population, numbering more than 126 million, do not speak Nahuatl themselves; nevertheless, many of them may consider it an important emblem of Mexican national heritage, and they may even feel that it is somehow also their language. They know that Nahuatl was once spoken by the Aztecs, who they may consider founders of their national community, and whose island capital was transformed into Mexico City, and became the capital of the Mexican nation. Indeed, the word "Mexico" itself comes from the Nahuatl language. This makes perhaps all of Mexico, in a way, a Nahuatl nation.

In the form of place names, the Nahuatl language is inscribed into the very geography of the Mexican nation, and many of its words exist as a common stock of localisms that give Mexican Spanish its particular flavor. The average Mexican may not be consciously aware of the etymological source of these words, and many consider Nahuatl and other Indigenous languages to be essentially an aspect of the national past, rather than its present (Gutiérrez Chong 1999). As Benedict Anderson ironically noted, when describing the development of Mexican nationalism, Mexico became a nation of "Mexicans speaking in Spanish 'for' pre-Columbian 'Indian' civilizations whose languages they do not understand" (Anderson 1983, 199).

In 2008, Marcelo Ebrard, then mayor of Mexico City, seemingly decided to do something about this discrepancy, and declared that from that moment on all public employees in Mexico City had to learn Nahuatl. "A people that forgets its origins and throws out its traditions," he stated, "will be at the mercy of those who dominate global culture."[1] He insisted that this was not a mere symbolic declaration, but that the city would indeed begin to publish public

---

[1] Jo Tuckmann. 2008. City employees learn language of the Aztecs. *The Guardian*. February 28. https://www.theguardian.com/world/2008/feb/28/mexico.

documents in Nahuatl, and that functionaries had to learn the language to be able to read them and carry out their jobs.

Even though they speak the language that Mexican national mythology holds so dear, Nahuatl-speaking Mexicans, however, rarely find that the fact that they can claim ethnic ties to the group that founded the Aztec Empire affords them any special status within the Mexican national community. In fact, just as all other Indigenous groups in the country, they experience systematic marginalization. All of their socioeconomic indicators—poverty, literacy, health, employment—are substantially lower than the national average, reflecting the fact that their access to health services, education, and legal services is limited and of lower quality than for the majority population (INEGI 2005). This marginalization is the result of a long history in which the Nahua peoples first fell under a regime of exploitative colonialism and were subsequently drafted into the creation of a nation that saw them as second-class citizens.

Social stigmatization of Nahuatl speakers has also had drastic effects on the language. In hundreds of rural towns and villages where Nahuatl was the primary vernacular only decades ago, today residents see that the language may be about to disappear. In these communities, the language was transmitted to the current inhabitants in an unbroken chain from their ancestors who experienced the rise of the Aztec conquest state in the 13th century. But now, at the opening of the 21st century, Nahuatl speakers are seeing that in their communities many youths no longer speak or understand the language, and that parents no longer speak it to their children, preferring to use it only in private homes when speaking with older relatives. In many towns where it was recently spoken, Nahuatl is now all but a memory; a few words remembered by the elderly, or recited in a song, or the name of a place, are now relics, or emblems, of a past form of communal life.

In his statement, Mayor Ebrard described the language as the shared property of Mexican citizens, identifying them as a collective, in contrast with citizens of other nations in a global context. But to those who have grown up speaking Nahuatl, the language is not primarily an element of a national heritage common to all Mexicans; to them it is not a national emblem, but a communal practice of meaning-making. Moreover, it is a practice that has for centuries identified them and the people of their own communities as being different from other Mexicans, and has marked them in many contexts as less than full members of the Mexican nation. Nevertheless, at the same time, those who still speak it do so because to them the language has not been simply a stigma to be shed. They have kept it because it held value to them for various reasons: as a system of meaning through which they have learned to make sense of the world, a code enclosing a form of life, a shared practice offering them a place in a community. So, in another sense, these communities of people, who have kept the language alive as their means of everyday meaning-making and social action, are the Nahuatl nations.

Mexico City is one of many examples of how a language can disappear from a community engulfed in rapid change; once a bustling metropolis of Nahuatl-speakers, it is now centuries since Nahuatl was a major language of public communication there. Today its central plaza, the Zócalo, stunningly juxtaposes the Aztec past, represented by the excavated ruins of the Great temple of the Mexica, with the contemporary political power of the Nation, represented by the palace of government and the huge Mexican flag that often flies on the plaza (see Figure 1.1). The megalopolis reached its vast size as people left rural communities, where Indigenous languages were often spoken, for the city, in search of opportunities that were not present in the countryside. Most of the new arrivals left their Indigenous languages behind, adopting Spanish as their only language. Because of this, even though Nahuatl was once the main language spoken in the region now covered by the sprawl of the Mexican capital, today the vast majority of the inhabitants of Mexico City do not speak Nahuatl. According to official statistics, at the turn of the millennium, only 37,000 out of the almost 8 million inhabitants of Mexico City spoke Nahuatl (INEGI 2005)—most of them probably recent arrivals

Figure 1.1 The fusion of the Aztec past and the Mexican present near the Zócalo, Mexico City's Central Plaza; in the foreground, the serpent heads at the foot of the staircase of the Aztec *Templo Mayor*, and in the background, the Palace of Government.

from rural Indigenous communities.[2] Perhaps predictably, Ebrard's visions of a corps of Nahuatl-speaking public servants did not come true. Today, more than 15 years after his announcement, it would still not be an easy task to find a public employee in Mexico City who can carry out a conversation in Nahuatl, and the city government does not routinely translate documents or information into Indigenous languages. Once a living language practice has crystallized into a mere emblem, it is not easy to thaw it into a dynamic practice again.

Nevertheless, the mayor's bold pronouncement was a reflection of a major change in the way that Mexicans perceive and talk about Nahuatl and other Indigenous languages. A gradual process, the changing view of Indigenous peoples and languages in Mexican society was first signaled with the 1992 Mexican Constitution, which defines Mexico as a pluricultural nation and makes specific reference to the Indigenous peoples and their cultures as the basis for the Mexican nation. In 2003, the *Ley General de Derechos Lingüísticos de los Pueblos Indígenas* [General Law of Linguistic Rights of Indigenous Peoples] recognized Indigenous languages as co-official "national languages" with the same validity as Spanish "in the domains in which they are spoken." It also created INALI, the *Instituto Nacional de Lenguas Indígenas* [National Institute of Indigenous languages], an institute charged with the responsibility of implementing the rights to equal treatment that the law promised Mexico's speakers of Indigenous languages (Hidalgo 2006). From this time on, Indigenous languages have received increasing attention from Mexican politicians and institutions, and a new set of discourses about Indigenous languages have become prominent within the Mexican public. Where previously Indigenous languages were primarily spoken of as an obstacle to the national project of reshaping Indigenous people into Mexican citizens, linguistic diversity is now generally described as a valuable asset to the nation.

Since Ebrard's statements in 2008, thousands of people across the country, and even in other countries, have taken a renewed interest in Nahuatl. Inhabitants of rural towns have organized language programs where youths study the Indigenous language of their parents or grandparents. Nahuatl courses in which Mexicans who do not live in Indigenous communities can learn the language are taught in urban cultural venues, educational institutions, and online. Having been previously seen by the Mexican public either as an arcane language of dusty history or an embarrassing "dialect" of uneducated peasants, the use of Nahuatl now proliferates in all sorts of hip

---

[2] This figure only counts the inhabitants of the city proper, not the larger metropolitan area. Today, 24 years later the official number of inhabitants of the city is 9 million.

venues in Mexican society: in books, poems, comics, movies, music, internet memes, online fora, public signage, and official communication, much more so than was the case 20 years ago, when not much more than an occasional primary school picture book or some missionary material was printed in the language. Nahuatl is experiencing a moment of resurgence and revival, and so are the country's other Indigenous languages, all of which are increasingly assigned positive value both by the communities that speak them and by the general public. This resurgence is of course tied to an increasing global interest over the past decades in combating language endangerment through practices of revitalization or reclamation. But it is also tied to cultural politics operating at national, international and highly local levels.

This dramatic change in the role of Nahuatl in Mexican public life is the central pivot of this book because it raises several big questions about the politics of Indigenous language vitality. At the core of these questions is the relation between the Mexican nation-state and the Indigenous micro-nations that it encompasses: What happens when the same state, whose nation-building project has been the driving factor causing Indigenous peoples to give up their languages, suddenly decides to present itself as the protector of these same languages?

This book explores some of the results of the 2003 law, focusing on the political and linguistic consequences of government-driven language politics meant to revitalize the Indigenous language in Nahuatl-speaking communities. Through ethnographic studies of communities that are reclaiming Nahuatl through education, it also explores the potentialities of the law, and its potential risks and benefits, for Indigenous political communities. Ethnographic data is interpreted in relation to an account of the long-term historical trajectory of Indigenous languages in Mexico which transcends, but also links, periods and events, and in relation to an analysis of contemporary Mexican nationalism. In exploring these relations, the book also develops a theory of the relation between language and Indigenous politics.

Nahuatl: A Language in the Plural

About a million and a half Indigenous people who speak the Nahuatl language live in town-communities scattered throughout the central highland states of Puebla, Hidalgo, Tlaxcala, Morelos, and Guerrero, along the Pacific coast of Michoacán, and the gulf coast of Veracruz, and even into Durango and San Luís Potosí in the north (INEGI 2005). Nahuatl belongs to the Uto-Aztecan language family, and as such it is related to languages spoken in the United

States as far north as Idaho and in much of northern Mexico (Caballero 2011). The earliest Uto-Aztecan speaking ancestors of today's Nahua peoples lived in the US Southwest and migrated south into what is today Mexico.[3] According to INALI's 2020 survey, 1,651,958 people in Mexico spoke a variety of Nahuatl, making it Mexico's most populous Indigenous language group. The number of speakers is rising and has risen steadily since the 1950s, although at a slower rate than the Spanish-speaking monolingual population (INALI 2012). INALI divides the Nahuatl linguistic group into 30 different varieties, based on a set of not entirely clear criteria, including self-denomination, mutual intelligibility, and region.

It has become customary in academia to refer to the people who speak Nahuatl or come from historically Nahuatl-speaking communities as "Nahuas," though few Nahuatl speakers refer to themselves in that way. This is because, more than an ethnic group with a common identity, this label describes a purely linguistic grouping. The term "Nahua" groups together people and communities with a wide diversity of ethnic and political identities based on the fact that the language they speak can be linguistically classified as one of the many varieties of the Nahuatl language.

Depending on how one sees it, Nahuatl may or may not even be a "language." Another way to see it is that the label "Nahuatl" covers several dozen languages, some of them quite similar and mutually intelligible, others as distinct in grammar, vocabulary, and pronunciation as Spanish is from Italian, or as modern American English is from the Middle English of Chaucer's Canterbury Tales. One might also consider it a "language" with many divergent "dialects." To the historical linguist a "dialect" is a regional variety of a "language," and a language in turn is understood to group together a bundle of regional varieties that are potentially in an early stage of a process of divergence to become separate languages. To linguists then, "dialect" is a potentially very useful word that describes a view in which every form of speech represents a "dialect," but always a "dialect of some language" (Van Der Aa and Blommaert 2014). In this book, and in linguistic usage (Chambers and Trudgill 1998), the term describes the fuzzy zone of divergence between two historically related linguistic varieties—before they become so different that they can no longer be considered the same language. Historically, for example, there must have been a time in the past, probably more than a thousand years ago, when there was a single Nahuatl variety, which then gradually split into two as one group migrated eastward and another stayed in the western part of Central Mexico. Today we can still see that the varieties of Nahuatl in the

---

[3] Shaul 2014; Hill 2019; Hill and Merrill 2017; 3.

eastern range of the Nahuatl-speaking area have commonalities that they do not share with those in the west, and vice versa (Pharao Hansen 2014). In the sense of spatially distributed linguistic variation and as closely historically related linguistic varieties, the concept of "dialect" is important for the arguments in this book, because the distinctive features of local language varieties do not only mark the boundaries of historical Nahuatl-speaking communities, but they very frequently also come to mark the boundaries of current ones.

In Mexico, however, *dialecto* is a dirty word. It is frequently used to describe, pejoratively, the vernacular languages of the rural working class, who in Mexico historically have happened to be largely Indigenous and speak Indigenous languages. Many Mexicans understand Indigenous languages to be these kinds of "dialects": deficient semi-languages with no grammar and no writing system. In Mexico, therefore, one has to use the word with caution—both because of the discriminatory associations of the word, and because it is not always clear where boundaries between dialects and languages can be drawn. Because of this usage, a frequent slogan and hashtag used in the struggle for linguistic rights in Mexico is *todas se llaman lenguas* [they are all called languages], calling to abandon the use of *dialecto* to refer to Indigenous languages altogether. To bypass the problem of distinguishing between macro-languages and their local varieties, INALI has introduced new terminology, according to which language labels such as "Nahuatl" or "Mixtec" are considered to name "linguistic groups" (*grupos lingüísticos*) consisting of a number of related "varieties" (*variantes*). Nevertheless, in English, "varieties" is often an imprecise word that can describe any identifiable variant of a language, from the personal idiolect of an individual, to a particular register of a language, such as slang, to a regional dialect. Consequently, I will use the word "variety" to describe any delimited and identifiable way of speaking the Nahuatl language, but will occasionally talk about "dialect groups" (groups of similar and historically related varieties of Nahuatl), "dialect areas" (geographic areas inhabited by such groups), and "dialectal differences" (differences characterizing the varieties of a dialect group or area).

The language label "Nahuatl" itself is also problematic. Not all speakers of the languages that linguists call Nahuatl consider themselves to speak "Nahuatl." Some do not operate with that concept at all. The ancient Mexicas of Mexihco-Tenochtitlan would say that they spoke *mexihcacopa* "as Mexicas." Whereas, following the colonial tradition of associating the Nahuatl language with the Aztecs of Mexihco-Tenochtitlan, today many Nahuatl speakers refer to themselves and to their language as *mexicano*—generally pronounced in Spanish as [mehikano], rarely in Nahuatl as [meʃikano]. This usage of *mexicano* as referring specifically to Nahuatl speakers is in fact the original one, from before the establishment of the Mexican nation-state. In many communities, "Nahuatl" is a new word, introduced by linguists or people who have read some scholarly literature, or more recently by the media and government institutions. But like *mexicano*, the word "Nahuatl" goes back at least to the early colonial period where it was used to describe a "clear sound," and interpreters who were able to translate from the many vernacular languages into the most widely used one (Nahuatl) were called *nahuatlahtohqueh*, "Nahuatl speakers/clear sound speakers" (in Nahuatl) or *Nahuatlatos* (in Spanish). Another great many speakers of "Nahuatl" call their language some variant of the word /ma:se:waltlahtol/ which means "language of the commoners" or "language of the Indians." This word is based on the root /ma:se:walli/ (pl. *ma:se:walmeh/ma:se:waltin*), which originally referred to a member of the commoner class in Mesoamerican feudal society, but which acquired the general meaning "Indian" in the colonial period. In the area around Tatahuicapan in southern Veracruz, the language is referred to as *mela'tahtol*, "true language," and one speaker told me that he found the use of the word *masewaltlahtol* to be offensive, because it equated Nahuatl speakers with colonial serfs. For speakers of many of the varieties, the word "Nahuatl" is impossible to use as the endonym for their variety because it ends with the [tl] sound which is not found in all varieties, hence they tend to call their language "Nawat," as speakers in the Puebla Highlands, Tabasco and El Salvador do. Nawat speakers in El Salvador are also opposed to the use of the label "Pipil," which has been applied to many of the Central American varieties at least since the colonial period, but which for them is derogatory, meaning "children" (Boitel 2021a, 2022b).[4]

So, as the Russian literary theorist Mikhail Bakhtin (1981, 293) teaches us, there are no neutral words, no one label that fits all. Given that a neutral term is impossible to find, in this work, following the prevalent usage in linguistics and scholarship, I will use the term "Nahuatl" when referring to all the

---

[4] In the ideal version of this book, there would be a chapter about the politics of revitalization of Nawat in El Salvador, which is in many aspects similar to the Mexican case, but also very different in some important ways. Nawat speakers migrated to El Salvador from Mexico probably in the 10th century CE, and the varieties of El Salvador are closely related to the varieties spoken in southern Veracruz and Tabasco. In the 1930s the Salvadoran dictatorship feared an Indigenous communist uprising, and reacted by conducting a genocide against the Nawa population. This caused the remaining Nawa speakers to disavow the language (since speaking it put them at risk), and at the end of the 20th century the language was often described as extinct. Nevertheless, there were small pockets of speakers secretly keeping the language alive, and in the early 21st century, several language reclamation movements began, some aligned with a new form of state multicultural nationalism, some aligned with Mexican and US ideologies of *mexicayotl* (see Chapter 6) and others based on local community projects in the speakers' hometowns. This fascinating, but at this point imaginary, chapter, however, must be published elsewhere. Meanwhile, interested readers may consult Gould and Lauria-Santiago 2008; Boitel 2021a, 2021b, 2022a; and Campbell 1985.

varieties of the Nahuatl "linguistic group." When referring to specific varieties, I will try to use the preferred nomenclature of its speakers, whether Nahuatl, Mexicano, Masewaltlahtol, Mela'tahtol, Nawat, or another—but inevitably I will be unable to satisfy everyone's preferences. There is no semantically or grammatically (or politically) satisfactory way to inflect the word *Nahuatl* in the plural.

Just as it is hard to say whether Nahuatl is one or many languages, it is hard to say whether Nahuatl speakers would conceive of themselves as an ethnic group, or whether "Nahuas" is more of an externally established ethnic category to which Nahuatl speakers have been ascribed. As will become clear through the book, this varies, depending on circumstances. Group identities are never static or totalizing, and Nahuatl speakers may of course identify with each other under circumstances where a notion of forming a language community comes to the fore. This is usually just one among many different ways of identifying, depending on context and the specifics of whom they are identifying with, or in contrast to, in a given moment. They may identify nationally as Mexicans, in contrast with people from other nation-states, or as *indígena* when such an identity is prompted in an interaction with the Mexican state and its institutions or representatives. Or they may often identify as *macehualmeh*, a Nahuatl word originally meaning "commoner," but today often used as a term that constructs a rural and racialized peasant-class identity, in contrast to typically *mestizo* city-dwellers (Sandstrom 1991). All of these forms of identities, whether based on language communities, class affiliations, or the political concept of indigeneity, may take on meaning for Nahuatl speakers in different social contexts. Among all these different sources of group identity, the local town-community holds a special significance for most Nahuatl speakers, and indeed for most Indigenous Mesoamerican peoples.

Such town-communities are known in Nahuatl as *altepetl* (pl. *altepemeh*), which literally means "water-mountain." The same word was used by pre-Hispanic Nahuatl speakers to refer to the type of self-governing city-state that was the primary political unit throughout Mesoamerican culture (Berdan 2008, 108; Horn 2014). In that period, Nahuatl-speaking communities were never united in a joint pan-Nahua ethno-political project, but rather formed loose networks of independent city-states that competed and waged war with each other, dominated and paid tribute to each other, and made alliances and federations with each other, but always with the interest of their own local polity at heart.

Today such local *altepetl* communities also make up the social spheres in which the Nahuatl language exists, and each community is likely to have its specific way of speaking the language. Towns in a specific region will usually have mutually intelligible varieties of Nahuatl, but nonetheless, there are still often noticeable differences, in intonation and speech melody, in vocabulary, or in grammar—even between varieties spoken in neighboring towns. From one region to the next, the language may be different enough that they could be considered distinct languages if one considers only linguistic differences or the degree of mutual intelligibility. These local varieties of Nahuatl are intimately bound to the local communities that speak them and to their local way of life. Nahuatl speakers in one town often speak the language only with other community members, but use Spanish to speak with outsiders, even outsiders who speak another variety of Nahuatl. Working with the concept of "communality," which has been central to theorizations of Indigenous political communities in Mexico, the late Mexican linguist Leopoldo Valiñas has suggested referring to the local forms of Indigenous Mexican languages as *communalects*—emphasizing the symbiotic relation between the language variety and the local communities and their communal forms of life (Valiñas Coalla 2010). The concept of the communalect and the way it emphasizes communal ownership of language varieties is central to my understanding Nahua language politics. While to the linguist, or to the Mexican nation, Nahuatl may be "a language" that can be an object for study, description, representation or celebration, to speakers themselves the linguistic entity of social relevance is likely to be the individual communalect.

Now that we have seen how the label "Nahuatl" covers what is really a mosaic of patterned linguistic diversity, I can proceed to reassemble it in a form where the patterns can be located and described. The following map (Figure 1.2) shows the areas where Nahuatl varieties are spoken in Mexico and El Salvador, marking out the main areas where Nahuan languages are spoken. Using the analysis of Nahuatl dialectology first developed by Canger (1988), the map represents the western dialect group, the central subarea of the western area, and the varieties classified as belonging to the eastern dialect group (Pharao Hansen 2014). As Faudree (2013, 31) notes, these "blotches of color" render some things visible, while obscuring others. The map tells us nothing about speaker demographics or language vitality, or degrees of intelligibility between varieties, or political identities. It glosses over the significant diversity within each area; it also doesn't represent any of the other languages also spoken in the same areas, and it doesn't show the many communities of Nahuatl-speaking migrants across Mexico and in the United States. It just tells us a little something about the spatial distribution of different Nahuatl varieties.

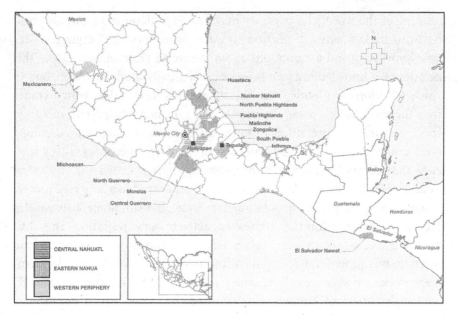

Figure 1.2 Nahuatl dialectology: map of the main areas where Nahua languages are spoken, including the varieties in Mexico and El Salvador. The areas are shaded to show the affiliations with the major dialectal groupings of Nahuatl: the Eastern, Central, and Western branches of the Nahuan language family. The towns of Hueyapan and Tequila, the ethnographic locations of Chapters 4 and 5, respectively, are also marked.
Map by Diego Mendoza Hernández.

Semiotic Ideologies: Valorizing Languages

The theoretical approach to language taken throughout this work builds on the tradition of linguistic anthropology that is informed by the semiotic theories of C. S. Peirce (see also Hanks 1996 for a formulation of this theory of meaning). Central to this approach is the concept of *indexicality*, which describes the way in which linguistic signs may point to, or *index*, other signs or concepts with which they are associated (Silverstein 1976). Indexicality is the way in which linguistic signs confer other kinds of meaning than that which is the strictly semantic or referential content of words. For example, how a subtle difference in the pronunciation of a word may tell us something about the identity of the speaker, or how we may understand the same word in one sense in one context and in different sense in another.

Indexicality works because whenever a human language user perceives a certain linguistic sign used by someone else, they interpret it to find its meaning. The act of interpretation includes finding not only the *denotational* meaning of the word (the sense we may find in a dictionary), but also how the word makes sense in relation to other aspects of the language user's basic knowledge and assumptions about the world (Kockelman 2010). This includes tacit knowledge about how a sign is usually used, by whom, and in which situations and with what objectives. This knowledge, which comes from the interpreter's prior experience and previous interpretations of the world, permits interpretations of indexical signs. And when shared among interlocutors, it enables shared understandings of sign meanings. This knowledge that allows interpretation of indexical signs is called the "indexical ground" (Hanks 1992). Whenever we encounter a word in a language that we recognize, we interpret its denotational meaning, but simultaneously we also interpret its indexes. It is the indexes that activate our expectations and ideas about the language—what it is called, where it comes from, how, when, and by whom it is supposed to be spoken, and so on. These ideas about how language works are what we call "language ideologies," and they operate silently and largely outside of our awareness as we weigh our own words and those of others in our everyday languaging activities. But they may also rise to awareness, especially as language itself becomes the object of discourse: when we talk about languages and express our otherwise tacit evaluations discursively, using *metalinguistic discourse* (i.e., "discourse about language") to speak about "correct language," "formal usage," "slang"—or about "Indigenous languages" or "the standard language." The importance of language ideologies and metalinguistic discourse for language activism can hardly be overstated, as it is only through their mediation that we may we communicate the relative importance of different languages in different contexts, and our ideas and evaluations of how and when to speak them.

This crucial importance of language ideology and indexicality may be best illustrated by example: a few days after first arriving in Hueyapan, Morelos, in October 2003, I was introduced to Javier, a teacher from the town. He was an elementary school teacher in Mexico City, but also taught Nahuatl language at a high school. He was a big gruff man, and when he heard that I had come to Hueyapan to study Nahuatl he became visibly agitated and launched into a diatribe: "No one speaks Nahuatl here! Nobody here knows how to speak real Nahuatl; they just know some words and mix it together with Spanish. If you want to learn Nahuatl, you have to go somewhere else. Go to Mexico City, there you can learn real Nahuatl at the University. What people speak here is not Nahuatl!"

Javier's reaction makes it clear that even the evaluation of what counts as "real Nahuatl" and what counts as "not Nahuatl" depends on an ideological stance. To Javier, only Nahuatl unmixed with Spanish was worth speaking, and he associated the local mixed language with illiterate peasants of his hometown (including his own parents), but he located the "correct, true, Nahuatl" in universities and cities. In this way, a language ideology—specifically an ideology that has been called "purism"—determines whether Nahuatl, and what kind of Nahuatl, is to be considered worthy of being spoken. Such ideologies underlie any decision about which languages to speak where and how, and fuel any decision to support or revitalize, or punish, the use of Indigenous language. For this reason, language ideologies, and the way indexicality ties together arrays of ideological stances, linguistic forms, and individual identities, are central to the study of language-revitalization practices in linguistic anthropology.

There is an irony or a paradox inherent in the ideology of linguistic purism when applied to minority languages. As pointed out by Kathryn Woolard, who has studied language politics and nationalism in Catalonia, even language activists fighting to save their own languages often proceed from the same "notions of language that have led to their oppression and/or suppression . . . imposing standards, elevating literate forms and uses, and negatively sanctioning variability in order to demonstrate the reality, validity and integrity of their languages" (Woolard 1998, 17). The literature on language revitalization within the field of linguistic anthropology has frequently pointed to mismatches between what actors engaged in language revitalization think they are doing and the methods with which they strive to achieve their objectives. Scholars in sociolinguistics working on the relation between nations and the construction of national languages have centered the role of authority in linguistic prescriptivism (Milroy and Milroy 1999). They study how political actors and entities can claim the authority to regulate what the national language is or should be, and how this authority is constructed by different national institutions, such as national language academies, or official language policies implemented through educational systems. While prescriptivism works primarily from the top down, as political institutions seek to regulate language use, another language ideology, purism, tends to work between individuals who police each other's language use. The ideology of purism holds that distinct languages must be kept separate by the speakers, in order that they may be conserved in their "pure state." Purism is interesting as an ideology, because it is often espoused by ordinary people who learn this way of thinking about language in school, and because its tenets contrast sharply with how linguists understand the nature of language. Most linguists would say that there is no such thing as a pure language, and that all languages show signs of having been influenced by other languages, through loanwords and through the ways multilingual speakers unconsciously and inevitably draw on resources from different linguistic repertoires, mixing them. The study of purism in minority languages has been of central interest to linguistic anthropologists because it provides a prime example of how practice is both different from and influenced by ideology. Those who espouse purist language attitudes may be highly attentive to certain kinds of language mixing, but at the same time, they may not even be aware of other ways in which their language is already mixed. And even as they forcefully enunciate purist stances, their actual language use is likely to unconsciously exhibit the same kinds of mixture that they are criticizing.

Purism and its role in regulating the use of Indigenous language has been a significant topic in sociolinguistic studies of Nahuatl since Jane and Kenneth Hill published *Speaking Mexicano*, the first sociolinguistic monograph on any Nahuatl variety (Hill and Hill 1986). It studied the variety spoken in the Malinche region of Tlaxcala, called Mexicano by its speakers. It was a detailed study of the linguistic practices and ideologies of Nahuatl speakers in the region. In many towns in this area, the process of language shift was already in an advanced stage in the 1980s, and the Hills' study focused on understanding the political dynamics underlying the shift. They noted that the Mexicano variety of Nahuatl spoken by most people in the Malinche region was heavily influenced by Spanish, having borrowed words, grammar, and sentence structure from the dominant language. But they also noted that the degree to which Spanish loanwords were used varied a good deal between different speakers and different social contexts. To understand the social processes behind this spectrum of language mixture, they theorized that the use of language intertwining was motivated by ideologies that tied the two languages to distinct social domains and functions. Because of its relation to the national sphere of politics and power, Spanish was considered a language of power and domination. Consequently, the registers of Mexicano that exhibited the highest degrees of Spanish influence could be used as a "code of power," used by speakers to position themselves as powerful individuals with important ties in the political sphere outside of the local community—for example, in public political speeches. In contrast, the Indigenous language was associated with the domestic sphere and interactions among family members and close friends, and registers that drew heavily on the Indigenous grammar and lexicon became a "code of solidarity" used primarily in intimate and private settings. The Hills posited that a process they referred to as "syncretism" served to suppress the distinction between the two linguistic codes in the context of speaking Mexicano, and made it possible for both codes to coexist in the same utterances. Their study was foundational for the field of sociolinguistic studies of code mixing, and sparked interest in the social context of language shift. A series of studies of language mixing between Nahuatl and Spanish followed the example of the Hills: José Antonio Flores Farfán, a Mexican sociolinguist, published a study of Spanish–Nahuatl code mixing in central Guerrero (Flores Farfán 1995). Like other sociolinguistic scholars studying language death, Flores Farfán sees language mixing as a stage in the process of attrition affecting moribund languages. Jacqueline Messing, a student of the Hills, continued their studies in the Malinche region, studying the inception of language-revitalization projects in the region, and the language ideologies leading Tlaxcalan youths to either abandon or study the Nahuatl language in school.[5]

In their descriptions of purist ideologies at work among speakers of the Malinche Mexicano, the Hills showed that the purist ideology goes hand in hand with certain other attitudes toward identity and society, and with a claim to status and power within the community. Similarly, Michael Silverstein conceptualized purism and attitudes about what language is, and how it should be used, as *metapragmatic* ideologies or discourses—the use of language to regulate language use.[6] This reflexive use of normative language to describe language and prescribe linguistic usage became the topic of many subsequent studies. This large body of work in linguistic anthropology has shown the important role of metapragmatic language ideologies, as a nexus of sociopolitical and discursive phenomena, in giving language multiple layers of social meaning in addition to its merely referential meaning. I draw on this work when I conceptualize how the various people who take an interest in the Nahuatl language and the many different ways of speaking it motivate their actions and opinions.

Efforts aiming to strengthen endangered languages can be based on different language ideologies. Errington (2003) distinguished between localist, comparativist, and rights-based language ideologies in language endangerment and revitalization discourses. The first values minority languages as intimately tied to local communities and what makes them culturally distinctive; the second values languages as representative of a shared human cultural heritage; and the last values minority languages as the expression of the basic right of humans to engage the world through the language of their community. Each of these ideologies comes with a built-in risk or drawback: localist language ideology risks promoting essentialist ideas of language, such as purism or nativism; comparativist language ideology values abstract diversity, but not necessarily individual people or language varieties; the rights-based

---

[5] Messing 2002, 2007a, 2007b, 2013.
[6] Silverstein 1976, 1981, 1992, 1993, 1998, 2003, 2014, 2018.

ideology risks making language shift a matter of only individual decisions, without attending to how such decisions are grounded in collective and/or class-based contexts of inequality.

In the metalinguistic discourse of language revitalization in Mexico, I have also found three different types of language ideologies that each motivate a different form of Nahuatl language activism: nationalist, ethnopolitical, and communal language ideologies. Each of these ideological types participates in different projects of language activism, and I believe that each of them appeals to different groups of people. Where nationalist purism sees linguistic authority as emanating from the myths of the nation-state, and ethnopolitical purism sees it as historically anchored in the origins of a specific minority ethnic group, communal language purism sees linguistic authority as tied to a place, a localized community from which a local set of norms emerge, and in which they hold sway. Often highly local varieties of languages, such as the varieties characteristic of individual towns or rural areas, have been deprecated by nationalist projects of standardization and homogenization. Or they have been occasionally used as a source of local flavor and authenticity, by elites addressing locals and wanting to sound like a local. Philosopher Dale Turner describes the relation between language and community: "to be an active language user means that you are a member of a community, you share and participate in linguistic practices that in a sense belong to that community" (Turner 2020, 177). This relation of mutual belonging between place, community, language, and speakers is what motivates communal language purism, and which makes it different from the appeal to notions of correctness imposed by authority, which are usually associated with linguistic purism.

Language participates in the creation of communities at all scales; from the micro-scale of the momentary community in a dialogue or group conversation; to communities based on shared practices or interests or residence in a place with their own specialized vocabulary; to the delimitation of larger and more enduring regions such as states, cities, or territories, with their own names and identifiable accents or linguistic varieties; to macro-communities of speakers of specific named languages such as English or Spanish or Nahuatl, who may share very little apart from the language. Recent scholarship in sociolinguistics and linguistic anthropology has used the concept of *sociolinguistic scales* to describe the process in which enregistered linguistic varieties map onto imagined communities with different scopes, some of which encompass others (Faudree 2014). In this line of thinking, ideas and discourses about "diversity" regulate and manipulate social scales (Faudree and Schulthies 2015; Faudree 2015b), and structure space (Blommaert 2013).

One might consider the process of mapping across scales and domains one of mutual constitution, in which localities constitute languages, while languages also participate in constituting locality—"producing locality," in the terminology of Appadurai (1996). However, I mean to suggest that in addition to the overtly political uses of language as a scale-making tool, there is also a less conscious and perhaps even intimate aspect to "diversity," which comes into being through the way that human subjectivity is shaped by experience and participation in concrete sociality. In the context of language activism, even minor linguistic differences can produce strong experiences in speakers who have grown up speaking the language, because they produce what Sapir called a different "form feeling" (1949), or an "intimate grammar" (Webster 2010). This aesthetic-subjective aspect of the relation between people, their places, and their communities contributes to giving communal ideologies of language a particularly strong appeal, and to making this a force to be taken into consideration in projects of language revitalization.

In Hueyapan, I have a friend, Don Rosalio. He is a farmer by trade, specializing in fruticulture. Behind his house, he tends to his blackberry vines, with large purple berries clinging to wires strung out between wooden poles, and to his orchard of sweet peaches and large Hass avocados. But he also likes to read and debate, and whenever we meet, we discuss everything from astrophysics and theology to European and Mexican history. He is bilingual in Spanish and Nahuatl, but he strongly prefers Nahuatl, and if he had a choice, he would use Nahuatl all the time. Speaking with him, I find I have to switch to Spanish when I can no longer find a way to make my limited vocabulary sustain a discussion about evolutionary theory or digital technology. He has used his acute linguistic awareness to develop his own system for writing Nahuatl, specifically for writing the Hueyapan variety and its distinctive features. Once, when we were discussing his orthography and the Nahuatl course taught in Hueyapan (described in Chapter 5), he expressed worry that one of the teachers in the course had lived for a while in another Nahuatl speech community. "They shouldn't be bringing in influence from other places," he said, "because if we are reviving a Nahuatl that doesn't belong to us, then what is the point? [Spanish: ¿que caso tiene?]" Javier's purism was the purism of the nationalist ideology, which holds that the Aztecs of the 16th century were the pinnacle of Indigenous civilization and everything that differs from that is wrong. Don Rosalio's language ideology is also a form of purism, but in contradiction to Javier's ideology, which deprecates the local variety, Don Rosalio takes that variety as the norm to be maintained, the variety that is tied to his own community, and his own experience of growing up as a Nahuatl speaker there.

Wittgenstein, in *Philosophical Investigations*, told us that to "imagine a language means to imagine a form of life" (2010, #19). In trying to capture the intimate relation between communities, language varieties, and the people who speak them, I rely on Wittgenstein's notion of "forms of life" to conceptualize the way linguistic meaning is grounded in the everyday life of a specific community. The habits of everyday life and the environment in which it takes place motivate the need for certain concepts and provide those concepts with their particular, concrete meaning. This relation creates an intimate experiential bond between our own way of speaking and our own way of life, a bond that can potentially unite us with people with similar ways of speaking and living. That bond is at the core of the political power of language.

Nationalisms: Nations with and without States

This book is also a study of nationalism, and an analysis of the relation between languages and nations. The case of Nahuatl as a national language illustrates the contingent and complicated relations between linguistic varieties, social identities, and the political movements that seek to unite them. The argument of the book proceeds from the observation that there is a disjuncture between the way the Mexican state motivates its decisions to engage with Indigenous language, and the way that Nahuatl is meaningful in the daily lives of those who speak it. This is of course partly a question of scale, the imagined community of the nation, and the face-to-face community of the *altepetl*, but that is not all; there is a qualitative difference as well. This requires us to begin by theorizing the relations between languages and the groups of people who speak them—whether conceptualized as nations, ethnic groups, or as *altepetl*-type communities.

European conceptualizations of the "nation" have tended to understand it as defined by group differences in cultural and linguistic traits. Among them, a *primordialist* understanding of nationalism would see language and linguistic unity as an element that precedes the nation and gives it its existence, whereas *constructionist* accounts have tended to see national unity, including cultural and linguistic unity, as a product of the establishment of a national state (Özkirimli 2010).

In Europe, political projects of nationalism have sought to turn patchworks of heterogenous communities into states that were relatively culturally and linguistically homogeneous, and to do so they have had to actively work to create unified cultural identities and to homogenize the national community. In doing this, they have often chosen to forcefully suppress or assimilate ethnic minorities, and to strive to erase regional diversity within the national border (Gellner 1983, 48–49). In postcolonial countries, ethnic and cultural diversity was often a much more salient starting point, where settler communities of European extraction lived surrounded by colonized Indigenous groups that happened to find themselves within the borders of the would-be nations. Postcolonial nationalists have faced the task of finding ways to create a convincingly coherent national construct as a bricolage of cultural and linguistic traits from settlers and from Indigenous groups. In the last decades of the 20th century, liberal thinkers of multiculturalism (e.g., Taylor 1994 and Kymlicka 1995) have sought to reconceptualize settler states as acultural civic states, where cultural difference is located exclusively in the private domain, outside of the public domain of civic engagement, and therefore does not threaten the state's hegemony. The state may be able to grant *recognition* of cultural difference, and recognition of citizens' membership in different ethnic communities, but it does so by depoliticizing Indigenous forms of life, and by conceptualizing their claims against the state as symbolic rather than substantial. Theorists of recognition would have it that the symbolic act of recognition is itself able to heal the damage done by colonial violence and dispossession, making further concrete, political concessions, such as reparations or sovereignty, unnecessary. This approach has been widely influential in the ways settler states have reorganized their nationalisms away from ethnocidal assimilationist policies, and toward taking a more tolerant and accepting stance toward Indigenous peoples within their boundaries.

Conversely, Indigenous groups have struggled to find ways to conceive of their own relation with the national community posited by the settler state; such struggles are documented in a substantial body of anthropological literature.[7] In practice, the process of postcolonial nation-craft, also in its liberal multiculturalist form, forces Indigenous groups to accept some kind of status along the lines of a "nation within a nation." That is, they find themselves in a liminal space, where they are at once recognized as having the defining traits of a nation, but not allowed the full sovereignty that a nationalist ideology would suggest as the appropriate manifestation of nationhood. In recent years, Indigenous intellectuals throughout the Americas have worked to conceptualize this liminal space that their communities find themselves inhabiting in order to point out directions toward potential political futures.[8] This new generation of Indigenous thinkers have continuously problematized

---

[7] See, e.g., Postero 2007, 2017; Povinelli 2002, 2012; Warren 1998; Hale 1997, 2004, 2005.
[8] See, e.g., Coulthard 2014; Simpson 2014; Aguilar Gil 2018; Tzul et al. 2019; Cayuqueo 2018; Díaz Gómez, Hernández, and Jiménez 2007; Rivera Cusicanqui 2012; Tzul 2018; Loncon Antileo 2020.

the liberal multiculturalist paradigm of recognition, and in so doing, the key question leading toward potential Indigenous futures has been the definition of "sovereignty." In the United States and Canada, Indigenous communities have been historically recognized as sovereign nations that have entered into a confederation with the settler state. However, this recognition has been largely symbolic and administrative, and rarely reflected in concrete political recognition of the sovereign right of governance of Indigenous communities.

Mohawk anthropologist Audra Simpson (2014) has described how the project of national sovereignty of the Mohawk Nation is continuously interrupted by the brute facts of a US–Canadian realpolitik. The Mohawk Nation straddles the border between two settler states that may at times be willing to recognize Indigenous nationality at a purely symbolic level, but refuses to do so in concrete ways that would constitute the Mohawk Nation as an equal to them. Arguing that this essentially noncommittal stance of settler states makes the quest for meaningful recognition futile, Yellow-knife Dene scholar Glen Sean Coulthard (2014) suggests that Indigenous communities should cease to strive for symbolic recognition from the settler state, since doing so reversely entails the recognition of the state's right to grant recognition. Rather, he recommends "turning away" from the settler state to pursue a self-recognition that would allow the Indigenous people to define their own political futures independently of the whims and wiles of the settler state. In Native North America, nationalism is not only the project of the settler state, but Indigenous nations have their own submerged nationalisms and national projects that they are increasingly prioritizing.

In Mexico, as we shall see in Chapter 2, colonialization proceeded differently from how it worked in the United States and Canada. The Mexican state never legally recognized Indigenous groups as equivalent to sovereign nations, with legal rights to self-determination. When Mexico became independent in 1821 after 300 years as a colony, a formalized political relation between Indigenous communities and the settler state was abolished. Since then, Mexican nationalism has been a project of the state, through which it has sought to forge a single coherent national unit, as an amalgam of Indigenous and settler cultural elements—the hybridizing project called *mestizaje* (Miller 2004). In this process, the state and its elites have picked out elements from Indigenous cultural repertoires, tacking them onto their own cultural heritage, to lend it distinct local flavor and authenticity. These elites have often belonged to the settler communities, but at times, Indigenous elites have participated in the project of *mestizaje* and nation-building, promoting traits from their own cultures as elements of a shared national culture. This has particularly been the case for Nahua elites, who have found themselves closer to the state apparatus than many other Indigenous groups. Just as Indigenous territories provided the natural resources needed for nation-building, Indigenous communities were a stock of semiotic resources up for grabs, from which the symbolism of this new nation could be forged. In the Mexican national project, these peoples were themselves destined for disappearance, as they were gradually incorporated into the national community, giving up the cultural signs that identified them as an ethnic group, adding them instead to the great national melting pot (Gutiérrez Chong 1999). Whereas in the United States, the early form of state nationalism explicitly excluded Indigenous communities by relating to them as nations that they aimed to gradually out-compete, in Mexico early state nationalism aimed to assimilate them—though when this became inconvenient, it sought to destroy them, as in the case of the Yaqui (Hu-deHart 2016; Haake 2007), the Cruzoob Maya of the Caste War (Rugeley 2009), and the Nahua Zapatistas of Morelos during the revolution (Pharao Hansen 2024).

Because of this history, in Mexico it is not commonplace to conceive of Indigenous peoples or their communities as "nations." Rather, the norm is to speak of *pueblos indígenas* (Indigenous peoples) or *pueblos originarios* (aboriginal peoples) that are organized politically and geographically into distinct local *comunidades* (communities), and are classified culturally into different *grupos étnicos* (ethnic groups) or linguistically into *grupos etnolingüísticos* (ethnolinguistic groups). The legal status of Indigenous Mexicans is simply as Mexican citizens, and though they may at the same time be members of a specific community and represent a specific ethnic group, such a relationship is not an official status that pertains to them as individuals. So officially, in Mexican law, there is no "Nahuatl nation," only a cultural-linguistic group of Nahua people, defined as people who belong to communities that speak, or that have historically spoken, Nahuatl.

Precisely because they are centered in local communities and not in a pan-ethnic identity movement, Indigenous linguistic revitalization efforts are not necessarily in opposition to the Mexican nation-state. Only the most fervent Nahua political activists would imagine themselves as members of a sovereign "Nahua nation," let alone seek to promote such an ideology as a basis for Indigenous politics. Indeed, Indigenous political movements since the 1930s and up until now have tended to struggle to achieve a more meaningful integration into the nation, sometimes under the slogan "Never again a Mexico without us!" They do not see language revitalization as a step toward some future independent ethnostate. Rather, they are "localist" or communal; their aim is to be able to maintain and cultivate the cultural and linguistic practices of their own *altepetl* communities—sometimes this entails working toward political independence at the municipal level. My impression is that most Nahua people consider the project of cultural revival, and even the project of pursuing a kind of political sovereignty through municipal independence, to be entirely compatible with participating as citizens and nationals of a Mexican nation-state. Vice versa, with the intentions laid out in the General Law of Linguistic Rights, the Mexican state signals that it finds the desire of Indigenous peoples for continued participation in their own forms of communal life to be compatible with the national project. Hence, the question becomes what type and degree of ethnic, linguistic, or political sovereignty is possible and desirable for Indigenous minorities within the Mexican nation.

Since Nahua communities and the Mexican state are not currently competing for exclusive dominion, but rather are seeking ways of coexisting, it may seem that there is a reasonable alignment between the wishes of Nahua people and the Mexican state's desire to use Indigenous cultural signs as an emblematic element of a broad national culture. If most Mexicans feel that Indigenous languages are valuable to the nation, and that therefore they should be supported and protected, then that should in theory make it easier for Indigenous communities to get the state to invest resources in supporting their struggle for cultural *survivance* (Gerald Vizenor's coinage referring to the act of surviving in resistance; Vizenor 1999). Indeed, this is the mainstream view in Mexican politics, and also a very common view among activists of Indigenous language and culture in Mexico. One aim of this book is to question this narrative of a mutually beneficial alliance between Indigenous communities and the Mexican state about the maintenance and revitalization of Indigenous languages. This questioning is animated by a doubt about whether mainstream understandings of the role of language in the political life of Mexican Indigenous communities are sufficiently well-developed for Indigenous communities to feel safe that the political projects they wish to pursue are compatible with state guardianship of Indigenous cultural and linguistic resources. The risk is that it may become yet another practice associated with forms of "internal colonialism" (Gutiérrez Chong 2010) and forms of intangible extractivism of the kind denounced by scholars like Simpson (2017; Simpson and Klein 2017), Grosfoguel (2016), and Rivera Cusicanqui (2012).

Anthropologists have interrogated the politics of language endangerment and revitalization, pointing out how official discourses that ascribe positive value to Indigenous languages are often prepackaged with liberal multiculturalist approaches to cultural difference (Duchêne and Heller 2008). Languages are represented as "culture," and therefore relegated to the private domain, outside of the civic public. Just as governments may subsidize clog dancing events or avant-garde art installations, they may also support the teaching of Indigenous languages as a form of recognition of this particular type of cultural expression—as long as it is relatively cheap, makes for good publicity for the state, and the responsibility if it does not succeed is placed on the Indigenous people themselves. Because it is seen as politically harmless, language revitalization risks becoming one of the ways in which the settler state produces what Hale (2004) has called the *indio permitido*—ways of being Indigenous that are acceptable to the state, precisely because they do not pose any demands on it and do not interfere with its everyday operations. However, the depoliticized view of language revival may also open new spaces for social action. Kay Warren (1998) has described how the fact that language revitalization was seen as apolitical and therefore harmless allowed Maya people in Guatemala to organize themselves and share crucial narratives that motivated cultural survival, right under the eye of a genocidal state that was determined not to allow political forms of Indigenous organization.[9]

Various Indigenous scholars have also described how sometimes the most political acts of resistance may not be overtly political: those that are not aimed outward at the adjacent settler public, and not seeking to alter or influence the relations that hold between Indigenous and settler communities. The most political acts may be those through which a community constitutes itself as a community vis-à-vis itself, not those that seek to define its outward relations. Coulthard (2014) talks about this as "turning away" from colonial relations, and seeking first and foremost to achieve self-recognition by grounding Indigenous conceptualizations of the political community in Indigenous lifeways. Nishnaabeg scholar Leanne Simpson (2017) makes a similar call to focus on traditional lifeways, and to invite Indigenous youths into these traditional ways by using land-based pedagogies as a form of radical resistance. In her study of the political implications of Kiowa craft production, Kiowa scholar Jenny Tone-Pah-Hote (2019) also urges us to understand how cultural practices may be politically meaningful not only in resisting domination and hegemony, but also in constituting social networks, and building communities. Common to these visions of Indigenous politics is that they propose a political vision that refuses to let their communities be defined through their opposition to the settler colonial hegemony, but which insists on a positive communal identity formed from substantial content, including kinship, craft traditions, subsistence practices, history, territory, land, and language. Sovereignty, in this view, does not come from being recognized as a sovereign nation by a settler colonial state, but emerges continually through practice.

---

[9] See also Barrett 2008; French 2010; Romero 2012, 2015.

One aim of this book is to use these thoughts about Indigenous sovereignties, which emerge largely through the experiences of Indigenous peoples in the United States and Canada, to analyze the political situation of Indigenous peoples in Mexico. What does sovereignty mean in Mexico, and what possibilities for maintaining Indigenous sovereignties are afforded by the particular political arrangements between the Mexican state and the Indigenous communities within it?

Where North American theorists of Indigenous politics have focused on the question of sovereignty, in Mexico, scholars of Indigenous politics have placed the *community* and *communal practices* (*comunalidad* in Spanish) as concepts that define the sociopolitical forms that characterize Mexican Indigenous communities. Since the 1980s, particularly in the state of Oaxaca, Indigenous social theorists, such as Floriberto Dìaz Gomez and Jaime Martínez Luna, have developed communality as the central framework for understanding the internal political cohesion of Indigenous local communities.[10] Currently, the most influential theorist of communality is Ayuuk (Mixe) linguist and thinker Yásnaya Aguilar Gil, whose perspectives on the political relations between Mexican Indigenous communities, Mexican nationalism, and Mexican language policy have won widespread resonance. Aguilar is a linguist and a member of the Ayuuk community of Tukyo'm (Ayutla), Oaxaca, as well as a prominent public intellectual publishing op-eds in both Mexican and American news outlets. In a collection of essays (2020a, 2020b), Aguilar formulates an account of the relations between Indigenous communities and the Mexican state in which language is not reducible to its function as a marker of cultural difference or as capital within a unified linguistic market.

Like Audra Simpson, Aguilar sees Indigenous communities as nations in resistance against the domination of a settler state, but where Simpson describes the Mohawk Nation's frustrated struggle for sovereign statehood, Aguilar eschews the state as an objective altogether. She proposes a classification of three different forms of nationalism: the nationalism of a state that assumes and strives for cultural homogeneity within its domain; the subaltern nationalism of stateless nations striving for statehood; and finally, the nationalism of Indigenous nations without the "desire of state." To Aguilar, the natural unit of Indigenous politics in Mexico is something like the Mesoamerican *altepetl* community: small local communities, governed through traditional forms of participatory democracy, mutuality, and cooperation, mediated by joint commitments to certain customary institutions and values. Rejecting

---

[10] Rendón Monzón 2003; Díaz Gómez, Hernández, and Jiménez 2007; Díaz Gómez 2001; Aguilar Gil 2013.

statehood as an objective, she also rejects state-based forms of nationalism as a vision for her people: while she understands the Ayuuk, or Mixe people, to be a nation, she rejects the idea of a single unitary ethno-national government, proposing instead the Ayuuk nation as network of "minuscule structures," self-governing local communities.

Having rejected state nationalism and the desirability of centralized state authority, for Aguilar there can also be no authorized standard language. Instead, she describes Indigenous language as a "cognitive territory" that belongs inherently and communally to Indigenous nations, and which is the medium of Indigenous forms of collective existence, and of communal politics. She accuses the Mexican state, not of suffocating Indigenous languages through neglect, but of actively using linguicide in its efforts to dominate and assimilate Indigenous peoples. Rather, Aguilar encourages Indigenous communities to use their languages against the state, to evade state control, rather than to cede authority over it. Language, in this conceptualization, becomes a potentially crucial element of the political infrastructure that enables Indigenous communities to maintain sovereignty.

In keeping with these current perspectives on Indigenous political theory, in this book, I approach Indigenous language revitalization as a field of political action. Even as language-revitalization projects may appear from the outside to be apolitical, or engaged in a project of multiculturalist civic development, Indigenous communities may at the same time be working to fortify their own sense of self-recognition—forging sovereignty through practice, in ways that may not be recognized as political by the state.

Communities: Of Nations and Publics

Beyond the exploration of the specific case of Nahuatl and nationalism in Mexico and the question of whether the state's expansive language policy may support or undercut Indigenous sovereignty, another more general aim of this book is to contribute to our understanding of the political aspect of language. Through its description of how Nahuatl speakers and activists use the language in different political projects, it provides an account of the process through which language differences come to be politically relevant, and through which they become tied to political communities and identities.

In the early romantic formulations of nationalism, language was a major constitutive element of the nation. Languages were seen as natural kinds, standing directly for the unbroken continuity of political communities emerging from deep history (Gal 1989). In the romantic tradition of German nationalism represented by Herder and Fichte, language was the soul of the people, an almost magical essence of the only natural political community (Özkirimli 2010, 13–15). Nevertheless, in order for language differences to be able to neatly demarcate political boundaries, all the messy variation and the dialect continua running across borders had to be reduced and standardized (Haugen 1966). Invariably, the most highly valued form of the language, which really expressed the national soul and which all national citizens would have to learn, was whichever dialect was favored by the upper classes. This naïve linguistic nationalism is still commonplace today, despite many valiant efforts to dispel it. It goes hand in hand with the equally common, primordialist conception of the nation, which sees it as a naturally arising political unit that perdures over long periods of time.

Eric Hobsbawm formulated his immensely influential constructivist account of nations as the product of nationalism; states actively produced the nation by politicizing ethnicity, using ethnic divisions as boundaries for projected states, and ethnic solidarity as a medium for generating popular consent to governance. Language, to Hobsbawm, cannot be a vehicle for community until it is standardized by the nation. The Hobsbawmian approach to language and nationalism has therefore focused on how nation-states (mostly European ones) have used language standardization, with marginalization of vernacular dialects, as an element in processes of nation-craft. A language, in this view, emerges as one of the "invented traditions" (Hobsbawm and Ranger 1983) through which a national community constitutes itself. In this view, there was no "language" before the nation, only the multitudinous vernacular traditions that it had to replace. These vernacular traditions in turn were not tied to political communities or identities, but were simply the medium of everyday communication of the dominated classes. In Hobsbawm's theory of nation and language, the relation between the two is one of symbolic reference. The national language is, like the flag, one of the nation's emblems; it is created by the nation itself to stand for it and to reproduce it. By enforcing the use of the national language, the nation recreates itself in every linguistic encounter. This, as argued by Aguilar (2020a, 172–74), is what makes Indigenous languages anathema to the nation: their very presence in the national territory negates its ability to reproduce itself through a linguistic monopoly.

In Benedict Anderson's account of the origins of nationalism (1983), language takes on a more generative role. While he agrees with Hobsbawm that the desire for a state is the original motivation behind the nation, he nonetheless sees language use, especially in the form of print media, as the major vehicle through which a community arises that can then come to desire a state. Print media deterritorializes language and circulates it in a public that is not place bound—the "imagined community." To Anderson, this is what makes it possible to transcend the local community of face-to-face interaction, and create the imagined community of the nation. Language is the medium of sociality, the medium through which we formulate a conception of a common good, through which we form a republic. So, in Anderson's theory of nation and language, language use in joint communicative action is prior to an emergence of national sentiment. Language is not only an emblem through which the nation perpetuates its own idea, although it also is that, but it is additionally the medium for the formulation of a joint intention through which the nation comes into being.

The nation and the solidarity of the members of its imagined community are preceded by the existence of human communities whose members share languages which they use to create narratives that define them as a group in a contrastive relation to other groups. In sociolinguistics, such groups have been traditionally called "speech communities." The term "speech community" has a long and contentious history of definitions within sociolinguistics—from Gumperz's (1968, 1962) and Labov's (1972) widely influential definitions, of communities defined by shared norms of language use, to contemporary definitions based on practice theory and the Habermasian concept of the public (Patrick 2008; Muehlmann 2014).

The speech community, defined by sharing a set of social and grammatical norms for language use, has been contrasted with the "language community," which unites people who share "a language" in the sense of a denotational code, without necessarily sharing any norms for linguistic usage, or political concerns, or even a sense of identity. In proposing this contrast, Silverstein (1998) cautioned us to remember that "locality," like "language" and "society," is scalable, which means that it has to be produced to fit a specific scale—and this scaling is done through discourse. What makes Nahuatl-speaking communities "local" is the fact that its speakers speak of it as being tied to certain types of locality, their own local communities or regions mainly, but also at times to abstract locations such as a pan-Nahuan ethnic community, or the Mexican nation. A central claim of this book is that the Nahuatl language takes on vastly different social and political functions depending on how it is discursively scaled to fit a community at a given scale; and that therefore the process of scaling is of the utmost importance if we want to understand, or manipulate, the causal processes that determine language vitality.

Communality and the Sphere of Indigenous Politics

Anthropologists have had a hard time trying to find adequate ways to conceptualize the organization and coherence of Indigenous, and other non-nation, political communities. The difficulty stems from the risk of describing Indigenous *altepetl*-type communities as internally homogeneous cultural islands, isolated from the wider society that they are situated within. Here I am of course alluding to the intense debates about the political cohesion of Indigenous *campesino* communities in Mexico started by Redfield's (1930) and Lewis's (1951) discussion of the Nahua community of Tepoztlan, Morelos, and its continuation by Wolf's (1957) proposal of the "closed corporate peasant community" as a characteristic political form of Mesoamerica. A more recent engagement in the debate, centered in the Nahuatl-speaking region of the Sierra Huasteca, is Schryer (1987, 1990), who concludes that Nahua communities may be corporate, but never closed (and rarely as egalitarian as some would have it). For the anthropologist, the challenges of defining what makes "the community" are many—because how do we define whether a group of people make up one community or many, when any posited community will have a heterogeneity of practices, traits, ideas, and opinions, and often no element that is shared universally within it? How can communities be entities that endure over time, when new communities can be imagined into being and existing ones can become obsolete and disappear within a few generations? How can communities be discrete units with boundaries, when community members, ideas, and defining traits can seemingly move fairly freely between them and be shared by multiple communities at the same time?[11]

The notion of the closed corporate community has also been criticized for seeing Indigenous communities as isolated from the broader flows of history, placing them outside of history and thereby denying them *coevalness* with the national societies they are located in. Refuting this view, historians have shown time and again how Indigenous communities have been actively engaged in political events and movements at the national and international scale. From their participation in the Spanish colonization of Central America and the US Southwest, to their engagement in movement of national independence, of resistance to or alliances with the forces of the French intervention and to fighting on various sides in the Mexican Revolution, Nahua people have never been trapped outside of history, but have always participated actively in it.

---

[11] The intensity of these debates about ethnicity, nationalism, and cultural politics and the various perspectives on the possibility of cultural communities of different types are reviewed well by Hylland Eriksen (1993).

They have appealed to the nation when they needed a strong ally against local rivals, or oppressive state governments, and they have fervently celebrated the symbols of the nation: the flag, the national hymn, and the national patron saint, the Virgin of Guadalupe. Nevertheless, there is something about the way that *altepetl* communities are organized and the way that Nahua people relate to them that feels a lot like a form of corporate nationalism. Frequently there is an intense pride in the local community, its specific language and customs, and a strong solidarity with co-*altepetl* members in conflict with outsiders, whether a neighboring *altepetl* or state officials. An *altepetl* in most cases is not simply a place where one lives; it is a political community that one is part of, and which contributes significantly to identity. Moreover, it is of course also a community that is often linguistically and culturally distinct from the national mainstream. Anthropological and linguistic conceptualizations of the "community" offer no theoretically neutral or unproblematic way of describing this type of social unit, but neither can it be ignored since this local "nationalism" is clearly a strong, if not the strongest, force in maintaining the use of the language, and in motivating linguistic revitalization locally.

For some reason, however, these questions do not seem to worry many of the Nahuatl speakers I have met—they are usually quite confident about which communities they are members of, about their social and physical boundaries, about what membership in a given community entails, and how membership in communities at different scales can be combined. It would appear that there is little need for them to theorize these aspects of the political community.

What Indigenous Mexican scholars have participated in theorizing, instead of seeking to define and delimit Indigenous communities as units, is the social principles that create its particular type of social cohesion; that is, instead of defining it negatively as separate from other communities, they define it positively, in terms of the social forces that produce it. As mentioned, the concept of communality (*comunalidad*) which is central to Yásnaya Aguilar's description of the relation between language and community has been central in these efforts by Mexican Indigenous thinkers to understand and describe Indigenous forms of social and political life. Among the principal early thinkers developing the framework of communality in Mexico have been the anthropologists Floriberto Díaz Gómez (1952–1995), from the Ayuuk (Mixe) community of Tlahuitoltepec, and Jaime Martínez Luna from the Zapotec community of Guelatao, both from the state of Oaxaca. Both of these thinkers were involved in the processes of the formulation of Indigenous political rights in the 1970s and 1980s, the processes that also led to the declaration of Barbados.

Díaz Gómez (2001) provisionally defined communality by a set of elements that generate it: (1) a kinship type relation between a group of people and the land and territory that sustain them; (2) a process of collective decision-making by consensus in public assembly meetings; (3) unremunerated service as the practical form of the exercise of authority; (4) the mutual participation in collective work for the common good as a form of "recreation" (repeated creation of the community, but also of the individual as a collective being); and (5) collective ritual celebrations and feasts as an engine of reciprocity and redistribution. Martínez Luna (2003) wrote explicitly of communality as the organizational form through which Indigenous communities in Mexico exercise their autonomy and self-determination. Significantly, this does not place self-determination as a future goal to be achieved, but as an already existing state of affairs—a kind of autonomy that can be maintained and cultivated and further developed.

Reading Díaz and Martínez Luna with the sensibility of an outsider anthropologist, one may feel uncomfortable with the seemingly essentializing and normative implications of positing distinctly Indigenous social forms in this way as a total package, because what about those Indigenous people and communities that understand themselves differently or create themselves through different practices? But if one reads it rather as a programmatic expression of the social form to which an Indigenous community may aspire as an alternative to nation-building, it need not be understood as any more essentializing than the Declaration of Independence, or any other political constitution. Any statement that aims to bring into being a political community must define itself as a distinct "we," before the properties of that "we" can proceed to be negotiated further by its members. The community, then, as it is understood in the framework of communality, is a public forum of people sharing a kinship relation with a place and a sense of reciprocal responsibility expressed in ritual forms, who make collective decisions through public discussion. When the formulation is stripped of its culturally specific wrapping, in this way, it is not so different from the Greek *polis*, or the *Öffentlichkeit* or *public sphere*, as it is theorized by Habermas.

The Altepetl as the Indigenous Public

Recent work in linguistic anthropology has precisely adopted Jürgen Habermas's concept of the public sphere in new and innovative ways.[12] As

---

[12] Gal and Woolard 2001, 1995; Cody 2011; Swinehart and Graber 2012; Muehlmann 2014; Kroskrity and Meek 2017; Rodríguez 2021.

originally formulated by Habermas, the public sphere is the sphere of public discourse where discussion and debate among private members of the bourgeoisie make it possible for them to generate consensus and advance claims and demands upon the state (Habermas 1962, 1989). Habermas sees the liberal public sphere as bound in time and place to the European bourgeois society of the 18th century, and he considers it to have declined as a result of the advances of capitalism in which the boundaries between private citizens and the state have been increasingly blurred. To be useful in anthropology, the concept has had to be pluralized, and stripped of its universalizing appeals to European traditions of rationality, and of the unconvincing pretensions that it can be a maximally inclusive and power-free space of discussion (Fraser 1990; Warner 2002). In this conception, publics can form wherever discussions about the common good take place, regardless of the kind of rationality it employs, and counterpublics formed as bubbles within or against publics as competing visions of the common good emerge. A public sphere, then, may describe any space of communicative action in which visions of a common good can be formulated, and in which the joint attention to this common good creates a sense of political community. Each public is grounded in a form of life,[13] which shapes its particular forms of communicative action, and provides it with its own particular rationality. Communality is such a political and social rationality that is tied to a particular form of life, and the *altepetl* type of community can be understood as a kind of public sphere.

Since publics are constituted through communicative action, language is the medium of the public. In this sense, the public is very similar to Anderson's conception of the nation; it is an imagined community that emerges through a sustained conversation among multiple participants, who understand themselves to be a "we" (in the intersubjective sense of Schütz 1967). This *we-ness*, which generates itself through the very act of conversation (and its accompanying practices such as collective work, or feasting), is the centripetal force that keeps the public together. So, while the "we" of the early Mexican nation was busy speaking for the Indigenous peoples whose languages they do not understand, those peoples were engaged in conversations of their own within their own communities and in their own languages. In every Indigenous community, there is a continuous conversation about what is in its best interest. Such discussions are often contentious and often do not generate a clear

---

[13] Habermas follows the phenomenological tradition and calls the intersubjective grounding of the public the life-world (*Lebenswelt*), but here where the focus is on socially produced meaning, I follow Wittgenstein and call it a "form of life," which may then generate (inter)subjective life-worlds in those who participate in it. In my conceptualization of we-ness as the manifestation of intersubjectivity, I follow Schütz and the Husserlian tradition as laid out by Duranti (2010).

consensus, but they emerge from a shared reality and a communal solidarity. In this work, I understand Indigenous *altepetl* communities to be the quintessential form of the public in Mesoamerica. And within the context of contemporary Mexican politics, like Martínez Luna, I consider the *altepetl* public (or its equivalent in non-Nahuatl-speaking communities) to be the Indigenous political unit that carries the potential of sovereignty.

The way I use the notion of the "public" differs from how some other linguistic anthropologists use it. It is sometimes understood as something that is created externally, through a particular relationship between a state and a group of people who advance claims based on their collective interests. An example of this use is when Juan L. Rodríguez (2021) describes how the Venezuelan state wished to use its "oil magic" to constitute the Warao as a public, that is, to make them take a particular position as subject to (and perhaps a client of) the state. In my conceptualization, this position is that of becoming a *constituency* within a national public, which also means giving up the independent status of one's own public. The difference in usage is subtle, but important, because for me it is presupposed that Indigenous communities will always have their own publics in some form or other, whether communicated in Xavante dream-retellings (Graham 1995), Mazatec song competitions (Faudree 2014), Samoan *fono* discourse (Duranti 1994), or Basque "outlaw radio" (Urla 1995)—the question for the anthropologist is how to locate it. Conversely, in this conceptualization, when an Indigenous public becomes a constituent (or a client) of another larger public, such as a nation-state, it risks causing the decline of Indigenous publics.

Language as the Medium of Political Community

By using the *altepetl*-type public as the unit of political analysis, it becomes possible to see one major difference between the way that the Mexican nation relates to Indigenous languages and the way that the Indigenous communities use them. For the Mexican national public, Indigenous languages are an *object* of communicative action. They are primarily something to talk about, something to describe, and something to ascribe value to. Indigenous languages are part of the nation's common good (though it is of course up for discussion how big a part they are and how much value should be ascribed to them). But the situation is different in an Indigenous language public. Here the Indigenous language is the *medium* of communicative action, and it provides the terms in which the public debate is conducted and the common good is formulated. This difference is not trivial, because it means, in effect, that the Indigenous community excludes the majority public from participating in decisions about its common good. Just as the Spanish-speaking national public sphere excludes monolingual speakers of Indigenous languages from participation, the fact that an Indigenous public uses the Indigenous language as its medium means that the monolingual members of the Spanish-speaking majority are unable to participate.

The terms of the Indigenous language enclose the Indigenous forms of life, and work as a protective *semiotic membrane* against outside influence and outside attempts to control the Indigenous conceptions of the public good. Any attempt by outsiders to intrude on Indigenous decision-making must pass through a *barrier of translation*: someone has to be bilingual and do the work of translating messages between the Indigenous public and the national public. But such intrusion also has to pass through a *barrier of contextualization*: the meaning of any message that is received will have been converted into the terms and concepts that are used in the Indigenous language; and it will be understood in relation to the forms of life that they pertain to. To be successful in relaying a message, the translator not only will have to know the local language, but also must be acquainted with the local form of life.

Today, of course, most Nahuatl speakers do speak Spanish, and messages pass readily from the national public and into the Indigenous publics, but the use of Indigenous languages still closes off Spanish monolinguals from participation in the discussions that subsequently take place in the community. For example, Yásnaya Aguilar (2020b) describes how during negotiations with state officials about some state project that would intrude on their lands, Mixe delegations would switch to speaking Mixe to change their strategy of negotiation, indicate a better argument, or warn of deceit. "The use of the Mixe language created a space that was impenetrable for the functionaries" (Aguilar Gil 2020b). The strategic use of an Indigenous language, kept alive through everyday language use in participation in an Indigenous public, lets the Indigenous community maintain control of their own communication and their own public matters, opening up or closing off and forming networks with other publics that use the same language.

One function of Indigenous language therefore is as an instrument to support the maintenance of sovereignty by sustaining and delimiting a political community. In Indigenous towns where Indigenous languages are spoken by most of the community members, they work as privileged semiotic vehicles through which local public spheres are formed. They are the vehicles through which Indigenous communities engage themselves in conversation, and in which they formulate their own worldviews, which in turn produce values, projects, and ideologies. Indeed, this book proposes that more than any other single factor, it is the function of language as the semiotic infrastructure of a political community that determines a minority language's value to its community of speakers, and consequently its vitality.

Indigenous languages thrive when the Indigenous public is politically vital, with a strong sense of communal identity and a shared common good, partly achieved by using its language in an ongoing debate about the future of the community. Moreover, when the local language thrives as a language of political conversation, it delimits the scope of the dialogue to those who share the language's inherent assumptions about the political and social world they inhabit. In turn, the challenge of translation that it poses to outsiders wishing to participate in the dialogue gives the discussion a degree of resistance to the intrusion of outside concepts and values from the majority group. The language forms a semiotic membrane that offers the community's political autonomy a degree of protection from outside spheres of politics. Moreover, reciprocally, the community protects the language by maintaining its use as long as the community needs it as a vehicle of their separate identity. When analyzing the consequences of language-planning initiatives like those of the Mexican government, it is important to pay attention to this symbiotic–semiotic relation between language and political community.

This means that the Mexican nation, when seeking to claim Indigenous languages as a national property, is threatening the sovereignty of Indigenous communities. But it also means that if the state is indeed invested in supporting the vitality of Indigenous languages, it could potentially also support their continued sovereignty. It is a major goal of this book to draw attention to the slipperiness of the ground of language-revitalization efforts, where benign efforts may risk slipping up and sliding along to much less desirable results.

Revitalization: State-Sponsored Languages, Semiotic Sovereignty, and Emergent Vitalities

If the relations between Indigenous publics and Indigenous languages are as I propose above, this has consequences for how to understand the ongoing crisis of Indigenous language vitality, and for how to understand the state's potential roles in supporting language vitality.

With the 2003 General Law of Linguistic Rights, the Mexican state committed itself to supporting the vitality of the minority languages spoken within its borders. In a sense, what the law did, even though the state probably did not realize this, was to announce a massive, nationwide, state-sponsored project of revitalization of hundreds of distinct linguistic varieties. Few of the world's nations have taken on such responsibilities for their minority languages, and so there is little ground for comparison; two relevant exceptions that it may be worth looking at are Ireland and Bolivia.

National Language Revitalization in Ireland

One example of a state that has invested massively in maintaining and supporting language vitality is Ireland. Already before the Republic of Ireland gained independence from the United Kingdom in 1922, nationalists were undertaking efforts to support the Irish language, which had been losing ground for centuries, but with independence these efforts were nationalized, and were integrated into the project of nation-building (Doyle 2015). The Irish state invested massively in language development and translation, making Irish a compulsory subject for all students, requiring Irish proficiency from all civil servants, supporting Irish-medium schools, and funding Irish-language media. Nevertheless, by all accounts the situation for Irish in the Republic of Ireland is considerably worse now than it was a hundred years ago: the Irish-speaking Gaeltacht areas that once covered the entire west of Ireland have dwindled into scattered enclaves. Compulsory Irish instruction has meant that as many as 42% of the population consider themselves to have a degree of fluency in the language, but only 3% of households use Irish as their language of everyday communication. Outside of schools, only some 83,000 people, out of the population of 5 million, report using Irish daily (Ireland 2010). Moreover, Irish is a language with several dialects spoken in the Gaeltacht areas, and an official standard taught in schools that differs from all of them, leading to conflicts over linguistic authority (O'Rourke 2011). Some observers have argued that the relative lack of success of Irish-language maintenance is caused by the fact that it is largely a top-down project, cherished by the elite who are able to make sure that their children have the best opportunities for learning Irish, but without broad backing in the working-class population (Weafer 2016). The 20-year plan for the Irish language that the government of Ireland published in 2010 sets as its specific aim to triple the number of Irish who speak the language on a daily basis from 83,000 to 250,000. Whether it is going to reach this goal remains to be seen.

Compared with Ireland, the task facing Mexico, if it is to succeed in reversing language shift for Indigenous languages, is greater and more complex by several orders of magnitude, with hundreds of different languages, a much bigger population, and a much less stable economy and political system.

Among the languages of Mexico, the situation of Nahuatl may be the one that is most comparable to Irish. Like Irish, Nahuatl is spoken in scattered communities, by speakers who often feel a strong pride in and attachment to their own local variety. And, like Irish, Nahuatl has been taken up as an emblem of nationhood by a postcolonial nationalist movement, creating potential conflicts over language ownership. Also like Irish, the version championed by the national establishment and taught in universities is different enough from the vernacular varieties spoken in the local communities that it challenges the status of native speakers as authorities of the language.

National Language Revitalization in Bolivia

Another, perhaps more comparable case, is Bolivia, where the system change that brought Evo Morales to power in 2006 also inaugurated a new approach to the country's Indigenous languages. In Bolivia, speakers of the 36 Indigenous languages are in the majority. According to a 2001 census, as many as 62% of the population spoke one of the Indigenous languages (Postero 2017, 26), the Andean highland languages Quechua and Aymara being the most widely spoken, and there were many other smaller language communities, such as Guaraní (a large language community in neighboring Paraguay), Siriono, and Tacana. The new regime instituted intercultural bilingual education across the country and extended support for language development of minority languages, and required all public officials to speak the main Indigenous language of the region in which they worked. But nevertheless, according to Gustafson (2017), there are significant disjunctures between the Bolivian state's legislation in support of Indigenous languages and their implementation in practice, exemplified for example by the fact that Morales, though himself ethnically Aymara, invariably spoke in Spanish. At the same time, though speakers of Indigenous languages now participated in networks of political power, and extended the currency of their languages into spaces that had been previously monolingual, the state's inability to address most of the fundamental inequalities in Bolivian society meant that, for many Bolivians, Indigenous languages remained tied to undesirable forms of life. Even as the classrooms were filled with would-be public servants diligently studying Guaraní, the teacher may lament that many of his fellow Guaraní "don't want to be Indigenous anymore" (Gustafson 2017, 54). Nevertheless, Bolivia, with its (then) Aymara president and demographic majority of speakers of Indigenous languages, is also not a straightforward comparison with Mexico.

The cases of Ireland and Bolivia suggest that it would perhaps be wrong to evaluate the potential for change inherent in these projects of state-sponsored revitalization simply by numbers of speakers. If higher numbers are achieved by making urban non-speakers learn the language in order to hold a job as a civil servant, then that number does not necessarily tell us anything about whether the language thrives in the communities where it is used as a language of everyday interaction (and which are supposed to benefit from these new language policies). In state-sponsored language revitalization, *language* becomes the object of interventive action, not the community of speakers.

Here lies the relevance of language ideologies as an instrument of analysis: In language revitalization, the construction of language vitality takes place in an ideological field where the ideologies of speakers, interested outsiders, colonizers, educators, missionaries, activists, linguists, and anthropologists interact. The difficulties posed by this complex interaction of ideologies and objectives have prompted Kroskrity (2009) to argue that early in the process of any project of linguistic revitalization, there should be a stage of ideological clarification, in which actors make their ideologies, assumptions, and objectives explicit so that a shared agenda can be formulated. While almost all language-revitalization projects involve multiple actors with differing ideologies, only relatively recently have linguists begun to examine how our own ideologies interact with those of native speakers, even though linguists and language educators are among the most important sources from which language ideologies flow into the public discourse (Collins 1998; Bucholtz 2003). By now, the literature on language-revitalization projects is replete with narratives of how different agendas among participants hamper projects of language revitalization or renewal, or even make them impossible.[14]

The Decolonial Critique of the "Reversing Language Shift" Paradigm

Linguists working within the "Reversing Language Shift" paradigm (Fishman 1991, 2000), have tended to see language revitalization not as a political project, but largely as a question of ensuring intergenerational language transmission by supporting the academic infrastructure of the language and raising its prestige within the community of potential speakers. The strongest expression

---

[14] Perley 2011; Shulist 2018; Nevins 2013; Wroblewski 2021; Meek 2012; Báez, Rogers, and Labrada 2016; Gustafson, Julca Guerrero, and Jiménez 2016; Davis 2017b.

of this ideology was Hale et al.'s (1992) article which called linguists to arms in a struggle against language endangerment, comparing it with the loss of biological species and making the conservation of linguistic diversity a matter of global importance. I was myself initially trained to study languages rather than the communities that speak them, and this rhetoric motivated in me a keen interest in language endangerment and in preserving Indigenous languages for the sake of science and humanity. Similarly to how Duranti (1994) arrived at the politics of language use by setting out to studying grammar, I arrived at the political community as the necessary crux of any interest in Indigenous language use and vitality. In this way, I am also arguing against my own former apolitical perspective, and simultaneously making a case for the continued relevance of language revitalization.

Linguists of course realize that the task of revitalization requires community support, but early on, linguists envisioned the alliance between community and linguists as an ideally apolitical process, not directly related to specific political struggles of the community. Recent scholarship on language reclamation has criticized many of the earlier discourses and practices of language revitalization, calling for all language-reclamation work to be led by Indigenous communities themselves and driven by their needs and respecting their wishes for the future of the language.[15] On the other hand, anthropologists who work with Indigenous rights and cultural politics from the perspective of social critique sometimes seem to consider language revitalization to be a superficial kind of activism based on essentialist assumptions about the relation between language, culture, and identity. They sometimes suggest that cultural revitalization, especially when supported by the state, may instead contribute to perpetuating and reinforcing stereotypical, essentialist notions of indigeneity, without contributing to solving the political issues of structural violence and racism that brought about the language's endangerment in the first place.[16] More recently (and with more focus on language as well as more theoretical nuance), Muehlmann (2008) has described how some Indigenous Cucapá youths in the US–Mexican borderlands experience the discourses and practices of language revitalization to be oppressive. Errington (2003, 2008) describes the current paradigm of language endangerment discourse in linguistics as potentially complicit in neo-colonial regimes of language. When positions of authority in the Global North take the authority to decide that minority languages must be saved in the South, it risks

---

[15] Perley 2011; de Korne, Haley and Leonard 2017; Davis 2017a.
[16] This I consider a fair, if much simplified description of research in the tradition exemplified by scholars such as Friedlander (1975), Kuper (1988, 2003), and Friedman (1993).

perpetuating the same colonial dynamics that are at the root of language endangerment to begin with.

This ambiguity is also found within decolonization perspectives on language revitalization. Some such approaches have seen language reclamation as an inherently decolonial practice, a way toward epistemological decolonization, a way of reclaiming the ontological categories of submerged Indigenous traditions through language. Language reclamation, in this view, becomes a way to decenter or bypass European epistemologies and upset the hierarchy of power that places settler languages at the top of a hierarchy of languages and excludes colonized languages from the spheres of academia and education. Nevertheless, several scholars have critiqued the epistemic approach to decolonization as being a depoliticized philosophical approach that locates decolonization in the mind, severing it from political change. Silvia Rivera Cusicanqui forcefully denounces this approach, particularly as it is practiced within the field of subaltern studies, insisting that "[t]here can be no discourse of decolonization, no theory of decolonization, without a decolonizing practice" (2012, 100). Decolonizing academia cannot be achieved simply by scholars from the Global North adopting Indigenous concepts into their theoretical vocabulary or giving their journals names in Indigenous languages.[17]

As Tuck and Yang (2012) have established, decolonization cannot be a mere metaphor. The same is the case when it comes to decolonizing language and linguistics: to be decolonial, revitalization practices must contribute to a substantial change to the colonial landscape of relations (including the relations between linguists and speakers of Indigenous languages), as Wesley Leonard (1998) has argued. These arguments caution us to critically scrutinize the effects of the concrete practices of language revitalization before making claims about their political or decolonial potential.

It follows from these critical arguments that not all possible uses of Indigenous languages necessarily contribute to making the language more vital or to the substantial benefit of the community of speakers. For example, the state may use Indigenous languages in ways that weaken, rather than strengthen, Indigenous sovereignty. They may use Indigenous languages to subvert the sense of political independence and self-sufficiency of Indigenous political communities. Therefore, state-sponsored language revitalization should be judged not solely on its ability to provide infrastructural support

---

[17] A salient example here is the concept of *nepantla* which, through the work of Gloria Anzaldúa, has been taken up by decolonial scholars in the United States—but which, although it means "center" or "middle" in Nahuatl (not "in between" as Anzaldúa and those following her usage claim; this is a misreading through Spanish *en medio*), it is not particularly central to Indigenous discourse in Nahuatl, and is rarely, if at all, used as a central concept by Indigenous activists or intellectuals in Mexico.

for the use of Indigenous languages in the mainstream public sphere, but also by its ability to support the political autonomy of Indigenous communities. A revitalization effort done wrong may threaten both the community and its language, if it compromises the intimate relation between community and language, and community ownership of the semiotic resources it represents. Several common strategies of large-scale language revitalization that some government and institutional initiatives use seem to be double-edged swords of this kind. This holds, for example, for interventions that teach Indigenous languages as second languages outside of the communities, and those that provide remedial education using Indigenous languages with the aim of easing Indigenous youths' access to the mainstream education system. The risks are that teaching Indigenous languages to non-speakers, who are not members of the existing speech community, may make the language less relevant to its original speaker base; or that offering access to mainstream higher education to Indigenous youths may be a scaffold, bringing them into an ideological infrastructure that encourages them to abandon the local speech community and the language and seek the realization of their life projects elsewhere and through other languages. In other words, language revitalization may become a form of *semiotic extractivism* (compare with Simpson and Klein 2017 and Grosfoguel 2016, 2019). Recognizing these risks prompts us to look closely at how government-driven language-revitalization efforts work in concrete practice, and how they affect Indigenous political communities, and whether they contribute to what Barbra Meek has called "linguistic self-determination" (Kroskrity and Meek 2017).

Language Activism as a Communal Practice

To adequately assess the value of language-revitalization projects, we should judge their degree of success not solely on their ability to produce new speakers, but also by evaluating the potential to counteract the processes that threaten to dissolve Indigenous publics into the mainstream, national public sphere. We must look at Indigenous language activism also as a communal practice.

Several scholars in linguistic anthropology have made this point in various ways. Studying language-reclamation projects among the White Mountain Apache, Nevins (2013) points out that even as the academic approaches of language endangerment and revitalization may be at odds with local interests and practices surrounding a language, there may still be potential for joint projects, and for synergistic emergence of empowering practices in the periphery of the official revitalization projects. Others have studied the intersections between social and linguistic resurgence and cultural production, from poetry (Webster 2016) to song contests (Faudree 2015a), to community radio (Valentine 1995), and to art workshops (Flores Farfán 2011). The key element in this strand of work is that language use is embedded in cultural activities, and that it is these activities that can support the development of new linguistic vitalities outside of a classroom setting. The concept of multiple vitalities tied to specific cultural forms has been proposed by Bernard Perley (2011) based on his work with his own Maliseet language. Perley troubles the idea that languages can only "live" as long as there are speakers who use them for everyday community communication. He suggests that rather than counting vitality simply as the number of speakers, there may be different kinds of vitalities that can emerge through other means, as language users engage with language artifacts such as books or texts, or sing songs or remember the names of places. Similarly, Jenny L. Davis (2017b) describes the language-revitalization programs of her own Chickasaw Nation, with a focus on how revitalization practices have a restorative function in fostering a sense of transgenerational community, and by providing semiotic means through which Chickasaw citizens may experience Chickasaw identity. Where early linguistic attention focused on how to make language revitalization "work in practice," understood as producing fluent speakers through educational interventions, scholars like Davis and Perley focus on how the practice of language revitalization works in the community. These studies encourage us to think with more nuance about what linguistic vitality is, and in what contexts it may emerge. In line with these arguments and perspectives, the objective of this study is not to find out whether state-sponsored revitalization in Mexico is good or bad. Rather, it seeks clarification in all of the different senses: to uncover the potentials and risks of state-sponsored language revitalization, as well as how the projects and interventions and their surrounding discourses come to afford different forms of life and different types of social action in Indigenous communities.

This perspective motivates a turn toward semiotics and the human ability to select and create different meaningful relations between themselves and the physical world, and to make those relations the foundations of their own subjective and intersubjective lifeworlds. A group of people may be able to semiotically constitute themselves as a separate community existing within a separate, but locally shared, conceptualization of the world, and they may be able to privilege the meaningful relations that are obtained within that local conceptualization. If so, then the degree to which they can be separate from the nation-state, even while also being a part of it, may be constrained only by their ability to hold on to their locally meaningful world in the face of pressures to abandon it. This suggests the possibility of another kind of "Nahuatl Nation," one that is now hidden inside the mist or beneath the rocky ground of the Zongolica mountains, or in the memories of the old people of Hueyapan, and which can perhaps only be imagined into existence through the semiotic resources of the Nahuatl language. Perhaps, this is a community of the radically "otherwise" (Povinelli 2012), where different ontological relations obtain between humans and the territory; or a nation of intimate affective relations of different sorts, a nation that has no physical infrastructure or official ideology, but serves only as inspiration for political projects in the present. By describing how political communities use the Nahuatl language as a vehicle for imaginations of alternative political potentialities, this work may contribute to also deepening the space in which anthropologists can imagine language, and language revitalization, as a potential field of radical minority politics.

Semiotic Sovereignty

In advocating this perspective, I propose the concept that I call *semiotic sovereignty* to describe how Indigenous communities protect the integrity of their publics by maintaining control of the semiotic resources required to access their public spheres. In naming this concept, I do not claim to have invented it, since everything indicates that Indigenous communities across the world already operate with a realization of its crucial importance to them. When Pueblo people in New Mexico restrict the ways in which outsiders are allowed to access and represent their language (prohibiting its representation in writing; Debenport 2015), they are effectively protecting their semiotic sovereignty. When Apache traditionalists seek to keep sacred stories and words out of the revitalization curriculum, perhaps they are similarly seeking to maintain control of a crucial element of their semiotic resources—while encouraging learners to acquire the language skills necessary to access those resources (Nevins 2013). If we recognize semiotic sovereignty as a key aspect of Indigenous political sovereignty, it may prove easier to understand the conflicts that often arise in Indigenous revitalization projects. It allows us to see that questions about what orthography to choose, what variety to teach, and who should be teaching are not simply questions of personal rivalries or entrenched arbitrary preferences, but part of essentially political conflicts over how best to protect semiotic sovereignty. The concept, and the description of the semiotic and political mechanism that it operates through, may also throw new light on the relations between language and nation that have been a constant topic of inquiry in studies and formulations of nationalism from Fichte and Renan to Hobsbawm and Anderson.

Chapter Road Map

Over the course of the book, I show that semiotic sovereignty may be a principle that operates in language-renewal efforts in different ways. In Chapter 2, I show that over the course of Nahua history it seems that political sovereignty is closely aligned with the ability of Indigenous groups to use their languages to close off their own publics to outsiders. After the Mexican revolution, many Indigenous communities "opened up" and sought the intervention of the state in support of their political projects, but they did so at the peril of becoming clients of the state, and of seeing the local public spheres dissolve into the national public. In Chapter 3, I describe how the Mexican state is seeking to claim ownership of Indigenous semiotic resources in an effort to brand itself in an international market, and I argue that this puts Mexico's marketing of its own identity at odds with Indigenous sovereignties. In Chapters 4 and 5, I show how specific Indigenous communities, a local *altepetl* community and a regional Nahua public centered around an intercultural university, strive to claim ownership of their semiotic resources using small acts of community-building and semiotic resistance. I suggest that such struggles are best understood as efforts to secure a measure of semiotic sovereignty in a situation where it is threatened. In Chapter 6, I look at Indigenous revival movements in the Mexican diaspora in the United States, and I show that these can also be seen as acts of semiotic resistance to an established order of ethno-political relations. I point out an inherent tension between Chicano activists' struggle to claim a rightful ownership of Indigenous Mexican semiotic resources and the struggles of Indigenous *altepetl* communities in Mexico to maintain their sovereignty. Semiotic sovereignties, like Perley's vitalities, should be conceived as emergent across a spectrum of intensities and a wide range of contexts, from mundane acts of meaning-making in support of subsistence in adverse conditions to open acts of rebellion against established glottopolitical regimes.

Methods: Interscalar, Transtemporal, and Translingual Ethnography

This book is also an ethnography of the Nahuatl language. As far as language can be an object of ethnography, it is a moving object—constantly flowing through time and space, continuously changing both form and meaning in interplay with social and historical circumstances. Paja Faudree and I have argued that because language always travels through history and society, in order to get the best view of it we should try to locate it through triangulation (Faudree and Pharao Hansen 2014). When we seek to understand the social context of language, we should look also at the history of that context; and likewise, when we try to understand the history of language, we must seek to understand its social context. Finally, when trying to understand history or social context, we have to look at it linguistically—allowing us in this way to see how language participates in the creation of social meaning, and how it is the medium of our historical narratives. This approach to the language–culture–history nexus is at the same time a theory and a methodological proposition: it requires the integration of methods from three sources of knowledge: ethnography, linguistic analysis, and historical contextualization. This is the approach taken in this work.

The book integrates research that has been conducted over 18 years, from my first research stay in the community of Hueyapan, Morelos, in 2004, and until the beginning of 2022 when I stayed two weeks in Tequila, Veracruz. In this period, I have collected data using a number of different methods borrowed from anthropology, linguistics, and history.

Ethnographers have traditionally seen ethnography as studying a place and a local community, which becomes the "field." With the development of multi-sited ethnography, ethnographers developed various methods of "following" in which the researcher explores a single theme, thing, idea, or group of people, that moves between different localities in various social contexts (Marcus 1995). Similarly, linguists often see languages as bound to places and to communities of speakers, but they are nevertheless aware that language is always on the move, as speakers travel or migrate, to meet and talk in new contexts. Therefore, when I study the relation between Nahuatl, the nation that claims it, and the people and communities that speak it, my method is to "follow the language," through contexts of different types and at varying geographical and historical scales.

I follow Nahuatl through time by analyzing historical sources that document the use of Nahuatl in its social context in different historical periods, making this also a transtemporal ethnography. Because history is a part of all of the analyses here, I do not have a traditional history chapter. Rather, all of the chapters are also history chapters. Chapter 2, however, is entirely dedicated to describing the social and political history of Nahuatl until the end of the 20th century. Here, I privilege the use of Nahuatl language sources, because I want to show the view of Nahua history as Nahua people communicate it within their own public sphere, so that I may come closer to understanding how their visions of a common good have been formulated at different intersections of time and space. And though I describe the colonial language situation, I focus on the postcolonial period, which is crucial for understanding the politics that led to the decline of Nahuatl. I also draw on the work of historians who have used Indigenous language sources or have focused on analyzing the internal workings of Indigenous communities. In the subsequent chapters, I rely partly on primary sources such as official documents, media accounts, my own conversations and interviews, and the work of other historians who have written about the relevant topics and areas. To get a better grasp of 20th-century history in Nahua communities in Morelos and Veracruz, I have worked in some historical archives: the municipal archives of Tetela del Volcán, of Orizaba and of Zongolica, at the Barlow papers at the Universidad de las Américas in Cholula, and in the Agrarian Archive in Cuernavaca.

I follow Nahuatl in space by studying it ethnographically at different social and political scales. Claudio Lomnitz (1992) has described Mexican society as an integrated system operating at three different scales: the nation, the state or region, and the local community—each of which is characterized by its own cultural and political logic. His model of nested social scales has inspired my choices and organization of ethnographic contexts. In Chapter 3, the first of the ethnographic chapters, I work at the macro-scale of the Mexican nation. Here, I analyze the way that Nahuatl is used by the nation-state in its communication with Nahuas and with non-Nahuas, and what this tells us about the state's engagement with Indigenous communities. Then, in Chapter 4, I work at the local scale of the *altepetl* of Hueyapan, Morelos, where Nahuatl revitalization has become part of a movement for municipal independence. In Chapter 5, I take a regional perspective, as I work in the Zongolica region in central Veracruz. This is one of the areas in Mexico where Nahuatl-speaking *altepetl* communities neighbor each other, and where there is consequently the possibility of the formation of a regional Nahuatl-speaking public, a possibility that I explore in the context of intercultural education at the Universidad Intercultural Veracruzana in Tequila. Finally, in Chapter 6, I zoom out to the transnational scale, across the border with the United States, as I describe how the use of Nahuatl is integrated into projects of cultural reclamation by Mexican American activists. In each case, I strive to show the articulations across scales—how events and processes at the transnational, national, and regional scales reverberate through the local scale and into the lives of individuals and families, and how social dynamics at the local scales fuel processes that play out at larger scales. This makes the ethnography not only multiscalar, but interscalar. I seek to achieve this in part by the addition of making frequent use of life history interviews. Such accounts of lived experience make it possible to access history as it makes itself felt, and as it is expressed in interpretation and narration (Ochs and Capps 2001). Life histories allow me to access subjective descriptions of how the effects of large-scale historical processes ripple through individual life trajectories. While it is possible to read the three ethnographic chapters as stand-alone case studies, it would be a mistake to approach them as separate mini-studies united only by a common theme of "Nahuatl language politics." Rather, they each contribute a piece of a larger argument, which can only be grasped in full when seen from multiple angles and in different contexts.

Each of the ethnographic contexts that I have worked in has required a different conceptualization of "the field" and of fieldwork, and different methods for collecting data. Therefore, rather than having a consolidated methods section, each chapter has information about the methods used for data collection within a specific context.

Positionalities

Each context has also motivated a wealth of different positionalities, more than I can reasonably describe in the traditional manner of the reflective ethnographer. Perhaps, the easiest way to describe how people have seen me is to mention some of the words, phrases, and titles that have been used to address me or to refer to me. I have been at different times in the field both a student (*el viene a aprender nuestra lengua* [he comes to learn our language]) or a teacher of Nahuatl (*el maestro sabe más Nahuatl que nosotros* [the teacher knows more Nahuatl than we do]; false, of course). I have been addressed as an honored guest with the exoticness and authority that comes from being a European foreigner, as *el profesor* (professor/teacher) or *doctor Jansen*. At other times I have been perceived as the odd stranger sitting with a laptop or a notebook in the corner and people have talked about me as *el muchacho de Dinamarca* [the lad from Denmark] or I have been assumed to be the son of the only other European to frequent an institution (*hablaste con el hijo de Günther*? [Did you speak to Günther's son?]).[18] When I was staying with the Sánchez family in Tlaquilpa, visitors would call me *pinotl*, a Nahuatl word meaning "stranger" or "non-Indigenous person."

In Hueyapan, I have been often described as *el güero* [the white/blonde guy]. But I have also been seen as a family member of respected community members (*es el yerno de Doña Mago* [he is Doña Mago's son-in-law], or as *sobrino del licenciado Fili* [the nephew through marriage of licenciate Filiberto], a *tio* or a *padrino* to someone's children, or a parent of a classmate to pupils in the local school (my daughter attended first class in Hueyapan when we were in the field). Especially through my wife Claudia, who is from Hueyapan and with whose family we have lived in the periods when we have been there, I have had the possibility of meeting many, many people in Hueyapan who received me cordially and openly because they knew her. The value of my access to her networks of kinship and friendship cannot be overestimated. Additionally, the fact that I have from the outset tried to speak as much Nahuatl as possible has also been a major source of access, since many people have found it to be excessively surprising to be able to speak Nahuatl with a foreigner, and have invited me into their lives simply because of this. My perspectives and the types of social contexts that I have had access to have of course been colored by these positionalities, and another researcher might have had a very different experience. Compared with Hueyapan, where I started work in 2004 and now have family relations, in most of the other contexts where I have worked my presence and positionality have been more traditionally ethnographic—a lone researcher staying in a community for a limited amount of time. Nevertheless, in many places I have maintained relations longer, and have returned to the same sites and met with the same people, returning to them, in various forms, the work that I have done. Because my approach, which is to understand as much as possible of the diversity of Nahuatl, requires visiting many places where the language is used, I have not always or everywhere been able to cultivate relations with as much dedication as I would have liked.

In studying the use of Nahuatl in the Mexicayotl movement in the United States, I have made use of digital ethnography, participating in online fora for the discussion of Indigenous Mexican cultures, language, and history, where mostly, but not only, people from the Mexicayotl movement participate. Here I have striven to be upfront with the fact that I was a researcher studying how they related to the language. Sometimes community members

---

[18] At the Intercultural University of Veracruz, many students apparently thought, or feigned believing as a joke, that I was the son of Günther Dietz, the university's director, who was from Germany.

have approached me to access my knowledge about the language, but in many other cases, they have been highly skeptical of me because of my positionality as a white European and an anthropologist (the word "culture vulture" has been mentioned more than once). Nevertheless, though I have not spent much time together with them physically, through the online fora, I have come to have friendships and professional collaborations with activists of the Mexicayotl movement, and I try to meet with them when I am in California and New Mexico.

Translation Practices

Rather than multilingual, I would describe my ethnographic method as *translingual*, by which I mean to refer to the part of the work that entails constant translation between multiple languages. My interlocutors in the field have, at different times, spoken different varieties and sociolinguistic registers of Nahuatl, Spanish, or English—and at any given time, I have had to strive to be maximally attentive to the nuances of meaning that can be expressed by minuscule variation (an impossible goal to achieve in full). Simultaneously, my own notes and thought processes have been carried out partly in my own native Danish, and partly in my adopted language of English. Often the analysis itself requires me to point out translational choices made by others working in two of these languages, or to note that texts in one language may be interpreted and represented in several different ways in the other. Moreover, all of this has to be represented now in English. Translation, then, is integrated into every single step of this work.

Translation is a central aspect of all ethnographies, even those where an ethnographer is studying their own community of origin among interlocutors whose language they share entirely. The old idea of anthropology as cultural translation has been critiqued for its tendency to see the task of ethnography as simply rendering the concepts of foreign societies into the concepts of one's own (Asad 1986). The "Writing Culture" anthropologists realized that this was a gross oversimplification of the task of the ethnographer. Crapanzano cited Walter Benjamin's quip that "All translation . . . is only a somewhat provisional way of coming to terms with the foreignness of languages" (Crapanzano 1986, 52). However, he noted that even this underestimates the complexity of the task, since it includes not only the act of interpretation of foreign words and concepts, but also the communication of those concepts intelligibly and clearly in another language, all while simultaneously making it appear as if their interpretation and translation are not provisional, but authoritative. The ethnographer "must render the foreign familiar and preserve its very foreignness at one and the same time" (Crapanzano 1986, 52). For all their interest in representation and translation, the "Writing Culture" anthropologists did not explicitly say much about the role of language differences in the work of ethnography. They seem to have assumed, reasonably perhaps, that the ethnographer understood the languages spoken by their interlocutors.

My impression is that many ethnographers working in Indigenous communities do not understand all the languages spoken by their plurilingual informants, but are content if there is one language shared between them, usually the majority language or a *lingua franca* that can be used to exchange information more or less without friction. They may then use a few key words in the Indigenous language strategically throughout the text, to achieve the effect of authority and foreignness mentioned by Crapanzano. Even today, few ethnographers are explicit about this process, and in many cases, it is not possible for the reader to actually assess how much or how little of the interaction took place in which language; and even direct quotations from interlocutors may appear only translated into English, without letting us know what language they were translated from (see also Tanu and Dales 2015).

This is a trap that I have tried to avoid as much as possible in this work, which is one of the reasons that whenever feasible, I reproduce the wording in the original language (usually Nahuatl or Spanish) in italics followed by my translation in square brackets. This allows readers both to see the original language and wording, and if they're able, to check my interpretation and translation against their own. Another reason that I use this representation, with large chunks of text that are likely to be unintelligible to the reader, is that, like Mannheim (2015), I do believe that "all translation is radical translation." Mannheim argues that since the meanings of linguistic expressions in different languages are grounded in ontologies that may be only partly commensurable, translations rest on *acts of transduction* (Silverstein 2003) where not only as much as possible of the denotational value of expressions feeds into the translational choices, but also as much as possible of their indexical relations and social and affective values. This requires a good deal of "thick description" (Geertz 1973) surrounding the translated text, including information about the ranges of meanings of the words used, how the range of possible meanings is constricted by context, other related words that could have been used but weren't, the sociolinguistic registers or genres that the expression draws from, and more. The work of translational commensuration is partial, and the translator should be able to account for the parts. This is the reason that in many cases, especially in the key examples, I give not only the original wording and my translation, but also in prose form my full interpretation of the original wording in relation to the context in which it appears, including, when necessary, analysis of the relevant grammar and vocabulary, sometimes in the main text and sometimes in footnotes.[19] With this method, I commit to a translational ethic that holds that every translation is fundamentally provisional and selected among many possible and potentially equally valid translations—and that each translational choice must therefore, in principle, be supported by arguments.

In terms of translation style, I have opted for a style that is relatively literal, at the expense of fully idiomatic English. This I do in order to attempt to convey part of the *feeling* of the language and its particular poetics, also in the translation, realizing that this is all many readers will have access to. It makes for translations that may be accused of being somewhat *foreignizing* (Leavitt 2015), but which also achieve the goal of keeping the foreign somewhat foreign while making it familiar; and perhaps activates the readers' imagination enough to offer them a glimpse into "an otherwise world" (Povinelli 2012).

---

[19] For example, "*Axan nehwa ahwel nan niyes semilwitl* [Nowadays I cannot be here every day]."

1b
Interlude

On Transcription

In the discipline of linguistics, when writing about languages that have no established writing system, one is generally expected to give a short description of the orthographic conventions used in the work, usually in the form of a key that ties specific graphic symbols to their related phones or phonemes. Such an orthographic key is often given in a footnote somewhere on the first page and then that is considered to have been taken care of. Since this book contains a good deal of written Nahuatl, it seems to be in order to give such a key. However, given that when writing Nahuatl any choice of orthography is itself an ideologically laden statement, it feels necessary to spend a little bit more than a footnote to reflect on the possible choices and their associated ideologies. Before embarking on Chapter 2, this interlude will show how the choice of orthography forms a powerful nexus that intersects both with the fact of linguistic diversity, and with ideological choices about how and whether to represent it. This section will also serve to introduce the reader to the different ways of writing Nahuatl, many of which will be used throughout the text when quoting or otherwise representing the language. The interlude may be excessively linguistic for some readers, who are more interested in the ethnography, and they can skip ahead to Chapter 2 without it affecting their understanding of subsequent chapters. In case they later end up having questions about Nahuatl orthography, they can jump back and read it.

Ideologies of Nahuatl Writing

One area in which language ideologies—about what Nahuatl is or should be and how this relates to the idea of what types of communities it represents—are often made explicit is the question of orthography. As is the case for many Indigenous languages of the Americas, there is no single orthographic standard for writing Nahuatl, but rather many different orthographic conventions exist and compete, each of them aligned with particular ideologies and perspectives. Paja Faudree (2015b) and Daniel Suslak (2003) have described how contestations over orthographic choices for how to write Indigenous languages of Oaxaca are politicized. In the Oaxacan context, such choices come to index membership and allegiance to different reading and writing publics, to interest groups, such as writer's collectives or organizations, or to specific local communities and their phonological variants. Nahuatl has a deeper history of literacy, and a much larger and more diverse base of speakers, readers, and writers than the Mazatec and Mixe languages studied by Faudree and Suslak. Nevertheless, there have been few attempts in the literature at comparing the different writing systems in use for Nahuatl, or at analyzing how they play a role in Nahuatl glottopolitics. In the following, I will sketch some of the relations between orthographic choices for writing Nahuatl and major structures of metalinguistic ideologies about the language.

One such question is whether the aspect of language to represent in writing is the pronunciation of the word. Linguists distinguish between two different levels of abstraction in the representation of word structure in writing. The phonetic level is the level of pronunciation, and phonetic transcriptions aim to capture objectively the sounds produced in a specific instance of speaking, each letter representing a specific position of the speech organs. The phonemic level, in contrast, is a representation of an abstract level based on a phonological analysis, and a phonemic orthography only represents those differences in pronunciation that are considered to differentiate between different referential meanings in the language. In notation, linguists distinguish between phonemic and phonetic writing by putting the former between slashes (i.e., /foˈniːmɪk/) and the latter in square brackets (i.e., [fəˈnɛtɪk]), and finally using angle brackets to represent the ortographic, written form <phonetic>.

The history of representing the Nahuatl language with the Roman alphabet had already begun during the earliest phase of the conquest when Cortés wrote his letters home representing names of Nahua people and places. Nahuas had been representing their language using logographic representations with a degree of phoneticism[1] already before that, but within a few decades after the arrival of the Spanish, they had adopted alphabetic writing as if it were their own. Young Nahuas were trained in writing by friars who also produced a series of *artes* (didactic grammars) that established a loose set of conventions for writing and analyzing the Nahuatl language. All of these writing conventions

---

[1] Whittaker (2021) engagingly describes how the native Nahua script worked by using signs for words to write words with similar sounds, e.g., a drop of water, a:(-tl) to phonetically write the syllable /a/, and a bean e(-tl) to write the syllable /e/.

were based on those that were in use at the time for writing Spanish, but just as there was no fixed orthography for writing Spanish, there was never a single convention for writing Nahuatl in the colonial period.

The reason that Nahuatl required a set of orthographic conventions that are different from those used for writing Spanish was that the Nahuatl language uses sounds that did not correspond to any sounds in the Spanish language, prompting the friars to make decisions about how to represent those, and each scholar made different choices. The result was that the orthographic conventions employed by Franciscan Andrés de Olmos in his 1547 *Arte para aprender la lengua mexicana* (which was the first grammar of an Indigenous American language) were not the same as those used by his Franciscan colleagues such as Bernardino de Sahagún and his Indigenous collaborators who wrote the Florentine Codex, which were not the same as the conventions of Alonso de Molina who wrote the classic 1571 *Vocabulario en lengua castellana y mexicana*. Their orthographies differed in turn from the Jesuit tradition of writing Nahuatl that was started by Antonio del Rincón (a native Nahuatl speaker) in his 1595 *Arte mexicana* and further elaborated by Horacio Carochi in his 1645 *Arte de la lengua Mexicana* (Carochi 2001). Even the individual friars themselves were not fully consistent in their orthographic choices. For example, they often used letters *u* or *o* and *i*, *y*, or *j* interchangeably, and the sound /w/ can be found written in several different ways in the Florentine Codex and in Molina's dictionary with the graphs <hu, uh, o, u, v>—even the same word may be written differently by the same author on different occasions. Colonial authors also frequently abbreviated and used shorthand, suggesting that for them the issue of convention was merely an issue of practicality of communication and not a question of choosing a single standard and sticking to it.

When linguists started writing about Nahuatl in the early 20th century, they had to establish conventions for how to represent the sounds of Indigenous languages. They strove to make sure that data about different languages were compatible, so that the same speech sounds were given the same letters, regardless of the language in which they appeared. Their ambitions were to make a single global system for the representation of all human speech. In the United States, one such system was developed by American linguists working with Indigenous languages. This system, dubbed the Americanist Phonetic Alphabet (APA), was used by the earliest scholars publishing about spoken Nahuatl varieties, such as Franz Boas (1917) and Benjamin Lee Whorf (1946). Meanwhile in Europe, phoneticians were developing a different phonetic alphabet, the International Phonetic Alphabet (IPA), which eventually became the standard used by linguists in writing all of the world's languages. Today one occasionally finds new texts that use the APA, but the vast majority of linguistics texts use IPA when giving phonetic representations of language.

There is wide agreement among linguists that in designing a writing system it is desirable to aim for a relatively phonemic rather than phonetic representation. This is not only because a phonemic analysis produces the minimal number of discrete phonological units necessary to reproduce all the sound contrasts that create meaning in the language, but also because there is good evidence that phonemic writing systems are easier to learn and use for native speakers (Seymour et al. 2003; Landerl 2005). This is presumably because they represent the specific contrasts that speakers learn to focus on during the process of language acquisition. Now, in principle, a phonemic orthography can use any set of random symbols to represent the phonemes of a language, but in practice the choice of which symbols to choose is based on adherence to some already existing conventions. That is, we can create a phonemic orthography based on the symbols of the APA or the IPA, or create it by adapting Spanish orthography or one of the conventions used by colonial grammarians. Unsurprisingly, this is where the discussions begin.

The Sounds of Nahuatl

To understand the intricacies of these choices, it is necessary first to know a little about the phoneme inventory and the sound structure of Nahuatl. First, we must point out that the different varieties of Nahuatl in fact have different phoneme inventories. This fact itself is not always recognized, and when people discuss Nahuatl orthographies, it is often assumed that it is possible to establish a single convention that can represent *any* variety of Nahuatl. When taking into account the diversity of sound systems used in contemporary Nahuan languages, it becomes clear that this is not necessarily the case. Typically, discussions of Nahuatl orthography start from the phonemic inventory of the variety of Nahuatl represented in the early grammars. This variety belongs to the central dialect area, based specifically on the way that nobles spoke in the polity of Tetzcoco, and it recognized only 15 different consonant phonemes. The consonants are represented here using the IPA sign corresponding to their most common pronunciation /p, t, k, kʷ, s, ʃ, ts, tʃ, /tɬ/, l, m, n, w, j, ʔ/. It recognized four vowel sounds /i, e, o, a/, with a contrast between long and short vowels, making a total of eight different vowel phonemes. Other varieties differ from this inventory, some having fewer, and some having more, distinct phonemes. In Table 1.1, I represent the consonant

Table 1.1 Nahuan Consonant Phonemes

	Labial	Alveolar	Palatal	Velar	Glottal
Stops	/p/	/t/		/k/, (/kʷ/)	(/ʔ/)
Voiced stops	(/b/, /ɓ/)	(/d/)		(/g/, /gʷ/)	
Fricatives	(/f/, /v/)	/s/	/ʃ/		(/h/)
Affricates		/ts/, (/tɬ/)	/tʃ/		
Liquids		/l/ (/r/)			
Glides	(/w/)		/j/		
Nasals	/m/	/n/		(/ŋ/)	

phonemes of Nahuan languages using IPA; the letters in parentheses are phonemes that are only found in certain varieties, whereas the letters with no parentheses are to my knowledge found in all varieties.

- The phoneme /ɓ/ is found in *Mela'tajtol Nawat* of Pajapan, where it is a development of the phoneme /kʷ/ which this variety now lacks.
- Some varieties have introduced voiced stops /b, d, g/ through Spanish loanwords, but in some varieties they are no longer limited to loanwords, but have become integrated into native vocabulary. The same goes for /r/ and /ɾ/.
- Some varieties in Zongolica have no [w] sound, but only the sounds [v] and [f], corresponding to the voiced and unvoiced allophones of the phoneme /w/ in other varieties ([f] corresponds to /hw/). It would be justified to argue that such varieties have a /v/ phoneme but no /w/.
- Some varieties have [h], others have [ʔ], as an expression of the phoneme often called *saltillo*, but the varieties of the Isthmus have both, since they have [h] for the original *saltillo* and have introduced /ʔ/ instead of a previous /k/ in syllable final position.
- The phoneme /tɬ/ has merged with /t/ in the varieties of the Sierra de Puebla, the Isthmus, Tabasco, and El Salvador. And it has merged with /l/ in certain varieties in Morelos, Guerrero, Michoacán, and Durango. Though the change of /tɬ/ to /t/ doesn't cause many problems of intelligibility, it is not a simple change, as speakers of t-varieties have no way to predict when a /t/ in their variety corresponds to a /tɬ/ in another variety. If they want to learn a central variety such as colonial Nahuatl, they have to learn it for each separate word.
- The velar nasal /ŋ/ is considered a marginal phoneme in Pipil Nawat of El Salvador by Lyle Campbell (1985).

For most phonemes, the choice of a letter is uncontroversial because there is wide agreement among Nahuatl scholars and speakers about how to represent them, but particularly the ones that are characteristic of the phonology of Nahuan, as opposed to Spanish, are the ones that tend to cause controversy. The most controversial phonemes are by far the *saltillo* (the phoneme that is a glottal stop in a few varieties and a glottal fricative in most others; see above), the bilabial glide [w], and the velar stops [k] and [kʷ]. However, before we proceed to describe how the different orthographies handle these phonemes, I will describe the different ideological bases for choosing how to represent them.

Linguistic, Historical, and Intuitive Orthography

There are three different types of logic that scholars, educators, and speakers use when deciding how to write Nahuatl. If we approach the question from an analytical perspective, as for example linguists typically do, it seems obvious that each phoneme should ideally correspond to a single letter. Under this criterion, the most rational alphabet is one that is maximally economical and uses a single symbol (or combination of symbols) for a single phoneme everywhere this phoneme occurs. Such an orthography is economic in terms of the different symbols used, and it represents the phonological structure of the word directly. Linguists know that such a structure is also easier to learn for the native speaker. This type of orthography tends to avoid the Spanish style digraphs, such as using the combinations <qu> to write the sound [k] before certain vowels and <c> before others, or using <hu> to write the sound [w]. Linguist Maurice Swadesh, who was a student of Edward Sapir, and who lived in Mexico during the 1940s and worked closely with the indigenist scholars who were working to promote Indigenous literacy, was the first to advocate this approach.[2] Perhaps due to Swadesh's influence, the Nahuas who participated in the First Aztec Congress held in Milpa Alta in 1940 adopted such

---

[2] Swadesh describes his preference for an APA-based orthography in a 1940 letter to Robert Barlow, located in the Barlow Papers of the archive of the Universidad de las Americas in Cholula, Puebla. He proposes that Nahuatl words in Spanish publications should use a simplified version that doesn't mark glottal stop, and which uses j for h, and which uses s for x. He follows the Asamblea de Filólogos y Lingüístas—not the Aztec Congress. He argues that the alphabet should be for Aztec monolinguals, and that it follows that the alphabet therefore need not follow the Spanish conventions. Also it is for them to know modern science, not to know their history, so following tradition is also not an issue, only ease of learning the script. He also critiques Juan Luna Cárdenas's idiosyncratic orthography which proposes to use the letter <ʒ> for the /tʃ/ sound and <ç> for /s/. This shows the interaction between American scholars like Barlow and Swadesh, and Mexican nationalist scholars like Cárdenas. As mentioned below, Barlow's Nahua friend and collaborator from Hueyapan, Miguel Barrios Espinosa, championed the APA-based alphabet, which had the virtue of neither being based on the Spanish convention nor incorporating letters not found on a standard typewriter as Luna Cárdenas's orthography did (although it did include the "English letters" <k> and <w>) (Barlow papers: [182.2–9]).

a convention as official. Today this system is advocated by linguist Andres Hasler (Hasler Hangert 1996), who has played a role in promoting this tradition in some Nahua-speaking areas, notably in the Zongolica region (see Figure 1.2 in Chapter 1). In addition, some Chicano groups prefer it, perhaps as a rejection of Spanish-type digraphs as part of a decolonization approach. Miguel Barrios Espinosa from Hueyapan, who studied linguistics with the American linguist Robert Barlow and promoted the use of the language in the 1940s, also considered the rejection of Spanish orthography to be important. He wrote "*inin totlahtol okse, tleka tikihkwiloskeh kemen kaxtillan?*" [This, our language, is different, why should we write it as if it were Spanish?].[3] Hence, this orthography can be motivated both by an ideological interest in representing each phoneme with a single corresponding grapheme (i.e., a letter), but also by an ideology that consciously rejects the colonial, Spanish-based orthographic convention as foreign.

However, if we were to adopt a perspective from the disciplines of history and literature, we might conclude that there is no need to introduce a new analytical orthography that differs radically from how the language was written during the colonial period, when so many written materials were produced. Instead, the most rational solution under this perspective would be to simply adapt the many colonial conventions into a single convention that allows us to read the many colonial documents written in Nahuatl with as little adjustment as possible. This way of writing assures that contemporary writers can see themselves as part of a continuous tradition of writing from the colonial period and up to now. Furthermore, it facilitates Indigenous readers' access to the colonial sources, since they do not have to learn a new orthographic convention. Finally, the fact that this writing system was highly successful in the colonial period could be taken to show that there really is no need to introduce one that is simpler, or which claims to be easier to learn. Proponents of historically based orthographies may sometimes argue that using other orthographic types constitutes a deliberate attempt to sever the sense of historical continuity between contemporary Nahuas and their colonial ancestors, in order to deny them of a sense of shared history and political community with the Nahuas of the past. This ideology is particularly common in the strand of scholarship that Paja Faudree (2013, 18–22) calls the "belletristic" approach, which treasures the comparison between colonial Nahuatl and "classical" languages of Europe, and which likes to draw direct links between pre-conquest poets and contemporary Nahuatl language authors (Faudree 2013, 213). Figure 1.3 shows an example of a document written in Nahuatl in the colonial

---

[3] Barrios Espinosa, Miguel. 1950. "Mexihkatl," *Mexihkatl itonalama*, Vol 1, p. 1.

Figure 1.3. Excerpt of the diary of Don Domingo de San Anton Muñón Chimalpahin, Folio 23, written in 1596.

Document located at the Bibliothèque nationale de France. Département des Manuscrits. Mexicain 220. doi: inark:/12148/btv1b8562411r; free permission for scholarly work).

period, the diary of Domingo Chimalpahin Quauhtlehuanitzin, a Nahua chronicler from the Altepetl of Chalco, south of Mexico City who wrote annals and chronicles in the late 16th and early 17th centuries using an orthography of the Franciscan style.

Some proponents of historically based orthographies also object to the use of the letters <k> and <w> on aesthetic or political grounds, for example calling them "American letters," or say that using them is too complicated. Historian John Sullivan (2011, 152), who is a vocal proponent of Andrews, Campbell, and Karttunen's historical orthography for use with contemporary varieties, objects to the "modern" orthography (with <k> and <w>), saying that "the new convention confuses the concept of everyday writing with that of phonetic documentation." Such an argument is not in fact meaningful, since the removal of Spanish digraphs (<qu>, <hu>, etc.) is entirely unrelated to the degree of phoneticity (pronunciation nearness) of the writing system. But it does demonstrate the degree of displeasure that the use of "new" letters may provoke in someone with a different orthographic socialization. Sullivan (2011, 152) summarizes the argument for using the historically based orthography by underscoring the feeling of historical continuity that it provides:

> We feel that spelling is the product of tradition and not of science. We are proud that our work builds on the great works of our fellow researchers, both past and present. Further, the conventions of the linguistic tradition are so different from older writing that they constitute an obstacle to the reading and study of the great corpus of works that constitute the written cultural legacy of the Nahua civilization.

In this way, Sullivan's historically based orthography forms part of an ideology of pan-Nahuan nationalism that values giving contemporary Nahuatl speakers, understood as a collective, access to the historical sources. In this perspective, a diversity of orthographies, or even a difference between the colonial and the contemporary orthography, becomes an obstacle for the pan-ethnic project.

Nonetheless, even among the proponents of historically based orthographies there are ideological differences that map onto the choice of orthographic conventions. Today, there are two historically based approaches to writing Nahuatl in use, and proponents of both are linguists who have studied the classical language, and both systems are developments of the system originally developed by the Jesuits. One system was promoted by American grammarians and historians J. Richard Andrews (1975, 2003), and R. Joe Campbell and Frances Karttunen (1989). The other system is used by the French linguist Michel Launey, whose monumental 1,600-page *thèse d'etat* was based on an analysis of the Florentine Codex (Launey 1986). Both of these orthographies use the Spanish digraphs such as <hu> for /w/ and <qu>/<c> for /k/, but they differ primarily in how they represent the *saltillo*. Andrews and his followers write it with the letter <h> which makes sense since this letter tends to be pronounced as [h] by English speakers, and since [h] is how most Nahuatl speakers pronounce the *saltillo*. Most colonial texts do not represent the *saltillo* phoneme, but one does occasionally find the use of <h> to represent the *saltillo*, although no texts use it systematically. Launey, on the other hand, uses the system proposed by Carochi, which represents the *saltillo* with an acute accent over the preceding vowel when in the middle of the word, and with a circumflex accent when word final. This way of writing the *saltillo* makes sense in reference to the Tetzcocan variety of Nahuatl, in which it was pronounced as a glottal stop. Many colonial linguists considered it not to be a distinct consonant segment but rather a type of accent, and the first to write the *saltillo* with a diacritic was Antonion del Rincón, who was a native speaker of Nahuatl, and whose intuitive analysis influenced Carochi (McDonough 2014, 52–55). Both Andrews and Launey adopt Carochi's convention of using a macron above the vowel to indicate vowel length. Today, Andrews's orthography is in wide use in the work of most North American historians who work with colonial sources. It is the standard adopted in Karttunen's important *Analytical Dictionary of Nahuatl* (Karttunen 1983), which gives it considerable weight.[4] Since Launey's pedagogical grammar was only available in Spanish and French until 2012, his orthography has been mostly used by Mexican and European scholars.

A further place of discussion is the representation of the phoneme [w], which Launey and Andrews both write as <hu> when syllable initial and <uh> when syllable final. Danish linguist Una Canger (2011b) has argued that although this convention of writing the sound [w] is found in many colonial sources, it is based on a misunderstanding of the orthography of Andrés de Olmos. Olmos was a careful listener and sometimes recorded differences in pronunciation that were below the phonemic level (that is, they don't distinguish different meanings). For example, in most Nahuan varieties the voiced consonant phonemes /l/ and /w/ are devoiced when occurring word-finally, where they are then pronounced as [ɬ] and [ʍ], respectively. These devoiced variants of the phonemes Olmos wrote as <lh> and <uh>, respectively, with a final <h> which represented the sound of aspiration. This suggests that Olmos

---

[4] It is sometimes called the Andrews/Campbell/Karttunen or ACK orthography, because it is also used by Joe Campbell and Frances Karttunen in their "foundation course," a popular Nahuatl learner's grammar (Campbell and Karttunen 1989).

had decided to write the /w/ sound with the letter <u> except when it was devoiced, in which case he added the h. Nonetheless, subsequent writers did not understand this subtle distinction of Olmos, and instead started using <hu> as a digraph representing /w/ in all contexts, instead of the simpler and more economic way Olmos had envisioned. Canger thus advocates a return to Olmos's original intent and no longer writes <nahuatl> but rather <nauatl>. This proposal also avoids the issue, implicit in the Andrews/Campbell/Karttunen system, that the letter <h> is used both to write the *saltillo*, and in conjunction with <u> to write the sound /w/, giving the letter two distinct values. This in turn causes orthographic ambiguity with the way of writing the phoneme /tʃ/ as <ch> in contexts where the sequence /kw/ is written <chu>—Canger's proposal avoids this ambiguity. Though even before Canger made her argument, some Nahuatl scholars, such as the native-speaker Luís Reyes García and his students, had followed this convention in their work, it has not yet gained widespread recognition, although it represents a significant simplification of the writing system, and simultaneously builds on tradition.

The use of colonial-type orthographies tends to privilege the variant sometimes called "classical Nahuatl," which is usually exemplified by the Nahuatl of the colonial grammars and the works of Sahagún, and based on the early colonial Tetzcoco variety. Proponents often assume that the standardized classical orthographies can be directly applied to all Nahuan varieties. This is, however, not necessarily the case. For example, it requires some significant accommodation to represent varieties that have introduced new vowel distinctions, such as the variety of Tetelcingo Morelos. In addition, given the use of <h> to represent both glottal stops [ʔ] and glottal fricatives [h], it becomes difficult to accommodate varieties that have both the stop and the fricative as distinct phonemes, such as the Isthmus varieties of southern Veracruz. These are all issues that do not emerge as long as one works only with colonial texts or with the most widely spoken contemporary varieties such as those of the Huasteca, North Puebla, or Guerrero, which tend to have phoneme systems fairly similar to colonial Tetzcoco Nahuatl. Figure 1.5. shows a sign written in a colonial style orthography, published by the Health Secretary of Puebla State; the Nahuatl variant it represents is that of Northern Puebla.

In spite of the large amount of scholarship produced in North America that uses the Andrews/Campbell/Karttunen orthography, a third perspective on how to write Nahuatl is even more influential among native speakers. This third perspective we may call the "practical" perspective, since it is primarily concerned with making a writing system that is acceptable to native speakers and easy for learners to acquire. From this perspective, it makes most sense to have a writing system that accommodates to the learners' preferences, and

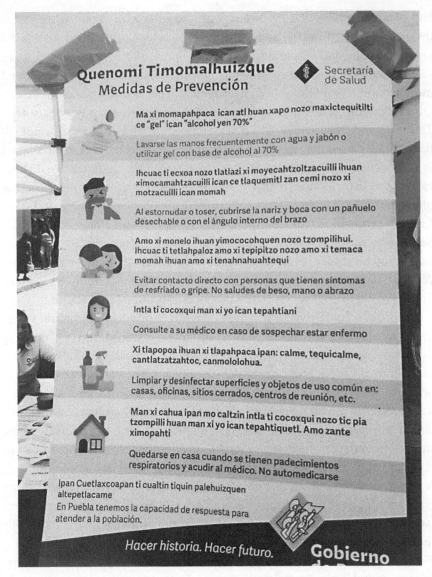

Figure 1.4. Nahuatl writing example, colonial/current, Huauhchinango 2020. Information sheet about how to avoid contagion with COVID-19, written in the Nahuatl variety of North Puebla, in a colonial style orthography, and published by the Health Secretary of the State of Puebla.
Photo by author.

which does not necessarily mark all phonological distinctions if these can be omitted without disturbing the reader's comprehension of the text.

"Practical" orthographies of Nahuatl have been produced within the Mexican system of Indigenous education, often by linguists working for the Summer Institute of Linguistics (SIL; or their Mexican branch, *Instituto Lingüístico de Verano* [ILV]), and promoted by SEP (*Secretaría de Educación Pública* [Ministry of Public Education]) since the 1930s (I have more to say about the collaboration between SIL/ILV and SEP in Chapter 2). In the case of Nahuatl, most of them have been based on using only the letters that children are assumed to already know how to use from having acquired Spanish literacy. SIL states this as one of their basic goals in orthography development (Benton 1999). That means that they often do not use <k> and <w>, which are not taught to children in Mexican elementary schools since they are not generally used in Spanish, and that they use the letter <j> for the sound [h], since Spanish does not have [h] and the <j> represents the sound [x] which is the closest equivalent. Today some SEP orthographies do use <k>; few if any use <w>. SEP orthographies also have local variants to accommodate dialectal variation, so that for example in the Isthmus, area where most varieties have both a glottal stop and a glottal fricative, <j> is used for the fricative and <'> for the stop. Practical orthographies generally do not mark vowel length, since in Nahuatl this very rarely distinguishes between word meanings, and can generally be inferred from context by native speakers. In some local SEP orthographies, vowel length is marked by underlining vowels, or by doubling them. During the 1950s–1970s, the Mexican branch of the American missionary organization ILV (*Instituto Lingüístico de Verano*) was responsible for the development of Indigenous orthographies for use within the Mexican education system. They often based their decisions about orthographies on surveys of the ease with which learners acquired the orthography, which formed the empirical basis for their orthographic choices. The consistent choice of Spanish-style orthographies by ILV linguists in their collaboration with SEP was a result of the fact that the goal of Indigenous language education during this period was to make it easier for monolingual Indigenous-language students to acquire Spanish. Literacy in the Indigenous language was generally conceived as a medium for acquiring Spanish, not as an end in itself. Today, the SEP often advocates SIL-style orthographies, and they are used by many bilingual teachers in the education system. Some important Nahuatl language authors, such as Natalio Hernández, continue to use and promote these SEP orthographies. They are preferred by many Nahuas both because they are easy to acquire for those who already know how to write Spanish, and because it is likely to have been the orthography first encountered by those Nahuas who have encountered written Nahuatl during their basic education. Figure 1.5 shows an example of Nahua elementary school writing, which mixes features of the SEP style orthography and the analytical orthography with <k> and

Figure 1.5. Nahuatl writing example, current. Child's drawing exhibited at the bus station of Tequila, in April 2013. Nahuatl text, written in an orthography using <w> and <k> but <j> for the glottal fricative /h/, mixing the SEP orthography with the analytical style orthography that is widespread in the Zongolica region. The text describes how one should open the windows at home and let the air through the house, to avoid getting sick frequently.
Photo by author

<w>, and also has some interesting phonetic spellings, probably reflecting local pronunciation of /ehekatl/ as [ehikatl] spelled <heikatl>

Finally, a large number of Nahuatl speakers have never encountered written Nahuatl during their education. When they decide to write their language, they have no choice but to improvise their own orthographic conventions. The process in which Nahuatl speakers reinvent their language as a written language can be observed online when native speakers begin to use the language on the internet. These intuitive orthographies tend to have some aspects in common. First, they tend to be pronunciation-near, that is, they reflect the pronunciation of the specific writer, without passing through a phonological analysis. This is probably because most non-linguist speakers are not consciously aware of the abstract structures of their language, and therefore do not have a concept of a sound structure that differs from the pronunciation they hear. Second, they tend to be primarily aware of those aspects of their language's sound structure that are significant in Spanish, the language in which they have learned to write. This means that intuitive writing systems often do not represent sound contrasts that do not exist in Spanish, such as vowel length. They also often overrepresent contrasts that are important in Spanish, but which are not a part of the Nahuatl sound system, such as the difference between voiced and unvoiced stops, or the difference between [u] and [o] (contrasts that are only found in some Nahuan varieties). For some reason, intuitive orthographies often use the letters <gu> to represent the sound /w/ (which is usually written as <hu> in historically based orthographies). This may be because in Spanish this convention is quite frequent, found in words such as *Guadalajara* [wadala'xara] (a city), *güey* [wey] "dude", *pingüino* [piŋ'wino], and so on, and because this is the spelling that Mexican primary schools teach as the "standard" representation of the sound [w] in first grade—even though the Spanish language also represents it in several other ways, for example, with <hu> in *huevo* [weβo] "egg" or *huacal* [wakal] "wooden box".

These intuitive orthographies also frequently do not use the letter <x> to represent the palatal sibilant sound [ʃ], but often uses <sh> instead, as in English. This is probably because many contemporary Nahuatl speakers are aware that these letters are used in English for the same sound as the one found in Nahuatl, but are unaware of the tradition of writing this sound with the letter <x>. Today many Mexicans, including Nahuatl speakers, pronounce the letter <x> as either [ks] or [s] when it occurs in Nahuatl-derived words and names. For example, the place name <tlaxcala>, originally pronounced [tlaʃ'kalla:n] in Nahuatl, is now often pronounced [tlakskala] or [tlaskala], or the name <xochitl>, meaning "flower" in Nahuatl and pronounced ['ʃo:tʃitɬ], today is generally pronounced ['sotʃitl] by non-Nahua-speaking Mexicans (among whom the name is most frequent). Intuitive orthographies also often do not distinguish consistently between words' affixes, so that bound affixes are often represented as separate words, if they correspond to a word in Spanish. For example, the subject prefixes, corresponding in meaning to the Spanish personal pronouns, which are free words, are often separated from the verbs that they are part of with a space, even though they cannot be moved into any other position relative to the verb, nor can they be pronounced separately as a meaningful word. This shows that when a person who has learned writing in Spanish begins to write in Nahuatl, they are generally only aware of the linguistic contrasts that they have encountered and learned how to represent in Spanish, which means that they unconsciously introduce Spanish influence in the way they write the Indigenous language. The unconscious nature of this process of Spanish-language influence means that it may sometimes contrast with conscious ideologies seeking to avoid

Spanish influence. Finally, when writing intuitively, native speakers of course use the letters that they feel best represent their specific local pronunciation. A speaker of a variety that has only [v] but no [w] may choose to use the letter <b> to represent this sound, since <b> is used interchangeably with <v> to represent that sound in Spanish. A speaker of a variety that voices the phoneme /k/ when occurring between vowels may choose to write that sound with the letter <g> even though it is not phonemic, and so on. This all makes the intuitive orthographies enormously diverse and sometimes very difficult for others to read.

Comparison of Different Conventions

The differences between the main orthographic systems can be demonstrated schematically as in Table 1.2.

The following is a side-by-side comparison of the different orthographies, writing the Nahuatl phrase, "I will write, you write too!".

IPA:	nehwa nitɬahkʷilo:s,	tehwa ʃitɬahkʷilo no iʍki!
APA:	nehwa niƛahkwilo:s,	tehwa šiƛahkwilo no: iwki!
Colonial style:	nehua nitlacuiloz,	tehua xitlacuilo no iuhqui!
Analytical style:	nehwa nitlahkwilo:s,	tehwa xitlahkwilo no: iwki!
A/C/K style:	nehhua nitlahcuilōz,	tehhua xitlahkwilo nō iuhqui!
Launey style:	néhua nitlácuilōz,	téhua xitlácuilo nō iuhqui!
Simple SEP style:	nejua nitlajcuilos,	tejua xitlacuilo no iujqui!
Complex SEP style:	nejua nitlajkuiloos,	tejua xitlakuilo noo iujki!
Intuitive style:	nejua ni tlajcuilos,	tejua shi tlacuilo no iujqui!

Table 1.2 Nahuatl Orthographies

Analytic/Hasler /Aztec Congress	Carochi/ Andrews	SEP/SIL	Carochi /Launey	Colonial	Intuitive
w	hu-/-uh	u	hu-/-uh	hu, uh, o, u	gua/guo/güe/ güi, -uh, u
k	qui/que, ca/co	k, qui/qui/ ca/co	qui/que, ca/co	qui/qui, ca/co	k, qu
s	ci/ce/za/zo	s	ci/ce/za/zo	ci/ce/za/zo, ç	s, z, c
h/ '	h	j, '	é, ê	-	j, h
x	x	x	x	x, s	x, sh
-	ē	ee/-	ē	-	-

Different orthographic choices emerge from different perspectives on what task is the most important function of writing, from different aesthetic preferences based on the socialization and experience of individual scholars and writers, and also signify adherence to broad ideological movements and arguments. When I have taught Nahuatl grammar to Nahuatl speakers, I generally tell them that they can use any writing system they like, but that I prefer they stick with one and use it consistently. I also tell them that regardless of which system they choose to use, they will eventually meet someone who will tell them that they are using the wrong one.

Orthographic Relativism

Given that there is no neutral choice of orthography, in order to be fair in my representation of the different ideologies of the Nahuatl speakers and writers that I describe in this volume, I will have to adopt a stance of "orthographic relativism." This means that I will not choose a single writing system to use consistently throughout the book. When I quote written Nahuatl, I will use whichever orthography is used in the original; when quoting spoken Nahuatl, I will try to use what I believe to be the preferred orthographic convention of the local community that the speaker's language represents. This means that when writing Nahuatl from Zongolica, as I will in Chapter 6, I will use an analytical system that uses <w> and <k>, because that has become the preferred system in most of the region due to the influence of linguist Andrés Hasler and the local collective of Nahuatl authors and activists *Xochitlahtolli*. When I write Hueyapan Nahuatl, as I will in Chapter 4, I will use a local convention that is closest to the intuitive system (for example representing the phoneme /k/ as <g> between vowels). The reasons for choosing this unconventional system will become clear in that chapter.

2
From Indian Republics to Covert Publics
Colony to Nation

Yz catqui	Here it is
nican humpehua, nican mottaz, nican ycuiliuhtoc	Here it begins, here it is seen, here it is written
yn cenca qualli, yn cenca nezcaliltlahtolli	The very good, the very exemplary speech
yn itauhca, yn ipohualloca, yn itlahtollo.	Its fame, its account, its story
yn inelhuayo, yn itepecho.	Its root, its foundation
Yn iuh peuhtica, yn iuh tzintitica	Thus it begins, thus it takes its base
yn motenehua huey altepetl	The mentioned great city
Ciudad México Tenochtitlan	The City of Mexico-Tenochtitlan
yn atlihtic yn tultzallan yn acatzallan.	Inside the water, among the reeds, among the rushes
...	
auh ynin huehue nenonotzaliztlahtolli	And this ancient word of council
ynin huehue nenonotzalizamoxtlacuiloli Mexico	This ancient written book of council of Mexico
yn oticahuililotiaque.	That we were left as they went
yn huel topial ynin tlahtolli.	It is our real treasure, this word.
ynic no tehuantin oc ceppa	Thus also we again
yn Topilhuan yn toxhuihuan	And our children, our grandchildren,
yn teçohuan, yn totlapallohuan	our blood, our relatives
yn totechcopa quiçazque	that will come forth from us
ynic mochipa no yehuantin quipiezque.	Thus, they will also always keep it.
Tiquincahuilitíazque yniquac titomiquillizque	We will leave it to them when we go on to die
o ca yehuantin yn intlahtolli huehuetque	And it is them, the words of the elders
yn nican tictlallia	That we put down here
yn antopilhuannican anquittazque	So that you who are our children, may see it
yhuan yn amixquichtin	And that all of you

Nahuatl Nations. Magnus Pharao Hansen, Oxford University Press. © Oxford University Press 2024.
DOI: 10.1093/oso/9780197746158.003.0003

yn amMexica. yn anTenochca	You who are Mexica, you who are Tenochca
nican anquimatizque	you will know here
yniuh peuhticatqui	how it was begun
yn oticteneuhque	The one we have mentioned
yn huey altepetl Ciudad México Tenochtitlan	The great City of the Ciudad México Tenochtitlan
yn atlihtic yn tultzallan yn acatzallan	In the water, among the reeds, among the rushes
ynon can otiolque otitlacatque	That wherein we lived, we were born
yn tinochca	The Tenochca people.

(§2 Crónica Mexicayotl, Hernando Alvarado Tezozomoc, 1609)

This text is one of the earliest and most evocative Mexican expressions of nationalism. It was written in the late 16th century, probably before 1581,[1] by Hernando Alvarado Tezozomoc,[2] a descendant of the royal lineage of Mexica rulers. His mother was a daughter of the last independent Mexica ruler, Moteczoma Xocoyotzin, and his father, a grandchild of the Mexica ruler Axayacatl, was the first of the Mexica rulers of Mexico-Tenochtitlán who were installed by the Spanish after the conquest of the Aztec Empire. As an heir to the royal Mexica lineage, the Mexican nationalism of Hernando Alvarado Tezozomoc was more accurately a *Mexica* or *Tenochca* nationalism, an identity centered in Mexico as an *altepetl*. This principle, of having a political identity centered, not in abstract ethnic affiliation, but in the local community of residence, has perdured widely among Indigenous peoples in Mesoamerica from precolonial times until this day.

Using primarily Indigenous sources, this chapter narrates a political history of Nahuatl-speaking communities from the decades after the conquest, through the colony, the independence struggles and the period of nascent nationhood, on through the Mexican revolution until the post-revolutionary establishment of the modern Mexican nation-state. The central argument advanced through the narrative is that throughout this period, Nahua communities have survived by cultivating their own publics through communal practices, also when their

---

[1] Peperstaete and Kruell (2014) argue that the original version of Crónica Mexicayotl was likely used by Diego Durán when he wrote his *History of the Indies of New Spain*, which he finished in 1581.

[2] The authorship of the main text of the Crónica Mexicayotl is debated. Susan Schroeder (1997) favors the Chalca historian Chimalpahin as the primary author, whereas others argue that Alvarado Tezozomoc wrote the main text, which Chimalpahin later copied and extended. Even Schroeder agrees, however, that the quoted text is written by Tezozomoc, though she does not consider it to be the introduction to Crónica Mexicayotl, but rather the afterword to another work.

survival depended on collaborating with, or making demands of, colonial administration or national governments. But I also argue that just as Habermas argued was the case for the bourgeois public sphere, this collaboration between Indigenous publics and the state carried the seed of its own undoing, because when Indigenous communities come to rely on the nation to address their needs, the communal practices of the local public risk losing their significance. The focus here is on the relations between projects of state nationalism and practices of Indigenous communality, and so I focus on the post-independence period, which has been relatively little studied, and dedicate less attention to the details of the much better described colonial period.[3]

Even though the royal descendant Alvarado Tezozomoc wrote at a time when his royal dynasty had been subjugated to the Spanish colonial regime for 60 years, he understood the interests of the Mexica tribe, not primarily in contrast to Spanish colonial dominance, but rather in contrast to the other Indigenous *altepetl*-polities that the Mexica descendants were competing with for prestige and privileges within the colonial order. To Alvarado Tezozomoc, an important group of competitors, the group with which he specifically contrasts the Mexica when he describes whose history it is that he is telling, were the Tlatelolca. The Tlatelolca were the neighbors of the Mexica and among their most bitter rivals. Mexico-Tenochtitlan, the capital of the Mexica tribe, and by extension of the Aztec Empire, was located on the southern part of an island, and the city of Tlatelolco had originated as Mexica rebels who broke away to settle their own city on the island's northern part. In 1463, Alvarado Tezozomoc's great-grandfather Axayacatl had conquered Tlatelolco and subjected it to Mexica dominance and taxation. But when the Spanish and their Tlaxcalteca allies besieged Tenochtitlan, Tlatelolco was the last refuge of the Mexica ruler Cuauhtemoc, who was captured in Tlatelolco as the city fell to the invading forces. And while Mexico-Tenochtitlan was demolished by the conquerors to erase all visible signs of the defeated Mexica rulers, Tlatelolco was spared the same degree of destruction; it even became the site of the first university of the Americas, the *Colegio de Santa Cruz de Tlatelolco*, where Nahua youths from the various noble lineages were taught to read and write in Nahuatl, Latin, and Spanish, and where many tomes of knowledge were produced. At the time when Alvarado Tezozomoc was growing up, the Franciscan friar Bernardino de Sahagún was working at Santa Cruz de Tlatelolco. There, Sahagún was training students to find and interview surviving Nahua elders

---

[3] For important work on the political organization of Nahua communities in the colonial period see, for example, Lockhart 1992, 1991; Haskett 1991; Wood 2012; Townsend 2019, 2016, 2009; Medrano 2011; Johnson 2018; Lee and Brokaw 2014; Mentz 2008.

who remembered the time before the arrival of the Spaniards, in order to produce the encyclopedia of Nahua culture which is today called "The Florentine Codex" after the Italian city where it is kept. Alvarado Tezozomoc writes that "as for Tlateloloco, there, we will never be dispossessed [of these stories], because it is not their patrimony that is being made" [*Auh in tlatilolco ayc ompa ticuililozque ca nel amo ynpiel mochiuhtiuh*];[4] it suggests that he was probably aware of this work in progress, and that he may have worried that the students at Tlatelolco might produce a view of history biased against the Mexica and skewed in favor of the Tlatelolca tribe. Hernando Alvarado Tezozomoc was writing exactly because he wanted to provide the Mexica perspective on their own history. The first Mexican nationalism was an Indigenous tribal nationalism, where political identities and loyalties grew from *altepetl* membership.

Hernando Alvarado Tezozomoc was also writing within a political order of colonial New Spain. In this system, the circumstances of one's birth determined one's category membership in the *casta* system, which in turn determined one's political, social, and economic status and rights. Spanish *peninsulares*, those who were born on the Iberian Peninsula, were the top class in the casta hierarchy. However, this category was also subdivided into social ranks that circumscribed the possibilities available in one's life, depending on whether one was born into a noble lineage or not, or whether one had feudal entrusted possessions such as *encomiendas* or not, whether one was suspected of having Jewish or Moorish ancestors or not, and of course whether one was a man or a woman. Below the peninsulares were the *criollos*, those born to pure Spanish lineage in the New World—also with an internal division along class and gender lines. Below the *criollos* were the *mestizos*, those with mixed Spanish and Indigenous lineage. Below them were the *indios*, the Indigenous population of the continent.

The *indios* were afforded a set of special political rights and protections, including the right to maintain their own separate territorial governance in so-called *Repúblicas de Indios* (Indian Republics), with *cabildos* (town councils) headed by a *gobernador* (Indigenous governor) (Haskett 1991). They were also considered by Spanish colonial officials to be morally inferior to Spaniards, in need of constant moral guidance by Europeans, and they were exploited for unremunerated labor and heavy taxes. Like the higher *castas*, the Indian *casta* was also subdivided along class lines, with poor *macehuales* (commoners) serving and paying taxes to the rich governing class of Indigenous *pipiltin* (nobles), who sometimes came to rival Spanish nobles in wealth and prestige. Within the Indigenous *casta*, there was also an ethnic hierarchy where

---

[4] Schroeder and Anderson (1997, 60) / MS374 fol. 18 recto, bottom.

some ethnic groups were more prestigious than others; those who had served as allies of the Spaniards in the process of conquest were afforded special privileges and land rights (Matthew and Oudijk 2007). The Tlaxcalteca people of Tlaxcala, whose alliance with the forces of Hernán Cortés had been decisive in the downfall of the Mexica, ranked among the most prestigious and privileged Indigenous ethnic groups. Below them followed the Mexica because of the prestige of having headed the Aztec Empire and for having assisted the Spaniards in their conquest of vast areas of Mesoamerica. Then followed the rest of the Nahuatl-speaking groups, who were considered among the most developed and civilized people of New Spain; then followed the many other non-Nahuatl speaking sedentary peoples, Mayas, Mixtecs, Zapotecs, Otomies, Tarascans, and so on. Lowest among the Indian groups were the nomadic or semi-nomadic peoples such as the Chichimecos and Guachichiles, who were considered uncivilized and largely uncivilizable, and who were frequently subjected to arbitrary massacres and enslavement by colonial officials. Figure 2.1 below, depicts (among other things) the Mixtón war of 1541 in which Spaniards and allies fought against the semi-nomadic tribes of Jalisco (depicted naked and with a bow). Together with the nomadic Indians at the very bottom rung of the *casta* hierarchy were the Africans, most of whom were enslaved and had almost no political rights.

In colonial New Spain, rights and privileges were determined by the circumstances and place of one's birth: a truly nativist political regime. Nevertheless, while it was resolutely nativist in that almost all significant rights, duties, and privileges were immutable and assigned by reference to one's category of birth, it was, like the Indigenous system of competitive ethnic *altepetl*-polities, also a multicultural political order. It established a highly stable, though also highly hierarchical, system of interaction between peoples from different cultural and linguistic groups, in which one was able to, and almost expected to, assert pride in and allegiance to one's own ethnic group. It did not presuppose any shared identity for all subjects of the Spanish Crown, nor for that matter for people who happened to speak the same language, such as all Spaniards or all Nahuatl speakers. The colonial political order, therefore, was nativist, but not nationalist.

Colonial Language Policy in Theory and Practice

The Nahuatl language had a special prestige within the society of colonial New Spain for several reasons: first, because of its association with the Aztec Empire; second, because it was a language that was already widely used in

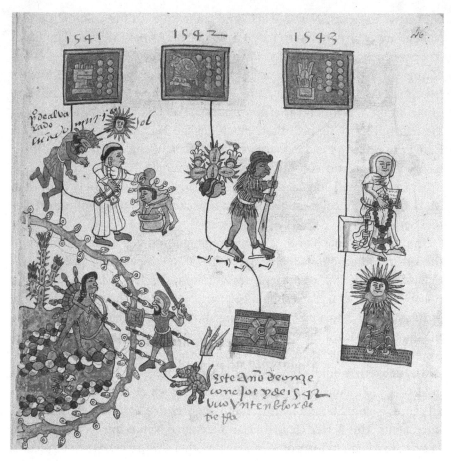

Figure 2.1 Folio 46 recto of the late 16th-century Codex Telleriano Remensis pictographically describing events in the years—"*10 House*"/1540, "*11 Rabbit*"/1541, and "*12 Reed*"/1542—including the death of conquistador Pedro de Alvarado (the attached glyph writing his Nahuatl cognomen *Tonatiuh* "sun"); a friar performing a baptism; a fight between a Spaniard identified with a name-glyph as ME-TOSAN (i.e., "Mendoza") and Indigenous archers (a reference to the Mixtón war); and an earthquake in Tenochtitlán/Mexico City. Though from an Indigenous perspective, the folio exhibits the blend of European and Indigenous cultural elements characteristic of the social order of the colonial period, see Rábasa (2011) for an extended analysis.
Source: Bibliothèque National de France, Département des Manuscrits. Mexicain 385.

interethnic communication before colonization; and third, because its usefulness increased as Nahua-speaking Tlaxcalteca, Mexica, and other auxiliary troops traveled along with the Spanish invaders, sometimes settling as a class of Indigenous colonizers wherever the Spaniards arrived, extending the reach of the Nahuatl language throughout the colonial territories from

Nicaragua to Texas, New Mexico, and California. In the colonial period, Nahuatl was most often referred to as *lengua mexicana* "Mexican language" in Spanish, or in Nahuatl as *mexihcacopa* "as the Mexica"—both labels taking as the prototype the variety of the language spoken by the Mexica tribe in Mexico-Tenochtitlan. This variety of Nahuatl was itself a mixture of the different Nahuatl varieties whose speakers had come to comingle in the metropolis of Tenochtitlán, which has led Nahuatl dialectologist Una Canger to refer to this language as Urban Nauatl, emphasizing the urbanized sociolinguistic context in which it emerged (Canger 2011a). This urbanized Nahuatl language was likely already a prestige variety in most of Mexico in the precolonial period, and it became even more so in the colonial period.

The language policy of the colonial regime toward Spanish, Nahuatl, and the other Indigenous languages spoken in New Spain changed substantially during the first centuries of colonization. Under Charles V, the basic policy was that all Indians should be instructed in the Christian faith and in Spanish. In 1565, this policy was changed by decree of Felipe II, now urging missionaries to learn the specific languages of the Indians among whom they were evangelizing. In 1570, Felipe II decreed that Nahuatl, because it was most widely spoken, should be the official language of New Spain.[5] This started a golden age of colonial Nahuatl writing, during which texts were written in all genres—from literature, history, and sciences to all sorts of administrative documents. This decree created a class of lettered Nahua intellectuals, such as Hernando Alvarado Tezozomoc and many others, who worked as interpreters, so-called *nahuatlatos*, scribes, and notaries, or who labored within the ecclesiastical system producing religious doctrinal texts or writing grammars and dictionaries of Nahuatl. Through collaboration between Nahuas and the friars who taught the natives to read and write, and also to read and write about Christianity in Nahuatl, a new form of Nahuatl was produced, that may be called "Missionary Nahuatl."[6] This register of Nahuatl, which was based on the urban Nahuatl of Mexico-Tenochtitlan, included new Nahuatl words for Catholic religious concepts and often subtly shifted the meanings of Nahua words away from their original meanings and into a meaning that fit within a Catholic worldview. The language policy of this period privileged not just

---

[5] "*Para que los dichos indios aprendiesen todos una misma lengua y que éste fuese la Mexicana que se podría deprender con más facilidad por ser lengua general*" [So that the aforementioned Indians should learn one single language, and that this should be the Mexican language which could be more easily acquired as it is the general language] (Archivo General de la Nación, México, Cédulas reales, vol. 47 [cited in Heath 1972, 52, 53]).

[6] Burkhart 1987, 26–28; Bierhorst 2009; Flores Farfán 2013.

the Nahuatl language, but specifically the Nahuatl language of the Valley of Mexico, and particularly the missionary register of the Nahuatl of the Valley of Mexico. This resulted in a sociolinguistic situation of the type Charles Ferguson (1959) called *diglossia*, in which many Indigenous communities used two different languages for different purposes—a vernacular language for everyday verbal communication, and another language, Central Mexican Nahuatl, for writing. Even in towns where people spoke Indigenous languages that were unrelated to Nahuatl, scribes would often write documents in Central Mexican Missionary Nahuatl; and in Nahua communities where the Nahuatl spoken was different from the Central Mexican standard, they would nonetheless write in the Central Mexican variety, although sometimes giving away hints of the vernacular. In effect, the Nahuatl-centric language policy created a language hierarchy to match the hierarchy between the ethnic groups: Indigenous vernacular languages at the bottom, Central Mexican Missionary Nahuatl at the top of the Indigenous language groups, and Spanish on top of the colonial hierarchy, superseded only by the Latin of the Catholic Church.

In 1634, Felipe IV reversed this Nahuatl-friendly language policy, decreeing that Spanish should be the sole official language of New Spain, and the only language of education and instruction (Heath 1972, 37–39). This decree, however, did not really undo the special status of Nahuatl among the Indigenous languages, which had by then become established, nor did it succeed in stopping what was by now a vibrant tradition of Nahuatl language writing (Carr 2012). Nevertheless, it did usher in a period in which Nahuatl and all other Indigenous languages of Mexico were slowly but gradually displaced by Spanish, first in the official sphere of language use, and then gradually in the Indian communities as well. This process of language displacement moved slowly through the second part of the colonial period (post-1634), as Spaniards increasingly encroached on Indigenous communities; settling inside them, although this was illegal, appropriating Indigenous lands and properties through dubious means, and dominating the sphere of commercial and economical transactions. In the local *altepetl*-communities (constituted now as *repúblicas de indios*) the process of language shift moved gradually. First, Nahuatl gradually stopped being used in the sphere of official written communication, making Nahuatl a primarily vernacular language, and then Spanish began also taking over the sphere of spoken communication, starting again with official or public speech genres, and finally coming to also dominate the speech of the intimate spheres of individual homes and family life. The dominance of Spanish was cemented with the royal *cédula* of 1770, titled "*Real cédula para que en los reinos de las Indias se extingan los diferentes idiomas de que se usa y sólo se hable el castellano*" [Royal decree that in all the kingdoms of the Indies the different languages that are used should be eradicated and that only Castilian should be spoken]. This decree abolished all education in Nahuatl, including for priests, made Spanish literacy a requirement for all public offices, and required Indigenous *cabildos* [town councils] to pay for Spanish-language teaching.[7] As the title of the decree establishes, this was a deliberate effort to move toward the extinction of the Indigenous languages of New Spain (Morris 2007, 439–40).

The Three-Stage Model of Colonial Language Change

Ethnohistorian James Lockhart spent half a lifetime studying the corpus of colonial Nahuatl text, investigating the linguistic signs of the process of language shift by examining the gradual changes in the number and kind of Spanish linguistic elements that crept into the Nahuatl-language texts (Lockhart 1991, 1992). He and the linguist Frances Karttunen proposed a model of language contact where the gradually intensifying contact between Nahuas and Spaniards correlates with gradually increasing contact-induced changes in the vocabulary and grammar of the Nahuatl language (Karttunen and Lockhart 1976). Lockhart based his subsequent analysis of colonial Nahua society on this model, and the method of tracing social change through linguistic analysis of colonial texts. Based on the documents they surveyed, Karttunen and Lockhart defined the first stage as spanning the period from first contact to approximately 1545. In this period, Nahuas were primarily reacting to all the new elements that the Spaniards brought with them, coining new words for the previously unknown technologies, animals, and social categories. Texts from this period mostly show newly coined words that describe the thing they refer to using Nahua lexical elements. For example, the word *quauhquauheh* "possessor of horns" was coined with the meaning "cow." Or the meanings of existing words were extended to new senses, such as when *ichcatl* "cotton" came to also mean "sheep" and "wool." In this period, Nahuas adopted few loanwords from Spanish, and when they did, they accommodated the loans to Nahua phonology, breaking up difficult consonant clusters that were not found in Nahuatl, and exchanging sounds unfamiliar to the quite small Nahuatl consonant inventory with their closest Nahuatl equivalent. For

---

[7] Heath 1972, 215–20; Tanck de Estrada 1989.

example, Spanish *almorzar* "have breakfast" was borrowed into Nahuatl as *almasaloa*, and *firma* "signature" was borrowed as *pilmah*.

In the second phase, defined by Karttunen and Lockhart as lasting from 1545 to approximately 1650, which was also the period when Nahuatl was the official language of New Spain, the contact with the Spaniards and Spanish administration intensified, and so did the linguistic signs of contact in Nahuatl. Nahuatl adopted many more loans from Spanish; borrowing Spanish words now replaced new coinage as the major strategy for finding words for elements originating in Europe or from Spanish society. Borrowings were also no longer phonologically adapted to the sound structure of Nahuatl, suggesting that Nahuas by now were familiar with Spanish and generally had learned to pronounce Spanish words, even if they were not necessarily bilingual. Texts from this period also saw the loss of some features of Nahuatl grammar. For example, the rule of Nahuatl grammar that had prevented the use of plural forms of inanimate nouns was now mostly suspended, most likely because Spanish had no such distinction between animate and inanimate nouns.[8] This change correlated with a loss of the traditional way of counting inanimate items, namely by using noun classifiers (a grammatical strategy similar to the way that English counts some mass-nouns, such as bread counted in loaves, or paper counted in sheets).[9]

In the third phase, starting in the mid-17th century, Nahuatl and Spanish intertwined even more. Loanwords were introduced profusely, almost willy-nilly—even for words and concepts that had adequate Nahuatl correspondences. Loans included grammatical particles and function words such as prepositions (which had not previously existed in Nahuatl grammar), and entire grammatical constructions were calqued into Nahuatl, changing core aspects of the language's grammatical structure. Spanish verbs were incorporated into Nahuatl discourse using the *-oa* suffix, which was appended directly onto the Spanish verb, turning it into a Nahuatl verb that could take Nahuatl grammatical inflection (e.g., Spanish *firmar* "to sign" became Nahuatl *firmaroa*, which could produce the inflected verbal form *nicfirmaroz* "I will sign it").

The three-stage model of language contact and change in the colonial period is a perspicacious and important analysis of the language of the documentary corpus from the period, and it tells us much about the social and

---

[8] In the early colonial period, inanimate nouns such as *tetl* "rock" or *xochitl* "flower" had no plural forms but were counted simply by adding the quantifier *ome tetl* "two rocks" or *miyac xochitl* "many flowers." Today most Nahua varieties allow them to be pluralized using the suffixes that were previously only used for animate nouns, *ome temeh* "two rocks" and *miyak xochimeh* "many flowers."

[9] Jensen 2008; Canger and Jensen 2007; Stolz 2018; Olko, Borges, and Sullivan 2018.

linguistic processes of the period. Recent scholarship on lexical change across the colonial period has confirmed a gradual increase in the use of Spanish vocabulary in Nahuatl language documents (Brylak et al. 2020). Nevertheless, the model cannot stand alone as a universal account of how the Nahuatl language changed in the colonial period, or as Lockhart also does, as a description of the linguistic situation in Nahuatl-speaking communities today. It relies on assumptions about the relation between written and spoken language that are not fully warranted, and on generalizations from certain sociolinguistic contexts to others, that may be warranted in some cases but not in others. A more nuanced model of the process of change undergone by Nahuatl in the colonial period would strive to understand the diversity of sociolinguistic contexts in which Nahuatl existed, and it would not take literate language to be a direct reflection of spoken language and its developments, but rather would recognize the diversity of sociolinguistic contexts of New Spain (and contemporary Mexico). The three-stage progression model describes the history of Nahuatl–Spanish contact as moving toward a supposedly inevitable endpoint at which Nahuatl disappears and all domains of discourse are colonized by Spanish. This is of course problematic from a political standpoint since most Nahuas, whether colonial or contemporary, have not thought of themselves as a vanishing culture doomed to disappear. It is also problematic because it is precisely contradicted by the reality observed in this book: that Nahuatl seems to be in some ways experiencing revitalization, even as contact between Nahuatl speakers and Spanish speakers continues to intensify.

Lockhart's model postulates causation between the intensity of contact between Nahuatl speakers and Spaniards and the degree of linguistic change and shift, but this causal link is not universally true. In many cases, Indigenous towns that are located in close proximity to major Spanish-speaking cities, and which have experienced intense contact with Spanish speakers for centuries, have maintained their language vigorously well into the 20th century, and even to this day. This is for example the case for the Nahuatl speech communities of Tetelcingo in Morelos (now within the urban zone of the city of Cuautla); also for Ixhuatlancillo in Veracruz (a five-minute taxi ride from downtown Orizaba), and for Milpa Alta (within the greater metropolitan zone of Mexico City), and for the Isthmus Nahuan towns next to the major port city of Coatzacoalcos and the oil refinery-town of Minatitlán (the political situation here is described by Chevalier and Buckles 1995). In all these cases, the fact that the Nahua community has been engaged in long-standing conflicts with the neighboring Spanish-speaking communities has seemingly *bolstered* their commitment to their local identity and to the Nahuatl language.

There, Nahuatl has persisted in spite of intense contact, with an emphasis on *spite*: one might argue that precisely conflict and competition between Nahuas and Spanish speakers has been the causal mechanism supporting the maintenance of the Nahuatl speech community. The process of language change and shift is mediated by the specifics of the sociopolitical situation, and the identity processes in which the contact situation is embedded.

The model also does not recognize the diglossic context in which the colonial Nahuatl texts were produced. Nahuatl-language texts exist from the entire colonial period and in almost all areas of Mexico and Guatemala, and therefore this giant corpus provides an invaluable source of information about the colonial process and how it affected language use. However, given that the people who produced the documents often spoke different languages and varieties than the one they wrote, we cannot extrapolate directly from the written language to what was happening with the vernacular languages (Madajczak and Pharao Hansen 2016). Literacy was not widespread, and those who wrote documents in Nahuatl most often learned to write through close contact with Spanish clerics. These scribes must be assumed to have generally been among the most proficient users of Spanish in their respective communities. Therefore, it is not enough to simply note the different ways in which Spanish gradually entwines more and more with Nahuatl in the colonial documents and then conclude that Nahuatl was gradually disappearing or turning into Spanish.

A paradox springs to eye when we compare the geographic distribution of colonial Nahuatl text production with the distribution of Nahuatl languages today. The paradox is that there is almost no overlap. The places that produced the most Nahuatl language texts were major cities whose inhabitants are not Nahuatl speaking today (and were mostly not Nahuatl speaking at the end of the colony), whereas the regions and towns with the highest concentrations of Nahuatl speakers today usually produced few if any Nahuatl-language texts in the colonial period. In Lockhart's causal framework, this paradox is a result of the more intense contact between Nahuas and Spaniards in cities. But the discrepancy also points to the fact that literary production in Nahuatl was *itself* a sign of the intensity of contact. In those Nahua communities where contact between Spanish and Nahuatl speakers was least intense because the colonial administration was less present there, there was less pressure for a constant production of written documentation, and the communities could maintain a largely oral public sphere using their vernacular languages. In contrast to the presence of texts written in the Latin alphabet, many of the rural towns where Nahuatl has endured the longest have maintained their histories and land claims in non-linguistic forms: in maps and land titles representing their territories in non-alphabetic form perhaps closer to pre-contact forms of writing (Ruíz Medrano 2011; Wood 2012). For this reason, we must not be misled into thinking that any production of Nahuatl-language texts can be understood simply as an expression of Indigenous nationalism: the written Nahuatl was not necessarily tied to the ethnic identities of the community where it was written, nor does it necessarily suggest the presence of a vibrant Nahuatl-speaking public in the community where the text was produced. Nahuatl texts in the colonial period were written, not necessarily for a local Indigenous audience, but rather were produced on the behest of a colonial regime that, for a time, had chosen this variety of Nahuatl as its favored means of communication between itself and the Indigenous population. This is not to say, of course, that texts were never produced for the use of Nahuatl-speaking local communities; they frequently were, and elements from the Missionary Nahuatl register of the Indigenous lettered class spread also to the vernacular languages of the communities. But it does mean that we must remember that in the colonial period, the Nahuatl that was written down did not belong to anyone—because it belonged to everyone, and particularly to the colonial system.

Nahuatl and *Criollo* Nationalism

This special status of the Central Mexican variety of Nahuatl as a colonial vehicular language of interethnic communication within an ethnic regime where certain groups of Nahuatl speakers held a privileged status is a key element for understanding the roles of Nahuatl in the development of Mexican nationalism in the 19th century. The colonial division of the Indigenous communities into elites and commoners, and the particularly privileged status of the Nahua elite, took on a crucial significance for the political development of many Nahua communities at the beginning of the 19th century, as the colony of New Spain became the nation of Mexico. Some Nahua elites managed to become powerful within the *Repúblicas de Indios*, amassing wealth and land, and achieved status comparable to many Spanish landowners. At the end of the colony, they were often able to pass from the colonial *casta* class of *indios* directly into the upper class of the Mexican nation, simply by giving up their visible ties to their local communities and to Indigenous culture.

At the same time, the *criollo* class of Spaniards, who were Spaniards but lacked the full political rights of the *peninsulares*, were becoming increasingly dissatisfied with this status. In their works, *criollo* intellectuals developed a suite of symbols of Mexican-ness that was to become central in the emergence of the national identity. Emergent nationalist authors used the literary variety of Nahuatl used in the colonial texts to tie the Mexican experience to the glorious national past it represented. Without doubt, the most important symbol taken up by the *criollos* in this way was the Virgin of Guadalupe. The first known description of the apparition of the Virgin of Guadalupe is from 1647, written in Nahuatl by the *criollo* lawyer Luís Laso de la Vega, and it tells the story of the Virgin appearing to the Nahua commoner Juan Diego (Poole 1995). Early *criollo* Guadalupanists included the polymath and antiquarian Carlos Sigüenza y Góngora (1645–1700), who collected Nahua codices and documents, and even integrated a sequence of Aztec rulers into the arch of triumph made to welcome the new viceroy, positioning him as the successor of the Aztec Empire (Brading 1991, 362). Similarly, nun and poet Sor Juana Inés de la Cruz (1602–1680), a friend of Sigüenza y Góngora, mixed Nahuatl into her works to evoke a *criollo* ambience, adding carnivalesque color to her representation of a uniquely Mexican way of life, inaccessible to the Spaniards. Later in the 18th century, Jesuit scholar Francisco Javier Clavijero (1731–1787), who had learned Nahuatl as a child in Veracruz, likewise strove to create an image of Mexico as being glorious in its own right by comparing it directly to the ancient world. In his *Historia Antigua de Mexico* (Clavijero 1844), he compares Texcoco to Athens and its ruler Nezahualcoyotl to Solon, and Cholula to ancient Rome, and Nahuatl to Latin and Ancient Greek (Bárbara Cifuentes 1996). Clavijero was also instrumental in changing the significance of the term *mexicano* [Mexican], to apply not only to speakers of Nahuatl, but in a sense of Mexican nationals—co-opting the term, and by extension the Mexican language, for the nation. Clavijero was also among the first to idealize the Nahuatl recorded in the early colonial sources for its large and nuanced vocabulary, with many concepts showing a highly developed state of intellectual life, and conversely he was also among the first to lament the "degenerate" state of Nahuatl spoken by rural Indigenous communities. This practice of idealizing the culture and language of ancient Nahuas and their language, while despising the contemporary ones, remains a highly damaging element of nationalist approaches to Nahuatl to this day.

Nahuatl was used by *criollos* as an aesthetic element in a new cultural identity, standing in for those aspects that made the *criollo* experience different from the implicit European norm. This hybrid identity was the seed from which Mexican nationalism, as the identity component of the independence movement, sprouted.

Independence: Nahuas and the Nation

> Mazehualzizinti nancate ipan inin Cemanahuac ihuan nan motlatotl mexicacopa, ihuan amo nan quimati caxtelancopa sanhuel yehuatl tianguis tlatole. ¿Nanquimati clen quitos nequi Constitucion? Amo nanquimati, ihuan amo nanquimatisquiaya semicac tia ipan nan motlatotl amo nan mechilhuisque. Xicaquica noso clen axcan nan motechi monequi, iquac mocentlales mochin clamancle ihuan nan ixclamatisque.
>
> *Macehuales* [Indian commoners] you who dwell here on earth and whose language is that of Mexico, and who do not know the language of Castile, just that marketplace language. Do you know what the word "constitution" means? You do not know, and you would never know unless someone will tell you in your own language.
> Listen here to what you will need to know now, as everything "will be put to together henceforth, and you will know".
>
> **(Bustamante 1820, "La Malinche de la Constitución"**
> **[As reproduced in Horcasitas 1969])**

In 1820, the year before Mexico finally achieved independence, the nationalist leader Carlos Maria Bustamante wrote a manifesto directed to the nation's *indios* urging them to support the cause of independence (Horcasitas 1969). Bustamante had collaborated with the revolutionary forces of Jose Maria Morelos y Pavón, ending up in prison in Veracruz with the fall of the Morelos revolution, and he wrote this manifesto from his cell. Bustamante titled his treatise "The Malinche of the Constitution," referring to Malinche, the Nahua woman who served as translator between Cortés and the Nahuas during the Spanish invasion. Its argument is a call for the Indians to recognize the liberating force of the national constitution, which Bustamante states will set them free from the abuses of the hacienda owners. It also includes an exhortation to dutifully take up the responsibilities of a Mexican citizen, refraining from alcoholism and embracing education and civil virtues. Today the document reads as a surprisingly explicit mixture of patronizing racism and liberal rhetoric. Tom Nairn has written that nationalism must necessarily present itself in culturally populist terms, because the people and their idiosyncrasies are all it has to go on; when the intelligentsia invited the masses into history "the invitation card had to be written in a language they understood" (Nairn 2003, 328). "The Malinche of the Constitution" is a clear example of such an "invitation card," however clumsy its execution.

Horcasitas proposed that Bustamante's letter was translated by a Nahuatl-speaking fellow prisoner, who might have been one of the many Nahuas who took up arms for José Maria Morelos's rebellion. There are a number of irregularities in the orthography of the Bustamante letter that makes me think that whoever wrote it had never before written in Nahuatl and improvised the orthography—for example, the /tl/ phoneme is consistently written with <cl> (the most similar sound in Spanish to the Nahuatl /tl/), and words are frequently divided, setting prefixes apart from the roots. This is all quite similar to how today's native Nahuatl speakers intuitively write their language when they have only received training in writing Spanish. The translation itself is clearly written by a competent speaker. This suggests that perhaps the translator was a Nahua person who had participated in Morelos's independence movement and ended up a prisoner in Veracruz alongside Bustamante.

Ten years earlier, in 1810, just as the independence struggle was breaking out in earnest, the liberal royalists[10] published a series of broadsides in Nahuatl urging the Indians to rally around the legitimate authority of the king of Spain (Morris 2007). The identities of the Nahuatl speakers who translated these independence war tracts remain unknown, but they must have been native speakers allied with opposing sides of the independence movement. It has been suggested that the 1810 royalist broadsides were translated by Rafael Tiburcio Sandoval, an Indigenous priest in the parishes of Ecatzingo and Tetela del Volcán, who also published a grammar of Nahuatl in 1810. Sandoval, if he was the translator of the broadsides, was not simply a loyal supporter of the Crown. In his 1810 grammar, he severely criticized the 1770 decree that abolished the use of Indigenous languages in evangelization, and, in fact, its very publication defied the decree (Morris 2007, 450).

In the Mexican historical imagination, the independence struggle has been understood as the result of the emergence of a new public sphere of *criollo* intellectuals who imagined into being a new public of independent Mexicans. As Eric van Young (2001) has amply demonstrated, this narrative leaves out the role of local publics, often Indigenous, that strived primarily to resolve local grievances against the hegemonic order, and seized on the new political ontology offered by the independence discourse as a way of inserting their local struggle into a broader political movement. Recently the Indigenous

---

[10] The Spanish realm was undergoing liberal reforms with the Laws of Cádiz at the time of the beginning of the Mexican independence movement. One way in which they practiced this liberalism was by advocating the abolition of the tribute paid by Indigenous communities to the Crown, which was also, according to Morris (2007), a selling point in the Nahuatl broadsides.

participation in the struggles that led to the end of the colony has received renewed attention.[11] While long ignored or minimized, today there can be little doubt that Indigenous people participated in the independence struggles to a comparable degree to all other segments of the Mexican population. This fact suggests that Indigenous people were also swept up by national and liberal ideologies that originated among the *criollo* elites, or, alternatively, it could be interpreted to mean that Indigenous people saw the independence movement as a way to achieve their own objectives and participated primarily as temporary allies. Probably both arguments would be true—Indigenous people did not form a homogeneous class, and their motivations for their participation in the independence struggle must have been varied.

The independence movement, however, turned out to be a double-edged sword for Indigenous communities. The introduction of the liberal Cádiz constitution in Spain in 1812 abolished the *casta* system and constituted Indigenous groups as Spanish citizens. The status as citizens with equal rights to all other citizens was retained in the Mexican Constitution of 1824. This entailed the abolition of Indian republics, and the dissolution of Indian *cabildos* and subsequent constitution of new bourgeois *cabildos* that were open for participation only for property owners. The end of indigenous cabildos also meant an end to the need for indigenous-language *escribanos*, and to the production of administrative documentation in Nahuatl, although the process that ended this tradition was not as complete or as abrupt as it has often been described (see, e.g., Melton-Villanueva 2016). In effect, this led to a kind of political decapitation of the Indigenous *altepetl* communities, as Indigenous elites such as governors and their families, who had better access to economic resources and to the Spanish language than lower-class Indigenous people, became able to participate in the new national public sphere as landowners with political representation. Landed Indigenous elites increasingly oriented their political attention toward the national political sphere, in which they had access to an unprecedented degree of social mobility. The lower classes, in turn, had to remain in place, now functioning as a working class of peons for the landed elite. Indigenous *altepetl*-communities had to struggle to maintain control of their collective land resources that were often targeted by the wealthy owners of *latifundios*. Sometimes these hostile landowners were even their own former leaders, who could now easily alienate land from the communal holders who now no longer had a political organization to represent them.

---

[11] Van Young 2001; León-Portilla and Mayer 2010.

The Cargo System as Indigenous Mutualism

Without an official structure of political organization and representation, Indigenous *altepetl*-communities were no longer recognized as political communities within the national order. Rather, from the perspective of national politics, they were simply groups of private citizens who lived close to each other and shared certain cultural and linguistic particularities. Nevertheless, from the perspective of the Indigenous members of each *altepetl*, they continued to be "communities," and merely reconstituted themselves in the form of civil societies within the liberal national order.

One way through which Indigenous communities reconstituted themselves as civic organizations in the early national period was through the development of widespread religious lay-brotherhoods known as *mayordomías* or *cofradías*, into a quintessential form of Indigenous social organization known as the cargo system. The cargo system, as it still exists in many Mexican towns today, is a hierarchic network of civic-religious offices that include offering public service in the form of labor, food, and goods for religious festivals, in exchange for increasing prestige within the community, and the ability to hold increasingly more prestigious offices. The origins of the cargo system have been much debated, but it seems established by now that while it clearly has particular functions in Indigenous communities and a degree of fusion with pre-Columbian cultural practices, it is best understood as a relatively recent introduction in its contemporary form (Chance and Taylor 1985). Colonial *cofradías* seem to have been primarily a network of religious education, whereas in the post-independence period they took on a much more political form, a development that can be understood as a response to the political decapitation of the Indigenous publics in which the lower classes regroup, organizing themselves in mutualistic collectives within the private sphere. The *cabildo*, the church staff, and the *cofradía* have been described as the three main pillars of social organization in the colonial Indian town, but because the liberal laws defined the religious domain as lying outside the public sphere, the latter two were not affected by the abolition of the Indigenous public. This made it possible for Indian *altepetl*-communities, which had never practiced a distinction between politics and religion in the first place, to use the *cofradía* as the space for the establishment of a new public sphere.

The *cofradía* system has the peculiar trait that it is organized as a colonial *cabildo*, a hierarchical structure with officeholders, but since it operates through voluntary association (at least in principle) and within the religious domain, it was and is not generally considered a forum of public politics. Nonetheless, in many contemporary communities there is clearly a significant overlap between public politics and the cargo system, since successful cargo-holders are often more likely to become elected officials of the public. Similarly, the related system of *compadrazgo* (ritual co-parenthood) also seems to have taken on political functions in this period as the venue for the establishment of individual client–patron relations, under the guise of mutual solidarity (Nutini and Bell 1980).

The cargo system, in which members share goods and services within a religious framework, is precisely organized around a collective discourse of the common good, phrased in both religious and material terms. While the cargo system tends to be seen as a private sphere organization from the perspective of the official national politics, for the Indigenous people who participate in it, it is a major forum concerned with promoting the common good of the community (Martínez Luna 2009). To understand Indigenous politics, and how Indigenous political communities have survived two hundred years of increasing assimilation into the Mexican national sphere of politics, we must acknowledge that they have thrived in forms that are invisible from the vantage point of national politics. They reconstituted themselves in ways that have the outward appearance of a civic society organization, but which have the inward function of *covert publics*, which combined a colonial conception of political organization, the *cabildo*, with traditional conceptions, and tied together religious practice and mutual sharing of wealth. Doubtless, Kropotkin ([1903] 2021) would have no difficulties seeing the development of *cofradías*, in the period in which Indigenous communities experienced the most vicious onslaught against their communal property and conditions of life, as an expression of the human tendency toward employing mutual aid as a political strategy of resilience in the face of adversity.

Nahuatl Text Production in the 19th Century

The change in the political status of Indigenous communities also changed the usage patterns of the Nahuatl language. As Nahua publics were increasingly "privatized," by being reinterpreted as belonging to the private sphere and not to the sphere of national politics, they also became increasingly oral. Central Mexican Nahuatl lost importance as a language of political organization, and the local vernacular languages, although often profoundly influenced by literary Nahuatl, became the codes in which local public spheres worked. Jane and Kenneth Hill have described how in the 1970s, in Tlaxcalan towns, Nahuatl served as a code of solidarity—the language of mutuality and respect—whereas a more Spanish-influenced variety of Nahuatl, lacking the grammatical signs of respect and mutuality, serves as a "code of power" and dominance. In many Nahua towns, the social life of the *cofradías* is the main social domain where Nahuatl is used, and the register of Nahuatl of the *cofradías*, also used between compadres, is that in which the honorific registers, with their complex grammatical markings of respect, are most vigorously maintained (Hill and Hill 1978). The *cofradías* became a sphere of solidarity and mutual aid; and Nahuatl, the most elaborately respectful and polite kind of Nahuatl, became its language.

Where the decree prohibiting the use of Nahuatl in print was unsuccessful in exterminating Nahuatl text production, the transformation of Indian republics into towns with no formal independent status, setting them aside from any other town, resulted in the de facto termination of the colonial tradition of Nahuatl language literacy. Even those towns that passed to become independent municipalities now had to communicate in Spanish with the other branches of government at the state and national levels. Because Indigenous communities lost the political infrastructure that required written documentation, and because the written documentation that was required from them now had to be conducted in Spanish, they also largely stopped producing texts in Nahuatl. In histories of Nahuatl, the 19th century is often skipped altogether as a sort of vacuum between the colony and the *mestizo* nationalism of the mid-20th century. However, there were texts produced in Nahuatl in the 19th century, and they do tell us something about the political status of speakers of Indigenous languages within the early Mexican mation.

Like "The Malinche of the Constitution," most of the texts published in Nahuatl in the 19th century, including those from the Reform War in the mid-19th century, were in the form of propaganda. They are official texts, translated and produced by Nahua intellectuals, and issued by the diverse factions invested in the struggles to determine the future of Mexico. While they speak on behalf of non-Indigenous authors, they address Nahua people as an audience. This shows that in the 19th century, when Indigenous people still made up a significant percentage of the Mexican population, the Nahuas were an important constituency. Even in the 1910 national census, *monolingual* speakers of Nahuatl alone counted above 500,000 and made up more than 3% of the country's total counted population (there is reason to believe that Indigenous peoples were particularly undercounted).

These texts show some of the functions taken on by literate Nahua intellectuals as mediators between the Mexican nation and their own Indigenous nations during this period. Now that Indian *cabildos* no longer existed and communal land claims had little weight, there was no official platform from which to address communal grievances. This meant that communities had to find new ways to access the public sphere and its officials, and to forge alliances with people and institutions in power. During the 19th century the main political division in the Mexican national public was between conservatives and liberals, and throughout the middle of the century Mexico was waging war, either between the liberal and conservative factions, or between the faction in power and external invaders such as the United States and France. In order to find a platform for advancing Indigenous concerns, Nahua intellectuals had to ally with different sides that they believed to be best able to provide solutions. Typically, the problems faced by Indigenous communities in this period were land conflicts, as haciendas and corporations aggressively encroached on Indigenous communities. In some cases, land conflicts between communities were fueled by the legal basis for the privatization of communal lands, which also allowed for the recuperation of lost patrimonial lands of communities, which could be reclaimed and then redistributed into privately owned plots. Because different liberal factions interpreted liberal legislation as either prohibiting communal landholding entirely and mandating disentailment ("disentailment" is the word used for the policy of privatization of communally owned lands), or as simply making it a possibility for communities to switch to private ownership, it was sometimes in the best interest of Indigenous communities to side with the liberals, and sometimes to side with the conservatives, in the quest for maintaining their land bases (Mallon 1995).

In the period between 1858 and 1876, Mexico was ravaged by wars between liberals and conservatives called the Reform Wars. In 1861 the wars were interrupted by the French Intervention, in which France sought to place Maximilian of the Habsburg family as emperor of Mexico. During this period, Nahuatl again came to be used in public statements calling on the Indigenous constituency to take sides. Best known among these are the propaganda treatises in favor of the emperor Maximilian, and Maximilian's decrees issued in Spanish and Nahuatl. The person behind these translations was the emperor's personal translator and Nahuatl specialist, Faustino Galicia Chimalpopoca. Probably the single most significant Nahua intellectual of the 19th century, Chimalpopoca was a descendant of the noble lineage of Tetzcoco. Before his involvement in politics, he was a member of the Society for Geography and Statistics, which was the main official institution that dedicated attention to Indigenous languages in 19th-century Mexico, and he was a professor of Nahuatl. He is well known for his controversial translations of Nahuatl codices, and for having translated a series of decrees by Maximilian into Nahuatl, as well as redacting a *proclamo* [proclamation] in Nahuatl urging Nahuas to join and support the emperor against the liberals (León-Portilla 2003). In her description of Chimalpopoca's life and times, Kelly McDonough (2014) represents him as a true organic intellectual working actively to defend the rights and interests of Nahua people, who were often adversely affected by the reform process that privatized communally held Indigenous lands. She describes how on several occasions he was consulted by representatives of Nahuan communities who sought his help in land disputes. She argues that it was exactly his interest in defending the rights of Indigenous communities that led him to become a close collaborator of Maximilian, whom he considered much more in tune with Indigenous needs and interests than the liberals. One might say that Faustino Chimalpopoca found liberal nationalism to be less attractive for Indigenous communities than a benevolent imperialism. In the end, this alliance cost him dearly when the liberals, led by Benito Juárez, ousted the French and executed the emperor. Chimalpopoca, who himself barely escaped execution, was basically written out of the intellectual history of 19th-century Mexico. His translations were disparaged, and his other writings forgotten.

Another member of the Society for Geography and Statistics was Miguel Trinidad Palma, a conservative priest from Puebla, who published a Nahuatl grammar in 1886, and who in 1888 produced a translation of the 1857 liberal constitution into Nahuatl. He dedicated the translation to Porfirio Díaz, the hero of the war against the French, who had by then been president for over a decade. Contrary to Chimalpopoca, Trinidad Palma seems to have picked the winning horse, and his translation can be considered a victory tribute to the liberal cause, more than a document aimed at an Indigenous public, which by 1888 was unlikely to be literate in Nahuatl. Cifuentes (2002) has described Trinidad Palma's primary interest to be that of educating and civilizing Indigenous peoples, rather than advocating for their rights. Under this perspective, the Nahuatl translation of the constitution could be understood to be similar to Bustamante's simultaneous admonition to Indigenous peoples to be good and decent citizens while holding up the promises of the liberal constitution as a guarantee of being treated as citizens once a sufficient state of civility has been achieved.

Again, the writings in Nahuatl produced in the mid-19th century primarily had the function of propaganda, trying to win Indigenous support for whichever political cause was espoused by the author. They do not seem to really tell us much about what was going on in Indigenous communities; they didn't write back.

Rebellions and Revolutions as Signs of Covert Publics

A Mexican nationalist perspective of Indigenous politics describes the dissolution of Indian republics as a kind of liberation, through which the subjugated Indians of the colony finally became Mexicans with full rights as citizens. In this chapter, I take a different perspective, one centered in the Indigenous communities that lost political recognition, and whose leaders defected to seek prestige outside of their communities. Under the former perspective, the persistence of Indigenous languages, coupled with the continued social and economic marginalization of Indigenous communities, becomes a sign of an incomplete liberation; it suggests that Indigenous culture and language are what hinders Indigenous peoples from accessing full rights and privileges as citizens. I suggest instead that the opposite is the case: the socioeconomic inequality that was perpetuated in the liberal regime of the independent nation forced Indigenous people to form new publics in which they could organize their local common good, sharing resources and maintaining their religious and civic traditions. These new publics were formed out of view of the national political system, because it formulated itself in the idiom of religion (which to the liberal mindset belonged to the private sphere) and because it used Indigenous languages as the medium of communication. To their members, the Indigenous publics functioned as public spheres, in which local politics were carried out, but these functions were hidden from the view of outsiders. These covert publics sustained the continued use of the Nahuatl language (and other Indigenous languages) in the 19th century, and were in turn protected exactly because their linguistic isolation made them relatively impenetrable and opaque to outsiders.

The propaganda texts in Nahuatl described above show that political actors in the early national public considered Nahuas an audience and a potential constituency, but there is little evidence of direct Nahua political agency in the 19th century, at least if we only consider written documents to be direct evidence of the workings of Indigenous political communities. However, there is another, indirect, form of evidence for the existence of local Indigenous political publics in the post-independence period: rebellions. During the "long 19th century," the political landscape of rural Mexico was riddled with armed "peasant uprisings," in which the rebellious peasants were usually Indigenous people. Such uprisings were commonplace both in times of peace and war. Although, in wartime, Indigenous rebellions often aligned with government forces (whether domestic or foreign), they were generally fighting to achieve local objectives, formulated as the common good of a local public.

In times of peace, such local counter-publics tended to organize themselves in resistance to and opposition against the developing Mexican nation-state, rather than fighting to be included in the national project. The presence of Indigenous rebellions indicates the presence of a public that sees its political objectives as being contrary to the projects and intentions of the state against which it rebels. Though we cannot always see Nahua publics in the historical documents of the 19th century, because they were often not lettered publics or because they wrote in Spanish when they were, we can sometimes see them emerge into history in the form of rebellious resistance.

The Indigenous rebellions documented throughout Mexican history from 1521 until today can be understood as expressions of Indigenous communality in resistance to external threats, and as such, as indicators of the existence of Indigenous publics. In her detailed review of the "peasant rebellions" in Mexico from 1819–1910, Leticia Reina (1980) demonstrates that throughout the 19th century, wide tracts of territory were in open armed rebellion against the state. Among historians, these rebellions have generally been considered "peasant rebellions," but it is clear, both given the ethnic composition of the rural population of 19th-century Mexico and from the sources presented by Reina, that these peasants were largely Indigenous people fighting to preserve their local land bases. Comparing Reina's maps of the areas in which the rebellions were most frequent and intense with contemporary maps, we see a significant overlap between the rebellious regions and the regions that have the highest density of Indigenous groups today—these were not simply agrarian movements, but also Indigenous ones.

In Antonio Gramsci's understanding of the intellectual, "Every social group, coming into existence on the original terrain of an essential function in the world of economic production, creates together with itself, organically, one or more strata of intellectuals which give it homogeneity and an awareness of its own function not only in the economic but also in the social and political fields" (1971, 5). In contrast to the more common view of the intellectual, Gramsci's definition does not privilege the lettered intellect, but is based on the social function of the intellectual in a community. Applying it would entail that Nahua communities must have always had intellectuals, persons who direct and verbalize the community's collective aspirations and interests. The constant presence of local rebellions in Indigenous communities points toward an active concern for the local public good in these communities, and so clearly must have required the presence of some kind of intellectuals to be able to take form. But these intellectuals were not the kind who left behind writings in Indigenous languages, probably because writing was not the medium through which these counter-publics sustained themselves. Rather, they must have existed largely within the intimate sphere of face-to-face contact between family members, neighbors, friends, compadres, and *cofradía* members, and sustained themselves in the medium of spoken language. Apart from the names of some of the leaders, we know very little of these local intellectuals, who organized their towns in armed uprisings.

Nahua Publics during the Reform Wars

One case in which we do have documentation of the Indigenous bases of rebellion is in the Puebla Highlands during the Reform Wars, which for various reasons has become the best documented of all the armed conflicts in which Indigenous peoples participated in the 19th century. Particularly the work of Florencia Mallon (1995, 1994) has provided a detailed account of the dynamics of political engagement by peoples in the Puebla Highlands. She describes how Nahua people of the towns surrounding Zacapoaxtla took up arms three times in the 19th century. First, they fought against the local *hacendados* (hacienda owners) in 1850–1855, and then subsequently allied with the liberal side during the Reform Wars (1857–1860). Then they fought on the nationalist side against the French during the French intervention (1861–1867), where they won national recognition as they played a decisive role in the Battle of Puebla on May 5, 1862, in which the French army was routed. The town of Xochiapulco, from which many of the Indigenous "National Guards" came, received a land grant and political independence as a municipality, thus rewarding their loyal support of the liberal and nationalist forces, even to the point of burning down their own town instead of allowing it to fall into enemy hands.

While Mallon's main argument is about the active participation of rural peasant communities in the construction of Mexican nationalism, her documentation of these struggles may also suggest that the nationalism of the people of Xochiapulco and the Zacapoaxtla region was secondary to their sense of town loyalty. While the Xochiapulquenses did destroy their own town rather than let it fall into the hands of the French and Austrian troops, the objective for which they were fighting was clearly the right to independently manage and control their lands. The people of Xochiapulco had originally allied with the liberal cause because of a local liberal leader who interpreted the new laws as warranting the local community's right to reclaim and redistribute tracts of ancestral lands claimed also by another town. This led to the division of towns in the region into conservative towns, organized against the expropriation and redistribution of lands, and liberal towns that believed they stood to gain from the redistribution. The liberal towns found leadership, first, in Manuel Lucas, a Nahua merchant from Zacapoaxtla, and subsequently under his son, the schoolteacher and later general Juan Francisco. The family had lived for a while in Veracruz, where Juan Francisco received his education, but returning to the town they became leaders first of the uprising against the *hacendados* and then against the conservatives and French. This dual background, which meant that they were intimately related to the local culture while also able to function in the national public sphere, could well have been what enabled them to take on the role of organic intellectuals and leaders of the local political community.

Mallon does not discuss the role of the Nahuatl language in organizing the rebellion, but it is clear from her descriptions that political fault lines in the highlands often coincided along ethnic lines, between Nahuas and Totonacs, or Nahuas and *mestizos* and *criollos*. If we accept that in cases where Indigenous communities explicitly aligned with national-level discourses, the underlying concern tended to be the control of communal land bases, then we may take the prevalence of armed rebellions in the North Puebla Highlands to be a sign that Indigenous publics continued to be alive and struggling throughout the "long 19th century." Moreover, Brewster (2003) has argued that the cacique hegemony of the Nahua Barrios family in the 1920s was a direct continuation of the tradition of ethnic localism of the 19th century, and that though they fought loyally under the banner of the federation, they were in reality engaged in local resistance. His argument further supports the significance of ethnicity and localist conceptions of community in military mobilization in the North Puebla Highlands.

The rebellion itself is one aspect of how a local community orients itself in relation to the national public, but another aspect is how the rebellion lives on in local memory. The physical act of rebellion and militarism is short lived, and generally is ultimately destructive for the local community. More important and persistent is the impression of the rebellion that remains in the local memory, and the way that this motivates future orientation toward, or away from, the national public. Regardless of whether the rebellion is ultimately able to achieve the goals of the local public, as in the case of Xochiapulco, or whether, as was more frequently the case, it was violently stamped out by the state, it may still motivate communities to take up the stance of the counterpublic. Whether it does so or not would seem to depend on the way in which memory of the rebellion is integrated into the local collective memory.

In this regard we also have particularly interesting data from the Puebla Highlands. Mallon (1995) herself, in her description of events in the 19th century, draws on local histories. She employs the account of local Xochiapulco historian Donna Rivera Moreno (Rivera Moreno 1991), who in turn drew on eyewitness testimonies recorded by Manuel Pozos in 1900. Mallon demonstrates that in Xochiapulco, locals frame the history of conflicts in contrast to official nationalist narratives that have described the people of Zacapoaxtla, the municipal seat that administrated Xochiapulco in the 19th century, as the Indigenous defenders of the nation, erasing the participation of the people of Xochiapulco. Xochiapulco historians actively reinscribe their town into the narrative. Just as the original rebellion did, this narrative looks at nationalism to the outside, but also has the simultaneous function of promoting a local version of community that is rooted in a local counterpublic tradition. This demonstrates how the history of the conflicts in which the people of Xochiapulco participated, as well as the local-level political divisions that motivated them, is still alive in the community today, and continues to motivate the construction of a local public. So, just as national histories have their foundational epics, and their stories of war and conflict with external enemies, Indigenous stories of rebellion can serve as a communicative action through which local public spheres are sustained.

The narratives of the independence period and Reform Wars form a local body of historical knowledge circulating within Nahua communities in the North Puebla Highlands. Comparing the historical narratives from Xochiapulco with those from the town of San Miguel Tzinacapan in the Cuetzalan region northeast of Xochiapulco is informative. The following narrative is one of those included in a collection of oral history from San Miguel Tzinacapan (Taller de Tradición Oral 1994).

Ualajkaj nikajkuín tateuianij analtekos franceses uan kichiujkej miak eliuisyot, kinimiktiayaj maseualmej uan ininka mauiltiayaj siuamej.

Overseas-people, soldiers from France came here, and they did a lot of evil: they killed the maseuales [Indians] and pleasured themselves with [raped] the women.

Motalijkej Sakapoastan. Tein ompa rikos iniuantiaj in analtekos, maj kinintamiskej in maseualmej.

They set themselves up in Zacapoaxtla. The rich people over there made friendly with the overseas-people, in order to finish off the maseuales.

Pero moyolchikauj ne general Juan Francisco Lucas iniuan ome Juanes para kinintokaskiaj.

But the general Juan Franscisco made his heart strong [resisted] in order to follow them along with the two Juanes [two other famous Nahua generals named Juan]

Ipapán ne Juan Francisco Lucas, kimiktijkej in analtekos ne noxolal Komaltepek. Satepan yajki in general kininsetilito xochiapolkah, sayoj amo kipiayak toni ika moteuiskej.

Juan Francisco Lucas's father was killed by the overseas-people over in Comaltepec. Then the general went to unite the people of Xochiapulco, although they didn't have anything with which to fight.

Entos in analtekos kichijchiujkah se kali ueyi omenepan, ompa ne Sakapoastan, kampa yetoyaj in soldados uan ompa kieuayaj ininteposuan.

So the overseas-people made a big, two-story house over there in Zacapoaxtla, where they stayed and kept their irons [arms].

Ne analtekos moinkitskilijkej seki siuamej uan kiniuikakej itech ne ueyi kali. Sayoj ne siuamej ipa kiniluijkaj ya toni in ompa kichiuaskej. Yejua ika mosenkaujkej uan kiniliuijkej in soldados maj kininchiuilikan tein yejuan kinekiskiaj.

The over-seas people grabbed some women and took them to the great house. But the women had been told what to do there. They let themselves entirely, and told the soldiers that they could do what they wanted with them.

Mientras ne takuatoyaj, in siuamej kijtojkej youij plasaj kikouatij toni in kikuaskej uan yajkej, sayoj kikoujkej se tamamal chiluak uan seki lometas de aguarras. Ijkuak mokepatoj, kitetenkej talpan chiluak uan kuali kitetekilijkej aguarras, kixotaltijkej uan siuamej niman kiskej nochin.

While they were eating, the women said they were going to the marketplace to buy something to eat, and they left, but they only bought a bunch of dry chile and some bottles of turpentine. When they came back they filled the floor with dry chile and poured out the turpentine, they set it on fire, and then quickly all the women ran out.

Nimantsin ne soldados nionó uel moijyotiayaj ok tsikuinteujkej tatastiuij, kitemotiuij kuali ehekat. Ompa kininchixtoyaj in maseualmej uan kinintamikokototskej ika machetej. Satepan yejuan kuali kalakkej uan kininkixtitoj nochi in teposmej. (Taller de Tradición Oral 1994, 120–21).

Right away the soldiers couldn't even breathe anymore, they ran out, they went coughing, they went searching for air. Outside the maseuales were waiting for them and they finished hacking them up with machetes. Afterward they could go inside and grab all the arms.

This narrative representation of the French intervention demonstrates how Nahua communities in the North Puebla Highlands have kept the history of the events in an emplotment very different from the one that exists in the national public sphere. First, in the nationalist myth of the battle of Puebla, the native forces of the Sixth Battalion under Juan Francisco Lucas are called "Zacapoaxtecas," an emplotment of the events that erases the fact that the mainly *mestizo* people of Zacapoaxtla were allied with the French, and it was the townspeople from Xochiapulco who headed the resistance. The emplotment also does not align *mestizos* and Indians against the foreign French enemy—but rather explicitly aligns rich *mestizos* with the French overseas-people, against the poor but resourceful *maseualmej* (used here as a pan-ethnic category of Indigenous, though prototypically Nahua, people). It also does not frame the struggle as a nationalist struggle, but as an entirely locally based resistance to abuse by outsiders. It is not the case that the people of San Miguel Tzinacapan remember the Indigenous participation in the reform war as a participation in a national struggle. Hence, though the national public sphere emplots the Nahua of the North Puebla Highlands as a particular kind of nationalist Indian subject—this emplotment is not found in the version of history that is reproduced for the consumption of the Nahua public of the Sierra Norte de Puebla.

Nahua Publics in the Mexican Revolution

The narrative of the Mexican revolution is often told as a chaotic and violent struggle between the urban constitutionalist factions of *Maderistas* and *Carrancistas* (led by Francisco Madero and Venustiano Carranza) and against the rural radicals such as the *Villistas* and *Zapatistas*, led by Pancho Villa and Emiliano Zapata. Indigenous people have often been depicted mostly as victims with little stake in the conflict.

Nevertheless, Nahuas also participated significantly on different sides in the Mexican revolution, though it has proved a controversial question to answer what they were fighting for. Did they fight as a segment of the agrarian sector for agrarian reforms, or did they fight as members of local Indigenous publics to recover land that had been taken over by the haciendas? Some scholars have argued that indigenism was not significant in the revolution, because there was no general movement that identified itself with a general Indigenous cause. John Womack, whose history focuses on the Zapatista revolution in Morelos, considers Zapatismo to be an agrarian movement, and he argues that the Nahua population of state of Morelos was negligible at the time of the revolution (Womack 1968). Alan Knight (1986) also downplays the role of local Indian parochial sentiment as a force in the revolution, distinguishing between *serrano* (highlander) and "agrarian" rebellions—where only the former had an Indigenous element. If we accept that Indigenous publics in Mexico are historically characterized exactly by their localocentric nature, and that they have no history of engaging in broader pan-ethnic or racial struggles, we see that we should not expect Indigenous rebellions to present themselves as engaged in ethnic politics. Rather, we should expect them to present themselves as fighting for whichever political cause is the major concern for their local public at a given time. The following paragraphs analyze the ways that Indigenous participation in the Mexican revolution has been represented, and argues that it has been largely erased from, or downplayed, in historiography.

In any discussion about Indian rebellions and their legacies, the Zapata revolution in Morelos looms large. The question of the possibility of an ethnic element in the Zapatista movement during the Mexican revolution has been contentious, and there are two distinct traditions of representation. One tradition sees Zapata as an Indigenous leader of an Indigenous community who defended his town's interests by allying them to a wider agrarianist social movement and the anti-Porfirian revolution. This tradition started with the scholarship of Sotelo Inclán ([1943] 1970), who depicts Zapata as the chosen representative of the traditional Nahua council of Anenecuilco and the keeper of ancient Nahuatl language land titles. The "Indigenous Zapata" tradition continues to live on in the contemporary Zapatista movement, with its clear coupling of the agrarian struggle with different forms of Indigenous worldviews, as well as among Mexican academic *indigenistas*, and in the traditions of many Indigenous communities. The other tradition sees Zapata as a *mestizo* agrarian leader whose success partly owed to his ability to recruit the Indigenous segment of the population to his cause. This tradition was founded by John Womack's seminal book *Zapata and the Mexican Revolution*, in which he argues that Zapata was a *mestizo*, who knew no Nahuatl, and that consequently the driving force behind the revolution in Morelos was the agrarian segment, making it basically a class conflict with only negligible or occasional ethnic elements. Womack's framing of the revolution in Morelos as an agrarian uprising with no significant Indigenous element has become the standard in historiography.

Womack's representation of Zapata as a *mestizo* leader (1968, 71) must be rejected for a number of reasons: first of all, Womack was unaware of the eyewitness testimony provided by Doña Luz Jímenez, who describes Zapata himself, as well as most of his men, as speaking Nahuatl when they arrived in

Milpa Alta in 1916 (Horcasitas and Jimenez 1968). Second, Womack's view of the ethnic demography of Morelos at the turn of the 20th century is erroneous, because it is literally based on an error in reading the main source for the number of Nahuatl speakers in Morelos. He cites a 1962 UNAM master's thesis in geography that analyzes census data in Morelos from 1900 to 1930, and concludes that Nahuatl speakers only made up 9.29% of the population of Morelos at the time the revolution broke out. However, the source cited misinterprets the census data, because the census in 1900 and the one in 1930 gave different instructions to the interviewer for how to count speakers of Indigenous languages. In the 1900 census, a person was counted as a speaker of an Indigenous language only if they did *not* speak Spanish; if they spoke Spanish they were counted as a Spanish speaker.[12] However, in the 1930 census speakers who were bilingual in Spanish and an Indigenous language were counted as speakers of their Indigenous language. So the 1900 census only counted monolingual speakers, whereas the 1930 census counted monolinguals and bilinguals. In 1900, when only monolingual speakers of Indigenous languages were counted, the number of speakers of Indigenous languages was 16.9% Nahuatl speakers. Today, there are very few Nahua communities with percentages of monolingual speakers as high as 16%, and in those communities, the vast majority of inhabitants tend to speak Nahuatl as a first language and Spanish as a second language. Towns with similar numbers of monolinguals exist, for example in the Zongolica region. Here census figures today suggest that a breakdown of 10% monolinguals would correspond well to a demographic breakdown with 10%–20% monolingual speakers of Spanish and 70%–80% Spanish/Nahuatl bilinguals. If, in 1900, the speaker demographic composition of the state of Morelos was similar to Zongolica today, then the state of Morelos had 161,000 inhabitants, out of which we would estimate approximately 16,000 monolinguals, and probably at least 100,000 bilingual Nahuas in the state. This of course means that when Womack takes the percentage of monolinguals to refer to the total number of speakers, he is vastly underestimating the number of Nahuatl speakers of Morelos at the time the revolution broke out, because most speakers would have been bilingual. This means that if we correct for these errors, likelihood

---

[12] The census questionnaire provided a field with the title "Idioma nativo o lengua hablada." The instructions to the person administrating the census stated clearly the procedure for filling out the field: "*En la columna 11 debe escribirse el nombre de la lengua nativa ó hablada comunmente, como castellano, francés, inglés, etc., ó bien el nombre del idioma indígena, como por ejemplo el mexicano ó nahuatl, el zapoteco, el otomí, el tarasco, el maya, el tzendal, el huasteco, el totonaco, etc., etc. A la persona que hable el castellano y un idioma indígena, como el otomí ó el mexicano ó cualquier otro, se le anotará de preferencia el castellano.*"

is that during the revolution, a majority of the state's population spoke Nahuatl.[13]

All accounts agree that Zapata's own engagement in the revolutionary fight stemmed originally from his responsibilities toward his own town of Anenecuilco, where he had been elected by a local council to be president of the defense committee, and in charge of the effort to regain lost land and water rights. However, where historians such as Womack have generally tended to see the Zapata revolution in terms of its relation to the simultaneous national struggle, and consequently foreground how Zapatismo articulated with other revolutionary movements and with national intellectuals, it is also possible to look at how Zapatismo articulates with local community-based movements in Morelos. One feature of the organization that is not generally explored is the relation between Zapatista generals and their home communities. Such an exploration is also beyond the scope of this discussion, but it should be noted that several major Zapatista generals were based in local Nahua communities and tended to undertake most of their fighting in their own local areas. Genovevo de la O fought around his native Huitzilac, Agustín Cázares around Indigenous Jumiltepec, Refugio Sánchez in Nahua Tepoztlán, Fortino Ayaquica in the northeast of Morelos around the Nahua town of Tochimilco close to his native Atlixco, Amador Salazár around Atlihuayan (also an important site of rebellion in the 19th century), and Zapata of course around Anenecuilco and Tlaltizapán. All of these generals seem to have been originally, and continuously, motivated by the desire to defend and serve their own communities (all of which were home to Nahuatl speakers well into the 20th century). Perhaps, then, an alternative perspective on Zapatismo would be to see it as a loose confederation of largely Nahuatl-speaking towns, each under their own leader and with local objectives, who joined forces temporarily to achieve the greater common good. Two further events provide support for this type of interpretation.

One of the enigmas of the Zapata revolution is the question of why Zapata, having taken the capital and celebrated his famous meeting with Villa in 1914, seemingly turned his back on the national revolution, turned toward rebuilding Morelos, and failed to provide the necessary support for Villa's operations, eventually causing the downfall of both of the radical armies. Womack ascribes the decision to disenchantment with the relations with the Villistas, but if we think of Zapata's revolution as primarily a localist

---

[13] Other contemporary sources, such as Gamio's *Forjando Patria*, also describe Morelos as a predominantly Indian state. See also Pharao Hansen (2024) for a detailed analysis of the probable Nahuatl-speaking population in Morelos before and after the revolution.

movement, it becomes perhaps easier to explain: he simply had no interest in the northern revolution or in securing the presidency for any particular faction. Supporting this interpretation is a leaflet circulated by Zapatistas in 1915 in northern Guerrero trying to recruit rebels to their cause: the headline read "*No peleamos por la presidencia. Nuestra revolución es la revolución del Indio*" [We do not fight for the presidency. Our Revolution is the Revolution of the Indian] (p.c. Gerardo Rios; see also Rios 2017). This strongly suggests that Zapata's constituency had little or no interest in national politics; they only wanted to live free and work their ancestral lands. Consequently, they were not willing to support the northern revolution by risking their lives far outside of their own territories.

Another critical junction for Zapatismo was the relations with the Nahua rebels of Domingo Arenas in Tlaxcala. Arenas had first been allied with Zapata, but had since switched sides to support Carranza. This was a blow to Zapata, who had probably counted on the Arenistas to keep Carranza busy in the valley of Puebla. Zapata's reaction was to circulate letters written in Nahuatl among the people of Tlaxcala, describing in grim vocabulary the Carrancistas and their cause. But the Tlaxcaltecas continued to be loyal to Arenas, until he was killed in a botched parley with the Zapatistas near Tochimilco. From the Zapatista perspective, Arenas is often depicted as a traitor, but historian Gerardo Ríos (Rios 2017) has argued that it is more likely that he was simply loyal to his own local community and their local objectives, and that it was this perspective that led him to consider an alliance with Carranza to be more desirable. The well-known Nahuatl manifesto of Zapata (León-Portilla 1978) was precisely produced by Zapatistas in their attempt to win the Arenistas as their allies—which we can recognize as a unique example of written communication *in Nahuatl* between two Nahuatl-speaking local counter-publics. In this way, by understanding the ethnic relations and community allegiances of the Zapata rebellion, we can also explain why it eventually failed; the local ties of its supporters simply made it too difficult to form a sufficiently broad base on which to continue the struggle. The close relation to the land and to their home communities was what the Zapatistas shared, but it was also what divided them—just as is the case with the Nahuatl language, which both unites and divides the Nahua peoples based on their ties to local publics.

In other Nahuan regions, communities responded in the same localist way to the revolution, which caused them to end up in different camps. In the North Puebla Highlands for example, the people of San Miguel Tzinacapan joined the constitutionalists because they were led by local Nahua cacique Gabriel Barrios, and because their traditional rivals in Cuetzalan had joined the Villistas and raided their town:

Kijtouaj ika nikan uín Kuesalankopa in viyistas amo katka tein semi pobres kemej itech in okseki xolalmej, amo tateuiayaj para maj amo kinintajyouiltikan in maseualmej, nikan in viyistas katka in koyomej de Kuesalan tein mero kinixyekantoya ipopauan kipiayaj ueueyij talmej yan kichiuayaj in refinoj, semi miak miak kininchiuilijkej in maseualmej. Yayaj ipa tachtekitij, kinintititilasayaj in siuamej uan kinimiktiayaj nochin maseualmej tein nemiaj nikan uín" (Taller de Tradición Oral 1994, 485).

They say that here around Cuetzalan, the Villistas were not the poor as in other places. They didn't fight so that the maseuales should not suffer. Here the Villistas were *koyomej* [mestizos/outsiders] from Cuetzalan who were being led by heads of family who had large landholdings and made cane alcohol. They did a lot to the maseuales. They robbed, they raped the women, and killed all the *maseuales* who lived around here.

The result of this particular history of struggle was that in the North Puebla Highlands, in a sense, Nahuas came out of the revolution well. Just as their local Nahua leaders had been considered loyal supporters of Porfirian liberalism, their revolutionary cacique Barrios was seen as an ally of the revolutionary regime in the national public sphere—able to command respect internally and to represent the region externally (Brewster 2003). The violent revolutionary war in Morelos had a similar result: the former Zapatistas were able to ally closely with the government of Obregón, and begin the country's most ambitious program of land reform, redistributing enormous tracts of hacienda land to the Nahua communities.

However, the alliance of Nahua community leaders with the government meant that Nahuas increasingly turned toward the national political system as the provider of the "common good." So the post-revolutionary transition instituted the client/patron relation between Indigenous communities and the state apparatus that characterized the *indigenista* period of Mexican history, and which is still evident in the way those relations play out today.

Nationalizing Nahuatl Publics

During the *Porfiriato*, the 30-year rule of Porfirio Díaz, a class of indigenista intellectuals, such as those working in the Society of Geography and Statistics, had already intensified the efforts to harness the Indigenous past to provide a legitimizing foundation for the nation. This continued the ideological-symbolic process of nation-craft, prominently including the usage of Aztec imagery and the Nahuatl language as a symbol of national identity. Mexican elites, some of whom saw themselves as descendants, in either a literal or figurative sense, of prehispanic Aztec royalty, promoted an image of the Aztecs based on the stereotype of the noble savage—bronze skinned and muscular, tragic heroes clad in feathers and gold ornaments (Keen 1971). (See Figure 3.0 for a prominent example of this image.)

This fetishism of a particular kind of Indian imaginary diffused from the urban elites to rural towns and communities, sometimes prompting local Indigenous intellectuals to reframe their own Indigenous identity in line with these stereotypes. Lomnitz (2001) describes how this process took place in Tepoztlán, where the Rojas family, hailing from the lineage of colonial governors, promoted an Indigenous identity in line with nationalist discourses and imaginaries of Indigenous nobility. One example of a prominent Indigenous intellectual who used his knowledge of Nahuatl to advance in the national public sphere of the Porfiriato was Mariano Jacobo Rojas (1842–1936). A native speaker of Nahuatl from Tepoztlán, and an advocate for Nahuatl language teaching, he became a teacher of Nahuatl at the *Museo Nacional de Arqueología, Historia y Etnografía* [National Museum of Archeology, History and Ethnography], and in 1927 wrote a well-known "manual" of Nahuatl (de Reuse 2010; Rojas 1927).

Such was the fervor of indigenist nationalism in the Porfirian period that it diffused even to the backwaters of northern Guerrero. Here, in Ichcateopan, Gillingham (2011) shows us how local elites created a tomb, complete with bones and a fake plaque, stating that it was the last resting place of Cuauhtemoc, the last Aztec emperor, executed by Hernán Cortés in 1525. Locals participated in the hoax to secure a place for their town and themselves within the narrative of the Mexican nation. Similar movements (although without the hoax) have been described in Milpa Alta by van Zantwijk (1960). Karttunen (1994, 1996) describes how another Nahuatl intellectual, Luz Jiménez of Milpa Alta, was recruited by the post-revolutionary nationalist movement to serve as a living symbol of the nation's Indigenous soul. Moving within the circles of Mexico City's cultural elite, she modeled for Diego Rivera and other revolutionary artists, and became a supplier of folkloric narratives for which she was rarely credited (McDonough 2014).

What seems ubiquitously true is that in the late 19th century, neo-Aztec revivalism was a cultural fad driven by nationalist cultural elites, rather than by Indigenous communities. When Indigenous people and communities participated in this kind of nationalism, their aim was often to amass social capital for themselves and their communities within the national public sphere. Within the mainstream public sphere, the *indigenista* and *hispanista* versions of Mexican nationalism were competing, and it seems that particularly rural

Indigenous intellectuals often saw the political advantage of supporting the indigenist version, even if it meant having to assume the role of the noble savage.

Lázaro Cárdenas and the Indigenous Constituency

Following the revolution, Mexico entered a period of nationalist reconstruction, with ideologies of nationalism, populism, and agrarian socialism reaching its height in the presidency of Lázaro Cárdenas. Cárdenas founded a Department of Indian Affairs in 1936, which later, under Miguel Alemán in 1948, became the National Indigenist Institute (INI), charged with the social and political development of the country's Indigenous communities. Cárdenas also allied his Institutional Revolutionary Party (PRI) closely with the teachers through the Ministry of Education (SEP), and the National Peasant Confederacion (CNC)—all of which had important functions mediating relations between the government and Indigenous communities. More than any previous period of Mexican nationalism, Cárdenas's presidency saw explicit elevation of Indigenous culture, and its integration into the nationalist imagination.[14] Some scholars, like Lomnitz (2001), have tended to focus on the post-revolutionary *indigenismo*'s use of Indigenous history as national symbolism. Nonetheless, in the 1930s, particularly during the Cárdenas presidency, the national engagement with living Indigenous culture and language, and with their political interests, was also intense. Indeed, the 1930s may be the only period in the history of the Mexican nation in which the state has dedicated similar amounts of attention to Indigenous peoples and their cultures and interests as they do in the current period. I also consider it the only period in which the intensity of Indigenous political organization compares to the one we see today. Following Dawson (2004), I consider it likely that Cárdenas made an explicit political choice of approaching the Indigenous population as an electoral constituency, and that his close attention to Indigenous interests reflects this choice, rather than a more superficial use of Indians as national symbols.

As mentioned above, it has been said that in Morelos the Zapatistas won the revolution. Many of the leading revolutionaries were incorporated into state and national governments. Through this alliance, many of the promises of Zapata's revolution resulted in concrete policy—most significantly the expropriation and redistribution of hacienda land to the Indigenous

---

[14] Heath 1972; Hartch 2006; Gillingham 2011; Dawson 1998, 2004; Gutiérrez Chong 1999.

communities. During the first decades after the revolution, almost all communities in Morelos filed requests for *ejido* land grants, and the Cárdenas government granted most of them. These grants were distributed through a laborious process in which lands were measured and expropriated. It was calculated how many persons could each receive a small *ejido* plot, large enough to sustain a family, and the lands were then distributed among the eligible individuals in each town. The process required a high degree of patience, organization, and political shrewdness from communities, as they had to find the ways to represent themselves to the state in the right way, demonstrating their necessity, justifying their claims to being the original owners of the lands they were requesting, documenting their eligibility. This in itself required a much more active relation between local community and state than ever before.

Nevertheless, starting with the presidency of Lázaro Cárdenas, the change in Indigenous policies also produced noticeable changes in many Indigenous communities. Cárdenas recognized that the Indians formed a powerful constituency, which if leveraged in favor of his socialist agenda, could prove a crucial pillar of support. Aligned with indigenista social scientists like Gamio, he considered that the objective of nationalism should not be to eliminate the Indians and the cultural diversity they represented, but rather to create a place for Indians within the construction of the nation (Dawson 1998, 2004). Cárdenas worked actively with social scientists to find ways to include Indigenous communities in the nation, and two of the most significant strategies were by promoting education and socioeconomic development in Indigenous regions. For the provision of education, Cárdenas allied himself with the North American missionary and amateur linguist William Cameron Townsend and his organization, the Summer Institute of Linguistics (Hartch 2006) (Figure 2.2 from Townsend's archive shows Cárdenas in 1937, visiting an indigenous community, perhaps Tetelcingo). They became instrumental in the efforts to provide Indigenous communities with primary education in their own languages, including the creation of education materials, curricula, and basic literature in many Indigenous languages. Being a missionary organization, although covertly so, they also became instrumental in further undermining local socio-religious organization in many Indigenous communities, creating the first inroads of Protestantism in Indigenous communities all over Mexico. Since conversion to Protestantism often entailed defection from the communal systems of mutual aid and the adoption of a gospel of individuality, in many places this seemingly benign state interest in Indigenous education indirectly affected the stability of Indigenous communality.

Figure 2.2 President Lázaro Cárdenas visiting an Indigenous community in 1937.
Photo by Antonio Carrillo Jr., March 20, 1937. From the collection of William Cameron Townsend, reproduced with permission of the Summer Institute of Linguistics.

Cárdenas also published two decrees in Nahuatl: one of them, titled "*Jn çiapopotl*" [the tar] (using the non-standard orthography of engineer and amateur linguist Juán Luna Cárdenas who translated it), explained the nationalization of the petroleum resources carried out by the president for a, probably nonexistent, Nahua readership (Hernández de León-Portilla 1988). This continued the 19th-century tradition of publishing select propaganda material in the country's major Indigenous language. Moreover, it also continued the tradition of publishing Nahuatl-language materials in ways that were not easily accessible or intelligible to native speakers, and without having a specific speech community in mind as audience. In the 1950s and 1960s, Juán Luna Cárdenas was a leading figure within the so-called *Mexicanidad* movement, which sought to restore Aztec culture and religion as the true national heritage for all Mexicans. As part of this work, he arrived in Hueyapan with the idea that restoring Aztec religion and language would be easier to do in an Indigenous Nahuatl-speaking community—and he was the leader of the group that Friedlander (1975) refers to as "cultural radicals," which will be described in more detail in Chapter 4. He also collaborated closely with Eulalia Guzmán, who promoted the hoax of Cuauhtemoc's tomb in Ichcateopan as a national treasure. Luna Cárdenas also plays an important role in the foundation of the Mexicayotl movement described in Chapter 6, which grew out of the *Mexicanidad* movement as its members migrated to the United States. The legacy of Lázaro Cárdenas's indigenism in this way flows through many of the entanglements between Indigenous symbolism and Mexican nationalism that still operate in Mexican national space today. But it also had significant effects in Indigenous communities, providing them with an avenue of access to the state, and a language in which to enter dialogue with its institutions.

The relation between Cárdenas and Indigenous people has been a focus of many analyses. Particularly salient has been his subsequent status as a kind of local saint in many of the communities that he visited in person and to which he frequently was directly instrumental in promoting the first visible signs of modernization. Cardenas's image among the Indigenous population as the first president to take an active and sincere interest in their situation led many Indigenous communities to begin for the first time to look to the national government for support. A clear example of this process is the situation of the Nahua town of Tetelcingo in Morelos. Ravaged by the revolution, the community was barely re-established in the 1930s when Cárdenas became president. Having recently left Guatemala, William Cameron Townsend chose the town as his first location for a missionary operation in Mexico; he made his residence there with the blessing of Cárdenas and gradually established a Protestant community in the otherwise traditionalist town (Hartch 2006). In 1936, Cárdenas held a much-publicized conference in the town in which he promised to bring the benefits of modernity to the town and pledged his allegiance to the Indigenous cause. Over the subsequent years, Cárdenas did indeed take a special interest in Tetelcingo (and some other Indigenous communities, such as the Purhépecha communities in his native Michoacán).

A particularly fascinating testimony of Cárdenas's relation with Tetelcingo is the narration of Martín Méndez Huaxcuatitla, or Ru Martín. Méndez was an orphan and former revolutionary fighter (having fought on all sides) who had resettled in his native Tetelcingo after the war, eventually becoming the local *ayudante* (main town authority). He was the one who had welcomed Townsend into town and became one of the most active leaders of the Protestant community there. When Townsend left Tetelcingo, he was replaced by the missionary linguist Richard Pittman, who continued work with Méndez. Méndez fluently read and wrote in his native language *Mösiehuali*, as the Tetelcingans call their local, highly distinctive variety of Nahuatl. On Pittman's suggestion, he typed up an account of his meetings with Cárdenas and his impression of Cárdenas's legacy, in which he describes the president as a Christ-like savior figure for the Nahua community of Tetelcingo, who brings to the town all the elements of modernity—technology, education, and the Protestant religion.

Ye cuaqinu naja niyeya de tlajtohuani ipa topueblo. Ipa inun tunalte oncä oyejyeya profesores amo tlamachtiyäya. Pero oyejya esfiela; ompa ochajchantijtaya. Belis otiyejyeya quiemi a las diez de ca isi cuac naja niyehuataya ipa ämäyetl ixpa ayudantía, cuac sa de repiente oniquijtac sente quixtiyäno ohualäya ca notlac, de tejano, de pantalo, hua de chaquieta. Naja amo onicchi cäso de yaja. Naja nicseguiro niyehuatica ipa ino ämäyetl. Por fin omopacho notlac hua oniechtlajpalo. Nuyijqui naja onictlajpalo, pero niyehuatica. Ye cuaquinuju oniechilfi inu quixtiyäno -?Amo tiniechixomati? Naja oniquilfi, - amo, señor. Yaja oniechilfi, Naja niPresidente de la República, Lázaro Cárdenas. Ye cuaquinuju onoquestiquis hua onitielfi ca en castilla. - "Señor Presidente! perdonemé! No le conocía."
(Martín Méndez Huaxcatitla, n.d.)[a]

And at that time I was speaker (ayudante) in our town. In those days there were teachers who didn't teach. But there was a school; there they were living. Maybe it was around ten in the morning, when I was sitting on an amate tree in front of the ayudantía (town hall), when all of a sudden I saw a Christian (a person) came toward me, in a cowboy hat, trousers and jacket. I didn't pay him any attention. I just stayed sitting on the amate tree. At last he came closer to me and greeted me. I greeted him back, but I was sitting. Then that was when he asked me, "don't you recognize me?"
I said, "no, sir."
He told me, "I am president of the Republic, Lázaro Cárdenas." Then in that moment, I jumped up and told him in Spanish,
"Mr. President, please excuse me, I didn't recognize you."

---

[a] This text is written in Tetelcingo Nahuatl, or *mösiehuah*, which is a variety characterized by its divergent phonological system. Where other varieties distinguish between long and short vowels, in Tetelcingo this contrast has become one of vowel quality, so that the variety has seven vowel qualities instead of four as most varieties. The orthography used here by Méndez used ä to write the vowel [ɔ] which corresponds to long /a:/ in other varieties. It does not represent the distinction between [i] and [ɪ]—writing both as <i>. Otherwise, it follows a SEP/SIL convention with <qu/c> for [k] and <j> for [h]. The English translation is mine. The text is published by David Tuggy at the SIL website: http://www-01.sil.org/~tuggyd/Tetel/F001e-Cardenas-nhg.htm.

Today, Méndez (portrait in Figure 2.3) is remembered by traditionalist Tetelcingans, not so much for the many modernizing developments he was able to bring to Tetelcingo through his relationship with Townsend and Cárdenas, but mostly for his association with the first group of Protestants, and the beginning lapse of the traditional socio-religious order. This at least is my impression after visits to Tetelcingo in 2018, when I interviewed some local intellectuals who were organizing the community's efforts to become an independent municipality.

Another element of Cárdenism that suggests that Cárdenas viewed the Indigenous population as a constituency, and that he also contributed to

Figure 2.3 Portrait of Don Martín Méndez Huaxcuatitla and his family.
From the collection of William Cameron Townsend, reproduced with permission of the Summer Institute of Linguistics.

making them increasingly see themselves as constituents, was the proliferation of Indigenous congresses during his presidency. Dawson (2004) describes how during Cárdenas's presidency Indigenous peoples began holding regional and ethnic congresses in which Indigenous intellectuals and representatives met and discussed their local and collective needs, and requested, or even demanded, attention from the government.

One such conference was the First Aztec Congress, celebrated in Milpa Alta, Distrito Federal (D.F.), August 13-18, 1940, during the last few months of Cárdenas's term in office. Nahuas from different areas in the Mexican republic attended the conference—at least representing the Huasteca region, the D.F., and Morelos. The minutes of the congress (excerpt in Figure 2.4) show two main points on the agenda: first, to establish a forum for the formulation of a general political will of the *raza aztekatl* ("Aztec race," which was the way that the Nahua pan-ethnic group is named throughout the minutes). The aim of the congress was to constitute itself as the sole legitimate voice of the *Aztekah* in relation to government. The congress, for example, claimed the right to decide an official orthography for the language to be followed by all (using <k>, <w>, <kw>, and <s>), and to be consulted about artistic and architectural decisions for all state-sponsored building projects in Nahua communities. Regarding education, it demanded that *Aztekah* communities should be served by Nahuatl-speaking teachers, and that education should be culturally and linguistically appropriate for Nahuatl speakers. It also requested specific government action in relation to infrastructure, focusing particularly on connecting Indigenous communities to the road-net and to assure fast and efficient postal communication, and for the establishment of specific educational *internados* (residential schools).[15] A subcommittee on women's rights exhorted the congregants to work to impede that *Aztekah* women should increasingly take on agricultural tasks fit only for men, and impede that they should continue to migrate to the cities to become domestic servants. Permanent committees were established to work for greater integration between the *Aztekah* and the other native "races" to fight for ending discrimination of *Indígenas* in the cities, and also a permanent subcommittee *De Lucha Contra el Vicio* [To Combat the Vice (presumably of alcoholism)]. The demands and concerns of the congress represented a will to

---

[15] Given what we now know of the residential school systems in the United States and Canada, it may seem contrary to our expectations that Indigenous communities would have wished for this, but clearly there was a demand for education in Indigenous communities at this time, and the remoteness of the communities must have made it the only solution that seemed viable. In many Indigenous regions in Mexico there are still schools with residence homes called *albergues* for students, often as young as six or seven, who live with other children and under the care of school staff, far away from their families, for most of the school period.

```
                    TLAYECALITIN.

        Icoentetl.- Monequi ce tlacatl ma quinmahahuiz huan axquioahuaz
            maquinoahcnyahuaca.
        Joontetl.- Monequi Temachtiani maquimati Aztecatl-tlahtolli.
        Ieyei.- Monequi tlalmohuolotene maquimati toquitiz cuali.
        Ionahui.- Monequi ma ce mocuitlahuia inic ax quieni ce chimiz.
        Temacuiltetl.- Tenahuatianime metoquitica quah monequi.
        Icchicuacentetl.- Tenahuatianime ma quah Aztecame huel mo-
        tlahuipano.


                            Ipal FELIPE CERECEDO LÓPEZ.
```

Figure 2.4 Excerpt from the minutes of the *Primer Congreso Azteca*, in which Felipe Cerecedo López, a delegate from Chicontepec, Veracruz, lists his community's requirements for a local municipal agent and other centrally appointed leadership figures: (1) a person who will defend them and not let them be cheated; (2) a teacher who knows the Aztec language [i.e., Nahuatl]; (3) a farmer who knows how to work well; (4) it is necessary that one should take care that one doesn't drink liquor; (5) leaders who work as necessary; (6) leaders who are similar to Aztecs [i.e., Nahua people].
From Barlow Archive, reproduced with permission.

become full national subjects, integrated into the Mexican nation state, with voice and vote, and with the same access to the benefits of modernity as other segments in society. A series of speeches by members of the congress stressed the cultural importance of using Nahuatl in the Mexican educational system. Invoking Nezahualcoyotl and Cuauhtemoc as founders of the national community, they pointed out that the study of Nahuatl etymology was no less relevant for Mexican Spanish speakers than the study of Greek and Latin etymology which was a required subject at all universities.

The political resurgence of Indigenous communities as they worked to insert themselves in the national imagination was surely a key moment in their history. More than ever before, they were able to engage in a relation with a state that recognized them as communities with political rights, and not just as minors to be cared for. Nevertheless, the moment was brief. When Cárdenas left the presidency in 1940, the inclusive indigenista agenda was sidelined, and only the basic programs of rural development were maintained, but the active political inclusion of Indians as a constituency quickly disappeared. This was no doubt because of the changing demographics that, starting in 1940, gradually made rural and Indigenous populations a less significant electorate. Rather than engaging with ethnic communities as political collectives, the attention to development of rural areas was undertaken by the INI, and by the different rural branches of the PRI, all of which worked with a thick bureaucracy and very limited possibilities for local community involvement. If during Cárdenas there was a possibility for Indians to organize around ethnic spheres of interest within the national public space, by the end of Second World War this possibility was gone, and they had ended up as clients to a patron state. In his analysis of the *Congresos Regionales Indígenas*, Dawson (2004) emphasizes how the congresses were a forum in which Indigenous peoples had to demonstrate loyalty to the revolution and proficiency in the revolutionary political idiom, even while emphasizing and promoting local autonomy. The client–patron relation that quickly replaced the inclusive *indigenismo* as the main form of political relation between Indians and state might have been the only possible outcome of this double-bind situation.

I believe that, more than any other factor, this change in the relationship between state and Indigenous political communities, embodied by the INI, SEP, and CNC, is what caused the accelerated decline of public use of Indigenous languages, and the disappearance of Indigenous symbolic idioms across Mexico in the 20th century. The primary function of these symbolic forms had been the maintenance of independent Indigenous public spheres opposed to the hegemony of the national public, but when Indigenous publics were now incorporated into the national public sphere as client publics, they became unnecessary. The demise of most Indigenous public spheres happened in a process that is surprisingly parallel to the process of decline of the Bourgeois public sphere described by Habermas (1989). By taking up a client position in relation to a benefactor state, Indigenous publics lost the ability to be counterpublics with their own locally distinct ideas of the common good and local strategies for achieving it. However, it was precisely their status as counterpublics that had allowed them to maintain their language and cultural distinctiveness throughout the adversities of the 19th century. Now, they had been invited into the national community, at the cost of abandoning their distinctiveness. But it was that distinctiveness that had made them a constituency, and in giving it up they joined the masses of the Mexican proletariat. This process of assimilation caused the demographic decline of Indigenous communities.

Modernity and the Decline of the Nahuatl Public Spheres

The decline of the Nahuatl public spheres need not be viewed as simply detrimental to Indigenous communities. The enforced ethnic separation that characterized the colonial period and the counterpublics that emerged from the liberal economic oppression and erasure of Indigenous communal experience in the early national period are certainly not periods of glory to which Indigenous people would be likely to want to return. On the contrary, Indigenous activism in contemporary Mexico often takes the form of movements to reinscribe themselves into national history, gaining a voice in the national public. The slogan, "never again a Mexico without us," used by Zapatistas and other Indigenous political activists, is exactly based on redefining culturally distinct Indigenous people as a recognized class of national citizens, with rights to self-determination at the local level, as well as rights to participation in the national public (Stephen 1999).

Perhaps because it was the period in which the nation listened the most intensely to Indigenous voices and demands, many Indigenous people do continue to idealize the Cardenista period (a Cardenista Party is popular in some Indigenous communities in the state of Veracruz, for example). However, the clear drawback of the form of inclusion that Indigenous peoples experienced in the Cardenista period and the subsequent decades is that it was paternalistic, motivated by a desire to bring Indians into a particular kind of modernity, without regard as to whether that was really what they wanted. And it was clientelistic, with government subsidies being exchanged arbitrarily in favor of political support, which suppressed the possibility of pursuing local political objectives and made it impossible for communities (Indigenous and non-Indigenous alike) to pose demands on the state.

Indigenous Activism and the Seeds of the Current Resurgence

While the decline of the Indigenous public spheres can be considered a broad and general process, starting with independence and accelerating with the nationalist policies of the 1940s, it is not the case that Indigenous publics have disappeared. Indigenous communities continue to form local publics, and to organize to obtain local political objectives through the different means at their disposal. Usually they do this at the level of a single town-community, but there have been times in the second half of the 20th century when, as in the 19th century, entire regions have organized temporarily to pursue shared political goals. The most significant of these is obviously the 1994 Zapatista rebellion of Chiapas, which continues to exist as a regional Indigenous counterpublic today, 30 years later. Nevertheless, other examples have taken place among Nahuas, already starting during the so-called Dirty War by the Mexican state against Marxist rural guerrilla groups which also included a strong Indigenous element.

In the 1970s, a group of Nahua communities on the Balsas River organized against the planned Tetelcingo dam that would have flooded most of their communities and required their forced relocation. The organization was successful in temporarily creating a shared front among the different communities, but disorganized as soon as the threat of the dam had been defeated (Hindley 1999; Flores Farfán 2011). The Indigenous guerrilla organizations that had their roots in Guerrero during the Dirty War also were influenced by social movements in the Nahuatl-speaking Zongolica region, described in Chapter 5. Here, Indigenous political organizations working in the spectrum from political protest and communal organization to outright guerrilla activity also formed during this period, and still have influence in the political climate of the region today (Díaz González 2016, 2019).

Also in the 1970s, in the Huasteca region of Hidalgo, Nahua communities began a process of reclaiming land from cattle ranchers. In the Huasteca, the end of the revolution had not brought about any significant redistribution of lands from non-Indigenous landholders, as it had in Morelos. The movement was community-based, as groups of Indigenous townspeople armed themselves and squatted on the ranchers' lands that they considered their communal patrimony. However, as the practice of squatting spread from town to town in the region, it eventually required enough critical mass that the government ceded to some of their claims, officially redistributing lands through a regional plan. Nahua historian Rafael Nava Vite (1996) summarizes his town's involvement in the Huasteca land reclamations of the 1970s:

Ken nesi ipan in ni tlajkuiloltekitl, nopa maseualolinilistli pejki ika ueuejakajtsij, pampa amo iuikal ken kintekiuiuyayaj maseualmej ipan se tlali, uan ken kintetesopayaj ipan sekinok tlali tlen ni Uextekapan. Pero kemaj sekij chinankomej pejke kikuij tlali tlen uejkajya kinkuilijtoyaj nopa tominpiyanij, sekij maseualmej pejkej kinpaleuiyaj uan mosenitskijkej iniuaya, maskej chikauak kinteuijkej nopa tominpiyanij inintekixpoyouaj, tlen nopa tlauel kinmauiliyayaj ipan ni tlali. Kejni, nopa maseualolinilistli mosemanki ipan nochi ni tlali. Nopa chinankomej mosenitskijkej mosenpaleuijkej ipan innemilis pampa san nochi motlajtlaniyayaj tlali.	As it appears in this work of writing, the maseualli (Indian/campesino) movement began in an incoherent fashion, because it was not the same how the maseuales were being worked on one land, and how they were being oppressed on another land, in the Huasteca. But as some communities began taking land that had been robbed by the rich long ago, some maseuales began helping them and joined with them, even though the rich fought their companions violently. In this way, the maseualli movement extended across the entire land [region]. Those communities united entirely and helped each other entirely with their lives, because they just asked for land.

Ni olinilistli nelia monelnekiyaya, pampa miakij maseualmej amo kipiyayaj tlali uan sekij tlen kipiyayaj nelia kuekuetsitsij eliyayaj, uan kemantika amo kuali tlali kipiyayaj. Yeka kampaueli on tekipanouayayaj, kemantika on tlapaleuiayayaj ipan potreros uan kemantika on ouatekiyayaj kampa nopa asukarchiuaj. Kemaj ni maseualmej kiitakej para nelia kuali sampa kitekiuisej nopa tlali tlen kinkuilijtoyaj, ayok kinelijlamijkej, kampaueli kampa mosentiliyayaj nopa maseualmej achtoui kiitayayaj kenijkatsaj kikuisej nopa tlali." (Nava Vite 1996, 79)

This movement truly was needed, because many maseuales had no land and some had too small plots, or sometimes had bad land. For that reason they worked where they could, sometimes helping at the cattle ranches and sometimes they worked the cane where they make sugar. When the maseuales saw that indeed they could take back the lands that had been taken, they didn't stop thinking about it. Wherever the maseuales met, the first thing they looked at was how to take back those lands.

A highly significant case of a Nahua rebellion in the 1970s is documented in the work of James Taggart (2008, 2010, 2020). He did long-term ethnographic fieldwork in Huitzilan de Serdán, a Nahuat-speaking town in the Puebla Highlands starting in the 1960s, a decade before a land reclamation insurgency broke out in 1977. Because of his long-term engagement, Taggart was able to document in real time the development of a movement, similar to the one described by Nava Vite, as he interviewed participants and other people affected by the movement, both before and after the events. Taggart's work demonstrates several key facts that resonate with my own conclusions. First of all, he shows that the uprising had a clear ethnic component, as Indigenous *maseualmej* organized in response to encroachment from *mestizo/coyomej* landowners who had also secured control of political power in the community, marginalizing the *maseualmej* from the official politics. Second, he documents how the motivation for the insurgency was emplotted in the narrations of the *maseualmej* in Indigenous mythico-religious terms, and motivated through a social need to sanction violations of sacred principles of reciprocity, humility, and respect for the rain deities. And third, his interviews show Indigenous intellectuals at work, carrying out the function of representing the community's aspirations and sociopolitical demands in the idiom that is grounded in a local Nahuat cosmovision. In recounting the events, *maseualmej* storytellers describe the rebellion allegorically as a storm, sent by the *quiyauhteot* (rain god) to punish the local municipal president for his lack of respect for them. In one version, told by Juan Mauro, authorities lock up a drunk for disorderly conduct, having accused them of scolding the rains. But the drunk is in fact himself a human representative of the rain god (some people's souls are tied to the rain gods). He lets the municipal president know that unless he is set free, the town will be struck by drought, but if they free him it will rain. The president, in his hubris, responds that if it rains tomorrow, he will free him. The next day the rains arrive with tempestuous force, and wash away the haughty *coyomej* and their goods and property, leaving unscathed only the drunk and the *maseualmej* who live up in the hills: "*Zayoh mocauhqueh libre tech in loma lo que ten viviroaya. Huan lo que ten ahmo, quinhuiac in ne at, ne creciente. Ne ciclon. Nihon catca pobrecito borracho que ahmo tei valoraya, cualquiera catca, como cualquiera. Como yahqueh a favor de rayitos, quipalehuihqueh in rayitos*" [only the ones were left free, who lived on the hillsides. And those who didn't were carried off by that water, that flash flood, that cyclone. It was that little poor drunk who was worthless, he was just like anybody. Since he went in favor of the thunderbolts [the rain gods], the thunderbolts helped him out. (my translation)] (Taggart 2020, 209).

In places such as the Huasteca, Guerrero, the Zongolica Highlands, Highland Puebla, and other regions and communities, strong and resilient Nahua publics continue to exist. Occasionally, they emerge into view of the national public sphere when they have to address some grievance, or obtain some political objective, but most of the time they are out of view, except to those who live in them. This chapter has now charted a history of the political relations between Nahuas and the state, first the colonial state, then the liberal state of the early independent nation, and, finally, the nationalist post-revolutionary state of the mid-20th century. In the social order of the colonial regime, Indian republics were states within the state, separate and unequal. In the independence period, Indigenous peoples were nominally equal to all other citizens, but in practice, Indigenous ways of life were excluded from the political sphere. The de facto exclusion from the national public left Nahuas with the choice to assimilate, to tolerate their marginalized status and reorganize in mutualistic corporate communities, or to engage in open rebellion. After the revolution, the state assumed a stance that was overtly sympathetic to the needs and wishes of Indigenous communities and promoted a nationalism in which there was room for some kinds of Indigenous identity. Nevertheless, the initial moves toward cultural development projects in which the state allied itself with Indigenous communities were quickly replaced by a general strategy of cultural assimilation. From the 1950s to the 1970s, the *indigenista* paradigm saw Indigenous culture as picturesque relics of the national past, but saw Indians as backward peasants that had to be educated to give them a useful place in the national productive economy. This also seems to have been the period in which parents in Nahuatl-speaking communities across Mexico stopped speaking Nahuatl to their kids, with entire towns abandoning the language of previous generations. Only in the 1980s and onward, this negative attitude to the cultural markers of indigeneity slowly began to change, and this change, and the question of whether it will contribute to reversing the decline of Nahuatl language publics, is the topic of the next chapter.

Figure 3.0. *Cuauhtemoc* by Jesús Helguera, an iconic painting of Mexican national romanticism from the 1950s, representing the last Aztec tlahtoani *Cuauhtemoc* "Eagle Descender." The aesthetics are representative of the Mexican nationalist imagination of indigenous peoples. The image is well known to most Mexicans, famously included in the paper calendars of Calendarios Landin that can be found in homes and shops throughout Mexico.

Reproduced here with permission from Calendarios Landin.

3
Nahuatl Is Very Fashionable Now
Nation Branding and Cultural Expropriation

Travelers arriving in Mexico City's Benito Juárez International Airport are faced with a dazzling array of impressions. A variety of restaurants and shops selling luxury goods and duty-free products, advertisements for international financial consultancy firms and expensive cars and watches—almost all of these are of much the same kinds as are encountered by travelers in any other airport in the world. Only in some of the restaurants that sell Mexican food and in the souvenir shop will one find things that present themselves as visibly Mexican. There are rainbow-striped Jalisco blankets, wide sombreros laden with tinsel, shiny bottles of tequila and jars of Mexican specialty foods, colorful dolls in *China-poblana* dresses, caricatures of Frida Kahlo, and Indigenous-style embroidered blouses. And there are the obligatory ashtrays and T-shirts featuring the striking imprint of the Aztec Sunstone with its central image of a deity sticking out its tongue, surrounded by the glyphs representing day-names of the Aztec calendar.

Having passed through the shopping areas, travelers make their way to the immigration line to have their passports checked. Here, the Mexican state makes itself tangible, as a customs official courteously helps first-time travelers fill out the customs forms before they arrive at the counter. In addition to the institutional presence of the state, the immigration space is also full of signs of the Mexican nation, and not only the tricolored flag and the national seal depicting the Aztec golden eagle on a cactus. It is also saturated with a mosaic of bright yet pleasant colors and a soft sound of children playing. The colors come from a dominating mural on the wall to the left; its painted fruits, tropical landscapes, ancient pyramids, and Mexicans in colorful costumes fill the room with an almost tangible air of Mexican-ness. The sound comes from a widescreen television above showing a looped video that announces a welcome message. The message is set to a series of National Geographic–style images of Indigenous children with embroidered shawls and wide-brimmed sombreros smiling to the camera, a woman in front of a colonial style church, a Yaqui dancer with his deer-antler headdress and a rattle, jumping right into the camera. The line and the counters with customs officials checking travelers' credentials are what Mitchell (1999) called a "state effect"—the tangible manifestation of the Mexican state regulating access to its territory. But the symbols represented in the mural and the video, and the way that they insert everyone in the room into a narrative of "Mexican-ness," produce a "nation effect," gently telling travelers that they are not only entering Mexican territory, but also Mexican national space—represented as a unique space of pleasant, colorful diversity.

When passing through the airport, travelers may also see a small sign in the official and national colors of green, white, and red with the heading "*QUEJAS e Inconformidades*" [COMPLAINTS and disagreements] in red (Figure 3.1). Below, in smaller white letters, we get translations into English, Portuguese, Chinese, Italian, and Japanese. Below this are four lines in Indigenous languages, and after each line the language is identified: Nahuatl, Maya, Mixteco, Mazahua. The text of the first line, identified simply as "Náhuatl," states: "*kla aka ixkualtsin mits notsa ¡ixteijle!*" This is the only text in Nahuatl in the entire airport—the only place within this space where the Mexican nation meets the world in which the Mexican state chooses to present itself by using Indigenous languages.

The text definitely looks like Nahuatl, though written in a somewhat improvised orthography, but if we ignore the Spanish heading that it is a translation of and try to read the text on its own, its meaning is not at all clear. In spite of my many years of working with Nahuatl, I had to do significant mental gymnastics to arrive at a possible interpretation of what it could even be saying. To test whether native Nahuatl speakers would have similar problems with understanding the text, I later posted the image with a request for translations from native speakers in a Nahuatl language forum on Facebook. Here it became clear that the text was immediately intelligible in its intended meaning only to those speakers who spoke a Nahuatl variety originating in Central Guerrero. Or rather, it was also intelligible to speakers of other varieties; they just understood it very differently. The literal meaning of the text, when translated in Central Guerrero Nahuatl is "If someone speaks to you ugly, report it!" To arrive at this meaning one has to interpret the syllable *ix-* in the word *ixkualtsin* as a negation, since this is its meaning in Central Guerrero Nahuatl. In Guerrero Nahuatl, *ixkualtsin* means "not-pretty," that is, "ugly." But in most other varieties, the main negation is the word *ahmo*, and the prefix *ix-* means "face." In these varieties, *ixkualtsin* would be understood as "handsome" or "pretty-faced." In the Facebook forum, the speakers from other regions, the majority, translated the text as "if someone handsome speaks to you, tell someone." Apparently, a speaker of Guerrero Nahuatl had been involved in the making of the sign, but the sign-makers had not considered that the

Figure 3.1. Multilingual sign found in Mexico City's Benito Juárez Airport in 2013, explaining how to complain about discriminatory treatment in various Indigenous languages.
Photo by the author.

text might not mean the same in other varieties of Nahuatl. In the Facebook forum, when it became clear that there were different ways to understand it, one of the speakers of Guerrero Nahuatl had a suggestion for what might have gone wrong in the translation process. He noted as a clue the word written *kla*. In Nahuatl, a word cannot start with a *kl* sound, but many Spanish speakers pronounce *kl* instead of the Nahuatl sound *tl*. So *kla* is not a possible word in Nahuatl, but the word *tla* means "if," and this is clearly what is meant in the context. He argued that, "The way they write kla grates on my ears, and makes me think that it is written by someone who doesn't actually speak Nahuatl, someone who maybe asked someone from Guerrero to translate for them." If they asked a random Nahuatl speaker to translate for them, that would also explain why they didn't consider that there might be other ways of understanding the message, and why they use a nonstandard orthography (because the person writing it down was not trained in writing Nahuatl, but simply wrote it as it sounded to them). If this is true, it raises some questions about the Mexican state's strategy for using Indigenous languages in public communication: Why have these four languages been chosen, out of the 63 officially recognized Indigenous languages, and why specifically a Guerrero variety of Nahuatl? Why is this sign, with information about how to report a complaint about bad treatment, the only sign in the entire airport to provide information in Indigenous languages?

In the rest of this chapter, I will provide an analysis suggesting that there is *no* reason for this. These signs may not reflect a strategy of communication at all, but rather a strategy of visibility. They may be intended not primarily to provide necessary information to speakers of Indigenous languages, but to demonstrate the inclusion of speakers of Indigenous languages into the Mexican national space, and to *brand* the nation in a particular way for a community of international consumers. This chapter examines the different roles and functions fulfilled by Nahuatl in the Mexican national public sphere, and it analyzes how they become meaningful within the context of Mexican Indigenous politics. In interpreting the state's use of Nahuatl (and Indigenous languages more broadly), I try to place these Indigenous language texts in their full semiotic context, both linguistic and sociopolitical, in order to understand the work that they carry out in the national public sphere. I show that the Mexican nation uses Indigenous peoples as a symbolic nexus that it includes as a central aspect of its national brand. And I argue that when the Mexican state uses Nahuatl in public communication, it is not always clear whether it is in fact trying to extend a service to its Nahuatl-speaking citizens and contribute to the revitalization of the language, or whether such usage is better understood as a part of this branding strategy. I show that, very often, the state's public use of Nahuatl *cannot* fulfill the communicative function that is ostensibly its primary intention. Therefore, I develop an analysis of the communicative intention of the Mexican state's public use of Nahuatl as a kind of *double-voiced communication* in the sense of Bakhtin (1981). I suggest that these texts are not primarily meant to communicate their informational content to Indigenous readers, but that their main communicative function is fulfilled by the connotational functions of simply writing in public in an Indigenous language. When the state writes a message in Nahuatl, it doesn't really matter what is being said, but by saying it in Nahuatl it communicates to Indigenous people that they are indeed included as a part of the nation, and simultaneously, to non-Indigenous people, it represents the state as diverse, inclusive, and respectful of the needs and rights of Indigenous citizens. The medium, in this case, is indeed the message.

When the State Speaks Nahuatl

Following the 2003 Law of Linguistic Rights, Mexican national space witnessed a proliferation of language-planning efforts, both public and private, implicitly with the intention of eventually complying with the law of linguistic rights. These results are most clearly visible to the public in the form of public writing in Indigenous languages, on public signs, information flyers and brochures, and even billboards. The Law of Linguistic Rights obligates all branches of government to provide its services in Indigenous languages to those who need it. It does not specify how this is to be done, nor does it, apart from the creation of the INALI (the National Institute of Indigenous Languages), establish an infrastructure in charge of accomplishing the change. Moreover, while the beginnings were auspicious, over the past decade government support for INALI has dwindled so that it now receives less government funds than the national baseball program (Aguilar Gil 2023). In 2014, INALI summarized its accomplishments of the previous 10 years in a public campaign focusing on three concrete results of its work: (1) the translation of the Mexican Constitution into 11 Indigenous languages (not including Nahuatl, since the Nahuatl translation was not funded by INALI, but by the Mexican Senate as part of their celebration of the centenary of the revolution and bicentenary of Mexican independence); (2) the elaboration of official orthographies for several Indigenous languages; (3) the organization of a corps of 500 Indigenous-language translators. It makes sense to look at the concrete impact of these accomplishments for the degree of accessibility of Indigenous-language speakers to government services.

The Constitution in Nahuatl

The Nahuatl translation of the Mexican Constitution (which is in fact the second such translation since the translation of the 1857 constitution by Miguel de Palma, and which was not published by INALI but by the Mexican Senate) was published in 2010 (Hernández Hernández and Hernández Ramírez 2010). It was translated by Natalio Hernández and Zósimo Hernández. Natalio Hernández is a poet laureate, member of the prestigious Mexican Academy for the Spanish language, a native speaker of Eastern Huastecan Nahuatl, with an educational background as a bilingual teacher. Printed in an undisclosed number of copies, it was distributed free of charge, but there was no organized effort to distribute it to Indigenous communities. Individual speakers of Nahuatl interested in reading it had to actively seek it in government agencies such as INALI, or its local state branches such as AVELI (Academia Veracruzana de Lenguas Indígenas) in Veracruz, or by downloading digital copies online. However, even if they had distributed it more widely, it is not clear how much that would have benefited Nahuatl speakers. Hernández is a speaker of Eastern Huasteca Nahuatl, which is one of the Nahuatl varieties with the most speakers, but also one that is markedly different from the more commonly studied varieties of the Central dialect area, as well as from the also very populous Nahuatl-speaking areas of southern Veracruz and Guerrero. Hernández and his collaborators, however, chose not to translate the Constitution into his own variety of Nahuatl, but chose, presumably in order to produce a translation that was accessible beyond his own dialect area, to avoid many of the grammatical features that distinguish his own variety from others—creating a kind of *koiné* consensus variety.[1] As a result, the translation uses the pronouns found in western varieties instead of the eastern ones that Hernández uses when he writes in his own Huastecan variety (i.e., writing <yehua> corresponding to /yehwa/, instead of <yaja> corresponding to /yaha/). It consistently uses a plural future ending with the suffix /-seh/, used only in the Huasteca and in Michoacán, instead of the ending /-skeh/, used in all other varieties. It generally uses the negation *amo* which is used in all the western varieties and some of the eastern ones, but also occasionally uses the exclusively Huastecan negative prefix /ax-/ which is unlikely to be understood by speakers from other areas. For example, the translation consistently uses *axcanah* in the meaning "nowhere" and *axcuali* in the

---

[1] In dialectology a *koiné* is a variety that emerges through contact between two regional dialects (as Koiné Greek emerged through the mixture of Ionic, Attic, and Doric Greek dialects), through a process of leveling and simplification in which the most highly marked forms in each dialect are lost, and forms that are shared or can be leveled remain.

meaning "bad." None of these expressions is readily intelligible outside of the Huasteca region. The decision of using an artificial *koiné* variety presents its own problems, as the translation then represents a Nahuatl that is not spoken by anyone, and which by virtue of its being reproduced in an official context is imbued from the outset with a higher level of prestige than the varieties of Nahuatl actually spoken.

Another choice made by the translators was to avoid Spanish loans, and instead create neologisms (or sometimes reach back to terms used in colonial Nahuatl texts) to express all those concepts that do not have well-established equivalents in contemporary Nahuatl, including most legal and political terminology, institutions of government, and so on. This type of terminology is of course densely used within the text of the Constitution. Here is an example of a very literal translation from the Constitution's paragraph two, which establishes Mexico as a pluricultural and pluriethnic nation with roots in the Indigenous pre-colonial communities:

Totlalnantzin monelchihua ihuan monelhuayotia ipa miaquintin masehual altepemeh tlen hualahuih ipan calpolmeh tlacamecayotl chanchihqueh ipan Anahuac totlalnantzin tlen queman opehqui yancuic chantilistli ihuan, mopialia tlen yehuan tlanahuaticayotl, tlapialistli, toltecayotl ihuan tlatocayotl, noso san achitzin tlen yehuan. (Hernández Hernández and Hernández Ramírez 2010, 16)

Our country [land-mother] truly makes itself and has its root in many Indigenous communities that come from the lineage of peoples [neighborhoods lineages] who lived in our country *Anahuac* when the new settlement began, and who have their own laws, property, culture and government, or only a few of the these.[2]

While there is a glossary included in the translation, it does not cover all the terms, and because of the density of neologisms in the text, the reader would have to familiarize themselves with the neologisms before being able to read even the first sentence. The glossary also of course only gives the equivalent term in Spanish, but does not otherwise define or describe the meanings, which means that the reader must have good knowledge of the constitutional

---

[2] My translation. Translated without consulting the Spanish text. *Toltecayotl* and *Tlatocayotl* here used in the meanings "culture" and "government" are terms re-adopted from colonial Nahuatl. *Tlalnantzin* (lit. "earth-mother") as "nation" or "country" can be guessed in context. *Yancuic chantilistli* (lit. "new homemaking") can also be inferred to mean "colonial settlement" in the context. The intended meaning of *calpolmeh tlacamecayotl* (lit. "neighborhoods lineages") is somewhat unclear but seems to refer to continuous habitation of a place from the pre-colonial to modern times. I tried reading this with some native speakers from Hueyapan and they achieved a general sense of the content of the paragraph, but found many of the highlighted words and phrases difficult or impossible to understand.

apparatus and its Spanish terminology before being able to understand the Nahuatl terms. Hence the translation is accessible only to a Nahuatl speaker who is literate, well-versed in political terminology, patient enough to use the glossary to learn neologisms, and able to cope with difficulties of intelligibility caused by regional variation—as well as able to find a copy of it through the internet or by traveling to a government office. This would describe only a very small subgroup of the population of Nahuatl speakers, and would a priori exclude all monolingual speakers. Furthermore, there is little reason to think that being able to read the Constitution is a necessity or even an interest of most monolingual, or even most bilingual Nahuatl speakers. The fact that even when provided in translation, the knowledge required to understand the details of the Constitution is not available to most members of Indigenous communities provides an excellent example of how the semiotic membrane of the hispanophone Mexican public sphere, consisting of the barriers of translation and contextualization, also effectively prevents outsiders from participating.

In sum, the communicative aspect of the translation does not seem to be the main motivation behind the project of translating the Constitution; rather, the main function seems to lie in its symbolic value as tangible expressions of the state's interest in and dedication to Indigenous communities and linguistic rights. Nevertheless, I would argue that by extension, it also serves as an expression of the incorporation of Indigenous communities into the nation-state and their integration into its political order. So in this way the translation constitutes a way for the state to legitimize its claim to authority and eminent domain over ethnic groups that could potentially see themselves as standing outside of its sphere of hegemony. It is a preemptive negation of any claim they might have to being politically independent of the Mexican nation.

INALI: Standardization and Translation

Another task undertaken by INALI is the elaboration of standardized orthographies. This project has the same kind of political implications, in which the state and its institutions constitute themselves as the unique holder of an authority through which the norms for how to represent Indigenous languages in writing can be established (INALI 2020). Reportedly, the *norma de escritura* [orthographic norms] for Nahuatl is finished and will soon be released.[3] Whichever orthography INALI chooses to give official status, the choice will

---

[3] Personal communication from Victoriano de la Cruz (autumn 2023) who has participated in the process of creating it.

carry with it political effects for Indigenous communities, and whichever orthography they select will alienate proponents of other systems. The choice will also affect the ability of communities to control what aspects of their language and identity they consider important to represent in writing. Figure 2.3 shows how, in 2014 before the process of creating an official orthoprgaphy began, INALI used Nahuatl in a colonial style orthography in signage at the Mexico City offices of the institution.

Finally, the education of interpreters is an essential step in achieving linguistic accessibility to government services for Indigenous people. However, the 500 interpreters that INALI claims to have educated must be seen in relation to the presence of at least 60 different languages and the 6 million people speaking them. They do not cover the entire Indigenous-language-speaking population; in practice there is a high degree of variation in where they are found and how they are employed. It is not at all the case that monolingual speakers of Indigenous languages can count on having interpreters in their interactions with the state anywhere in Mexico. There are many reports, particularly from the state of Oaxaca, with its extreme linguistic diversity, of Indigenous people being arrested, convicted, and imprisoned without ever having had a fair chance to know the charges against them or to respond to

Figure 3.2. Photo of the entrance to the headquarters of INALI in Mexico City in 2013, stating in Nahuatl and Spanish "welcome here to INALI, the place of many languages" and noting that the translation of the sign has been carried out in accordance with the Law of Linguistic Rights.
Photo by the author.

them. According to one article, 10,000 speakers of Indigenous languages were imprisoned around 2015, and only 10% of them had access to an interpreter. The article also critiques the practice of not remunerating translator services and using unprepared interpreters. Other reports tell of Indigenous peoples traveling to court appointments multiple times, only to have them canceled for lack of an interpreter. Others tell of prison inmates being used as ad hoc interpreters for other inmates. Some studies describe a practice of using Indigenous janitors or food vendors in the court buildings as interpreters (Kleinert and Stallaert 2015). Outside of the legal system, for example in medical contexts or in the context of municipal government, there are no systematic attempts to provide interpreter services at all. In some Indigenous-majority municipalities I have visited, I have been able to converse in Nahuatl with officials, and even in some cases with the municipal president. However, in other municipalities, also inhabited by a majority of Nahuatl speakers, I have observed monolingual Nahuatl speakers having to request help from strangers when trying to understand the information given to them by monolingual Spanish municipal officials. There is currently no requirement, nor even a general practice of hiring native language interpreters at the municipal level; rather, the presence or absence of interpreter services is left to chance.

In the spring of 2020, I was working in the community of Tequila Veracruz, when the coronavirus (COVID-19) pandemic reached Mexico. I was working closely with Gabriela Citlahua, a local Nahua woman with a BA degree from the Intercultural University of Veracruz. In the municipality of Tequila, most people speak and understand Nahuatl. The exceptions are in the central barrios of the town of Tequila and within the local political elite, and many children who have only learned Spanish in spite of being brought up by Nahuatl-speaking parents. There is a considerable number of elderly people who are not comfortable speaking Spanish. Nevertheless, almost all signage in the town is in Spanish, as well as all public information. A few days after the first cases of COVID-19 had been declared in the state of Veracruz, the municipal government began informing its citizens of the correct precautions through the town's loudspeaker system. The information was entirely in Spanish. One evening the mayor called Gabriela to ask her to produce an information spot in Nahuatl that could be run on the speakers along with the Spanish version. He needed it tomorrow. He didn't offer any resources for producing it, nor did he mention how she would be paid or compensated. Gabriela decided to do it, thinking that it was an important cause, and that she might accumulate some goodwill with the mayor's office, and create some visibility for the Nahuatl language, and so she spent the night doing the translation and recording the sound in her own voice. The following week it was playing from the town's loudspeakers, but she had not received as much as a thank you for the time she took to make it. Fortino Ramírez, a Nahuatl-language activist friend of mine in southern Veracruz, also independently made information material in the local variety of Nahuatl, which he printed and circulated in town and on social media. In early April, I traveled to the state of Puebla. Here their state government and the office of the State Health Secretary had made official information materials in Nahuatl and Spanish, posted in the streets of Huauchinango, a large municipality with many Nahuatl speakers. Meanwhile, the official social media accounts of INALI were still circulating a Nahuatl-language information sheet about how to use self-exploration to detect breast cancer. So clearly, there is a lot of variation in how different political dependencies approach the task of producing informational materials in Indigenous languages. If the Law of Linguistic Rights is seen as setting an ideal for the provision of state services that governmental institutions aspire to achieve, then the process remains in an incipient state. If the law is understood as establishing an actual obligation for that same provision, then it is one that the state cannot currently be said to be seriously trying to fulfill.

Particularly revealing of the lack of systematicity in the application of linguistic rights by the Mexican state was a lawsuit won by Mardonio Carballo, a Nahua poet and journalist, in 2015. In 2014, a new Federal Telecommunications Law was approved by parliament, and its article 230 stated that in order to obtain a permit to broadcast radio, broadcasters were required to broadcast "in the national language." Carballo, who was hosting programs in Nahuatl on a local radio station, recognized this as a denial of the right to broadcast in Indigenous languages, challenged the law in court, and won, whereafter the law was changed so that it now specifically mentions the right to broadcast in Indigenous languages (Guevara-Martínez 2021). The fact that simultaneously, with the increased attention to Indigenous language rights, such a law could be approved and put into force without anyone noticing the problem, shows how lightly the topic weighs on the minds of Mexican legislators.

There is little systematicity or apparent reason behind the decisions of the Mexican state to use, or not to use, Indigenous languages in addressing Indigenous communities—not when addressed as citizens with a right to receive important public information, and not even when politicians address Indigenous communities directly as a democratic constituency of potential voters. I have yet to hear a Mexican politician or official (with the exception of the director of INALI) address an Indigenous audience fluently in an Indigenous language, but occasionally they will sprinkle a few words or phrases into their speeches—particularly to say thanks. In Nahuatl, there is considerable local variation in how to express gratitude, but the most commonly known and taught expression is the word *tlasohkamati*. A simple word to pronounce as Nahuatl words go, it is, however, a rarity that these attempts by politicians to say "thank you" in the local language are fluently pronounced. Variations abound, such as *tlaxokomatli* (said by the governor of Morelos, Graco Ramirez, when visiting Hueyapan),[4] *tlaksokámati* (said by a state official visiting Hueyapan),[5] and *tlakosamati* (written by an academic in a poem honoring the memory of the famous Hueyapan intellectual and healer Modesta Lavana).[6] The most widely circulated *tlasohkamati*-gaffe, however, was made by the then presidential candidate Enrique Peña Nieto. In an address to a Nahuatl-speaking town in Guerrero, he managed to say "*tlaxkalli miyak,*" which in fact means "many tortillas." This odd mistake was recorded on video and circulated on YouTube and Facebook by his opponents, as evidence of his intellectual unfitness for the presidency.[7] Though perhaps understandable and relatively insignificant, such anecdotal gaffes serve as poignant illustrations of the superficial and primarily symbolic level of the Mexican state's engagement with Indigenous languages.

Mikhail Bakhtin's (1981, 324) notion of "double-voiced discourse" invites us to attend to how multiple intentionalities can be co-present in the same utterance, and how they may struggle for control of the final interpretation. Most of the Mexican states' communication in Indigenous languages have the quality of such double-voiced texts: intentionally ambiguous signs calculated to be interpreted in one way by the language public they explicitly address, and in another in the national public from which they are delivered. From the perspective, or rather *angle of listening*, of the national public, they are meant to index the progressive stance of the government, and the official integration of Indigenous communities into the national public sphere. This communicative strategy is largely successful insofar as it is communicating to the progressively minded, urban, middle-class Mexican. Nevertheless, when Indigenous publics are listening—to the degree that the messages ostensibly intended for them ever reach them—the semiotic process is much more volatile and susceptible to unpredictable interpretations. When heard from the Indigenous angle, the attempts to signal interest in the Indigenous communities by using their language come off as sufficiently insufficient to be insulting, or at least enough to undermine any impression of sincerity.

[4] http://morelos.gob.mx/?q=version-estenografica-del-gobernador-graco-ramirez-durante-la-inauguracion-de-la-feria-hueyapan-2013.
[5] Recorded in fieldnotes.
[6] https://hormega.wordpress.com/2012/08/06/volver-al-viento-72/.
[7] It should be noted that in Central Guerrero where he was speaking, the word for "thank you" is not *tlasohkamati* but *tlaxtlawi*, an abbreviation of the phrase *totahtzin mitztlaxtlawis*, literally "Our Father will repay you," which sounds a little bit more like *tlaxkalli*.

Nahuatl Belletrism and the Indigenous Heritage of the Nation

Another way that Nahuatl is present in the national public sphere is in the cultivation of the cultural heritage of the Aztecs, a form of intellectual and aesthetic pursuit that is closely tied to the construction of national identity. Paja Faudree[8] has referred to this vein of scholarship, whose primary exponent has been Miguel León-Portilla (1926–2019), as Nahuatl "*belletrism*," an approach to the study of Nahuatl texts that seeks not only to access knowledge of Nahua history and culture, but also to inscribe it into a national literary canon. Within Mexico, the significance of this school of Nahuatl studies is such that any Mexican humanist scholar will be familiar with the phrase *flor y canto* [flower and song], the Spanish translation of the Nahuatl metaphor for "poetry"—*in xochitl in cuicatl*. Similarly, every Mexican will be familiar with the Texcocan ruler Nezahualcoyotl, described as the quintessential poet-king of the Nahuas and represented throughout the country on statues and even on the 100-peso bill, and many will have had to memorize by heart the Spanish translation of a poem ascribed to his authorship.

As previously mentioned, the impulse to draw on Aztec history and incorporate the Nahuatl language as a local stock of symbols was found already in the proto-nationalism of the Mexican *criollo* class during the colony. In the 20th century, the intellectual and aesthetic approach to Aztec culture and to Nahuatl became a significant current in the *indigenista* movement. Starting with Sigüenza y Góngoras's comparisons between Aztec culture and the Old World, and on to Gamio's comparison of Aztec art with classical European art in *Forjando Patria* (Gamio [1916] 2010), continuing with Garibay's volumes on Nahuatl poetry and literature (Garibay K. 1937, 1953), and reaching a peak with León-Portilla's *La Filosofía Náhuatl estudiada en sus fuentes* (1956), this approach came to form the main academic approach to Nahuatl language and culture in Mexico (Payàs 2004; Keen 1971, 534–35). As pointed out by Faudree (2015a, 231), belletrist Nahuatl scholars should be recognized for their insistence on working from within the Indigenous languages and from a deep philological approach to the texts, and for establishing the study of Indigenous language texts as a field of scholarship in its own right. And one should not minimize their importance for those Nahuatl speakers, of whom I have met several, whose first experiences of Nahuatl as a language of beauty, art, and history came through pocket editions of León-Portilla's work.

---

[8] Faudree 2015a, 18–23, 213–14, 231. See also Gutiérrez Chong 1999; Payàs 2004 for descriptions of this tradition.

Nevertheless, in its quest to represent the "classical Nahuatl" of the colonial sources as one of the world's major classical traditions, Nahuatl belletrism has also contributed to the marginalization of other Indigenous literary traditions relative to Nahuatl, and of the living Nahuatl languages relative to the colonial variety. This aesthetic indigenism, idealizing the Aztec heritage and classical Nahuatl as a key aspect of Mexican national culture, and as the pinnacle of Indigenous aesthetic achievement, is still very much present in the Mexican national space. It stands in a fraught relationship to the struggle for recognition of contemporary Indigenous artists, as it establishes Indigenous artistic expressions as a valid tradition with a deep and valuable history, but simultaneously lifts up the classical form as an ideal against which contemporary art is judged, and largely places the role as arbiters of the value of Indigenous art with non-Indigenous intellectuals. It puts contemporary Nahua intellectuals who seek to take up a voice in the national public sphere in the situation of having to constantly articulate their own relevance in relation to the forms and themes of their colonial predecessors (McDonough 2014, 15; Coon 2014, 2015, 2019).

In June 2014, Mexican media were teeming with praise for the opening at the National Auditorium of *Xochicuicatl Cuecuechtli*, an opera composed by Gabriel Pareyón based on a poem in Nahuatl from the 16th-century collection *Cantares Mexicanos*. The music of the opera was performed by the ensemble *Lluvia de Palos*, using only pre-colonial Indigenous percussive instruments. The plot of the opera concerns a Huastec man being seduced by three *ahuianimeh* (Aztec courtesans) before taking on the guise of the Aztec corn deity. The poem *Xochicuicatl Cuecuechtli* [Shameless Flowersong] that serves as the basis for the opera is not explicitly erotic, although we know that the dance accompanying this type of song was considered indecent by Spaniards. Mexican Nahuatologist and philosopher Patrick Johansson has published an analysis of it, in which he argues that it is in fact permeated by a veiled sexual innuendo, expressed metaphorically and only accessible through deep cultural and linguistic analysis—according to him, the first example of the Mexican verbal genre, the *albur*, a kind of double entendre (Johansson 2002). Pareyón based his interpretation of the poem's meaning on Johansson's. However, at the performance, the Nahuatl libretto of the opera was nowhere represented in writing—neither in the program nor in the running light "supertitles" above the stage, which were only in Spanish. The sung Nahuatl was very difficult to make out, due to the unusual singing technique employed by the singers. The text in the supertitles had a very indirect relation to the words of the poem, and to what was actually being sung. At times, the titles approximated Johansson's translation, but at other times it deviated completely from the Nahuatl words, creating dialogue between the characters; or it added more explicit sexual innuendo, such as "we women do not subsist on corn and beans alone, we also need chili" or "I erect my flowery pole," neither of which was present in the sung words. The supertitle functioned more as a guide to the plot, and a representation of the composer's interpretation of the poem, than an actual translation of the sung text. This made the Nahuatl sung words stand alone, isolated from the meaning of the plot. The use of Nahuatl became simply an instrument to achieve an aesthetic effect, but not a language of communication. As far as I could ascertain by reading the program and the actors' biographies, there were no Nahuatl speaker or persons from Nahua communities among the main participants. After the performance, I attended the reception, and made small talk with some members of the audience. I recognized Francisco Baranda, a well-known Nahuatl teacher and native speaker from Milpa Alta and founder of one of the Nahuatl language academies. I asked him (in Spanish) what he thought about the performance: "It was very beautiful and interesting," he said smiling under his huge moustache, "but I wish that the language had been featured more prominently."

The use of Nahuatl in the *Xochicuicatl Cuecuechtli* shows the ambiguity of how Indigenous languages are currently fashionable in Mexico. On one hand, such engagements explicitly claim to be ways of honoring Indigenous peoples by exalting the quality of their cultural production, but on the other hand, contemporary Indigenous people have little voice or participation in the interpretation of the meaning of the signs that ostensibly represent "their" cultural production. The interpretation and execution are carried out entirely by cultural specialists from within the national public sphere. This exoticism and appropriation of the right to interpret Indigenous culture is the dark side of the "belletristic" approach to Indigenous culture, in which cultural elites take the responsibility of converting native "folklore" into "art." Rather than being works of cultural translation that seek to represent the meanings that Indigenous people attribute to their art to an audience of cultural others, such works risk ending up as a colonization of the Nahuatl text, and the erasure of the voices of the Nahuas who wrote it.

Fashionable Nahuatl: National Expropriations of Indigenous Culture

> "You should find some company that could be interested in sponsoring the Nahuatl course. What about the Tres Palomas *bakery?*"
> "They went out of business last year."

"Oh...."

I was at lunch with four of the people working in the office of the State Secretary of Culture, including the secretary herself and the director of the municipalization project, who was using my presence at the meeting as a pretext for asking for increased funding for the Nahuatl courses. But his request was not seriously considered. I tried to support him, commenting that I thought that the current project in Morelos was unique worldwide, in that it actually pays youths to study their community's language, and that the state could get a lot of positive publicity from the project. "No," said the secretary, "What we should do is tell everyone that being bilingual makes you more intelligent. There are neuroscience studies proving that! We should make it clear that all children ought to learn to speak Nahuatl and to play the violin. That is the way to rescue these languages." And with that, we moved on to other topics. On our way back, I asked her more about how she was working to support the Indigenous languages. She told me about two projects she had recently carried out: one was the production of a memory game to learn Nahuatl vocabulary. The memory cards were illustrated by a famous Mexican cartoonist; they were printed in color on thick glossy paper and the design was absolutely gorgeous. Another was a children's book with poems in Nahuatl and professional color illustrations. Arriving at her office, she gave me one of the memory games, and showed me the book. "You can't have the book, we didn't make very many copies and this is the only one I have left." I wondered where the other copies were, and guessed that they probably were not in the hands of schoolchildren in the Nahua communities, just as the beautifully designed memoryvgames probably never would be. "Why do you think spending all these resources on creating Nahuatl language art is important?" I asked. She looked at me seriously, with a look that suggested that I had finally understood what it was all about: "You see, Nahuatl is very fashionable right now. Everybody wants to learn Nahuatl and support Indigenous peoples." *I knew she had studied design in Paris, and dressed as she was, in a black designer dress with a matching broad-brimmed hat and a white scarf, it seemed clear that she knew what she was talking about.*

The approach to Nahuatl language revitalization of the Morelos State Secretary of Culture in the introductory vignette shows clearly that the field of language revitalization and its discourses and practices are embedded within a wider field of cultural production. It shows that actors in this field may understand the significance of their acts in radically different ways from those of linguists and language activists. Most linguists, for example, would consider language revitalization to be important for the sake of the language itself, as a part of a universal human patrimony of knowledge and for the sentimental or cultural value it has for the members of the speech community who developed it.[9] Another view is simply that language revitalization is valuable because it is part of a fashion trend. The secretary's statement in which she made fashion the key to understanding the importance of Nahuatl to the state prompted me to try to understand the role of fashion (both in the sense of changing norms, and in the sense of changing ideas and design patterns in consumer goods) to the politics of Indigenous linguistic and cultural revival.

But what is fashion, and how does it apply to language revitalization? The first anthropological engagement with "fashion" was Kroeber's analysis of the changing fashions of dress length.[10] He observed a certain regularity of the cycles through which dress length became progressively shorter until reaching a practical minimum length, and then progressively longer until it reached a practical maximum length and started becoming shorter again. He also posited that social volatility, for example during wars and revolutions, was reflected in increased volatility of styles. A perspective on fashion based on Bourdieu's concept of "distinction" (Bourdieu 1979 [English: 1986]) seems more in line with current anthropological thinking. Such a perspective would see fashion changes as driven by the process through which higher classes engage in conspicuous consumption in order to distinguish themselves from the lower classes, who in turn, in a process of mimicry, strive to gain access to the symbolic capital through which the upper crust of society semiotically consolidates its power. A synthesis of these two perspectives might come from a semiotically informed approach seeing changing fashions as a process of interpretation and reinterpretation in which shifting indexical grounds motivate new conceptualizations and cultural expressions, which in turn become the ground for further interpretations in a chain of indexical orders. Greg Urban (2001) has posited that metacultural ideologies are an important factor in providing a certain structuredness of long-term processes of cultural change. In Urban's formulation, metacultural ideologies congeal semiotic repertoires into registers that are then differentially valorized (Agha 2007, 147–50). For example, in a context where cultural innovation is particularly valued, one may expect a different type of fashion dynamic than in one that values faithful reproduction of tradition. The beauty of this idea is that it allows us to look at change as a process through which the present fashion emerges from a past, which it then appropriates by converting it into "history," before proceeding to project itself into the future. Fashion, then, is not random; it is a semiotic process that works through reactive dynamics. Each

---

[9] See, e.g., Hale et al. 1992; Woodbury 1993; and for an alternative formulation of the value of Indigenous languages, Davis 2017a; Muehlmann 2012; de Korne, Haley, and Leonard 2017.
[10] Kroeber 1919; Richardson and Kroeber 1940; Kroeber 1963.

new idea builds on the previous idea (which it either emulates or distances itself from), and so fashion forms genealogies across semiotic contexts.

The indexical ground relative to which Mexican Indigenous languages and cultural expressions have become fashionable is characterized by a metacultural ideology that values "the national," and which sees Indigenous tradition as manifestations of a particularly authentic kind of national culture. At the same time, "diversity" is in high currency on the global marketplace—travelers are attracted to it, and travelers are big business. Through the past decades, the realities of cultural globalization and the ideologies of multiculturalism have attached value to the exotic and the authentic as perhaps never before. Within this system of values, cultural expressions that are indexically tied to concepts of global capitalism and US consumer society are devalued, and those expressions that invoke authenticity, autochthony, and locality are positively valued. This diversity economy causes a cultural dynamic in which nations increasingly turn to narratives of national authenticity in order to brand themselves and so better become able to compete with other nations and with global corporations and their brands (Comaroff and Comaroff 2009). This is the global cultural field that sociolinguistic studies have also described as characterized by the condition of "superdiversity."[11] Though originally theorized for European nation-states in their reaction to immigration, this marketized "superdiversity" and its surrounding discourses of value would seem also to be at work in Mexico. In response to earlier nationalist narratives that saw diversity as a threat to national cohesion, these new discourses are working to reconceptualize cultural diversity as a value in and of itself. In this diversity-based market, Indigenous languages and cultural resources become a cultural resource that nations can expropriate and exploit, as long as they at least appear outwardly invested in progressive ideas of Indigenous peoples' rights.

Indigenous Signs as Nation Branding

The literature on the semiotic process of branding conceptualizes the brand as a way of indexically tying products, ideologies, and experiences together across contexts, making commodities recognizable and desirable, and adding value to the material commodity.[12] In this context, the nation may come to work similarly to a corporation whose brand adds value to its

---

[11] Vertovec 2007; Blommaert 2013; Duchêne and Heller 2009.
[12] Manning 2010; Nakassis 2012; Moore 2003.

products by indexing desirable narratives, and thereby assures their desirability abroad (Volcic and Andrejevic 2011, 2015). Comaroff and Comaroff (2009, 122) have described how African nations appropriate ethnic symbols as capital in projects of nation-branding, noting how some countries actually take out trademarks on brands meant to fortify their national rights to marketing certain cultural commodities considered national property. Recent work on nationalism has even suggested that the ideological fabric of nationalism has entered a new phase in the 21st century, within the context of an increasingly globalizing consumer capitalism, and an ever increasing focus on the trade balance. The intensification of a global market economy has made it imperative for the world's nations to market themselves in order to attract investments, making all nations essentially into corporations. Ravinder Kaur (2020) has shown how this "nation branding" takes place at the absolute top level of world politics, as nations strive to brand themselves in Davos at the meetings of the global economic elite.

Mexico also brands itself, and it increasingly uses Indigenous symbols to do so. One unmistakable example of this is the 2012 premiere of the movie *Hecho en México* (Made in Mexico), a musical-film by English filmmaker Duncan Bridgeman, depicting Mexican cultural life as a seamless blend of technological modernity, postmodern eclectic hybridity, and colorful Indigenous heritage. The movie itself, with its delicious graphic presentation of a Mexico in vivid saturated colors, with smiling faces, delicious meals, and beautiful exotic landscapes, was in effect a postcard or a tourist brochure turned cinema. It was partly funded by *Televisa*, the Mexican television company closely aligned with then President Peña Nieto and his wife Angélica Rivera, making it hard not to consider it basically a 90-minute-long ad for Mexico.

The colorful visual scheme of *Hecho en México* is also echoed in the branding of the *Pueblos Mágicos* [magical towns] program, which promotes particularly picturesque towns as destinations for domestic and international tourism. Casper Jacobsen (2018) has observed how this "multicultourism" simultaneously recruits Indigenous peoples as extras in the colorful spectacle, promising them a part of the bounty of tourism, while in reality it often ends up being extractive, with profits flowing to the already rich and powerful. Tourism is a major sector of national econocmic growth and development, the third largest contributor to the Mexican GDP after oil and remittances, and given the global prospects of the petroleum industry, the tourist sector is only expected to grow in importance (OECD 2020). In 2019, before the pandemic, it supplied 8.7% of GDP, and already in 2021 this number was back to 7.1%.[13] It is hardly surprising that shifting governments have sought to energize this sector through various campaigns and initiatives, the promotion of cultural or heritage tourism being one of them. For the current president López Obrador, the *Tren Maya* [Maya Train], cutting a swath through the pristine jungle of Yucatán, is the major prestige project for heritage tourism. With it, he seeks to entice tourists to venture away from the beaches of Cancún and toward the less visited states of Campeche, Tabasco, and Chiapas—promising opportunity to Maya communities along the track, though many fear these are empty promises that only cover up a more likely result of dispossession and environmental damage.[14]

Fashion as Nation Branding

The use of Indigenous cultural emblems as a national marketing strategy is also evident in Mexican fashion design. Mexican designers have increasingly used Indigenous emblems and symbols as part of their designs and media strategies through the past five years. Important designers such as Ricardo Seco, Carmen Rion, and Francesco Cancino incorporate elements that either directly copy or indexically invoke Indigenous crafts. Seco's sneakers, for example, incorporate not only the colors and technique of Huichol beadwork, but also the sacred imagery of the peyote cactus flower. Cancino's designs draw on the iconic Tzotzil Maya dress styles from Chamula, and Rion fabricates her shawls in collaboration with Oaxacan weavers' collectives. All of them have narratives about the significance of the Indigenous element of their designs that both discursively appropriate the Indigenous tradition as a national or regional heritage that also belongs partly to the designers through their own heritage, and they also use discourses of "honoring" and "generating visibility" for Indigenous artisans in order to explain and justify their choices.

In the spring of 2015, French designer Isabel Marant was chastised on social media for marketing a nearly exact copy of the traditional *huipil* (blouse) of the Mixe town of Santa Maria Tlahuitoltepec—produced in India, and without so much as mentioning where the "inspiration" for the design originated (Díaz Robles 2020). Mexican designers, as well as anthropologists and Indigenous activists, lined up to join the campaign condemning this blatant example of cultural appropriation. Marant unconvincingly defended herself

---

[13] https://www.statista.com/statistics/977929/mexico-tourism-share-gdp.
[14] Ansotegui 2020; Casanova Casañas 2021; Rosado-Zaidi 2021; Gasparello, Núñez Rodríguez, and Gasparello 2021.

by saying that the design was meant as an homage to the Mixe, in spite of there being no indication of the blouse's Mixe origins in the narrative surrounding the design, and not even an oblique attempt to include Mixe people in the discourse. Clearly Marant had made a misstep, but it is less clear if the misstep was the dubious use of Mixe heritage, carried out without the moves and social narratives that would license it as being legitimate and ethically sound, or if it was the fact that being French, she could make no convincing claim to being a co-proprietor of the heritage. A Mexican designer might have been able to do so more effectively.

Also in the spring of 2015, the New York Fashion Institute announced that Mexico would be included as one of the world's up-and-coming fashion capitals. News coverage in *The Guardian* included a picture of the presidents' wife, actress Angelica Rivera, dressed in Mexican fashion. An article titled "Designs from Tribal Past Make Mexico a Fashion Hit" mentioned the prominent use of Indigenous designs:

> "I want to show the cool Mexico with pieces you can wear on the street," says Seco, who is among many Mexican designers who capitalize on the country's diverse culture, mixing old and new. Inspired by the landscape, Alejandra Quesada often clashes floral and fauna prints for her modern maxi dresses, sweatshirts and more, while Francesco Cancino of Yakampot adapts indigenous shawls and Tzotzil tribal craft processes for his minimalist slouchy silhouettes."[15]

The piece also interviewed a fashion analyst who notes that the Navajo-inspired designs that are circulating in the United States, and which famously got Urban Outfitters in trouble with the Navajo Nation (Moynihan 2018), are simply too kitsch for the Mexican scene, which is why Mexican designers prefer Oaxacan fabrics and patterns. In this way, Mexican design was, not so subtly, distanced from US designs and its appropriations of the North American Indigenous tradition, probably Mexico's closest competitors on the global pseudo-Indigenous fashion scene. The use of Indigenous symbols is not restricted to *haute couture*, but in fact permeates all aspects of Mexican elite culture. In Mexico City's posher neighborhoods, one may find ads for yoga and meditation with Tibetan crystals and mantras in Nahuatl—offering participants the chance to simultaneously connect with the elements of nature and their national heritage by chanting in ungrammatical Nahuatl while

---

[15] Melanie Abrams. "Designs from Tribal Past Make Mexico a Fashion Hit." May 9, 2015. *The Guardian*. http://www.theguardian.com/fashion/2015/may/09/mexico-fashion-capital-indigenous-design-angelica-rivera.

listening to the sound of gongs and Tibetan singing bowls.[16] Through the process of distinction and mimicry, the high fashion quickly reverberates down through the class hierarchy, so that many of the product types pioneered by high-end designers, such as Huichol-style beaded sneakers or baseball caps, can now, five years later, be found in ordinary tourist markets.

Linguistic anthropologists have also noted how languages become increasingly commodified, as they are integrated into bundles of brands, identities, and flows of value (Heller 2010). The increased exchange value of Nahuatl could be expected to place Nahuatl speakers, with privileged access to the resource, in an improved position, and perhaps in some ways it does, but often other, more powerful, actors on the linguistic marketplace are better positioned to reap the dividends. Often non-Indigenous actors have better access to the means of production (including media, publishers, theaters, universities, as well as other more concrete forms of capital) and to the varieties and genres of Nahuatl that are authorized by national cultural institutions and therefore most prestigious and more highly valued.

The Semiotic Economy of National Nativism

In his 2001 essay, "Fissures in Contemporary Mexican Nationalism," Claudio Lomnitz insightfully points out that the increasing integration of Mexico into global material and ideological networks is causing the otherwise solid construct of the Mexican nation-state to crack. He relates the wave of nationalism of the mid-20th century to the economic situation of the period, when the Mexican economic strategy worked by strengthening the domestic market through an economy of "import substitution"[17]—creating a link between the national imaginary, the consumption of national products, and the symbolic power of the pre-colonial Mexican past as accessed through archaeology. He describes how fissures in this construct began to form as the enchantment with local products faded, when both upper and lower classes increasingly tired of locally produced commodities and began to crave consumer products from the international market. These were first accessible only to the upper

---

[16] "*Resonaron en la Fonoteca Nacional cuencos y mantras en náhuatl. El instrumentista Humberto Álvarez ofreció un concierto y explicó los beneficios para la mente, cuerpo y espíritu*" [Bowls and mantras in Nahuatl resounded in the National Phonoteque: The musician Humberto Álvarez gave a concert and explained their benefits for mind, body and spirit]. Secretaría de Cultura. September 13, 2015. https://www.gob.mx/cultura/prensa/resonaron-en-la-fonoteca-nacional-cuencos-y-mantras-en-nahuatl.

[17] The policy called *Import Substitution Industrialization* aimed to industrialize the Mexican nation by producing national imitations of foreign products and placing tariffs on imports, or even prohibiting the importation of certain luxury products (Moreno 2003, 41–43).

classes, but later through migration they also became available to the working class. This caused a reaction of distinction as the upper classes needed to distance themselves from this emerging pattern of consumption. Lomnitz describes how the category and epithet of the *naco* replaced the concept of the *indio*, as the instrument with which to castigate lower-class consumption patterns. Whereas *indio* was used to stigmatize the consumption of basic domestic goods such as corn tortillas and beans, the label *naco*[18] was introduced as a way to stigmatize lower-class consumers of international, mostly US-American, goods and aesthetics. Through the introduction of the *naco* stereotype, global consumer culture, which in the 1980s and 1990s was still the main source of cultural capital in Mexico, was devalued and re-signified as gauche, kitschy, and inauthentic. Writing in 2001, Lomnitz leaves his analysis open, pointing toward the possibility of different future developments of Mexican nationalism, and it is the outline of this future—which is now the present—that is represented in this chapter. The fissuring Mexican national space has attempted to repair itself, by reaching once more into the treasure trove of Indigenous symbolic resources, to find there the glue to mend its own crumbling construct. Current Mexican nationalism has responded to the threat of the global market by increasingly marketizing what it considers "its own" cultural heritage; that is, the heritage and symbols of what it frequently describes as "our" Indigenous peoples.[19] This is the context in which discourses of Indigenous rights, Indigenous languages, and the well-being of Indigenous communities have come to play once more a significant role in Mexican national space.

Lomnitz's argument advances from the symbol of the *naco*, the kitschy consumer of lower-class international symbols. By constituting the living link that indexically associates consumer goods from abroad with lack of class and refinement, the *naco* caused the metacultural devaluation of "the international," particularly "the American," as a brand (Lomnitz 2001). This devaluation in turn also indexically tainted those upper- and middle-class consumers who lagged behind the times and still preferred foreign products. The concept

---

[18] The concept itself likely originated as an anti-Indian slur, "Totonaco" likely originally referring to the Totonac Indigenous group, but it was eventually stripped of most of its ethno-racial referential meanings (if not its indexical meanings) and came to refer to people of low socioeconomic class and their consumption patterns (see also Báez-Jorge 2002). Another proposed etymology for *naco* claims it comes from the word *chinaco*, meaning "naked."

[19] "*Sintamos orgullo de nuestros pueblos indígenas, reconozcamos y protejamos sus derechos*" [We should feel proud of our Indigenous peoples, let's recognize and protect their rights]. Instituto Nacional para el Federalismo y el Desarrollo Municipal. August 9, 2017. https://www.gob.mx/inafed/articulos/sintamos-orgullo-de-nuestros-pueblos-indigenas-reconozcamos-sus-derechos-y-promovamos-su-desarrollo-dia-internacional-de-los-pueblos-indigenas. For comparison, see also how within the context of Venezuelan nationalist language politics, Juán L. Rodriguez describes officials referring to the Warao as one of "our" Indigenous peoples (Rodríguez 2021, 89).

of the *fresa*, in turn, ridicules this kind of upper-class consumer (Báez-Jorge 2002)—corresponding to what in the parlance of the mid-20th century would be called a *malinchista*[20]—a traitor to the *patria*. Resultantly, where a Mexican consumer of the cultural elite in the early 2000s could still be seen sporting Armani suits and Tiffany jewelry, today the more progressively minded elites can be seen wearing artisan-crafted suits of Oaxacan silk, Indigenous woven shawls, Huichol-style beaded bracelets, and embroidered huipiles, or even the simple two-piece *traje de manta* [white cotton pants and shirt] iconic of the Indian peasant. It is hardly a coincidence that this change in fashion has accompanied the introduction of the category of *indígena* (defined as a rights-bearing class, replacing the category of the *indio* as a class seen as requiring remedial development), and the institutionalization of international concepts of Indigenous people's rights. The positive valorization of the Indigenous and the corresponding devaluation of global consumer culture are the two sides of the coin of Mexican cultural economy.

Anti-Indigenous Backlash and Mock Nahuatl Online

It would certainly be false to imply that everyone in Mexico shares the positive valorization of Indigenous signs presented above. Many of the country's political elites remain ambiguous, if not directly disdainful, toward Indigenous peoples. The conscious use of political discourse to increase the value of the Indigenous sign on the market of Mexican cultural production equates to a devaluation of the traditional dominance of the European culture. Even if the change in value is predominantly driven by the consumption preferences of progressively minded non-Indigenous Mexicans, who also predominantly profit from it, this devaluation leads to resentment among non-Indigenous Mexicans. This resentment sometimes shows itself as further fissures in the narrative of national unity under the banner of shared Indigenous roots. In many cases, such fissures take the form of the kind of linguistic gaffes described by Jane Hill (2009), where an underlying deep-rooted racism is momentarily displayed through a rift in the thin veneer of civility.[21] Frequently, such gaffes occur when powerful persons mistakenly think they are acting

---

[20] This insult refers to Malintzin or Malinche, Hernán Cortés's native Mayan translator and concubine who assisted the Spaniards in conquering Mexihco-Tenochtitlan. A highly complex character, she came to symbolize the fetishization of the foreign in the context of post-revolutionary nationalism (Karttunen 1996, 1–23). Today she is also reinterpreted as a feminist Indigenous, or even Chicana, icon.

[21] See Navarrete Linares (2016) for an analysis of Mexican racism, including examples of anti-Indigenous gaffes.

in the comfortable and intimate space of the backstage, but suddenly find themselves performing on a mass-mediated front-stage (see Goffman). As in the context of the United States, where the racist gaffe momentarily exposes the illusion of the post-racial society, in the Mexican context, the racist gaffe demonstrates that the *indio* and its related racist stereotypes are not yet truly gone.

Another way that latent racism manifests itself is in the trappings of humor. As previously mentioned, Mexico has a long tradition of making fun of the *indio*. Depicted as lazy, naïve, uncultured, and passion-driven, such stereotypes have permeated Mexican cultural forms for most of the 20th century. While some figures, such as the famous character India Maria, can be argued to contain a certain element of social critique, others, such as Lucila Mariscal's character Doña Lencha, are simply clowns using the Indigenous element and its associated lack of grace as a prop; or they are dastardly villains whose ethnicity is used to suggest an element of unpredictability and lack of basic moral values.

While the *indio* as a comedy stereotype has become less prevalent and is now widely seen as lacking in taste, it continues to find new ways to reproduce itself, now often using new, less formal, and more anonymous media than the mainstream television channels. In the spring of 2014 a new class of internet memes began to circulate on Facebook and Twitter, seemingly mostly among middle-class urban youths. These memes combined images of Indigenous persons with captions of hybrid English/Spanish expressions, always with the ending *-tl*. The *-tl* ending an obvious reference to the absolutive suffix, which is a ubiquitous grammatical element on Nahuatl nouns, here iconicized to stand for Indigenous languages in general. The memes are clearly racialized and racializing, in the way that phenotypical, cultural, and linguistic traits are fused into a single caricature of the Indigenous (Aguilar Gil 2020a, 57–61). Not all of the memes were explicitly racist in their content, but nonetheless they were all predicated on the stereotype of the *indio* as an inherently humorous figure—and defined as a genre by the iconic reference to the Nahuatl language achieved by the addition of *-tl* (Figure 3.3).

The memes' use of Nahuatl was fully parallel to Jane Hill's (2009) concept of "mock Spanish," a "humorous" register of English that reproduces stereotypes of Spanish speakers, indexed through the use of iconic representations of Spanish phonology such as the suffix *-o* (e.g., "*no problemo,*" "*el cheapo*"). The meme trend spread so virally that eventually CONAPRED, *Consejo Nacional para la Prevencion de la Discriminación* [National Council for the Prevention of Discrimination], published a blog post describing why the "mock Nahuatl" *-tl* memes were discriminatory. Following the strategies of

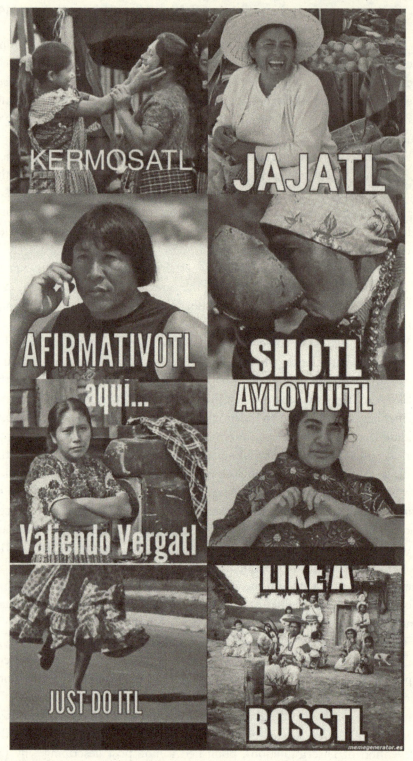

Figure 3.3. A collection of tl- memes that circulated on social media in 2012 and 2013. Public domain.

deflection described by Hill for users of mock Spanish who are confronted with the racist implications of their statements, online apologists for the memes, such as the Facebook group "*Yolotl*," maintained that the memes were just for fun and were not meant to be racist.

Many of the memes worked by simply adding the *-tl* to a well-known Anglicism, and juxtaposing them with an image of an Indigenous person performing some vaguely related act. For example, the Nike slogan "*Just Do It*" combined with a picture of an Indigenous woman in skirts and sandals running, or an Indigenous person taking a "selfie" and the caption "*selfietl.*" Thus the memes work exactly by indexically associating the foreign, and by extension *naco* and "low prestige," with the Indigenous person. The semio-political implication is that the Spanish/*mestizo* Mexican sign is normalized and idealized, exactly by virtue of its absence among the unattractive exoticness of the Anglo/Indigenous. The meme constitutes a covert, but easily accessible form of Spanish-centered Mexican nationalism, which seems motivated exactly by the marginalization of this perspective in mainstream public discourse. By using anonymous memes, the middle class, whose status is threatened by the revalorization of Indigenous symbols, strike back by reaffirming their own sense of superiority.

Since the semiotic logic of the fashionability of Indigenous symbols in Mexican society appears to be largely reactive and driven by distinction, there is also a strong undercurrent of anti-Indigenous sentiment. With the arrival in power of leftist President Andrés Manuel López Obrador of the MORENA party in 2018, this undercurrent has coalesced around resistance to his government and its values. During his decades-long campaign, AMLO, as he is usually named in the press, was even more actively trying to claim an alliance with the various Indigenous and progressive movements. Once he was in office, though, he quickly broke many of the promises he had made to these movements. His detractors quickly seized on these failures to deliver to his progressive base, tagging his followers as *chairos*. *Chairo* refers pejoratively to the kind of Mexican progressives who on the surface align themselves with Indigenous peoples, consuming their artwork and displaying their symbols, and speaking out for their causes, implying that this dedication is superficial or hypocritical. *Chairos* in turn now label anti-Indigenous cosmopolitan elites as "*whitexicans*," which serves to alienate them from the national community by making them out as Mexican representatives of a basically Anglo-American US culture. These terms, *naco, fresa, chairo, whitexican*, that various Mexican sociocultural and racial demographic groups use to insult and delegitimize each other, encapsulate the complex cultural politics of the Mexican nation. And somehow Indigenous peoples always figure as the pivot of these cultural struggles, reduced to a symbol to be either idealized or denigrated, depending on what kind of nation the loudest voices in the national public sphere sees themselves as part of. The underlying trope of the *indio*, as the undesirable uncultured other, however, still lurks just below the surface, as became clear when an elderly lady at a rally against AMLO's proposed electoral reform was filmed as she expressed her rage toward the president, yelling "*Indio de Macuspana, tienes unas patas rajadas que ni el mejor zapato que te pongas te quita lo naco, pendejo!*" [*Indio* from Macuspana, your feet are so dirty and cracked up that not even the finest shoe will make you less *naco*, moron!].[22]

National Promotion of Indigenous Languages: A Critical Evaluation

In this chapter, we have followed the Nahuatl language around in the Mexican public sphere. We have seen its use in official state communication ostensibly aimed at an audience of Indigenous language readers, but often with a highly questionable degree of communicative efficacy. We have seen it used by the intellectual and cultural elite as a symbol of the Mexican national heritage; and we saw how this "belletrist" tradition idealizes the colonial variety of Nahuatl, but does not include contemporary speakers in its endeavors. We have seen it as an element within a fashion trend that uses Indigenous symbols as a way to brand products as authentically Mexican in a global marketplace, and as a commodity that allows non-Indigenous Mexicans to feel connected to their national heritage. And we have seen a counter-reaction to these positive valorizations of the language, in which non-Indigenous middle- and upper-class Mexicans use elements of Indigenous languages as a stigmatizing racial marker.

If we want to know how these different uses of Nahuatl in the Mexican national public sphere affect the vitality of the Nahuatl language, whether it can really be considered a form of language revitalization or as working toward the actual fulfillment of the state's obligations of the linguistic rights of Indigenous peoples, then we must be skeptical. There is nothing to suggest that any of these activities in which Nahuatl is being used in the public sphere are aimed at creating new speakers, or that they are performing more than the most

---

[22] Macuspana is the town in the state of Tabasco where the president was born, and *pata rajada* "cracked feet" is a slur against Indigenous people that points to the habit of some Indigenous peoples of going barefoot and the resulting coarse soles of the feet.

perfunctory act of recognition of linguistic rights of speakers of Indigenous languages. They can be interpreted as testifying to the state's determination to normalize Indigenous languages in public space and to comply with the letter of the law. Nevertheless, if we analyze the efforts it becomes clear that while they are highly visible, they are not effective means of achieving the main provisions of the law, nor are they serious attempts at providing crucial linguistic services to the Indigenous population. In this sense, while the state ostensibly seeks to comply with the obligations the law puts it under, in the more meaningful sense of fulfilling the actual necessities of speakers of Indigenous languages, the law continues to be *letra muerta* ["dead letters," i.e., only on paper]. This insight poses the question of what it is, then, that is being achieved with the considerable expenditure invested in Indigenous language projects by the state, and whether it benefits Indigenous people at all.

Rather, what all of these different uses of Nahuatl have in common is that they are symbols of the inclusion of Nahuatl speakers (and of other Indigenous languages) as subjects of the Mexican nation. Simultaneously, as they demonstrate this inclusion, they also execute the expropriation by the Mexican state of Indigenous semiotic resources, such as language, artwork, intellectual creations, as national heritage of the nation and as part of the Mexican brand.

Gabriel Pareyón, the composer of the Nahuatl opera *Xochicuicatl Cuecuechtli*, read my critique of his work as it appeared in my 2016 dissertation and reacted to it in his own book: "*Resonancias del abismo como nación: aproximaciones transdisciplinarias a la filosofía de la música y la musicología en México*" (Pareyón 2021, 363–64). Here, in turn, he criticizes me for setting up too sharp a dichotomy between the Indigenous and the non-Indigenous or *mestizo*, as I evaluate the political implications of the public representation of Nahua culture and language. He claims that this division is in effect a form of cultural apartheid, motivated by an aversion to cultural ambiguity. I do agree that the distinction is anything but simple, and that perhaps in speaking of Nahuatl language and culture as morally pertaining primarily to Nahuatl communities, I simplify the matter, as millions of *mestizo* Mexicans have grandparents or great grandparents who spoke Nahuatl, and that Nahuatl culture could also, perhaps with equal right, be said to belong to them. I do not agree, though, that this is a form of cultural purism or apartheid, forcing a distinction onto something that is essentially hybrid. Rather, my argument is motivated by a critical perspective on the role of power disparities, and differential access to leveraging Indigenous signs as cultural capital, which points to the injustice of semiotic expropriation for the nation without corresponding political inclusion and material gain for Indigenous communities.

This critical view of state usage of Indigenous languages as a strategy for the legitimization of its expropriation of Indigenous semiotic and natural resources in general may suggest that when the public sphere suddenly assigns positive value to Indigenous semiotic resource, it is fundamentally harmful for Indigenous communities—harmful, because it is hypocritical, serving mainly the interests of the state and nation, while not fulfilling its own promises toward its indigenous citizens. However, drawing this conclusion based only on the apparent insincerity of the state's actions would imply a denial of the ability and agency of Indigenous communities to find ways of taking advantage of the sudden increase in the value attributed to their semiotic resources.

As demonstrated in the previous chapter, Nahua people do have agency (as if it needed demonstration), and the discussions that take place within Indigenous public spheres harness this agency and direct it toward collective goals. Even if the state is not truly invested in improving the conditions of Indigenous communities or in ceding the civic rights it has promised, and even if the national public sphere is mainly interested in Indigenous culture and language as a resource to be exploited, the high value of Indigenous semiotic capital furnishes Indigenous communities with new possibilities. By leveraging their semiotic capital, and by positioning themselves as authenticators of its value in the national marketplace, they can strategically use this value to reach political and economic goals that they could perhaps not otherwise have done. The next chapter describes how Hueyapan, a Nahua community in the state of Morelos, has achieved a long-time goal of political autonomy from its neighboring town by strategically using Indigenous identity, bolstered by language revitalization efforts, to support its demand for municipal independence.

Figure 4.0. Panorama of Hueyapan, looking north toward the town center, with Mount Popocatepetl in the background. The church dome (since destroyed in the 2017 earthquake) is seen between the trees and hills.
Photo by the author.

4
Language, Autonomy, and Indigenous Politics in Hueyapan, Morelos

Hueyapan, Morelos, February 2014: A couple of hundred people are gathered at the central Plaza to celebrate *día de la lengua maternal* [Day of the Mother Tongue]. Don Isabel Lavana, a retired schoolteacher who now lives in the nearby town of Jonacatepec, took the microphone to give an improvised speech to the assembled audience. Giving the initial greetings in Nahuatl, he went on to explain in a clear and soft voice:

Axan nehwa ahwel nan niyes semilwitl. Nan niyes tsitsigitsin ivan kwak okseppa tololoskeh, kwak okseppa amololoskeh an annechtlalwiskeh, tel nigan niyes. Nigan niyes porkeh nigan onitlagat. Nigan oniveyak. Nigan onoskaltih. Tos inin nin no . . . nigan nochan. Nigitta kah itech, nochi amehwan ken noknivan! Ken toknivan. Ihkon ninamechmoittilia. Ihkon ni . . . namechmoittilia, an ihkon man ye, an ihkon tigimmachtiskeh in tsitsigitoton. Nehwa axan namechmolwilia: niyolpagi. Niyolpagi kwak amehwan antlahtoah, ankipalewiah in totlahtol. *An ankipalewiah nochi tlen tehwan otikpixkeh.*[1]

[Nowadays, I cannot be here every day. I will be here a little and when we gather again, when you gather again and you invite me, I will be here. I will be here because here I was born. Here I grew up. Here I was raised. So this is my . . . my home is here. I consider this . . . all of you are like my siblings. We are like siblings. That is how I see you. That is how I see you, and that is how it should be, and that is how we will teach the little ones. Now I will tell you: I am happy. I am happy when you speak, when you help our *language*. And you help all that which we have received.]

A few years earlier, a similar event in Hueyapan—in which members of the community gathered to pay tribute to the language that many of them grew up with but now no longer speak in public—would have been, if not

---

[1] In my transcriptions of Hueyapan Nahuatl, I represent the pronunciation variants that speakers there tend to consider distinctive of their own variety, such as voicing of /k/ to [g] and lenition of /w/ to [ʊ] written <v> between vowels.

Nahuatl Nations. Magnus Pharao Hansen, Oxford University Press. © Oxford University Press 2024.
DOI: 10.1093/oso/9780197746158.003.0005

unthinkable, then highly improbable. But simultaneously with the sudden fashion of Nahuatl and Indigenous languages in the broader society, the attitudes of people in Hueyapan have also changed.

When I first arrived in Hueyapan in 2003, in my very first experience of fieldwork with the Nahuatl language, I had a hard time finding people who would admit to speaking the language. Even among those who spoke the language fluently, it was common to lament that nobody really spoke the language well anymore. A small group of activists, several of whom had a high social standing in the community, seemed to have fueled this self-deprecating sentiment by promoting the idea that the true Nahuatl language was the one spoken by the Mexica in Tenochtitlan five hundred years ago, before the language was debased and mixed with Spanish. They were offering their fellow townsfolk the opportunity to learn this "true" [*melauak*] Nahuatl instead of the "mixed-up" [*tlanenelki*] version they had grown up with. In this period, the youngest person I met who spoke Nahuatl as their preferred language was a 14-year-old boy named Rodrigo, who had grown up with his monolingual grandmother. Otherwise, most speakers were 30 years old and up, the majority over 50. Nahuatl was not used in public functions in Hueyapan. Its main function was in the domestic sphere, where it was used as a language of family solidarity, and among close friends who had grown up speaking it together. Many speakers told me that they had not learned the language from their parents, who had wanted them to learn only Spanish, but that they had picked it up "in the street" with their friends. At the same time, they would lament that their own children were not interested in the language, and that they didn't want to learn it. So the general feeling tended to be that the Nahuatl language spoken in Hueyapan was no good, that kids didn't want to learn it, that parents didn't want to teach it, and that it would probably soon be gone. Its predicted disappearance was generally lamented, but not seen as something that one could really do anything about.

Today, Nahuatl is still spoken mostly by elderly members of the community, but there are younger speakers, including children, some of whom have made their parents teach them the language. There are youths who clearly want to be fluent speakers, and who practice together, and who win prizes in "Nahuatl oratory" competitions. There are weekly Nahuatl language lessons, and Nahuatl is used in many public functions where it previously never was—for example, in official speeches by local authorities at cultural events and even at public political meetings on the main plaza. It can be found on some street signs, in shop names, and at one time, during the presidency of Mayor Javier Montes, even in the municipal logo of Tetela del Volcán, written on all public buildings and vehicles: "*Tiktekitigan tonochtin sejkan*" [Let's all work

Figure 4.1. Welcome to Hueyapan: a homemade sign at the road arriving in Hueyapan from Tetela del Volcán, welcoming visitors in Spanish and Nahuatl. The Nahuatl text says *xipanoh, nan tikpia mochan Hueyi-apan* ["Welcome, here in Hueyapan you have your home"].
Photo by the author.

together]. Figure 4.1 shows a handwritten sign someone has made (perhaps the youths in Chimalnahuatlajtole described later in the chapter), announcing a welcome to Hueyapan in Spanish and Nahuatl.

In this chapter, I describe how the change toward an increasingly positive valorization of the Nahuatl language has taken place in Hueyapan, and how that development has taken place in parallel with, or perhaps has been entwined with, changes in the political landscape within and around Hueyapan. When I arrived in Hueyapan in 2003, it was one of several secondary towns in the municipality of Tetela del Volcán, whereas today it is an independent municipality. Then the local authority was an *ayudante*, serving as a locally elected but unremunerated deputy of the mayor in Tetela, whereas now Hueyapan is governed by a *Concejo indígena* [Indigenous council] led by a *vocera concejal* [council spokesperson], also referred to as *tlahtoani* [speaker/ruler] in Nahuatl. The changing attitude toward the Indigenous language and the achievement of municipal independence have not occurred independently of each other, just as they are not independent from the trend toward a positive valuation of Indigenous languages in the national public sphere. Nevertheless, the relation between these distinct processes is not straightforward; one way to interpret it is that the people of Hueyapan have been able to use the increasingly positive discourse around Indigenous rights to achieve a political goal of political autonomy. This suggests that embracing the Nahuatl language and other symbols of Indigenous identity was a political strategy that bolstered the claim to the Indigenous status that could position them as deserving political independence from the non-Indigenous *cabecera* [municipal center] community of Tetela (Pharao Hansen 2018). But, importantly, during the process of becoming independent, the language also came to be a potent symbol of local community belonging.

The chapter begins by giving a political history of Hueyapan after the Mexican revolution. This history describes the community's internal divisions and conflicts, its relation with the neighboring community of Tetela del Volcán (see Figure 4.2), and with the government and institutions at the state level. The ways in which the people of Hueyapan have conceptualized their own hometown and its place within the political landscape at different times have been influenced by the development of its economy from a dependence on agriculture, both licit and illicit, toward an increasing dependence on remittances and commerce. It is emphasized how, throughout the past century, the community of Hueyapan has been engaged in a continuous

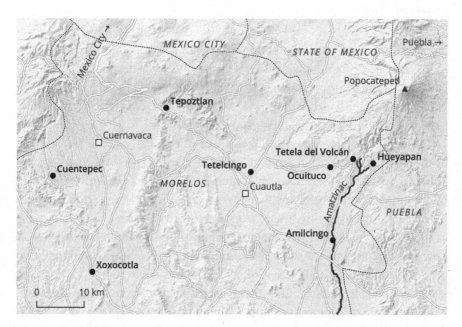

Figure 4.2. Map showing the location of Hueyapan and surrounding towns in the states of Morelos and southern Puebla.
Map by Joe Roe.

discussion about how best to manage its political relations, at times opting for more integration into the system and its infrastructure, and at other times opting for relative isolation or autonomy. Hueyapan is, in this sense, a public sphere, its members united by the realization of a shared good. Whereas in the 1970s, most people in Hueyapan probably would likely have agreed in seeing Nahuatl as an obstacle to improving the community's integration into the mainstream economy, today it has come to be seen as a common good that provides a certain political currency for the community.

The second half of the chapter gives an ethnographic description of the Nahuatl language youth program that began in 2014. This program formed a key part in the political interface between Hueyapan as an Indigenous community seeking autonomy, and the Morelos state government, which would eventually grant it. The teachers managed to use the program as a venue for political communication with the state, while also succeeding in using language and cultural revitalization practices to engender a sense of appreciation and community belonging among the students. Even though state policies may encourage empty folkloric performance of Indigenous identities for an audience in the national public, the same performance may well be full of meaning for the performers and for the people in their own local public. They may find ways of using the venues for such performances as platforms for staking political claims, and as instruments with which to achieve concrete political objectives for their communities.

Hueyapan's Municipal Independence

Tlalolintle: The Earthquake

On September 19, 2017, the ground moved under the town of Hueyapan in the Mexican state of Morelos. An earthquake of 7.1 points on the Richter scale shook the region southeast of Mexico City, causing devastation in Morelos and southern Puebla. It was just after one o'clock in the afternoon, on the exact anniversary of the great earthquake of 1985 that cost the lives of 10,000 Mexicans. This quake was much less lethal than that one, but the town of Hueyapan was severely affected, with nearly 80% of the houses sustaining enough damage to render them uninhabitable. The domed roof of the 16th-century church caved in, and the people attending a funeral there had to flee into the main plaza as the casket was crushed under the debris. Also on the main plaza of the town, the *ayudantía*, the building housing the local administration, was damaged beyond repair, as all of the pillars of the portico crumbled, leaving the upper level only halfway supported. Most of the town's old adobe houses, many built around the time of the Mexican revolution and considered part of the town's "architectural patrimony," were also destroyed as walls caved in, roofs came down, and foundations shifted. One house was swallowed by the ground so that what used to be the second floor was now at the ground level. Those who experienced the quake described the movement of the earth as unlike any earthquake they had felt before; rather than moving laterally, the ground seemed to pulsate up and down in a vibrating motion. One person described watching a stone wall fall down on the side and then immediately stand back up again, another described the telluric movement as if gigantic snakes were writhing just under the earth's crust.

Independence

Precisely three months after the earthquake, another ground-changing event occurred, this time affecting the sociopolitical landscape of Hueyapan. On December 19, 2017, the official state *diario official*, the newsletter publishing changes to laws and regulations in Morelos, published Decree No. 2343, by which Hueyapan was officially created as an independent municipality, severing the town from its previous *cabecera* [municipal center], Tetela del Volcán. This had been a change long in the making, as the people of Hueyapan had spent almost a decade lobbying for municipal independence (Pharao Hansen 2018). Nevertheless, the social and political effects of the completion of the process were of comparable magnitude to the material effects of the earthquake. With a stroke, Hueyapan went from being the minor partner in an uneasy political union with its rival town Tetela on the other side of the Amatzinac river canyon to being its own *cabecera* with its own internal rivalries and divisions. Where the people of Hueyapan had previously been able to often overcome internal divisions and rally around a joint political platform in opposition to the dominance of Tetela, this change brought new forms of politics to the surface of community life in Hueyapan, including internal rifts and competitions, and also new formulations of local identity, culture, and community.

Just like most of the infrastructure that transforms the physical landscape in and around Hueyapan, the town's municipal independence became possible thanks to transnational flows of migrants, remittances, and influence, but it was made meaningful, and therefore desirable, by the local political landscape.

The fact that the political changes described above have occurred in parallel with the changing attitudes toward the Nahuatl language in the community, and to other symbols associated with Hueyapan's Indigenous identity, poses the question about the type of relation between these two developments. If Indigenous language vitality is intimately tied to the vitality of Indigenous publics, as proposed in Chapter 2, we should expect a mutually reinforcing dynamic between the two processes. This chapter argues that such mutual reinforcement has been present, and that this has been caused not only by explicit decisions of the involved groups, but also by a sort of invisible hand–type process in which the increased value attributed to one of the elements (community/language) has rubbed off on the other in a self-amplifying process.

In the history of Hueyapan, as I tell it here, the process of language shift was initially caused by a tendency toward abandonment of the local public. This happened as the political attention of community members gravitated increasingly toward the national public, making them see Nahuatl culture more as an element in the Mexican national narrative than as their own local property. Similarly, the process that has led to the current period of cultural and linguistic revival is motivated by a number of political factors: first, it has been supported by the resurgence of the local public sphere as the center of political identity. This resurgence, in turn, has been caused by a socioeconomic and political florescence of the town relative to its traditional antagonist "other," the *mestizo* town and municipal *cabecera* of Tetela del Volcán. Secondarily, it has been supported by the emergence of nostalgia, idealization, and local patriotism springing from the experiences of Hueyapan's many expatriates and migrants, as well as their understanding of the town as the locus of a cohesive community with a shared assemblage of cultural resources.

Friedlander's Hueyapan

A couple of generations of anthropologists are familiar with Hueyapan, as it was described by Judith Friedlander in the 1970s, and it makes sense here to summarize Friedlander's argument and the observations that she based it on. In relation to language shift, the 1970s were a crucial period in the history of Hueyapan, because it was the generation of Hueyapanecos who were parents between 1970 and 1980 who stopped teaching their children Nahuatl. The process started earlier, probably as early as the 1950s, but during the 1950s and 1960s not a few Hueyapaneco children, most in fact, were able to learn Nahuatl without being exposed to it from their parents, instead picking it up from their playmates and friends.

Friedlander's main argument, for which her book became famous, was that the category of "Indian," or *indio* in Mexico, did not work as a label of an ethnic or racial group defined by shared cultural markers with a history going back to the pre-Hispanic period. Instead, she argued, it was a label that the nationalist Mexican state actively used to marginalize some rural communities, pushing them into a position of subordination and inferiority relative to the mainstream Mexican population. She argued that in order to be taken into consideration by the state, "Indians" were forced to assume the Indian identity and its emblems, such as speaking the "traditional" language, wearing the "traditional" dress, making "traditional" crafts, making a living through "traditional" subsistence patterns, and so on. This idea of "tradition," she argued, was largely fictitious, since many aspects generally considered "traditional" were in fact at least partly of colonial origin, and often not exclusive to communities identified as Indigenous. In this way, the discourse of "tradition" and "history" worked to deny groups coeval status within Mexican national society and trap them in a role as historical relics and living symbols of the national past.

In 2006, Friedlander published a second edition of the book, which included a foreword in which she rearticulated her critique in the light of the political changes brought about by the Chiapas uprising, and its apparent success in formulating a form of oppositional Indigenous politics that challenged the state's monopoly on defining Indigenous identity. In the foreword, Friedlander recognized the way that these developments had vindicated the potential of Indigenous identity politics as a platform of radically transformative movements, but she remained skeptical of the sincerity of the state's involvement in Indigenous politics, and wary of its continued engagement with the circulation of ethnic symbols and identities. As demonstrated in the previous chapter, Friedlander's fundamental skepticism regarding the effects of state involvement in ethnic revival is certainly justified. At the same time, however, there is a risk implicit in writing off Indigenous communities' work with defining and developing their own tradition as a form of complicity in producing their own "forced identity," when such work may be leveraged in the pursuit of political strategies. Doing so risks denying Indigenous individuals and communities the agency that they can deploy strategically to contest, manage, or refigure the representations circulated of them in the national public sphere. It denies them the right to the desire and aspiration to become "this impossible object and to transport its ancient pre-national meanings and practices to the present in *whatever* language and moral framework prevails *at the time of enunciation*" (Povinelli 2002, 6). Moreover, it denies that recognition not only results in the psychological violence of misrecognition, but may also be a catalyst for renewing fading Indigenous identities and creating new forms of self-recognition (Coulthard 2014). In Hueyapan's case, the agency of the community took advantage of a positive discourse around Indigenous rights at the level of the state government, which enabled the achievement of the long-desired goal of political independence, and the reinvigoration of a waning communal unity and the reaffirmation of the local public.

The next section of this chapter describes the history that led to Hueyapan's municipal independence, providing an interpretation of the development of Hueyapan in the 20th and 21st century that differs from Friedlander's in significant ways. In her work, Friedlander focused on the process of identity-making in the interactions between people of Hueyapan and discourses and actors representing the state, including the "cultural radicals" from the capital led by Juán Luna Cárdenas who propagated *indigenista* ideologies and discourses in the town. In contrast, I will emphasize the relation between Hueyapanecos and their neighbors in the municipal *cabecera* of Tetela del Volcán. Where Friedlander described the internal politics of Hueyapan as motivated largely by interactions between outsiders and locals, I will look at how internal social and economic divisions motivated how Hueyapanecos reacted differently in their contact with the state and representatives of the national public sphere. Friedlander did not dedicate attention to the Nahuatl language, and seems to have worked primarily through Spanish, and with people who preferred speaking Spanish. In contrast, I will argue that the ways in which the people of Hueyapan have used their language, and the times at which many Hueyapanecos have stopped speaking the language to their children or at which they have worked to revitalize it again, are closely tied to local political developments.

The long period in which the people of Hueyapan continued to speak their language, in comparison with other communities in the state of Morelos, I ascribe partly to the town's lack of political integration with the national public sphere in the 20th century. The decline of the use of Nahuatl accelerated beginning in the 1950s with the steadily increasing political integration of the town. Nonetheless, because there were powerful political forces within the town working against such integration, the turn toward the national public was never complete, and a separate vision of Hueyapan as a local public opposed to the local political authorities coexisted side by side with the push toward greater integration. In the 21st century, two things changed: first, as described in Chapter 3, the attitude toward Indigenous peoples and languages in the national public sphere became increasingly positive. Second, Hueyapan's status in political relation to the surrounding communities changed, as did the way in which Hueyapanecos saw themselves relative to these communities. These changes meant that enacting local political identity through the use of the Nahuatl language was no longer a strategy exclusively used by those who opposed the town's integration into the national public; now, it also became a viable strategy through which the local political community could articulate a specific, favorable, position for itself within the national public sphere. In this way, Indigenous symbols and the Nahuatl language became a currency that could unite both the modernizing and the traditionalist faction of the town's political environment.

Another History of Hueyapan in the 20th Century: What Caused the Decline of Nahuatl?

> *Nigan gente kigagih an nechnankilia in "kanin tiyoh" o "axkan kanin tiyas," pero togente maski kema kiliah se palabra, mati ammo techinteresaroa para man salogan in topipiljuan.* [People here do understand and answer my "where are you going?" or "where will you go now?," but even though our people here do say a couple of words, it seems we're not interested in teaching our children.]
>
> —Don Bulmaro Hernández Escobar, explaining the sociolinguistic situation in Hueyapan

Tetela and Hueyapan: The Story of a Rivalry

In the state of Morelos, most town-communities have gradually shifted from using an Indigenous language to using Spanish. Historically, in Mexico, such a shift, when an Indigenous language is no longer spoken, has been considered the point when a town is no longer "an Indigenous community," even if other traditions such as political organization or religious practices have been maintained. In Morelos, the genocidal disruption of the revolution caused Indigenous languages to almost disappear from the state, except for a handful of localities, one of which is Hueyapan (Pharao Hansen 2024). Before the revolution, it would have been hard to argue that Tetela was any less "Indian" than Hueyapan; instead, the difference between the towns emerged gradually as Tetela integrated itself into the national political mainstream at a quicker pace than Hueyapan.

At the beginning of the 20th century, Tetela del Volcán and Hueyapan were both minor satellites within the municipality of Ocuituco. Tetela was itself a rural town and Nahuatl was still spoken there, but in contrast to Hueyapan, it had a handful of elite families who had established themselves as merchants there in the late 19th century (Arias and Bazán 1979). While Tetela and Ocuituco had *mestizo* elites who were merchants, the elite group of Hueyapan was composed of local Nahuatl-speaking families who supported their elite status through ownership of agricultural lands. In the 1930s, elite families of Tetela and Hueyapan led a movement for municipal independence from Ocuituco. This was achieved in 1937, but with two important conditions: the municipality would not be eligible for state resources, nor was it allowed to levy taxes. These conditions made for a very tight economy for the new municipality, and provided little occasion for conflict about resource allocation between the two communities. The question of which of the two main towns in the new municipality would become the *cabecera* was not difficult. Even the people of Hueyapan realized that Tetela, with its local elite, would be the logical choice, and they even signed a document known locally as *El Pacto* ["The Pact"], in which it was stipulated that the presidency of the municipality would always be occupied by a Teteleño, and that Hueyapan would only be represented in the *cabildo* [municipal council] with two *síndicos* [syndics]. There were two main reasons this was acceptable to the people of Hueyapan at the time; one was that they realized that hardly anyone in Hueyapan had any formal schooling. The town had a small rural school, but probably no one in Hueyapan at that point—including the teachers—had received more than elementary school education. The other reason was that Hueyapan was physically separated from the *cabecera* by the wide Amatzinac river gorge, making the trip to non-remunerated *cabildo* meetings in Tetela strenuous and time consuming. In the municipal archive of Tetela, I located a complaint filed in the 1950s by the two *síndicos* from Hueyapan who refused to attend *cabildo* meetings, since the costs in lost labor time made it too hard on their families.

Tetela initially established its dominance over Hueyapan not because it was less Indigenous, but rather because elites there had better access to the national economy and political system. Hueyapan simply did not have the geographical and educational infrastructure that gave Tetela access to the process of development and modernization. Therefore, Hueyapan remained politically isolated and dependent on Tetela, while receiving little or no resources from the *cabecera*, and continued to have only symbolic political representation. In both towns, however, there was a gulf between the elite families, who were in favor of the revolution and its ideals of secularism, economic progress, and social development, and, on the other hand, more traditionalist families. In Hueyapan, the elite was centered in the central barrio, and included schoolteachers who were the main local representatives of the PRI ruling party. Less convinced by revolutionary ideals were the families of subsistence peasants in the outlying barrios, many of whom remained largely skeptical of the government and sometimes were attracted to the different radical political movements opposing PRI rule (Friedlander 2006, 76–79).

Traditionalist Farmers and Progressive Teachers

The popularity of the traditionalist and isolationist stance can be understood as related to the fact that the mode of production for many of Hueyapan's subsistence farmers was partly based on the community's isolated status. In the 1890s, Mexico experienced a boom in the consumption of marijuana among the lower classes, which made this plant an important cash crop for many rural Mexicans. When marijuana was outlawed in 1923 it became an even better cash crop due to the rising prices, but it had to be produced in out-of-the-way areas where the *federales* had no access. Marijuana had a long presence in Indigenous communities where it had been integrated into the local herbarium (not as a stimulant) since the colonial period (Campos 2012; Smith 2021). For much of the 20th century, marijuana was an important crop in Tetela and especially in Hueyapan, which was better protected from government control. This meant that the political and geographical isolation of Hueyapan was beneficial to a significant segment of Hueyapan's population. Marijuana production was concentrated in the town's outlying barrios, whereas the central barrio was the seat of the town's cultural elite, including those with church affiliations and the teachers—mirroring the division between progressive and conservative political views.

Nonetheless, gradually the progressives won the day by constructing the necessary infrastructure piece by piece. They built schools in all five barrios, and in 1947 they succeeded in building a road to the neighboring community of Tlacotepec, connecting the town with the rest of the state. The road-building project was promoted by the teachers, who lobbied the state government for dynamite and a truck. The teachers then used the schoolchildren as a source of labor, working on the road with picks, shovels, and dynamite in class time. In an interview, one man, who participated in the project as a boy, described these experiences as a formative moment in his sense of community. As described by Friedlander (1975), with the help of the SEP [Ministry of Public Education] and the cultural missions, more schools came to town, and by the 1940s several locals were studying to become teachers. In the same period, Hueyapan began being serviced by the *Instituto Nacional Indigenista* [National Indigenist Institute] (*INI*), which provided some services and economical support, but which required the community to be visibly "Indian" to qualify for handouts. Simultaneously with the arrival of the INI and the SEP in Hueyapan, a group of neo-Aztec cultural activists, led by the charismatic engineer and nationalist Juán Luna Cárdenas, arrived in the town. These representatives of the urban Aztec nationalist movement took it as their responsibility to make sure that the Indians of Hueyapan were the right kind of Indians—and legible to the state as such. This dynamic of a culture-based patron–client relation between the state and the community led to the paradoxical situation described by Friedlander as "forced identity." At the time when Friedlander wrote her famous ethnography of the community, progressive ideas were clearly dominant, particularly in the town center. In the progressive view, being an *indio* was clearly and unequivocally a bad thing, but in the view of those Hueyapanecos who lived outside of the town center and relied on subsistence agriculture and marijuana production, the signs and traditions that designated them as *indios* were also the signs of solidarity with the local community, its values, and its forms of life. Hence, the "traditionalist" Hueyapanecos of the outlying barrios were the ones to maintain the cultural forms that are today embraced by much of the community as constitutive of a local ethnic identity, and upon which the town's claim to political independence rests.

The process of decline of Nahuatl as the main community language also broke along the internal class divide within Hueyapan. It was the families of the town center who were more outward oriented, valuing education and the relations with the outside world, who first started emphasizing the use of Spanish over Nahuatl, whereas the people in the outlying barrios maintained the language longer—and do so to this day. This class-based difference between relatively culturally progressive or modernist *plasahkah* (the Nahuatl word for the inhabitants of the Barrio Centro) and the relatively cultural conservative attitudes of the inhabitants of the other barrios must be considered when analyzing the meaning of the cultural emblems of indigeneity to the people of Hueyapan. For example, Friedlander stayed with a family of teachers in the Central Barrio, which may explain why she got the overwhelming feeling that the Indigenous language and culture were undesirable to them, and were imposed by the "cultural radicals." Juán Luna Cárdenas's radical neo-Aztec movement was precisely allied with a family of teachers in the Central Barrio, who eventually distanced themselves from Luna Cárdenas when he fathered a child with the teacher's daughter and claimed that his son was a reincarnation of the Aztec god Huitzilopochtli (Pharao Hansen 2008). At the same time, many families in the more rural barrios were still raising their kids in Nahuatl, but without any interest in notions of reviving ancient Aztec culture.

Simultaneously with the opening of Hueyapan to new ideas, technologies, and infrastructure, the marijuana industry became more lucrative and more violent. A few families had prospered particularly from the trade, and they began feuding (Pharao Hansen 2016). Throughout the 1980s and 1990s, violence was endemic in Hueyapan, and it gained the reputation of being a closed-off *narco*-town. It had its own justice system, in which outsiders who committed crimes in the community were occasionally lynched as a deterrent, and, in some periods, police patrol cars entering the town were attacked and burned on sight. Hueyapan became for a while a sort of outlaw public, where being closed off and isolated from the view of the outside world was considered a public good by the town's most powerful *marijuanero*-families. With the beginning of the "War on Drugs," the army began to conduct frequent drug raids in Hueyapan and arrested hundreds of local people. This offensive finally ended the marijuana business in town, but it also sent many Hueyapanecos to search for other places to live and work. Many hundreds, or perhaps thousands, of them traveled to the United States as undocumented migrants, and began sending money back to their families. As Hueyapanecos increasingly integrated themselves into the (legal) national and global economy, the power balance began to shift between Tetela and Hueyapan.

Political Resurgence of Hueyapan in the 21st Century

Around the turn of the millennium, the economic situation changed for Hueyapan. Remittances from abroad enabled the creation of a multitude of new businesses, from grocery shops and hairdressers, to construction work and wholesale of building materials. Many bought cars, enabling a fleet of local taxis and an unofficial route of collective minivans running between Hueyapan and Cuautla. Remittances were invested in intensifying agricultural production focusing on cash crops; and as the local farmers developed an extensive system of irrigation and planted new peach and avocado groves, others used their connections in the United States to establish a plant in which local produce was packaged and shipped to the California market. This cash flow produced economic growth in the community, and increased access to education and increased social status of the community of Hueyapan relative to Tetela.

Concurrently, Hueyapan also experienced a political resurgence. In 2006, Mario Soberanes Pérez became the first Hueyapaneco to be elected mayor of the municipality. The Soberanes presidency was turbulent, as Teteleños were reluctant to accept being ruled by an "*indio*" from Hueyapan. In the spring of 2009, tensions turned into violence when Teteleños disputing Hueyapan's ownership of the main aquifer of the municipality formed an armed group, kidnapped Soberanes, and subjected him to a mock execution. They threatened him to sign over the right to the water source to Tetela, and they cut off the water supply to Hueyapan. The aggression only steeled the people of Hueyapan, who resolved to travel to Cuernavaca to support their mayor and denounce the violence. This was the first time that Hueyapan used their Indigenous identity politically against Tetela, as they framed the conflict as an attempt by a colonial power to strip the Indigenous community of their lands and natural resources. When, at that point, masked men killed Hueyapan's *ayudante* (the local deputy mayor elected through customary law) who had been a strong voice against Tetela, public sympathy quickly favored Hueyapan. As a result, it was legally established that the Amatzinac water source was within the territory of Hueyapan.

Having discovered their political strength, the main challenge for Hueyapanecos was to settle on a single candidate, and two factions quickly emerged: one faction formed around the Montes family, who had become powerful through their export industry, and the other formed around Mario Soberanes, the first mayor from Hueyapan. The failure of Hueyapanecos to rally around a single candidate meant that the 2009 election was won by the Teteleño Jorge Hernández, whose platform was explicitly formulated as a rejection of Hueyapan-centric politics, and who systematically marginalized Hueyapan in word and deed. Whereas earlier Teteleño presidents had used clientelistic practices such as vote-buying with success, the strategy of Hernández, and subsequent Teteleño candidates in the 2012 and 2015 elections, was one of overt antagonism. In 2012, perhaps in a kind of backlash against the explicit marginalization of Hueyapan's interests, Javier Montes Rosales, also from Hueyapan, was elected mayor; and in 2015 he was elected as the first Hueyapaneco delegate to the state congress, while at the same time Ana-Bertha Haro Sánchez, the wife of former mayor Soberanes, was elected mayor.

As municipal president, Javier Montes even changed the municipal motto to the Nahuatl phrase *titekitigan tonochtin sejkan*, meaning "let's all work together." Ironically, the new motto was simultaneously a plea for reconciliation between Tetela and Hueyapan, but as it was phrased in Nahuatl, it also symbolized the new political status of the Indigenous community of Hueyapan, and the political importance of indigeneity itself. Hueyapan had finally established itself as a full-fledged competitor for political authority within the municipality, and the use of Nahuatl as an emblem of governance symbolically emblazoned its Indigenous voice on all the municipality's official buildings, vehicles, uniforms, and stationery.

In the 2015 campaign, the candidate of the leftist MORENA party (Movement for National Regeneration) was successfully establishing a group of followers in Hueyapan. But during a rally in Tetela, he made an offhand reference to "sending truckloads of sandals to Hueyapan" (*indios huarachudos* [sandal-wearing Indians] being a traditional Teteleño slur against Hueyapanecos), and he lost any support he had there. The Hueyapan constituency instead rallied around the local candidate Haro Sánchez. The deployment of Indigenous rights discourses emerged out of an increasingly polarized political relation between Hueyapan and Tetela, and became an important tool with which Hueyapan could address local grievances. The goal of independence from Tetela, a goal that just 50 years ago Hueyapanecos could not even have imagined, emerged from the same process.

Multicultural Governance in Morelos

In addition to its renewed economic and intellectual strength, Hueyapan's transformation into a political force was also facilitated by developments that were taking place in the wider political spheres of the Mexican nation and in the state of Morelos, and which made the "Indigenous slot"[2] a more favorable position to inhabit.

Beginning in the 1990s, the Mexican state, like several other states in Latin America, changed its cultural politics away from idealizing a culturally homogenous nation, toward multicultural policies based on discourses of inclusion and diversity. This change emerged from a series of critiques of the ethno-national state, and the emergence of global human rights discourses that increasingly focused on cultural rights of minorities (de la Peña 2006). As a result, indigeneity and Indigenous peoples' rights are currently a hot topic in the Mexican public sphere, and one that is actively used

---

[2] In her work about Indonesia, Tania Murray Li (2000) describes the "tribal slot" as a particular social position in which Indigenous or minority groups may seek to position themselves, in order to articulate with the government demands and expectations for tribal people—in Mexico the equivalent "slot" would be the Indigenous or *indígena* slot.

by media and politicians (though note the relevant critique of Hale 1997. Today, overt public racism tends to be called out and castigated; and generally, media are sympathetic with Indigenous causes, even when politicians may not be.

Multiculturalist governance also reached the state of Morelos. After two periods of right-wing rule by the PAN (National Action Party), leftist Graco Ramírez of the PRD (Democratic Revolutionary Party) was elected state governor in 2012. Even though Morelos's Indigenous communities account for only around 2% of the state population, his election platform prominently included several promises aimed at the state's handful of Indigenous Nahua communities. Significantly, he promised to work to offer Indigenous communities a chance to become independent municipalities under the principle of *Usos y Costumbres*. Among his first actions as governor was appointing a director for the process of municipalization, and he chose the local filmmaker, anthropologist, and activist Francesco Taboada.

A major project undertaken by the new administration promoted education by offering all college-age youths an education stipend—the *Beca Salario* ("salary stipend"), on the condition of participating in one year of social work. Conditional cash transfer programs have been one of the main social policies with which the Mexican state has promoted social development and education, and one such program, *Oportunidades*, has been considered widely successful in promoting education (Behrman, Parker, and Todd 2011). But whereas in *Oportunidades* development is seen as a family-based process and the conditions are predicated at the family level, the *Beca Salario* program is community oriented and sees participation in community projects as a way to improve social cohesion and promote development, and furthermore the communities had a role in deciding which specific projects would count toward the stipend. In several communities, community organizers requested support from the state to organize Nahuatl language classes for youths, which would then fulfill the conditions for their stipend. Responsibility for organizing these courses fell to the state director of the municipalization project, since it was argued that to qualify for status as Indigenous municipalities, having a living Indigenous language in the community was a requirement. In this way, state policy made the teaching of Nahuatl a key point both for youths' individual access to economic resources and for the collective political project of becoming independent municipalities. This created a strong incentive for communities to start Nahuatl revitalization projects, and for youths to participate in them. The next section describes this revitalization project and its relation to the political movement for Hueyapan's municipal independence.

Summarizing, across the 20th century and into the 21st, the political situation in Hueyapan has influenced the vitality of the Nahuatl language in different ways: after the Mexican revolution, Hueyapan was a marginal community in the municipalities of first Ocuituco, then Tetela. In this period, contact between people of Hueyapan and the Spanish-speaking public sphere was infrequent and superficial; Hueyapan was basically an Indigenous public with its own political system, and Nahuatl remained the main community language. From the 1940s on, the state came increasingly closer, primarily through teachers and nationalist cultural activists: both of these groups encouraged the people of Hueyapan to stop speaking the local language in order to better integrate into the nation and obtain access to the benefits of social and economic development. From this period on, the community was divided between "modernists" who would abandon Nahuatl because they saw it as an obstacle for development, and "traditionalists," farmers and *marijuaneros* who would rather keep the town relatively isolated from the rest of the state, and who used the Nahuatl language as a kind of code of solidarity. The period as an outlaw public between the 1970s and 1990s protected the language from suffering a very rapid decline, as in some neighboring communities. With the beginning of the migration to the United States, the language in turn came to embody a certain nostalgia and became a potent symbol of belonging, which, along with the increased ability to challenge the Tetela hegemony and the discourse of Indigenous rights, fueled the move toward reclamation of Nahuatl as a valuable asset of the community, even among the "modernists."

Chimalnahuatlajtole: Ethnic and Linguistic Revival and Independence in Hueyapan

The emergence of Hueyapan as a political force to compete with Tetela, and the Mexican state's promotion of Indigenous culture, interacted to provide support for a local movement of cultural resurgence in Hueyapan. Under these conditions, the community experienced a renewed attachment to the traditions and symbols that marked the town and its inhabitants as ethnically different from Teteleños.

Another important factor in this revalorization took place among the Hueyapanecos abroad. Many of them had now been outside of the community for decades, only maintaining contact with their families and community through phone calls and packages shipped back and forth across the border. The largest expatriate community of Hueyapanecos in the United States is in

New York City, and Hueyapanecos there began using the internet as a platform for cultivating hometown nostalgia. Websites and Facebook pages with idealized photos of Hueyapan started appearing around 2010, and today several web fora exist in which Hueyapanecos abroad reminisce and share the things they love about their community of origin. These online media have become a forum through which expatriate Hueyapanecos engage in "diversity talk" (Faudree and Schulthies 2015), a kind of local patriotism in which the signs of the community's ethnic identity are idealized and reaffirmed as a shared property. The combination of nostalgia and localocentric pride motivated a renewed perspective on their cultural traditions among the Hueyapanecos in the United States—who increasingly came to idealize their local heritage and tradition. In these celebrations of ethnic heritage the folkloric elements are foregrounded, with images of young couples dressed in *traje típico* [folk dress] in pristine landscapes beset with flower and fruits, or photos of a girl in a *chincuete* dress standing under the Brooklyn Bridge with longing in her eyes.

The folklorization and indigenization of Hueyapaneco identity also affected the way Hueyapanecos relate to their culture, resulting, for example, in the local Indigenous identity suddenly taking a new centrality in town celebrations. In total, the year of 2013–2014 saw no less than three townwide celebrations of Hueyapan's Indigenous heritage: in October, a festival of local gastronomy, in which the virtues of local cuisine were exalted as the people flocked to the central plaza tasting and selling each other's mole chili sauces, pickled fruits, and tacos (Figure 4.3). A banner welcomed visitors from other towns in Nahuatl—"*ximopanoltitigan toaltepechan*" [Welcome to our hometown], but the vast majority of visitors were locals. Then, in April, the community celebrated a festival of local cuisine, with a strong element of also celebrating local identity and language, in which local elders took the stage, speaking Nahuatl and Spanish to the crowd, and imploring the gathered youths and children to learn the language and appreciate local customs. Finally, in August, the annual celebration of the patron feast of Santo Domingo in 2014 included several performances in the Nahuatl language, some by the youths of the Nahuatl course, and some waving a newly designed Hueyapan flag, featuring the name of Hueyapan written in Aztec glyphic writing. In contrast to the public expressions of Indigenous culture described by Friedlander, which she saw primarily as empty performances of indigeneity for political dignitaries, these events were organized by locals and primarily were targeted at local audiences and the migrant community, who participated by watching the videos online. Figures 4.3 and 4.4 show two of the celebrations in 2013, in which the Nahuatl language featured prominently as a symbol of local identity.

Figures 4.3 and 4.4. (4.3) Celebration of local gastronomy in october 2013, and (4.4) celebration of "Día de la lengua materna" on February 21, 2023.
Photo by the author.

Migration and Local Identity

Many of the individuals who have participated centrally in the current wave of ethnic resurgence in Hueyapan are also themselves migrants who have had the experience of seeing and remembering Hueyapan at a distance. It was also a migrant youth, Alex Maya, who had grown up in New York and returned to Hueyapan, who took the initiative to organize a Nahuatl language course through which local youths could fulfill their requirement for social work under *Beca Salario*. The course became a definite success, as 80 youths signed up for the first semester and began following classes every Saturday. Among the three teachers in the project was Alex's mother Guillermina, who had also lived in New York for 10 years before returning. The second was a local teacher who had taught in the Indigenous bilingual school system and had taught several years in the community of Cuentepec—the only fully Nahuatl-speaking community in Morelos. The third teacher had taught for two years in a Nahuatl language academy for Chicano children in Los Angeles. The fact that these individuals had grown up in Hueyapan, left, and are now "returning to their roots" shows the effect of migration, education, and economic development, and the role of education and experience outside of the community in making locals reconsider the value of the language. It also means that whereas the Nahuatl language in the 1970s was associated with a lower-class peasant identity, it is now connected to a middle-class identity and is seen as a sign of cosmopolitanism and educational ambition, while at the same time a sign of local communal values and solidarity. Doña Guillermina, Alex's mother, expressed it this way in 2016:

An kuak se kah, kuak se kah vehka, kuak	And when one is, one is far away, like that
inon ogachi se gimachilia tlon ipatin,	One feels more what its value is
tlon ipatin tlonon tikpiyah nan,	What the value is of what we have here
tlonon tikmatih, tlonon otikkuayah,	What we know, what we ate,
kenin otiveyageh, nochi nochi non	How we grew up, everything, all of that
ogachi se gimachilia, ogachi se gimachilia	One feels it more, one feels it more
an se ginemilia tlonon	And one thinks about what
tikpiya tlen oksigi ahmo kipiyah.	we have that others don't have.

Alex Maya took the initiative for the language course in the summer of 2013. Twenty-four years old, he had been given the position as *Secretario de Asuntos Migratorios y Indígenas* [Secretary of Migratory and Indigenous Issues] in the municipal government of Tetela del Volcán. This post was a promotion from a position in the DIF (*Desarrollo Integral de la Familia*), the branch of local government devoted to social development. Because of his young age and his former position, which he held only shortly, he had a close collaboration with youth groups in Hueyapan, and therefore he was tuned in to the development of the *Beca Salario* program, and to the wishes of the youths. The *Beca Salario* program required youths to participate in a community-based project in exchange for a scholarship, but in Hueyapan there were few obvious projects of that nature. The only one seemed to be the local health clinic, where some youths had already been participating in light volunteer work as part of their required social services, and others in exchange for their *Oportunidades* family stipends. However, the number of youths eligible for the program was much too large for them all to volunteer at the clinic, and many of them had no interest in doing so. So, drawing on his own personal interest in the cultural heritage of the community, he took the initiative to ask the liaison in the program at the state level, Francesco Taboada, whether it could be possibly to create a program of Nahuatl classes for youths that could then count toward the *Beca Salario* requirements. Taboada was in charge of the implementation of the municipalization program which was Governor Graco Ramirez's main initiative in Indigenous policy. The creation of Nahuatl classes fit well with his vision of cultural development in the Indigenous communities, which he saw as best driven by local identity and what he describes as the reintegration of the community through rekindling traditional forms of social organization and cultural practices. Taboada supported the creation of the program and promised to pay the salary of one teacher, if the other could be paid by the municipal coffer.

Alex Maya was born in Hueyapan to a single mother, but when he was 10 years old, the little family of his mother, himself, and sister left Hueyapan for the United States. After passing under the border in Arizona through the sewers, and wandering through the desert, he arrived in New York in early September 2001. His first week of school in the United States was marked by the chaos of 9/11 and his experience of being unable to communicate. Need being the best teacher, he quickly learned English, and became a good student, taking elementary school through to high school in Queens, New York. He participated in the community of Hueyapaneco expatriates in New York, feeling with them the nostalgia for their hometown, their families, their traditional dishes and celebrations. Then in 2012, his mother decided that she had saved up enough from her work in a beauty parlor that she could return to Hueyapan and set up a business of her own. Alex and his elder sister followed her home to the town they had not seen since they were kids. Arriving in Mexico, Alex realized that he hadn't brought his official high school diploma; the one he had was not accepted by Mexican colleges, and his plans of starting an education (which as an undocumented migrant he couldn't have done in the US either) fell apart. Luckily, the same year, Javier Montes was elected president, and with Montes being a relative of his mother, Alex was offered a job in the *ayuntamiento* [municipal administration]. Here his will to work, his contacts in the New York expatriate community, his experience as a migrant, and his social engagement, as well as the fact that he spoke fluent English, made him a good choice for one of the many positions in municipal governance that entail lots of tasks and responsibility and little remuneration.

The Nahuatl Course

An kemman otipehkeh   And when we began
'ka inin tegitl den pipiltoton,   this work with the youths
nehhua onomohtiaya porkeh ahmo   I was scared, because I don't know how to
nikmati kenin nikihkuilos correctamente,   write correctly,
ahmo nikmati de fonética, de ortografia,   I don't know about phonetics or orthography
ahmo nikmati,   I don't know it.
pero kuak onechilhuihkeh de keh nin tegitl   But when they told me that the task isn't
este ahmo san yehon, se kipalevis,   just that, but one has to help
sino huan totlahtol de nan,   rather with our language, from here
de nan Hueyapan,   here from Hueyapan
pos nikihta entoces kualle nikchivas   well, then I said, I can do it
porkeh nehhua kualle nitlanonotza.   because I do know how to speak well.
    —Doña Guillermina Maya Rendón

The two teachers eventually chosen to teach the course were Guillermina Maya, Alex Maya's own mother, and Alejandro Abad, one of Hueyapan's few bilingual teachers. Doña Guillermina had never taught before, but during her stay in the United States, she had grown particularly fond of her native language, often speaking it with her friends and relatives of her own generation. This motivated her interest in encouraging the use of the language, and the feeling of community among the youths. Her Nahuatl was fluent, and her pronunciation unmistakably *Hueyapanecatl* [from Hueyapan]. Maestro Alejandro was born in Hueyapan's San Felipe barrio, but did not acquire more than passive knowledge of the language in his upbringing. However, upon graduating as a teacher, he was stationed in Cuentepec, the only community in Morelos where Nahuatl is the main community language, and he taught the children there for more than a decade, learning fluent Nahuatl in the process. When he got the chance to return to Hueyapan to become the sole teacher in the tiny Indigenous primary school of the colonia *Matlakohtlan*, he took it. The children there did not actually speak Nahuatl when he arrived, but the school was run by the DGEI (*General Direction of Indigenous Education*, the Indigenous Education branch of the Ministry of Education), making it officially a bilingual school. Maestro Alejandro, with his experience from Cuentepec, took this seriously and in fact taught the children Nahuatl. Back home in Hueyapan, it cost him some efforts to adjust to the local variety, which differs from that of Cuentepec in several ways, but he actively sought out conversation partners and worked to adopt a more local accent.

Alex Maya was able to convince Javier Montes, the municipal president, to pay the salary of one of the teachers, and Francesco Taboada's *Dirección de Asuntos Indígenas* paid the other salary. The teachers received 200 pesos (approximately 16 USD at the time in 2014) for each three-hour class, which they gave every Saturday. The students who participated in the course were students of the *bachillerato*, a college preparatory high school for youths typically between 16 and 20 years of age. They were nearly all locals, except for a youth from the neighboring community of Alpanocan, Puebla. They represented all the barrios of the town, but given that not all students continue on to the *bachillerato* after finishing their *secundaria* [secondary school], they can be assumed to represent those students who achieved well academically in primary and secondary school. There were also representatives of all social classes in Hueyapan, from subsistence farming families of the *colonias* and outlying barrios, to youths from the Barrio Centro and from families that could be classified as "middle class."

From the inauguration in October and until the *clausura* closing ceremony the following June, students and teachers met every Saturday in two small classrooms in the administrative palace on Hueyapan's central plaza. During the week, the rooms were used as improvised classrooms by the *bachillerato* of Hueyapan, which does not yet have its own installations. The rooms are the same rooms where the first elementary school classes in Hueyapan were given in the 1930s and 1940s. In total, some 80 students enrolled in the course, but generally only around 60 would attend any given Saturday. This was probably a good thing because even with this number of students the two rooms were overcrowded. The ceilings in the rooms are high and the walls are plastered concrete, creating a soundscape where every whispered comment or squeaky chair resounds and echoes, requiring the teachers to raise their voices frequently, and ask the youths in the back rows to be silent.

The class was taught in traditional classroom style with the teacher writing basic vocabulary on the blackboard, students repeating words or phrases one after another, and the teacher correcting their pronunciation, or asking students to translate single words from Nahuatl into Spanish or vice versa. The result was that during the three-hour class each student spoke Nahuatl only one or two words at a time and only a couple of times during class; the rest of the time other students were repeating the same words, or the teacher was giving instructions. Sometimes the teachers would use exercises where students would form conversation chains using greetings, or asking each other's name, or stating and asking about what something is called:

> *Nehhua notoga Jaime.* [turning toward another student] *Kenin timotoga?*
> *Nehhua notoga Alicia.* [turning toward another student] *Kenin timotoga?* (etc.)

["Me, I call myself Jaime. What do you call yourself?"
"Me, I call myself Alicia. What do you call yourself?" (etc.)]
   Or
Ken otlathuilivak? ["How did it dawn?"]
Kwalle tlasohkamati. [turning toward another student] *Ken otlathuilivak?* (etc.) –
["How did it dawn?" "Well, thank you. How did it dawn?"]

The teachers maintained that it was the specificity of the local pronunciation that makes the language "ours." They would meticulously correct the students' pronunciation to soften consonants like /k/ and /w/ to sound like [g] and [ʊ] between vowels. This voicing and weakening of consonant sounds between vowels are a salient feature of the pronunciation that people in Hueyapan consider what makes their variety distinct from other varieties of Nahuatl (Campbell 1976). They also made sure that students added the strong preaspiration that makes /l/'s and /w/'s sound like [hl] and [hʍ] (as pronouncing l and w while blowing air out of one's mouth) when occurring after other consonants. For example, an exchange would go:

Student: *Nikneki nitlakwas* [I want to eat]
Teacher: *Ammo. Ihkon:* "*niknegi nitlagüas*" [No. Like this: "I want to eat"]

To emphasize the pronunciation, teachers chose an intuitive approach to orthography, adopting one which consistently marked those small differences in pronunciation, even though they do not affect meaning—for example, writing the phonemes /k/ and /w/ as <g> and <b> between vowels. Writing the [g] like this caused additional complications since in Spanish the letter <g> represents the velar fricative [x] when occurring before the vowels /e/ and /i/. This required the teachers to do as in Spanish and insert the letter <u> before these vowels, gui/gue, to force the correct pronunciation of the [g] before i and e. This choice in turn required them to introduce an umlaut over the subsequent <ü> when representing the phonemic lip rounding in the labialized velar stop /kʷ/ [gʷ]. Hence, the possessed form of /kalle/ "house" was <igal>, the verb /ƛakʷa/ "he eats" was written <tlagua>, and /i:kʷe:/ "her skirt" was written <igüe>. These are the complications that arise when Nahuatl speakers intuitively adapt Spanish orthographical conventions to the sounds of Nahuatl. Their writing system overrepresents the sound system by specifically providing extra information about detailed pronunciation contrasts that do not distinguish referential meaning. But it does so only in those cases where the contrast was ideologically emphasized as a "typical Hueyapan pronunciation" (and, ironically, only when it coincided with sounds they were accustomed to recognizing and writing in Spanish). Hence, detailed linguistic awareness, originally acquired through the habituation to the phonological contrasts of Spanish, was recruited to fulfill a political function of differentiating the "local" Nahuatl taught in class from other "foreign" Nahuatl varieties. In the same way, Guillermina, who was sometimes insecure in her role as a teacher, often emphasized that her main qualification as a teacher was exactly that she had the local pronunciation with no outside influence.

Sometimes classes would not involve conversation or practice at all, but rather took on the shape of lectures about aspects of local culture: the names and histories associated with places in the community, the traditional ways of celebrating different feasts, the genealogies of certain persons, or the way that social participation worked in the past. These lectures would often involve cultural words and phrases in Nahuatl, such as place names, kinship terms, the names of foods or the verbs describing their preparation, and so on.

Engaging Government through Cultural Politics

A few weeks into the course, the teachers decided that they were going to ask the students to learn the Nahuatl place names around their homes, and bring them to class to make a list or a map of the places. This project required students to engage with their parents or grandparents, and to learn about the local toponymy where they lived. Doña Guillermina had planned that the students should make signs to be placed around town with the Nahuatl names of the different localities. She organized wooden boards and paint, bought with their own money, and with the students, they created some 40 colorful signs to be posted around town. The multicolored handwritten signs read "*Ojtenko*" [Roadside], "*Tlalogan*" [Tlalok Place], "*Tzitzintitlan*" [Ailetree Place], "*Pajtlan*" [Medicine Place], and so on, and when placed in their locations would provide visual proof of the re-Nahuatization of the community (see Figures 4.5 and 4.6). I could immediately see the educational value in having the students engaging with their local environment through Nahuatl, reclaiming in this way the local cosmology. But there was another aspect of the exercise that I had not considered.

For the inauguration of the signs, once again Doña Guillermina invited the dignitaries: Francesco Taboada from the state government, the local delegate of the *Comisión para el Desarrollo de los Pueblos Indígenas* (CDI), and the municipal president Javier Montes. Both Montes and the delegate had been invited before to see the course, and Doña Guillermina had been disappointed when they canceled at the last minute, after she had cooked and organized gift

Figures 4.5 and 4.6 The day of the inauguration of the signs with Nahuatl place names; photos taken in the central plaza of Hueyapan.
Photos by Alex Maya.

baskets of local produce for the visitors. But with the inauguration of the signs, she knew that they would be more likely to come, figuring that the possibility of a photo opportunity and ribbon cutting would be irresistible. Particularly the municipal president Montes had been annoyed at not having been personally present at the inauguration of the course when he saw the amount of media coverage it generated. She was right; they did come for the inauguration of the signs (Figure 4.5). In front of an audience of community members, including many of the students' parents, the municipal president gave a speech emphasizing the Nahuatl motto of the municipality: *"tiktekitigan tonochtin sejkan"*—"let's all work together." Taboada's speech emphasized the importance of language as a vehicle of culture. Both promised additional resources for the course. Montes promised that for the next year he would pay for 10 more teachers, and he would have official signage created in Nahuatl to match the signage created by the students. Neither promise was kept in the end, but the fact that he would make them shows that at that point the Nahuatl course was seen as a source of political currency. The CDI delegate brought T-shirts printed with a Nahuatl logo for all the students, talked briefly about the importance of the course, and stated that she would continue to support it in the future whenever something was needed. The delegate did keep her promise, and later supported a request for money for a class trip to the Cacahuamilpa caves later in the season. The outcomes of the ceremony showed how well-considered Doña Guillermina's idea had been. By making sure the politicians felt that they had something to gain from supporting the class, she was able to garner additional resources that would not otherwise have been forthcoming.

Toward the end of the semester, the course had changed, the number of students was smaller, and the students who were there were more focused. They were very comfortable in the class and very attentive and engaged with each other and with the teacher, and they were clearly enjoying themselves. The conversation was happy, almost in tones of banter. A good handful of students were able to converse in basic Nahuatl and to translate most of the words asked by the teacher. The most attentive and engaged of the students had clearly been able to advance as Nahuatl speakers, in spite of the difficult learning environment.

When talking with the teachers afterward, they told me that they had been very active lately. They had founded an organization called *Chimalnahuatlajtole* [the Nahuatl language shield], dedicated to Hueyapan's cultural and linguistic revitalization. Two of their students had participated in a competition of Nahuatl oratory organized by the CDI in Cuernavaca, and one of them had won third place in his age category—winning an iPad. They had given him special preparation outside of class, and he had practiced intensively with his parents before the competition. They also said that a delegation of students had traveled to Cuernavaca to attend a ceremony at City Hall where they publicly thanked Governor Ramírez for his support of the course—making the speech in Nahuatl. And they said that now they were organizing a dance drama, representing the traditional wedding ceremony of Hueyapan for the official *clausura*, to which they invited me. The students had organized traditional dress from their parents, found the props for the dance in their houses (clay pots, *metate* grinding stones, woven reed *petate*-mats, and other traditional tools and artifacts), and they met to rehearse the dance in Doña Guillermina's house several times a week. At least for a good number of students, participation in the class was not simply a way to access the 800 monthly pesos of the *Beca Salario*, but also gave them something else that they valued. Furthermore, the parents of the students in the course had organized a support committee aimed at providing support for the teachers, and to lobby for more resources with the authorities, and in case of no resources being offered, to cooperate to cover the costs of the course. The course was apparently taking on the shape of one of the many civil society organizations and committees that people in Hueyapan participate in, most of which combine elements of collective bargaining with a cooperative economy similar to the traditional cargo systems, just as when the people in Hueyapan had built the road to Tlacotepec, and the *comité pro-carretera* had lobbied the government for technical and monetary support, but eventually constructed the road with their own labor when their lobbying efforts did not bear fruit. Today the public good that they were organizing around was the language course.

Thinking about these new developments, it struck me that perhaps the objective of the course had never been that youths in Hueyapan should start speaking Nahuatl fluently, or to dramatically expand the social domains in which Nahuatl is used. Maybe the language was simply a medium to achieve another set of political goals: a way of formulating a new idea of the common good for the entire community of Hueyapan, and of actively integrating local youths into a new local public sphere. In such a project, achieving linguistic fluency would not be a requirement, only achieving "cultural fluency" in the sense of being able to feel a part of the cultural and linguistic traditions that the community has defined as its own, and of being recognized as competent participants in that local tradition.

Having spent 10 years abroad, Doña Guillermina and Alex Maya understood that the local community was threatened with dissolution as youths oriented their perspectives outside of Hueyapan to find their sources of identity. By reconstituting Hueyapan as a public sphere, with a body of cultural heritage as a common resource, and a new set of discourses of community, they were taking on the threat that Hueyapan might disintegrate into a mosaic of political factions, special interest groups, and rootless youths waiting around for a chance to leave town. The acquisition of the Nahuatl language, then, and particularly its locally specific idiosyncrasies such as the accent, the toponymy, and the "culture words" described in the beginning of this chapter, came to serve as a way of mending a fractured community. The acquisition of discursive and grammatical fluency in Nahuatl came to be only a secondary objective of the language course. The main goals, as they emerged in the practice of the course, were to use the language to reintegrate the students into an experiential community of local practices, and to use this integration for achieving larger political goals, such as promoting the community's interests in relations with outsiders or even becoming an independent municipality.

Conclusion: From Outlaw Public to Indigenous Pride

The history of Hueyapan in the 20th and 21st centuries provides a case in support of my argument about the way that language loss and reclamation are often tied to developments at the local scale. In Hueyapan, Nahuatl has been socially meaningful to its people because of the way that it provided a medium of social cohesion and protection before an abusive state. Then, as Hueyapan turned its attention toward the national public sphere as the source of political identity, its usefulness declined, only to be revived again at a moment when the language was tied to the community's ability to leverage political currency in the national public for use in the local political relations with their neighboring communities. Undergirding this wider political development is the flux of Hueyapaneco lives and feelings: meetings with national and global publics, as Hueyapanecos migrate or as these publics enter into Hueyapaneco lives in other ways, cause appreciation for the safety and comfort offered by experiences felt as intimately tied to the local. The Nahuatl language, at least to that majority of Hueyapanecos who have heard it in their homes as children, or who know the names of the places around their houses, becomes such a vehicle through which a connection to something intimate and local is *felt*.

It seems that political developments at multiple levels of society have converged to produce a situation where many Hueyapanecos are increasingly interested in indexing their local identity, and in using Nahuatl to do so. Among the most important components in this change at the different political scales involved, I have identified three main processes:

- Changing discourses at the global and national level (described in Chapter 3);
- State and federal policies encouraging communities and individuals to revitalize languages through economic incentives;
- Political and economic resurgence at the community level, which decreased Hueyapan's political and economic dependency on Tetela and increased the value of cultural difference as capital.

If viewed through Roland Terborg and Laura Garcia Landa's (2013) ecological model of competing pressures, the changes look like the result of a simultaneous reversal of pressures against the Nahuatl language that had impeded its use at several different levels of the ecology. Terborg's model is individualistic in its focus on social pressures and their effects on the linguistic choices of individual speakers. Such a speaker-centered, rational choice-based model may well be used to explain why some individuals suddenly develop an interest in the language. For example, some youths may have been interested primarily in receiving the *beca*, and only secondarily in the language. But it is harder to explain within a model centered on the individual actor how a group of people came together in what appears to be a shared interest in relating to their community through language; that is, it begs the question of what social processes preceded, and produced the circumstances for, the chain of "individual choices." The model posits that language choice happens in an ecology of pressures, and consequently it explains language change as a result of changing pressures—but it does not allow us to understand what sparks a change in the ecology, and which pressures are more likely to become decisive.

Rather, my observations of Hueyapan suggest that instead of focusing on how social pressures mold individual behavior, it may be relevant to look at language shift and its reversal at the community level, less as a psychological process, and more as dynamics of political, economic, and semiotic ones. We might look at it as a process in which individuals orient toward or away from a specific community, and adopt whichever language serves as that community's privileged medium of discourse and identity. While we can see that each of the political changes taking place did create new motivations for individual choices, they would have been unlikely to manifest in the form of the current revitalization project except within a sociopolitical context where it was a feasible strategy for Hueyapan as a community to use its language as an ethno-political marker.

The fact that the Mexican state plays an active role in creating a political climate that makes it feasible for Indigenous people to feel pride, joy, or nostalgia for their community and its traditions, and to express that publicly, can hardly be a cause to dismiss the entire project as a "hot house phenomenon" (Faudree 2014:237) or an expression of "forced identity." Today, with the strengthened political position of Hueyapan relative to Tetela and to the state, the people of Hueyapan seem to be in quite a strong position from which to negotiate. Now they are able to decide how and when they want to inhabit the Indigenous slot for the sake of others, and when they want to do it for the sake of strengthening their own social bonds.

Like Friedlander, Indigenous political theorists have critiqued the politics of recognition as the paradigm through which settler states interface with Indigenous communities. However, where Friedlander originally saw recognition as a kind of paternalist condescension that denies the Indigenous community integration into the majority nation, they tend to see it in the opposite way—as a way for the state to claim the moral right to represent Indigenous nations that have not consented to such representation. Coulthard (2014) argues that rather than seeking recognition from the settler state, Indigenous communities should strive to achieve self-recognition by reconnecting with the "ground," as represented by their territories, languages, and traditions, which they can use as the basis for asserting political and moral autonomy. It is of course true, as Friedlander argued, that states frequently do seek to manipulate Indigenous people by supporting Indigenous communities' freedom of cultural expression while stifling their freedom of political expression. But the case of Hueyapan points to the possibility that Indigenous communities may choose to pursue local political goals through the strategic use of ethnic essentialism or nationalism. It seems that language revival can be an effective instrument with which to simultaneously pursue political goals in the local public sphere and in the national public.

In her essay "*Un nosotrx sin Estado*" [a we without the state], Yásnaya Elena Aguilar Gil encourages Indigenous people to reimagine their communities as small autonomous nations. Rather than echoing the Zapatist lemma of "never again a Mexico without us," she urges her fellow Indigenous intellectuals to envision an "us" without Mexico, and to work toward achieving that vision (Aguilar Gil 2018). Hueyapan's quest for autonomy followed many of the steps that Aguilar sees as fundamental for achieving Indigenous autonomy, but it was not motivated by a desire to opt out of the Mexican nation, and its strategy was carried out by engaging the state, rather than turning away from it. A key element that Aguilar stresses in the establishment of Indigenous autonomous nations in Mexico is language, in the sense of the "communalect" of the town-community (Aguilar Gil 2013). She argues that the fact that boundaries of Indigenous communalects tend to coincide with the borders of self-ascribed Indigenous political units demonstrates the importance of these political ties and of the linguistic differences that they structure to the speakers. That is, in many Indigenous regions, patterns of dialectal variation are organized by the speakers' political identities, and function as markers of membership in specific local communities. The importance of the communalect was also central in Hueyapan's revitalization project, where the local of anchoring pronunciation, knowledge of locally specific vocabulary (such as place names) and idioms (such as greetings and phrases of courtesy) provided the authenticity and intimacy that made project succeed both as revitalization and as community building.

In this radical vision, Hueyapan continues to be, as it was before the arrival of the Europeans, a very small nation, a city-state unto itself, with its own territory, and a population united by a set of national symbols, a language, and a vision of a shared fate and a common good. It is now, as it was also then, located within, but not inseparable from, the sphere of influence of a very large state, which constrains, but does not nullify, its independent agency in the pursuit of its local common good. When the ground moves, sometimes even visions of a radically different world can come closer to reality.

The first season of state-sponsored Nahuatl classes in Hueyapan and in the state of Morelos ended with a closing performance at the *Teatro Ocampo* in downtown Cuernavaca, where students from the different communities presented some of what they had learned. There were at least 500 persons in attendance for the event. Billed as a "Celebration of the Linguistic Diversity of Morelos," it was the *clausura*, the official closing ceremony, of the first year of state-sponsored Nahuatl classes in the state of Morelos. The old theater was packed. Most of the audience were families and relations of the youths and teachers who were going to be on stage, but in the front rows were dignitaries such as the state governor's wife, representatives of the state secretaries of education and culture, and even the director of the INALI (*Instituto Nacional de Lenguas Indígenas*). After an introduction and welcome, given almost entirely in Nahuatl by the announcer, a teacher from Cuentepec, a group of teachers and students from the municipality of Ayala performed the Mexican national anthem, singing in Nahuatl and in Mixtec about roaring cannons and the cry to war for the fatherland. Then the stage filled, as more than 100 children from an elementary school in Cuentepec organized themselves in neat rows. Dressed as little Aztecs, in white garments and golden plastic headdresses, they demonstrated an awesome musicality and discipline. They played "precuauhtemic"[3] instruments such as conch shell trumpets, *teponaztli* slit-drums, and upright standing *huehuetl* drums, never missing a beat, and going from sounds as soft rain to violent thundering crescendos. The percussive sound of wood on wood and wood on skin was colossal. During the performance, one of them, a girl of about 12, stood up and recited a prayer to the four world corners, mentioning them with the classical Nahuatl terms, and invoked the Aztec deities of *Quetzalcoatl* and *Tezcatlipoca*. In her speech, the

---

[3] This term, switching Columbus for Cuauhtemoc, the last Aztec emperor, as the fixture relative to which European contact is dated, is used in Mexicanidad circles as a substitution for "pre-Columbian" as a way to avoid defining the period by the name of a hated conqueror.

governor's wife stressed that this was an attempt at revitalizing the Nahuatl language, not through folklorization, but through engagement with the everyday Indigenous reality. I was waiting to see the delegation from Hueyapan present their performance, a short dance-theater representing a version of a traditional wedding ceremony of the community, and they went on last. The students wore the colonial style Hueyapan dress which is now considered the traditional dress, the girls in *huipil* blouses and black woolen *tzinkweitl* skirts, the boys dressed in white cotton pants and shirts, with woolen ponchos and sombreros. Their performance represented a version of the traditional ceremony of bride petition in Nahuatl. The groom and his parents asked the bride's parents, then the family collected and brought the bride-wealth, dancing slowly, swaying from side to side, with their sandal-clad feet stomping the rhythm. All the students from Hueyapan were on stage, although only about 10 of them had speaking parts. The wedding music, played from a tape, was a Huastec *son*.[4] A beautiful performance, it was obvious that the performers and organizers had put sincere efforts into achieving the feeling of an authentically traditional wedding. Nonetheless, I could not quite escape the feeling that there was something wrong about all this. After all, what did this fancy dress-up show for state dignitaries and patrons have to do with true community revitalization of the Indigenous languages?

When the show was over, the dignitaries were called on stage one after another to receive their diplomas and rounds of applause: first the politicians and subsequently the teachers. Now Doña and Maestro Alejandro would get their chance to enjoy the spotlight. But when the Hueyapan teachers were called, no one came to the stage. After calling a couple of times, the announcer said their diplomas would be given on another occasion, and proceeded to call the next group of teachers. I went down from the balcony where I had been sitting, through the backstage area and down into the cellar where the performers had their dressing area. There they were, the teachers and the students, smiling, talking, and playing, sitting around on the floor and on their props. They offered me homemade *mole poblano*, tamales, and fresh tortillas brought from Hueyapan by the parent group, who had organized an entire feast around the excursion. We sat around for a while talking about the event, and about their performance, and we took group photos of the students and teachers and myself (Figure 4.7). "But now," said Doña Guillermina in Spanish, "this was just the rehearsal. They didn't even let us finish here, they only gave us 15 minutes. The real performance will be at the town feast in August. We will perform the entire wedding ceremony on stage there."

---

[4] In Mexican traditional music, a *son* is a type of tune.

Figure 4.7 The youths of the Nahuatl language program with their teachers in the basement of the Teatro Ocampo in Cuernavaca after their performance of the wedding ceremony.
Photo by the author.

And so it was. In August, when Hueyapan celebrated the feast of Santo Domingo, its patron saint, the students performed the full version of the wedding dance in Nahuatl, in front of a crowded plaza full of Hueyapan locals, many of whom understood the words in Nahuatl, and remembered the traditional ceremony from their youths. There were no dignitaries or politicians present then to perform for, just the community, enjoying the performance as an expression of something that was uniquely their own. In 2021, Doña Guillermina Maya Rendón went on to be elected as the second *vocera concejal* [council spokesperson] of the Indigenous municipality of Hueyapan.

Figure 5.0 Don Félix Sánchez and the *yuntero* Don Basilio, getting ready to plow the flat part of the sowing terrain on a misty May morning in Tlaquilpa, Veracruz (described on page 197).
Photo by the author.

5
Land, Language, and Higher Learning in the Zongolica Highlands

The Man Who Visited Tlalokan

Once there was a man whose wife was in love with St. Anthony. She had an image of the Saint, and he was her lover, and she gave him food to eat. This St. Anthony ate human food and was alive. Every day she would send her husband to hunt for deer, because venison was the favorite dish of the Saint. The husband sought out deer far and wide in the woods and mountains, bringing only his faithful dog to help him. And they were not allowed to return home unless they brought meat for the Saint to eat.

One day he was stalking a stag through the hills and gullies, and he followed it without realizing that the stag was leading him into a cave. Inside the cave, the man suddenly found himself in Tlalokan, *the underworld kingdom where* Tlalokan Tata *and* Tlalokan Nana *guard all the wildlife and plants. The stag itself was* Tlalokan Tata, *lord of the underworld, and he scolded the man for having killed so many of his deer, and he told him to cure all the animals in* Tlalokan, *using as medicine the same herbs that he would use as a condiment when cooking their meat. The dog, complicit in killing the game, was beaten by all the animals, which down here in the underworld appeared to the man as humans. One of the animals, the frog, advised the man to use the leaf of the avocado tree to cure the animals. He had to toast the leaf and have it ground on the metate by the women of* Tlalokan *along with ashes. Smearing this powder on the dead and wounded animals that he had hurt as a hunter, they would come back to life.*

Tlalokan Tata then charged the man with the task of growing corn to make up for his crimes against the animals. He worked the earth, sowed the corn, and hoed it when it sprouted. But one day, when the tall stalks were just about to flower, the wind blew so hard that it broke all the cornstalks. The man found them lying on the ground and he despaired and went to tell Tlalokan Tata *about the misfortune. The lord of the underworld told him to use forked sticks to raise up all the cornstalks, but the man refused. "That is impossible," he said.* Tlalokan Tata *then told him to go gather two bags of the insect called* tzintijeras, *the earwig, and to empty one sack at the edge of the cornfield and one in the middle. The tzintijeras helped the man raise all the broken cornstalks—and that is indeed their job in the cornfield until this day. Soon, the cornflowers became cobs and the man harvested many sacks of corn.*

Nahuatl Nations. Magnus Pharao Hansen, Oxford University Press. © Oxford University Press 2024.
DOI: 10.1093/oso/9780197746158.003.0006

Tlalokan Tata *released the man from his obligations of penitence, and gave him a sack of money to take with him back to the human world. But when the man returned to* tlaltikpak, *the surface world, he found that not one, but seven worldly years had passed, and his wife had taken him for dead, deciding instead to marry her lover St. Anthony. The wedding was planned for the next Sunday. Confused and frightened, the man called once more on the animals of* Tlalokan *to help him. The ground squirrel came to him and told him to make a wooden mask, resembling the face of a stag. It also brought him food,* xokotamal, *sour tamales, and some meat. He made the mask in time for the wedding, and arrived there wearing it. The other guests asked him to lend them the mask so that they could dance with the bride, but he refused. "Bring me the couple, and they will wear the mask," he said. And so it was done, the couple came and put on the mask and started dancing to the wedding* son, *a lively dance. The man pulled out a stick and struck each of the pair one time, and before the astounded guests, the bride and groom turned into deer and ran out of the house into the wilderness. That way they paid their crime of having made the hunter kill so many deer.*

This narrative is a retelling in English of a story that is well known in the Nahuatl-speaking towns in the Zongolica region in Central Veracruz.[1] I first heard it in the spring of 2014, from Adán Sánchez Rosales of Tlaquilpa, who was then a student at the Intercultural University, and whose family I was staying with as I carried out several periods of fieldwork at the university over the course of 2014. Adán Sánchez retold the story in Spanish in his BA thesis, which he submitted to the Intercultural University of Veracruz (UVI) in July 2014. His thesis was an exploration of the agricultural ritual cycle in his home community, based on ethnography and interviews with local elders. In his thesis, the narrative supplies a description of the relation between humans and the earth, represented mythologically by the underworld of *Tlalokan* where the animals dwell and are cared for by their owner *Tlalokan Tata*. This is just one of many possible uses of this evocative narration and its layers of meaning. Another motif in the story is the idea that Indigenous people have become estranged from themselves through imposed religious and cultural ideas that have led to moral excess and social decay, and the idea of returning

---

[1] There are two other versions, both quite different from this one, collected and published by Luís Reyes Garcia (1976). In the longest of them, collected in Cuahuixtlahuac close to Zongolica, the hunter receives a ring that produces money in Tlalocan, but he loses it and must get help from various pest animals to retrieve it; the explicit moral is that humans owe our wealth to these animals which must therefore be treated with respect, by allowing mice to take grain, vultures to eat carcasses, and hawks to take chickens. In this version from Tlaquilpa, the moral is less explicit, but also points to the need for humans to respect animals and observe religious taboos.

to the ground and the sacred territory, to come to recognize oneself anew by performing penitence and restoring the balance.

The way the story became part of Adán's thesis research also shows how *intercultural education* at the UVI may motivate students to engage their local cultural traditions, and to find ways of understanding their region and the landscape they inhabit, which are not taught in the standard curriculum at Mexican universities. As a philosophy of education and as an institutionalized practice, intercultural education has been criticized as an ill-conceived and superficial engagement with diversity. It has been described by critics as an empty exercise in inclusion: chronically underfunded, with staff and students who are not necessarily from Indigenous communities themselves, and who really just want a normal education that can get them a stable job in industry or local government. My observations of and interactions with intercultural education as it is practiced at the UVI's campus in Tequila have caused me to take a more optimistic stance. This chapter argues that the way in which it is sometimes practiced in the intercultural universities of Mexico may provide a space where Indigenous students may engage in a process of self-discovery, as students engage with the languages and traditions of their communities in ways that code Indigenous culture in positive terms. This aspect of cultural self-discovery, as students recognize their own communities as carriers of valuable knowledge, may be a significant element in a process of Indigenous self-recognition.

In terms of its concrete educational outcomes, interculturality, as it is practiced in the UVI, seems to be providing Indigenous youths with new options that may make their goals of socioeconomic mobility more compatible with an interest in participating in the maintenance and development of local communities' cultural values and traditions.[2] In providing this option, intercultural universities in particular may hold the promise of becoming loci of the construction of new Indigenous public spheres, where Indigenous people can discuss their own shared affairs using language, concepts, and perspectives developed by themselves and grounded in their own lifeworlds. The analysis here uses space as a central analytical concept. Spaces are not simply empty, they are coded and read by those who inhabit them as particular kinds of space, with particular affordances that invite particular activities. Some ways of reading spaces constrain possibilities and force specific courses of action, whereas others create openings for different kinds of possibilities within them. In Adán's narrative, two different views of the landscape and the wild space of the Zongolica mountains are in conflict—one that sees the region

---

[2] Perales Franco and McCowan 2020; Mateos Cortés 2017; Dietz 2012.

primarily as a source of resources to be harvested, and another that sees it as the visible surface of a much larger space beneath, a space in which abundance of life is possible for the one who adopts the appropriate perspective.

Regions of Refuge: The Zongolica Highlands

A number of scholars in different disciplines have theorized the relation between the semiotic coding of spaces and social, economic, and political practices, on the one hand, and the forms of experience they generate in their inhabitants, on the other. From Foucault's focus on man-made spaces in relation to discipline (Foucault 1977) and the creation of politically docile subjectivities, to Harvey's geographies of difference (Harvey 1996)—such scholarship has tended to look at how spatial politics play a role in strategies of dominance and hegemony. In anthropology, Biehl (2005) introduced the concept of "zones of abandonment" in his description of how the absence of political investment in certain areas and their inhabitants creates conditions of life that are stripped of everything but the barest necessities—making "bare life" the only form of life possible.

In Mexican anthropology, a famous example of spatial analysis is Gonzalo Aguirre Beltrán's concept of "regions of refuge" (Aguirre Beltrán 1967), which describes spaces depleted of options, formed as the historical process of violent marginalization pushed Indigenous populations into the periphery. The Zongolica Highlands (*Sierra de Zongolica*), the inhospitable mountainous margin between the fertile plains of Veracruz and Puebla, was one of the areas that Aguirre Beltrán considered such a region of refuge. Short on natural resources and inaccessible due to the rough terrain, in the colonial period it never attracted many Spaniards, and consequently experienced relative independence from the colonial world. This relative independence came at the price of material hardship, though, as the cold rugged climate and meager soil provided only enough for basic subsistence.

When Aguirre Beltrán sees the Zongolica Highlands as a region of refuge, he does so from the external perspective of the *longue durée* of Indigenous history in Mesoamerica. Indeed, colonial history is the force that has produced that particular kind of spatiality. From the view of the Mexican state, the highlands are often coded as a region of underdevelopment and economic marginalization—one that consistently figures in the bottom tiers when INEGI, the Mexican Institute of Statistics and Geography, publishes indices of social development. A similar, though less empirically based view is often echoed in the news media of Orizaba, the major town located in the warm lowlands just north of the highlands. Here, the Zongolica region is depicted as a primitive and uncivilized outback where the colorful, but poor and essentially primitive *indígenas* live. From the perspective of a sociologist, the highlands could be coded as a "push zone" or a "sending zone" from which migrants move into the rest of national space and across borders. In the perspective of the UVI, it is one of four "intercultural regions," which means that it is a zone of Indigenous occupation with a resulting high degree of cultural and linguistic diversity. All of these possible constructions of the highlands as a space take a bird's-eye view of the region—the way it looks on a map, as a region shaded in according to some specific quality that we are illustrating. But as we know, the map is not the territory, and for the people who know the region not from maps, but from walking on its hills, tilling its lands, eating its fruits, and engaging with its inhabitants, it looks different.

In the Nahuatl language, there is no traditional word that describes the highlands as a region. The town of Zongolica is called *tzonkolihkan* [place of curly hair][3] in Nahuatl, but this label applies only to that specific community, not to the region. For locals, the region tends to be conceptualized as divided into three major zones, the cold, warm, and the temperate zones, and into specific town centers, each with a network of communities around them. The town centers are the main nuclei of local identity, and they tend to be the municipal seats [*cabeceras de municipio*], and the communities [*comunidades* or *congregaciones*] are considered its satellites. In Nahuatl, each town center is referred to as an *altepetl*. Even today, the *altepetl* constitutes the primary political unit in Nahua society, and the words used to describe regions, *weyi altepetl* [Great Altepetl], and communities, *altepemayotl* [altepetl arms/branches], are derived from that word.

The *altepemeh* (plural of *altepetl*) of the cold zone are Atlahuilco, Tlaquilpa, Astacinga, and Tehuipango, and those of the temperate zone are Reyes, Zongolica, Mixtla, and Texhuacan (Figure 5.1). The *altepetl* of Tequila is the access point to both zones, as it lies where the road leading south from Orizaba forks, leading to the temperate zone to the north, and the cold zone to the south. In the warm zone west of Tequila, the communities of Tenejapa, Tlilapa, Tezonapa, and Rafael Delgado are located. The three zones differ markedly in the richness of their soils and climates, and consequently in the type of agriculture they sustain. In the warm and temperate zones coffee grows well, and from the 19th century until the coffee market crashed in 1997 it was the main crop of the area. Today coffee is still grown, but it is not very lucrative, and many

---

[3] From *tzon-* "hair," *koliwi* "to curl" and *-kan* "place." Karen Dakin has suggested that here the word "hair" could be a reference to a landscape element such as a mountain top, and this is certainly possible. *Tzontli* also means a stub or a trunk of a tree.

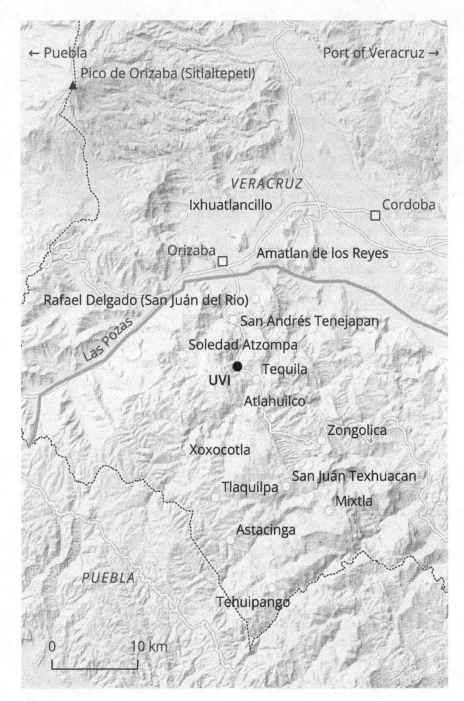

Figure 5.1 Map showing the Zongolica region in central Veracruz state and the major towns and cities in the area.
Map by Joe Roe.

growers produce it on a small scale only for local consumption, and supplement with fruits such as bananas, citrus, avocado, and peaches. In the warm and temperate zone, corn agriculture is often good for those who have relatively flat pieces of land to sow. In the cold zone, growing anything edible at all takes hard work, and the main natural resource is the cloud forest with its abundance of lumber, mushrooms, and game. These ecological and economic conditions of subsistence sustain different ways of life—some slightly more profitable and comfortable than others, but none that can be described as abundant.

In the conception of space that exists within the oral tradition of the Nahuas, the source of abundance is located underground, inside the hills and mountains, out of sight, in the underground realm of *Tlalokan*. Those Nahuas who share this conception consider its abundance accessible only in small portions, through diligent observance of ritual practice, and intensive labor. This is the lifeworld that grounds the narrative of the "Man Who Visited Tlalokan," and which undergirds most of the ritual practice of the Zongolica region, for example the ritual of *xochitlalis* or *xochitlalilistli* [lit. "Placing of Flowers"] in which offerings are made to the earth before opening the land for sowing, requesting permission to receive a share of its abundance (Morales Carbajal and Casas Mendoza 2020).

This view of space grounded in a Mesoamerican Indigenous ontology is challenged by a newer conception, tied to the same modernist tropes that also ground Aguirre Beltrán's "regions of refuge." This modernist view locates all sources of abundance and possibility outside of the region altogether, within the mainstream economic system, accessible by leaving to work in the cities, or crossing north into the United States. The Nahuatl phrase used to describe migrants, *tlen yawi ne wehka* [lit. "those who go there, faraway"], locates the migrants simply in an unspecified space far away, almost outside of the established world system. Luis Alejandro Martínez Canales, a former faculty member at the UVI in Tequila who wrote his doctoral dissertation about the effects of labor migration on the community of Tehuipango, noted how the discourses of migration tended to code the region as being empty of possibilities, making leaving the only feasible choice for those who embrace this view (Martínez Canales 2010).

Indigenous Education as Development in the Zongolica Region

The Zongolica Highlands region traditionally has had few educational options available, and those that it has had were of relatively low quality. Before 1966, all education in the highlands was monolingual in Spanish. In 1966 a group of Nahua schoolteachers from the Huasteca region in the state of Hidalgo arrived and founded the first 26 bilingual primary schools in the area, one in each municipality. By 1982 the number of bilingual schools in the highlands had risen to well over 100: 111 of them preschools and 75 elementary schools, as well as 18 school homes for children who lived too far from the schools. This was achieved largely by the support from the INI, the National Indigenist Institute, and its local *Centro Coordenador Indigenista* (CCI). The surge in schooling in turn led to a surge in bilingualism, and started a process very similar to the one that has led to language shift in many other Nahuatl-speaking areas. Through the CCI, the INI pursued the objective of increasing bilingualism, improving basic infrastructure (roads, schools, health clinics, public transportation), and generating better possibilities for the people of the highlands to produce and market their goods. The CCI sought to achieve this by easing local access to credit and facilitating logistics by improving infrastructure. They also promoted production by teaching skills and encouraging and supporting the establishment of production cooperatives (Hernández Orellan 2011). This was a basic neoliberal plan, based on the premise that by removing the obstacles limiting the free flow of goods and services, the locals would become able to pull themselves out of poverty by their own bootstraps. As in most such projects, development was framed in entirely materialist goals, as the simple increase of income and consumption levels. Education was conceptualized as a means to this end. One result of this policy was a view of the Nahuatl language as an obstacle to be overcome by teaching Nahua youths Spanish earlier and more intensively. This has contributed to a decline in the vitality and intergenerational transmission of the language in many communities in the region (Sandoval Arenas 2017). Indigenist education, in this way, has aimed largely at undermining the feasibility of Nahuatl public spheres.

Severiano Hernández Orellan, whose 2011 master's thesis in anthropology I cited above, wrote precisely under the direction of Gonzalo Aguirre Beltrán, one of the last of the major *indigenista* anthropologists (Nahmad Sitton 2008). Hernández Orellan himself worked at the CCI through the 1980s and 1990s. In his thesis, he summarized the positive achievements of the INI in terms of engendering economic improvement. He also extended a severe critique of the heavy bureaucratic system of the INI, which tended to crush local initiatives and favor the institutionalization of clientelism. He did not mention, however, how the same period saw an increase in outward migration from the highlands, toward Northern Mexico and the United States, nor how local cultural practices and social networks of reciprocity were affected by the INI's focus on individual social mobility. Hernández Orellan's sense of the achievements and problems inherent in *indigenista* education provides a salient example of how the *indigenista* perspective accepted a universalizing narrative of modernity as the only framework for development. It also provides an important contrast to the perspectives inherent in the types of intercultural education and development typically envisioned at the UVI.

Compared to primary education, secondary and post-secondary education has been slower to make it to the highlands. When the UVI opened its campus in Tequila (Figure 5.2), in the temperate zone of the highlands in 2004, it was the first institution to offer a BA-level career in the area. Previously, anyone who wanted to study further after having completed their *bachillerato* (equivalent to high school) had to travel out of the highlands, either to Orizaba or Córdoba where trade schools and small universities are present, or even further away to study at one of the state universities. Now, in addition to the UVI located in Tequila, the private university *Instituto Tecnológico de la Sierra de Zongolica* offers BA degrees in business, engineering, and agriculture. Most recently, after years of planning, in the spring of 2020, the UVI opened the *Maestriah Ipan Totlahtol Iwan Tonemilis* [MA in our language and culture], a monolingual MA program in Nahua language and culture. This program is unique in Mexico (and to my knowledge in Latin America) in offering a full master's degree in which an Indigenous language and culture are not only

Figure 5.2 A classroom at the UVI; the text on the screen shows part of an essay in Nahuatl that the students were collectively writing. The title is ¿*Tlen tlaki itech toaltepeyo?* "What grows in our community?"
Photo by the author.

the topic of study, but also the medium of instruction—that is, an MA degree aimed exclusively at fluent speakers of the language. Through the *Maestriah Ipan Totlahtol Iwan Tonemilis* (Bernal-Lorenzo and Figueroa Saavedra 2019a, 2019b), the UVI and its campus in Tequila are now attracting Nahuatl-speaking students from other states. Having been once described as being far out in the periphery of Mexican education, the Zongolica region is now a center for *Nahua education*.

A Region of Covert Abundance: An Indigenous Conceptualization of the Highlands

Adán collected the same story, the one that tells of the deer hunter's trip to Tlalokan, twice, in two different versions. The Spanish language re-narration in his thesis fused both versions. I was with him when he collected it the second time.

It was *Dia de la Cruz*, Day of the Cross, which is celebrated on the third day of May, and the cold part of the Zongolica Highlands was covered in a dense fog. From the slopes of *Vista Hermosa*, the community in the Municipality of Tlaquilpa where the Sánchez family lives, it was impossible to see the few hundred meters down to the municipal seat. Everything was gray and humid.

Over the winter, I had been staying with the family a week or two every month, going with Adán, his wife Ana, and his brother Malaquías to the intercultural university where Adán and Ana were in the last semester, and where his brother was now working as a faculty member. But now, spring was on its way, and Adán and Malaquías had convinced their father Don Félix to sow corn. Don Félix had been reluctant; it was a lot of work, including a substantial investment in the help of a *yuntero*, a plowman with an ox-plow, and the harvest is notoriously meager in the highlands. It might not be worth it, Don Félix had thought. But his sons had convinced him, and now he was fully determined. "It is always worth it to sow, even if the harvest is little, it means that whatever you can harvest of your own crop, you don't have to buy," he argued. I had asked if I could help sowing, and while they seemed a little amused at the thought of me in the field, they were happy to have me come along. I borrowed Malaquías's rubber boots and walked with them down the rocky slope to the slightly less rocky slope that would become the cornfield.

The Zongolica Highlands have been home to Nahua people for centuries, maybe even a thousand years. The town's church stands on the foundations of a stepped pyramid that is still clearly visible today, and locals say that before the Spanish invasion the people of the Altepemeh here were paying tribute to the Aztecs of Mexico who conquered the Cuauhtochco province in the 14th century. Tlaquilpa, in spite of its name, which probably means "place of fruits," is not a fertile place. It consists of pine-covered rocky hills, with arable land on the slopes and in the steep valleys. With cold temperatures and the year-round rain washing most nutrients out of the soil, growing corn requires much work, and gives little bounty. Corn is not a cash crop, and those who sow it harvest it only for their own consumption. But as Don Félix says, at least that means that one does not have to buy it. The main exploitation of the mountains is forestry for wood and lumber, but all the communal lands of Tlaquilpa have been depleted of forest. Only those who have private lands and exploit them sustainably can maintain this business.

As we arrived in the bottom of the steep valley between the ridge where Don Félix's family lives, and the next ridge over where his neighbor lives, I saw that the *yuntero*, Don Basilio, had already arrived. His oxen, not yet tied before the plow, were grazing on the unprepared land around a small hawthorn tree, which the thick mist made the only visible landscape feature. We all greeted him. While Don Félix stayed to speak with Don Basilio about how they would do the work (depicted in Figure 5.0 opening this chapter), Malaquías, Adán, and I walked around the other side to the small sheds where they used to live before they moved up on the ridge. Here a black tarp covered a small mound. Adán pulled off the tarp and told me to look. "It's organic fertilizer," he said, "we learned how to make this at the UVI." The mound beneath the tarp was gray and dry, and looked like ashes, but looking closer it also contained sheep manure, pine needles, compost, and lime. I grabbed a handful and it was warm, heated by the chemical reactions of fermentation. "Up here you can't grow anything without fertilizer," Adán told me, "but at the UVI we learned that chemical fertilizers deplete the earth quickly, and makes the dry corn less resistant to pests. It's also expensive." We filled the fertilizer into plastic sacks, and carried them down on the slope. This part of the slope, most of it actually, was much too steep for the oxen to plow (Figure 5.3). So instead of sowing into a furrow, Malaquías dug into the earth with his hands and dropped four or five maize kernels, red, white, yellow and blue, and a couple of dried black beans, into the hole (see Figure 5.4). I walked behind him with a bucket full of fertilizer, trying to keep my balance on the steep slope, so as to not roll all the way downhill into the stream on the bottom, and I dropped a handful of fertilizer directly on the seed, covering it with a couple of handfuls of earth. Hole by hole, and kernel by kernel, we worked our way down the slope as the morning hours turned into midday.

Meanwhile, Don Félix and Don Basilio sowed the flat part of the slope, using the ox plow. Later in the afternoon, Doña Cristina, Don Félix's wife,

Figures 5.3 and 5.4 Adán Sánchez Rosales sowing maize on the hillside in Tlaquilpa, in May 2014.
Photo by the author.

Felicitas, their youngest daughter, and Ana, Adán's wife, came down with food for us, and we took a break to eat. I sat next to Don Basilio, but was too tired and shy to make conversation. Don Basilio spoke Nahuatl rapidly, talking about the food, the field, the animals, and I gradually lost my concentration. But Adán in turn took the moment of rest as an opportunity to work on his own ethnography for his BA thesis. Being in the final stages of his thesis writing, he was struggling to find an interpretation of the stories that he had heard of Tlalokan. Tlalokan is the underworld in Zongolica Nahua cosmology, but it isn't an unpleasant, terrifying underworld of the dead, as European tradition tends to depict it, but rather an underworld of fertility and abundance, with water and plants. It is home to all the wild animals, which reside there under the protection of *Tlalokan Tata* and *Tlalokan Nana*, the ruling couple. At the beginning of the agricultural cycle in late March, the people of the highlands used to perform the *xochitlalilistli* ritual. In this ritual, an offering of flowers, corncobs, and candles is placed in a hole in the ground, accompanied by prayers to Tlalokan and its entities, asking them to provide water and to allow the corn to prosper. The ritual is expensive, because it is enjoyed among friends and neighbors with turkey and *mole*, and *pulque*, the fermented juice of the maguey cactus, and because of its costliness, many people in the highlands, including Don Félix, no longer practice it. Adán had sensed that there was a relation between the taboo on deer hunting observed by many communities in the highlands, and the cosmological relation between humans and the earth implicit in the *xochitlalilistli* ritual, but he had not been able to ascertain the nature of this relation. Sitting there by the fire with the *yuntero*, Adán took the chance to ask him, an elder of the community, about the relation between the deer and Tlalokan. Don Basilio told Adán the story that began this chapter, one that Adán had already heard once from his wife's grandfather. But whereas the first version described the role of the deer simply as a ploy to lead the hunter into the cave to meet Tlalokan Tata, in Don Basilio's version the deer is really a guise of Tlalokan Tata himself. This added spin on the tale gave Adán the ideas he needed to finish his analysis, linking native cosmovision to agricultural and ritual practices. In his thesis defense, he argued that knowledge of the native oral tradition and the way that it represents Indigenous cosmovision is crucial in order to be able to engender the kinds of social and economic development that respect Indigenous tradition and practice. Through the study and analysis of Nahua oral tradition, he was able to formulate an account of the highlands and the relation between people and environment, which was different from the "regions of refuge" conceptualization—one that recognizes the highlands as a zone of abundance when the ritually correct method is followed.

Interculturality and the UVI

Adán's ethnographic work among members of his own community, and the way that he tied it to themes of development, can be considered a typical example of what students do at the UVI. As such, it can be taken as a practical example of interculturality at work. Interculturality, besides being a practice, is also an influential set of metacultural discourses that provide an ideological framework for how state institutions can approach cultural diversity in a way that may be more ethically correct than previous approaches.

Interculturality is an educational paradigm that has been developed in Latin America starting in the 1990s. Its development has been tied to a social and political critique of mainstream neoliberal multiculturalism[4] and also to the defense of Indigenous people's rights and interests.[5] In Mexico, interculturality has become increasingly institutionalized as the main paradigm of cultural politics through which the state engages with its minorities. The 1992 Constitution defined Mexico as a multicultural nation, and was followed by the 1994 Zapatista uprisings, which created an even greater sense of urgency for the state to address questions of cultural diversity within the nation with a higher degree of sophistication than previous *indigenista* policies that had by that time become obsolete. In 1997 the branch of education aimed at Indigenous populations changed its name from "Bilingual Bicultural Education" to "Bilingual Intercultural Education." In 2001 the *General Commission for Intercultural and Bilingual Education* (CGEIB) was established, and the promotion of interculturality in the entire educational system became part of its mission. In 2003, The *General law of Linguistic Rights* established the right of all Indigenous peoples to receive public education at all levels in their native languages. And in 2003, as a result of a collaborative effort by the CGEIB and the CDI, the first of eight Mexican intercultural universities opened, offering careers in "intercultural development" to students (Schmelkes 2009).

In 2014, with the *Programa Especial de Educación Intercultural* 2014–2018,[6] the Mexican Ministry of Education (SEP) established interculturality as a paradigm "permeating all levels and modalities of education," emphasizing the need to use the pedagogical principles also in contexts that do not involve Indigenous groups. As pointed out by several researchers, there is not a single dominant conceptualization of what interculturality is, or what educational

---

[4] Povinelli 2001, 2002; Postero 2005, 2007.
[5] Gustafson 2009; Rappaport 2005; Loncón Antileo and Hecht 2011.
[6] The program can be accessed from the ministry of education webpage at http://dof.gob.mx/nota_detalle.php?codigo=5342484&fecha=28/04/2014.

principles it entails. Often actors within the intercultural system describe interculturality in opposition to multiculturalism. Multiculturalism is understood as the simple recognition of the existence of a plurality of cultures within the state. Interculturality, on the other hand, posits that this recognition must result in an intercultural dialogue in which members of the various cultures exchange views and positions, learning from and about each other, and negotiating a shared future on what is ideally supposed to be equal terms. The formulation of interculturality as a process in which cultures and their members interact on equal footing lends itself easily to the critique of naïveté. How, even in theory, can it be possible to bridge a cultural difference, created and sustained largely by colonialism and oppression, through the fiction that intercultural interlocutors are on equal footing? Or we may ask how discourses that posit cultures as stable entities, and encourage the use of forms of strategic essentialism, may pretend to be used to overcome an oppressive system that is exactly based on enforcing (and commercializing) exclusive and essentialist concepts of identity.[7] Others dismiss interculturality as a new guise of neoliberal multiculturalism, or paternalist indigenism, or as a version of other oppressive systems used to capitalize on cultural difference, or to make it otherwise compatible with whichever system of political domination is currently in place.[8]

Interculturality and the intercultural universities have faced these critiques and many others from different actors in Mexican society since their foundation.[9] I am not, however, going to engage these critiques at a discursive level to take a stance of either defending or critiquing "interculturality" as a set of ideologies or institutional practices assumed to have a particular ontology. Instead, I see interculturality as a heterogeneous network of interactions between Indigenous and non-Indigenous actors of different political persuasions, all with different goals and objectives, who operate with different instruments and under different constraints in their attempts to achieve them. Within this network, spaces of possibility may appear;[10] spaces in which Indigenous actors can work to realize and develop their life projects in ways and with degrees of agency that might not have been otherwise possible. The value of interculturality for Indigenous people must lie not at the level of its

---

[7] Hernández Reyna 2013; Arías Sandí and Reyna 2010; Hernández Reyna and Cocom 2021.
[8] Ávila Romero and Ávila Romero 2014; Rebolledo 2021.
[9] See, e.g., Dietz 2009; Dietz and Mateos Cortés 2011; Sartorello 2009; Arías Sandí and Reyna 2010; Lehmann 2013.
[10] Nygaard Folkmann (2011) has written about "spaces of possibility" in design, and Harvey (2000) has written about spaces of hope—the way I write about the existential affordances of different conceptualizations of space draws in part on their thoughts.

abstract ideology or the discourses that reproduce it, but in the concrete and practical effects that it has on their lives and communities. In this, it seems that the Indigenous critics of interculturality and intercultural education largely agree. P'urhépecha scholar Martha Dimas Huacuz critiques the way the intercultural university of Michoacán was underfunded from the outset, and lacked the basic resources to be meaningfully called "a university" (Dimas Huacuz 2006b, 2006a). She points to the fact that the decolonizing ideology of the institution rings hollow when it remains tightly controlled by the state, without any practical autonomy for the Indigenous groups it claims to serve. Yucatec Maya scholar Genner Llanes Ortíz considers interculturality to be a priori impossible in contemporary Mexico because of the unequal ground of power on which the intercultural meeting would have to take place. For example, he considers the close alliance between interculturality and modernist ideas of "development" to be highly problematic. Nevertheless, he also notes the importance of looking at the negotiation of interculturality as it happens on the ground in the institutional setting. He argues that such a perspective will motivate scholars to broaden the way they conceptualize "knowledge" within the intercultural framework to also include lived and embodied forms of knowledge (Llanes Ortiz 2008, 2010). These effects emerge within a nexus of institutional constraints and possibilities, and through the choices and practices of specific actors and collectives.

The program that created the Mexican intercultural universities was established during the presidency of Vicente Fox, and the movement toward creating the universities was spearheaded by sociologist Sylvia Schmelkes, who was the head of the CGEIB, and Xochitl Gálvez, who was the director of the CDI. The universities themselves were not founded by the federal government, but rather by the state governments, and the rectors in most cases were personally appointed by the state governors. The exception to this rule was the UVI, which was founded in 2004 within the politically autonomous Universidad Veracruzana, as a semi-independent branch within the university structure. In addition to the campus in Tequila, where I did my fieldwork, the UVI has campuses in three other "intercultural zones" in the state of Veracruz, and its central headquarters in the state capital of Xalapa, location of its mother institution, the Universidad Veracruzana. The "intercultural zones" are the four main zones of Indigenous presence in the state. Apart from the Zongolica Highlands with its large concentration of Nahua people, there is the *Huasteca* region with the presence of Nahua, Otomi, Totonac, and Tepehua people; the *Totonacapan* region with a concentration of Totonac people; and the *Selvas* region in the southern part of the state with the presence of Nahuas, and speakers of different Mixe-Zoquean languages.

Each campus is located in rural municipalities with a high concentration of Indigenous people, clearly in an effort to draw their students from among the Indigenous groups, although being public institutions they cannot limit their admissions along ethnic lines.

There is no single conceptualization of interculturality within the UVI, although some elements of interculturality are institutionalized into the curriculum. The curriculum, for example, institutionalizes the idea of intercultural dialogue as a "dialogue of knowledges." This means that a diversity of perspectives and practices is seen as an asset that is multiplied through sharing. In this way, interculturality differs from previous approaches to Indigenous education in acknowledging that Indigenous groups have knowledge, and in recognizing Indigenous knowledges as valuable and potentially equal to non-Indigenous ways of knowing. Practically, this epistemological pluralism is embedded in the organizational structure of the UVI, in which the leadership of each local campus is supposed to work in collaboration with a committee of community members and cultural authorities from Indigenous communities, to make sure that local knowledges are represented in the curriculum. Furthermore, among the core classes taught to all incoming students are topics such as *cosmovisions* (note the plural) and "local language" (note the singular)—meant to introduce the students specifically to epistemological, cosmological, and linguistic pluralism, and to specific local knowledges. All core classes use anthropological theory and method to mediate between pluralities of perspectives and meanings. Günther Dietz, an anthropologist who became interim director of the UVI in 2013, built on the theories of Nestor Garcia Canclini in his ethnographic work on the institution. He describes in ethnography how a possible achievement of the UVI could be the creation of a new kind of "hybrid subjectivity," the ability to move fluidly between modernist and traditionalist, Indigenous and Western, conceptualizations of the world (Dietz and Mateos Cortés 2011; Dietz 2012).

Nonetheless, while basic tenets of appreciation of diversity and cultural dialogue are respected by all within the intercultural system, among the faculty, different approaches to interculturality exist and are constantly debated. Some are, like the *indigenistas* of the previous phase of Indigenous education in the region, focused on creating students who will fit into the existing labor market and who will be able to produce economic development in their communities in terms of market access. A main discussion among proponents of interculturality pits a model based on liberal democratic rational dialogue within a power-free public sphere against a more radical vision that sees interculturality as a way of empowering Indigenous groups to form their own political community, in opposition or defiance to the neoliberal nation-state and against other hegemonic groups. Part of this dialogue also turns around the concept of modernity, and how discourses and ideologies of modernity can or cannot be reconciled with Indigenous perspectives on social change. It is not uncommon to overhear faculty members in the hallways discussing how best to understand the relations between interculturality and democracy, or how best to empower the communities. Education scholar Sartorello (2009) sees the diversity of understandings of interculturality, and the conflicts they sometimes cause, as a challenge to be overcome through consensus building. I would argue in turn that this plurality is both natural and necessary for the ongoing reflexive development of the intercultural model of education.

A clear goal of intercultural education as practiced by the UVI is to provide an educational space in which Indigenous values, perspectives, and practices are both welcome and specifically accommodated. This is in itself a new thing in Mexican Indigenous education, which has traditionally been constructed as a space of acculturation (or perhaps better put, "deculturation"), where heterogeneity could be replaced (or perhaps only reframed within) a common national culture. Through their focus on participating in processes of development and organization of Indigenous communities, the intercultural universities bring intercultural ideology, with its skepticism of universalizing narratives, into the field of "development," which has traditionally been dominated by absolutist modernizing discourses. This means that the ambitions of the UVI are not only to create a new kind of subject within the institution, but also to be a catalyst of social change outside it. This ambition of being a platform for social change, but without necessarily having a prepackaged idea of what kind of change this has to be, is what gives the UVI the potential to become a "space of possibilities."

Indigenous Languages in Intercultural Education

The role of Indigenous languages in intercultural education in general, and at the UVI in particular, is constantly being negotiated. Some educators see it as an optional part of the curriculum, one of many ways of engaging with interculturality. Others consider it a necessary element for achieving interculturality that Indigenous languages should first be institutionalized as equal to Spanish, and given the same importance and validity in the educational system. The way in which the Nahuatl language was used at the UVI changed substantially over the course of the year I visited there. When I arrived at the UVI, and told people about my project, I explained it as being an investigation of how the Nahuatl language was used in the intercultural context of the UVI. When I asked about the language situation at the UVI, the first response I received from a faculty member was, "The students speak Spanish here. It's only really in the communities of Tehuipango and Mixtla that there is a lot of Nahuatl, in the other communities everyone is already bilingual so there is no language problem there." This kind of discourse, framing the use of Nahuatl as a problem, and taking bilingualism and the consequent use of Spanish as the main language of communication as the solution, was not what I had expected to find at the UVI. Among the most common responses to my queries about the relative absence of Nahuatl on campus were comments such as, "most of the students speak the language, but not on campus," "they're embarrassed," "we hardly ever hear Nahuatl here." Mostly, the faculty members ascribed the students' reluctance to speak Nahuatl to embarrassment over their Indigenous roots. One faculty member, Adán's brother Malaquías, himself a native speaker and alumnus of the campus, noted that many students are there because they want to be *licenciados* (college graduates), and that they have the ideology that "*licenciados* don't speak Nahuatl." Malaquías was clearly opposed to this way of thinking. He argued that the UVI was not a place to study if you want to be the kind of *licenciado* who wears a tie and sits behind a desk. At the UVI, he argued, the purpose is to be at work in the communities, and the communities speak Nahuatl. My own interviews with students pointed to another possible explanation for the Nahuatl-speaking students' reluctance to speak the language on campus: all of them were highly proficient Spanish speakers who had spoken Spanish since they were children, and who had succeeded in the educational system exactly because of their ability to speak Spanish well. Speaking Nahuatl in an educational context had simply not been part of their *habitus* since elementary school (for those who had attended bilingual elementary schools).

In terms of the curriculum, when I was there in 2014, Nahuatl was only taught for a single semester during the first year's "core classes" taken by all first-year students under the title of "local language" (*lengua local*); another semester was dedicated to "national languages" (*lenguas nacionales*)—a general introduction to the linguistic diversity of Mexico. In comparison, two semesters are dedicated to learning English, which everyone I spoke to agreed is an important language to be able to use in a university setting. Apart from that, language is used as an optional "node" (*nódulo*) in the curriculum, meant to allow students on the language track to specialize in language on their own or in small groups with the support of faculty.

In the spring semester of 2014, things changed. A new school counselor was hired, Carlos Octavio Sandoval—who is a native speaker of Spanish, but fluent in English, Nahuatl, and Portuguese—having lived and studied in Canada. He had acquired Nahuatl as a second language, studying on his own. He speaks it fluently, and he insisted on speaking it in as many different contexts as possible. He brought a new way of thinking about language with him, as well as a new approach to interculturality. It seemed to me as if, by their combined energies, Rafael Nava and Carlos Sandoval infused a completely new approach to the role of language in interculturality. Both Carlos and Dr. Nava would converse with students in Nahuatl in the halls, occasionally use the language in the classroom as a medium of instruction, and also speak to each other in the language. Several times, Carlos caught me off guard, addressing me in Nahuatl in front of students—forcing me to do my best to respond in the same way—but talking about topics that I had never spoken about in Nahuatl before, such as making plans for class, talking about the theoretical points about Nahuatl, or interculturality, and so on. I also began hearing students speaking Nahuatl in the classrooms and among themselves out of class.

Dr. Nava had participated in the development of the UVI from its early days; coming from a background as an Indigenous education teacher, he had taught at the campus in La Huasteca, his native region, before coming to the Tequila campus. We talked about the way that Nahuatl was integrated into the curriculum. He told me that originally it had been the idea that the Indigenous language should be implemented not as a single subject, but as a "transversal axis," throughout the four years of study. For practical and bureaucratical reasons this was not the way it worked out. Indigenous language was confined to a single semester course of *lengua local*. At the Tequila campus, where the only local language was Nahuatl, this was less of a problem than at other campuses. The La Huasteca campus in northern Veracruz and the Selvas campus in the south are both located in regions with significant linguistic diversity, and at any given time the campuses had students speaking not only several highly distinct varieties of Nahuatl, but also Totonac, Tepehua, Otomí, Popoluca, and Zoque. At the other campuses, a given cohort entering first year would only be exposed to one of the local languages, and the decision about which that would be was not based on composition of speakers of different languages among the students, but on practical criteria, such as the availability of an instructor. At both campuses, and of course in Tequila, this generally meant that the language taught was most likely to be Nahuatl—for all students, regardless of linguistic background. Both Dr. Nava and Carlos Sandoval, as well as the director of the UVI Günther Dietz, found the way that Indigenous languages were officially included in the curriculum to be unsatisfactory, and were actively working to find better solutions to the practical problems. According to Dr. Dietz, the obvious goal for the Tequila campus was that Nahuatl should be the default language, which he considered a feasible plan given the relative linguistic homogeneity of the zone. Recognizing that the presence of Nahuatl in the system relied largely on the presence of faculty members who would actively use it, Dietz had been instrumental in placing all of the Nahuatl-speaking faculty members at the UVI as a strategy of linguistic normalization based on the language-planning strategy used in Catalonia.[11]

The culmination of the changes in the use of language at the Tequila campus occurred in the fall of 2014, when Dr. Nava and Carlos Sandoval organized the research colloquium to be held entirely in Nahuatl. The colloquium is a forum in which first-year students present the results of their field research projects for each other, using PowerPoint presentations and other forms of audiovisual tools. Usually colloquia were held in Spanish, the language of the majority of the faculty members who supervised the field projects, but for this colloquium it was organized that all students would present their research in Nahuatl. The purpose was to demonstrate the equality of Nahuatl as a medium of academic dialogue, and to incite students to speak Nahuatl on campus. The controversial aspect of the decision was that even monolingual Spanish students, who made up about 10% of the cohort, would be required to present in Nahuatl, and that only the Nahuatl-speaking faculty members, Carlos, Dr. Nava, and Malaquías Sánchez, would be able to give feedback on the presentations.

In the colloquium, about 10 four-person groups presented their research results with projects such as "promotion of domestic gardens as a way to food security," "violence and gender at the Indigenous school-home in Los Reyes," and so on. The students presented their results with little difficulty, considering that they probably were neither used to using Nahuatl when speaking about such topics, nor when speaking in public. Remarkably, several of the non-native-speaking students had managed to translate and memorize their parts of the presentation entirely in Nahuatl, some with considerable enthusiasm.

The presentations received constructive criticism from the three Nahuatl-speaking faculty members, regarding both form and content. The inconsistency of Nahuatl orthography in the PowerPoint slides was a general critique. This critique reflected both the students' lack of experience in using Nahuatl as a medium of written communication, as well as the teacher's goal of holding Nahuatl to similar standards of rigor as Spanish would have been—thereby cementing its legitimacy as a language of academic communication. The Nahuatl monolingual colloquium was the first major initiative by the new language teachers, and the first major step at the campus to actively promote the use of Nahuatl there. But it was not the only one: Dr. Nava and

---

[11] Aspects of this normalization strategy at the UVI are described by Figueroa Saavedra, Bernal Lorenzo, and Hernández (2013); Figueroa Saavedra and Hernández Martínez (2014); Figueroa Saavedra (2021).

Carlos Sandoval also organized to begin the publication of a bimonthly bilingual magazine *Toyolxayak* [The face of our hearts] with content written by the students. The same semester, Carlos Octavio Sandoval and Malaquías Sánchez started offering a Nahuatl course for monolingual faculty members, which four of the Spanish-speaking faculty started attending regularly. The semester after I left, Sandoval organized a series of "poetic action" events, in which groups of UVI students painted Nahuatl language poetry on publicly visible walls in the city of Orizaba, in order to draw visibility to the presence of the language (See Figure 7.0).

The novelty of the approach offered by Dr. Nava, Carlos Octavio Sandoval, and Malaquías Sánchez was to change the perspective on the Nahuatl language from being something that was primarily the interest and concern of the students who spoke it, to being something that was of concern to the entire university—including monolingual Spanish-speaking students and faculty members. In the period leading up to the colloquium, student groups would be working on their presentations, discussing among themselves how best to express a specific concept in Nahuatl, or how best to spell it. The native-speaking students would help the learners by translating for them and coaching them in pronunciation. In the language courses, Malaquías Sánchez, himself recently graduated from the UVI, was coaching other faculty members who were used to teaching communication or winning prizes for their mastery of the literary Spanish language. In a short semester, the linguistic order had been turned upside down, and Nahuatl became a valid form of linguistic currency at the campus in a way that it had not been before. This development toward increased integration of Nahuatl in the UVI at the Tequila campus eventually culminated in the foundation of the *Maestriah Ipan Totlahtol Iwan Tonemilis*, described below.

A significant element of this experience at the UVI is how the cultural change in this institutional setting was dependent on a very small shift in the composition of the faculty. Only a couple of faculty members with new attitudes and the desire to change the status quo were able to do so, without experiencing significant opposition or nonconformity from their colleagues and students. I wonder if this would have been possible if there had not already been a strong discourse of interculturality in place to support precisely this kind of initiative. The fact that the discourse of interculturality was universally adopted as the regulator of values and practices at the UVI meant that the innovators were not working against the established cultural norms when they were trying to implement change. In fact, it would have been difficult for anyone who had wished to challenge their projects to do so, because of the way they were solidly grounded in the shared discourse of interculturality.

Similarly, because of the discourse of interculturality, when teachers were now offered the chance to study Nahuatl outside of class time, the weight was on them to explain why they were not interested or able to participate, inverting the question from "Why should I study Nahuatl?" to "Why wouldn't I study Nahuatl?" In this way, the discourse of interculturality does not in itself create social change, nor does it force anyone to act differently from what they usually would, but it establishes a space of possibility where creating new approaches to teaching and learning, and to the relations and hierarchies of the everyday, can be challenged and experimented with.

A Space of Possibilities: What Grows at the UVI

Given that the UVI is founded and funded by the Mexican state and that most of its faculty are urban non-Indigenous intellectuals, the university may seem an unlikely place for any new developments in Indigenous ethnic politics to emerge. Nevertheless, it is also in some ways a novel and marginal institutional space that is not fully within the mainstream, and one that leaves room for agency for a variety of different actors, from administrators and teachers to students and community members, and for shaping new practices through interaction. In spite of the structural limitations under which it operates, the UVI provides students and families with spaces of possibility for envisioning approaches of development that fit their individual and communal necessities, and provides room for individual and collective agency. Nevertheless, it is not completely clear what impact, if any, an intercultural institution such as the UVI may have on the development of Indigenous ethnic politics.

When the UVI is seen as a space of possibilities, one that is not circumscribed by, or reducible to, the theories and ideologies through which it has been created, it should be evaluated by the ideas and initiatives that are allowed to grow and give fruit within its garden. Perhaps some of the things that come out of the UVI educational space can contribute to the development of new Nahuatl language publics, or to strengthening the existing ones. The rest of this section gives examples of concrete activities at the UVI that seem to have such potential effects.

Community-Grounded Research

The research projects of UVI students urge them to take their local communities to be the sphere of political action. This means that the local community is represented both as the sphere at which authority and authoritative discourse are produced, and also at which they are challenged.

Adán Sanchez did this in his thesis project, when he sought out local elders as cultural specialists whose knowledge he could synthesize into a collective perspective on agricultural rituals and their meaning in the community of Tlaquilpa. Furthermore, in his case, the narrative that he collected, and with which I began this chapter, had as its main theme the negotiation of cultural authority between an Indigenous ontology and an outside, national one. Don Basilio's narrative of the hunter's meeting with Tlalokan Tata explicitly reproduces a vision of Indigenous reality as ontologically and politically distinct from and superior to the outside ontology represented by the greedy and lascivious wife and her saintly lover, and it explains a series of cultural practices as a form of obeisance to this reality. In this way, in recollecting the story, Adán was in fact also recollecting a local perspective on intercultural relations between Nahuas and outsiders. The perspective he found was one that clearly posits the existence of a separate Nahua political sphere, in opposition and contrast to the mainstream one. By being able to recirculate it as a thesis, with the stamp of authority from the two local narrators who recounted it and from the UVI, this perspective came to be legitimized as an authentic "Nahua" way of understanding Nahua political existence.

Another example is the project of Maribel Salas Tentzohua, another student at the UVI, also from the community of Tlaquilpa, whose thesis project addressed the problem of deforestation affecting her community. The communal forest (*monte comunal*) of the community of Tlaquilpa had been depleted through over-exploitation in the early 1980s when the municipality abandoned the previous policy of requiring a permit to cut down any tree in the communal forest. This happened when community members suspected the municipal president of being about to sell the communal lands to outsiders (perhaps a well-founded suspicion, since this kind of occurrence is commonplace and privatization of communal lands has been a long-term strategy of the Mexican state). The people decided to expel the potential buyer and take over the management of the woods under an every-man-for-himself principle. This led to the rapid depletion of the forest, and presently only some privately owned terrains in Tlaquilpa are being sustainably managed. The continued depletion of the large communal forest means that young trees are cut down as soon as they can be exploited, before reaching their maximally profitable stage. The lack of old trees leads to erosion of the soil, and to a general decrease in biodiversity in the area, threatening for example the many local species of orchids. As her thesis project, the UVI student decided to work to reverse this development by speaking with local authorities and the many stakeholders who exploit the communal forest, in an attempt to convince them to go back to earlier ways of managing the forest sustainably by enforcing quotas and by participating in a reforestation project. In this part of the project she came up with more resistance than she had imagined; no one in her community was willing to commit to a moratorium on exploitation, or to support the introduction of a new set of regulations. And what surprised and aggravated her more, was that many cited as the reason for their unwillingness the fact that she was "just a young girl," assuming that if the project had a woman as its primus motor, it would not have sufficient clout to enforce any regulations. This made her decide to defy what seemed to be the public opinion and instead collaborate directly with several local elders, whom she convinced to participate in establishing a reforestation plan. The plan involved creating a tree nursery in the middle of the communal forest, six miles off the main road and only accessible by walking. With trees from this nursery, areas of the communal forest would be slowly reforested while she worked to gain the confidence and respect of the locals and formed alliances with more local authorities.

In these and many other projects at the UVI, the sphere of action is the local *altepetl* community, but rather than simply accepting and working within the existing communal structures, the projects also challenge established authorities and the communal status quo. The research projects that UVI students undertake participate actively in dialogues about how to move their local communities forward, both discovering local ways of understanding development, and proposing new ideas about which direction "forward" is.

Intercambio de Semillas

An annual event at the UVI was the organization of an *intercambio de semillas* [seed exchange], a one-day festival in which local farmers from the entire region meet and exchange their corn for sowing. Mexico is home to a surprising variety of native corn, even though native cultivars are quickly being outcompeted by commercial ones, many of which are hybrid and render the farmer dependent on buying new seed each year. The idea behind the seed exchange is to raise awareness of the value of protecting local cultivars among farmers, and to allow farmers to experiment with trying out new varieties that have not previously been cultivated in a given locality and microclimate. In 2014, the exchange was in Tlaquilpa, and at least 50 farmers from the different climate zones of the Zongolica region attended. Each of them brought 5–10 of their finest dried corncobs—from the long, straight, and even-grained white cobs of Rafael Delgado, to the short, large-grained blue and red cobs of the cold highlands. Everyone could take home seeds from the other varieties to try to plant them in their home soil. The majority of the dialogue and speeches were in Nahuatl, as well as some of the written materials handed out at the event.

La Escuelita "*Nikan Tipowih*"

Having graduated from the UVI with a thesis about Nahuatl language revitalization written entirely in Nahuatl, Gabriela Citlahua Zepahua of Tequila founded a community school in her own home: the "*Escuelita: Nikan Tipowih*" [Little School: We Belong Here]. Here, she gives children in her neighborhood, many of whom were otherwise alone most of the afternoon after ordinary school, the chance to come, get help with homework, play, and carry out creative activities (Uribe 2021). In her work with the children, Gabriela Citlahua integrates her intercultural educational philosophy, with particular focus on the value of community and cultural roots and heritage. Some of the children are Nahuatl speakers, others have not acquired the language, and she provides a space for children where, unlike in ordinary school, the two languages can exist on an equal footing, and each be considered valid educational languages. It seems likely that the experience of the *Escuelita* will leave a significant positive imprint in the lives of the children who attend regularly—and consequently also for the community as they grow up. The school also hosts cultural events, such as talks by visiting Indigenous intellectuals whom Gabriela Citlahua knows through her extended network (for example, Me'phaa poet laureate Humberto Matiuwáa gave a talk there in the spring of 2020). *Nikan Tipowih* is not part of the UVI, but it draws on its founder's experiences with intercultural education and the authority and legitimacy as a teacher inherent in her UVI degree. The activities of the UVI and its students are embedded in the local publics of the Zongolica region and grounded in its territory. But another way in which the UVI contributes to the development of local publics is through the participation in the formation of a vibrant intellectual community.

Indigenous Theorization

Part of strengthening the ability of a local public to encompass a wider range of social functions is to create vocabulary and concepts that can be used to fulfill the various social and cultural domains from which Nahuatl has traditionally been excluded. Rather than simply translating preexisting concepts into Nahuatl, the UVI invites students to develop such concepts *desde la cosmovision* or *desde la cultura* [from the worldview, or from the culture]. Students and teachers at the UVI participate actively in producing social and educational theory that draws on Indigenous worldviews and conceptualizations.

In his thesis, though written in Spanish, Adán Sánchez created the concepts that he used to analyze local ritual practice using Nahua words and concepts. Given that the focus of the investigation was the ritual cycle of the community of Tlaquilpa, Adán needed a theoretical framework within which he could approach the issue of cultural difference, and he dedicates a section to this question. He starts out by criticizing the folkloric concept of culture that is often used in Mexican discourses of "culture" to describe what makes Indigenous groups "different" and "unique"—the production of certain crafts, the Indigenous language, the use of *traje típico* [folk dress], and so on. He argues that there is need of a broader concept of culture that encompasses everyday life, forms of experience, work, and social relations. This critique of simplistic and essentialist concepts of culture is a staple theoretical point at the UVI. Rather than stopping at the critique, Adán makes a different turn, arguing that the problem is best avoided by using a native concept. He posits two Nahuatl terms that he proposes as native conceptualizations of "culture": *masewalixtlamachílistli* and *masewaltlatekpankayotl* (Sánchez Rosales 2014, 28). The first concept is based on the verb root *mati* "to know," from which the concept *tlamachilistli* "knowledge" is formed. To this word the prefix *īx-* is then aggregated, which is a body part prefix referring to the eyes and face. It creates the word *ixtlamachilistli*, which refers more specifically to knowledge derived through experience or study. By prefixing the noun stem *masewal-* "Indigenous," the word is restricted to mean a knowledge type which is derived from the type of experience shared by Indigenous Nahua people. The root *masewal-* is the base of the word *masēwalli* which originally referred to the commoner class in pre-conquest Nahua feudal society, but in today's usage commonly refers to all Indigenous people, prototypically Nahuas; the Nahuatl language is often referred to as *masewaltlahtol* "the language of the *masewales*." *Masewalixtlamachilistli* in Adán's usage then refers specifically to what anthropologists would call "Indigenous knowledge" of the Nahua of Zongolica. The other concept, *masewaltlatekpankayotl*, is based on the verb *tlatekpana*, which means "to put things on top of each other," "to put things in a row," or "to put things in order." The abstract noun derived from this verb *tlatekpankayotl*, then, has a meaning of "orderedness," "layered structure," or "sequence." Adán explains that by this concept he means to refer to the layered nature of practices shaped over time by repetition, and to the social order that emerges organically from this process. Again, by prefixing *masewal-* he restricts the concept to the orderedness produced by or characteristic of Indigenous forms of life. The concept strikes me as particularly potent because it encapsulates both the historical–genealogical aspect of culture, which is necessary to be able to talk about cultures as distinct units, and the structure, characteristic of the synchronic holistic culture concept. With this word, Adán becomes able to write about the culture of his community with a high degree of theoretical sophistication, yet in a way that is immediately intelligible to other community members.

Monolingual Nahuatl-Language MA Program

The *Maestriah Ipan Totlahtol Iwan Tonemilis* accepted its first generation of students in the spring semester of 2020. The process of creating the program and its curriculum had taken almost four years. The program is the first and until now the only one in Mexico to offer an MA-level education using an Indigenous language as the medium of instruction, and with the specific aim of producing MA-level professionals who can produce new academic knowledge in and through the language (Bernal-Lorenzo and Figueroa Saavedra 2019a).

I had followed the development of the program as an external consultant in the process of curriculum building, and I had the chance of giving a guest lecture in the class on Nahuatl grammar in the opening semester. Given the fact that there is no educational literature in Nahuatl, or even an established vocabulary for discussing most academic topics, a crucial part of the plan of the MA program was that as part of the curriculum, students themselves should participate in elaborating Nahuatl language teaching materials that can be used and expanded on by subsequent cohorts. Most of the students accepted into the program's first cohort were already educated as teachers within the bilingual or ordinary educational system. They had opted to participate in the MA program as a way to strengthen their professional profiles, and especially concerning the use of the language in the educational settings they were already working in.

Activism and Counter-Publics at the UVI

In her work on Mazatec ethnic revival which, similarly to what happens at the UVI, takes place through the establishment of local fora of discussion of communal issues, Faudree (2013) points out a key problem for minority activism in contemporary national democracies: namely, that expression may be free, and everyone is allowed to pose demands on authorities, but there is no guarantee that anyone will listen. This problem, of course, applies equally to the UVI case. Who listens to the cultural and social critiques advanced within the bubble of intercultural education?

But perhaps this problem can be sidestepped if we move beyond the conception of Indigenous communities and their local matters as merely private spheres of local "special interest" located within the scope of the Mexican national public sphere, as the Mexican state has tended to do. If the UVI is creating a counter-public that interfaces between different Indigenous publics, the critique may resonate beyond the local town-community, even if it does not reach the national public sphere. Nevertheless, UVI students also engage in different kinds of activism in the national public, suggesting that they can also take on the role of representatives of their communities' interests in the national public.

On February 27, 2016, the students of the UVI organized a protest in the center of Orizaba, against the state governor's open hostility to the University, which he stated would not be receiving any of the federal funds that the federal government had destined for it. For the past two years, students and faculty had suffered under an extreme lack of resources, and the contempt with which the governor now stated plainly that the university was among his lowest priorities brought the students' anger to a boiling point. After a march through the streets with signs and posters, they congregated on the main plaza of Orizaba. Gabriela Citlahua, then a second-year student, took the microphone, speaking in a powerful voice:

Kwaltis titlapowaskeh ika tlahtol tlen tehwan tiknekiskeh, ihkon yitos nawatl ihkon yitos español! [Deep breath]. Todos podemos hablar el idioma que querramos, y todos nos podemos entender . . . la lengua no puede ser una frontera . . . ¡*Axkan xikakikan*! [Interruption by applause and cheers from the crowd]. ¡*Axkan xikakikan*! . . . *Nikan tikateh tefan, ya miyak otechkixtilihkeh ik ich toaltepewan.* ¡*Tomin*! ¡*Tlalli*! ¡*Atl*! *Miyak otechkixtilihkeh.* ¿*Axkan tlen oksiki tehckixtiliskeh*? ¿*tokaltlamachtiloyahwan*? ¿*timokahkawaskeh*? ¡*Ahmo*! ¡*Ahmo timokahkawaskeh*! *ahmo*! [Interruption by cheers from the crowd] A los pueblos indígenas nos han quitado tierra, agua, territorio. Ahora nos quieren quitar también la educación, ¡no lo vamos a permitir! ¡La educacion pública es para todos! [The crowd begins to chant]: UV, SOMOS UV! UV, SOMOS UV! UV, SOMOS UV!

[*We can speak whichever language we want, whether it is Nahuatl or whether it is Spanish!* [Deep breath]. *We can all speak the language we want to, and we can all* understand. The language cannot be a barrier. ¡Now listen! [Interruption by applause and cheers]. ¡Now listen! ... *Here we are, they have already taken much away from our communities.* ¡Money! ¡Land! ¡Water! Much they have taken away from us. ¿Now what else are they going to take away from us? ¿Our schools? ¿Will we allow that? ¡No! ¡Will we allow that! No! [interruption by cheers from the crowd] They have taken land, water, and territory away from us, the Indigenous communities, now they want to take away our education, ¡we will not allow that! ¡Public education is for everyone! [Crowd begins to chant]: ¡UV, WE ARE UV! ¡UV, WE ARE UV! ¡UV, WE ARE UV!] [Transcription conventions used here: Italics = *Nahuatl*, plain = Spanish, ¡exclamation!, ¡YELLING!, ¿question intonation?]

Gabriela's speech was video recorded by the local newspaper *El Mundo de Orizaba*, which posted it to their Facebook page.[12] The next day it went viral, as more than 250 people shared it, and thousands "liked" it. A Nahua counterpublic had formed at the UVI, and had struck back at the mainstream public, now claiming a space in the heart of the conservative city of Orizaba—and online. In response to the attention, Gabriela posted from her Facebook profile:

Onechpakti tlen otikchihkeh yalla pampa omokak totlahtoltzin iwan axan kimatteh ke masewalmeh noihkeh timomachtiah iwan amo san timomasewaltlakentiah ihkuak tikxochikoskatiskeh se tekiwah. ¡Ma titlayikanpankisakah!" [It made me happy what we did yesterday, because our language was heard, and now they know that we *masewales* [Indians] also study, and that we do not just dress up in our traditional clothes to adorn some politician with flowers. ¡Let's come out ahead!]

The way Gabriela Citlahua puts her message first in Nahuatl, then in Spanish, effectively shows how she is addressing two audiences at once. Speaking in Spanish, she addresses the political officials of the state, who may see the protests as simply another annoying conglomeration of ordinary people trying to impede them in their work. They are highly unlikely to listen to such demands. But at the same time, by speaking in Nahuatl she also addresses her own community, the one that is the deictic center of her entire discourse. The "we" in her discourse represents simultaneously the Nahuatl-speaking communities that have been subjected to the appropriation of resources by the state and the nation, but also the student body of the UVI. Her statement construes the UVI as one of the basic resources of the Nahuatl-speaking communities of

---

[12] The video can be watched at: https://www.facebook.com/ElMundodeOrizaba/videos/1272917156068560/.

the Zongolica region—a public good that belongs to them, rather than to the state. The fact that she was acting on behalf of the Nahuatl-speaking public is evidenced by the fact that her subsequent Facebook message was entirely in Nahuatl: the "we" is not simply the students participating in the protest, but the entire community of Nahuatl speakers. She underlines the importance of the language as a unifying medium when she says that what made her happy was that "our language was heard." Here she even uses the honorific form of the noun "language" *totlahtoltzin*, emphasizing the Nahuatl language as a cherished possession of the Nahua community, adding its own enunciative force to the message. The message also explicitly counterposes the Nahua *masewales* against the "politicians" of the national public, maintaining that Indigenous people are not simply picturesque adornments as they dress up in *traje típico* as extras in public events honoring outside political officials; they have their own agendas, which also may run counter to those of the mainstream public.

When UVI students take roles representing their communities of origin, their communities are listening, commenting, and sharing the videos online. Seeing a strong young Nahua woman speaking truth to power, and using their own language to address the state and place demands, is bound to have an effect on their own confidence to do so as well. Even if the demands are unlikely to be heard or accepted, it is likely to have the effect of strengthening the Nahuatl-speaking public's recognition of itself as a community that has both the right and the ability to voice demands to the state.

Michael Warner (2002) has argued that the Achilles heel of the counter-public is its tendency to take on the form of a social movement and enter into relations with the state as a movement within the mainstream public sphere. In doing so, it is forced to adapt to the discursive regimes of that political scale, which jeopardizes its ability to remain a true counter-public with its own distinct idiom. Though perhaps not able to field claims on authorities at the national level, they are able to critique and challenge authorities within their own public with a real chance of being heard, and with a chance of being able to develop alternative perspectives on the public good. Nancy Fraser's (1990) rethinking of Habermas's public sphere concept introduced the possibility of envisioning subaltern counter-publics that operate at different political and semiotic scales from the national public sphere. The bourgeois public sphere emerged through collective discussions about the common good at the microscale of the city or town, before becoming the vehicle for the emergence of the national community. In the same way, we should not expect the members of an Indigenous counter-public to field claims or critiques against authorities at the national scale, but rather at the scale at which the counter-public sphere operates. In the case of Zongolica, these are the regional, municipal, and community levels.

Knowledge, Self-Knowledge, and Territory

The tendency to see the highlands as completely devoid of possibilities is common, both among its inhabitants and outsiders—partly because in one sense it is true: there are very few of the type of features commonly understood as possibilities; few options for subsistence, few options for education and paid work, few options for engaging in creative, recreational, or political activities. The important difference between the view grounded in the Indigenous lifeworld and the modernist view is not just how it conceptualizes the highlands as different kinds of space, but also that it motivates two different subjective stances in relation to the region, its population, and its future. By discursively privileging the traditionalist view that they call "Indigenous cosmovision," without essentializing this but leaving it open to interpretation, negotiation, and creation, the UVI does cultivate and support a subjective stance in its students that motivates them to engage in a different kind of relation with the territory and its communities. Through the interactions, activities, discourses, and social engagements between the UVI, its students, and the local communities in the sierra, new perspectives and possibilities are created, that may enable the UVI, and perhaps by extension also the wider Nahuatl-speaking public of the sierra, to imagine their landscape *otherwise*. This makes Nahuatl language revitalization, in this case its integration into higher education, a truly political practice, that has the potential to function as a concrete form of decolonization through self-recognition in the sense of Coulthard (2014), and to reshape conceptions of Nahua political communities.

Moreover, one of the possibilities enabled by the UVI is for it to play a role in the formation of a Nahua counter-public as "parallel discursive arenas where members of subordinated social groups invent and circulate counter-discourses, which in turn permit them to formulate oppositional interpretations of their identities, interests, and needs" (Fraser 1990, 67). This possibility is significant, because it suggests a possible new role for the Nahuatl language as the language tied to a public sphere that is wider than the individual Nahuatl-speaking *altepetl* communities. By producing Nahuatl intellectuals, and creating a sphere of Nahua-discourse that unites the entire region of Zongolica, and even reaches out to connect to other Nahuatl-speaking regions, the possibility of a wider pan-Nahua public emerges.

Elizabeth Povinelli describes the political order of "Late Liberalism" itself as a "cramped space" that is driven by a capitalist geontopower—the power to place the border between the living and the dead (Povinelli 2016). These cramped conditions drive the hands of the Nahua people of the highlands when it gives them little choice but to deplete the forest or to allow large-scale mining or power extraction projects to refigure their local landscape. While the UVI and the intercultural ideology are definitely a creation of Late Liberalism, they have, by opening the doors to Indigenous perspectives and actions, also opened up a pocket of possibility in this cramped space. The use of the Nahuatl language at the UVI enables the constitution of a Nahuatl public that is grounded in the Zongolica region and its Indigenous lifeworlds, and it permits the reproduction of "otherwise" construals of the relation between land and power, life and death, territory and community, innovation and tradition.

Figure 6.0 Still from Alicia Smith's video artwork *Hueyatoyatzintli—Great River* (which can be watched at https://vimeo.com/450855035). The artist sits singing in a shallow bend of the Rio Grande.
Reproduced here with permission of the artist.

6

Nahuatl across Borders

Mexican Transnationalism in the United States

Huēyātoyātzintli
Alicia Smith
(Translation into Nahuatl and from the Nahuatl back into English by the author)

Original	Translation	Back translation
How much time Great River	Quēmman, Huēyātoyātzintli,	When, great river
Since you heard the good song	Achto ōticcac īncuīcauh	Did you first hear the song
of the people who remember?	tlalnamiccātlātlācah	of the rememberer-people
I will sing to you	Nimitzcuīcatilīz	I will sing for you
Great River	Huēyātoyātzintli	Great river
The good song,	inin cualli cuīcatl	This good song,
long	nōihqui quēn tehhuatzin	Also, like you,
like you,	īca huēyac	it is long
until you remember	mā mitzilnāmictili	May it remind you
The good burial song	in cualli tētlāltōquilizcuīcatl,	Of the good burial song,
Great River	Huēyātoyātzintli	Great river
You who watches	tehhuatzin in titēchchīxtica	You who are watching us
like a mother	quēmen titonān	like you are our mother
Watching our breath	ticmoittitia in toihiyoh	You see our breath
slow	cēhuihtica,	become calm,
Great River	Huēyātoyātzintli	Great river
Dancing	titohtiticateh	We are dancing
in your arms	īhuān titēchnapalohtica	and you are embracing us
and our eyes cover	īhuān titēchīxpachōz	and you eye-cover us
The-people-who-remember	tlalnāmikkātlātlākah	the rememberer-people
Great River	Huēyātoyātzintli	Great river
The Blue-Not-Fish	in itztic ahmīmichtin	The cold not-fish
of your water	īihtec moāhua	inside your water
We crossed once before	ye ceppa otimitzpanoqueh	Already once we crossed you
Great River	Huēyātoyātzintli	Great river
Now we wait here	Axcān nicān titochīyāzqueh	Now here we will keep watch
forever.	mochipa	Forever

Nahuatl Nations. Magnus Pharao Hansen, Oxford University Press. © Oxford University Press 2024.
DOI: 10.1093/oso/9780197746158.003.0007

The poem *Huēyātoyātzintli* describes the Rio Grande, the river that traces out a long section of the border between Mexico and the United States. In the poem, and in reality, the river stands as a physical, tangible, and natural manifestation of the political border, an obstacle that has to be crossed in order to pass between the two countries. The poem was written for a piece of video art, which shows the artist, Alicia Smith, performing the poem, addressing the river in song. As she sings, she sits in the water with her back to the camera and with strips of red cloth fastened to her flesh, symbolizing bleeding wounds that tie her to territory, and to the past.

The poetic voice that addresses the river is a "we," and it talks about how this "we" crossed the river long ago. The voice relates how the river, like a mother, watches over those dead bodies, the not-fish, who have drowned in its waters, and how its perpetually rushing waters sing their burial song. The "we" that the poem voices is a historically deep collective that may be understood as uniting a lineage of people who have crossed and interacted with the river through time immemorial. It includes the ancient Uto-Aztecan nomads who left their homelands and wandered into Mexico—and it includes their descendants, the Nahua people, who established themselves as founders of the Aztec Empire. It includes those Nahua people, warriors, muleteers, and craftsmen, who accompanied Spanish expeditions as they expanded the Spanish colonial empire north across the river—and it includes their descendants, the Chicanos of mixed Spanish-Indigenous heritage who are now US citizens. It also includes the Aztec descendants who remained in Mexico, among them Mexican migrants who today cross the river north, back into the ancient territories of their distant ancestors that are today the home of their Indigenous relatives. This epic "we," spanning across thousands of years and thousands of miles, is cast as the children of the river and of the landscape through which it winds.

The "we" of the poem is the people of *Aztlán*, a mythical name given to an ancient homeland of the Aztecs (*Aztecatl* means "person from *Aztlán*" in Nahuatl), which is sometimes claimed to have been located in the US Southwest. The poem casts the crossing of the Mexican migrant into the United States as a sacred journey back toward those ancient roots. This motif is a core trope of contemporary Chicano thought, one which ties the existence of Chicano people in the United States to a history that is deeper than both the United States and Spanish colonialism, and which represents Chicano people as essentially Indigenous to the US Southwest, alongside the other Indigenous groups of the region. The salience of this trope, in Chicano thought, is testified in Gloria Anzaldúa's "The Border," in the work of the poet Alurista who wrote the "*Plan Espritirual de Aztlán*" which was a major manifesto of the Chicano student movement MeChA (*Movimiento Estudiantil Chicano de Aztlán*) in the

1970s, and in countless other works by Chicano intellectuals (Pharao Hansen and Tlapoyawa 2020).

Having grown up in Albuquerque, New Mexico, Smith does not speak Nahuatl, nor do any members of her immediate family, but she wanted the song of the river to be performed in that language, which to her represents her genealogical ties to the Indigenous peoples of the Rio Grande Region. She contacted me on Facebook, asking me to translate it into Nahuatl for her. The text, appearing here with her permission, is that translation, and the translation of the Nahuatl back into English (not Smith's original English-language text).

Smith is not alone in considering Nahuatl to be an important part of the cultural heritage of Chicano people. Hundreds, if not thousands, of Chicano people share the feeling that Nahuatl, not Spanish or English, is their most significant heritage language, and they often study it precisely as a way to reconnect with a Mexican Indigenous heritage.

The previous two chapters have described communities fighting to maintain and strengthen the Nahuatl language, as youths have given up learning the mother tongue of their parents and grandparents. I have argued that the survival of the language is closely related to the strength of the political community of speakers and of their desire to keep that community from being absorbed into the Mexican national community. If the vitality of the Nahuatl language is so closely tied to communal identities in Indigenous communities that are striving to maintain their political independence from the Mexican nation-state, we must ask what is happening among the Mexican Americans who use Nahuatl as a heritage language. As in the Mexican communities, also in the United States the language seems to be experiencing a kind of "revival," or at least a drastically increased usage, but in a context where there is no tie to a historically continuous Nahuatl-speaking public, and where there is no threat of being absorbed into the Mexican state.

Scholarship on "neo-Indian" identity movements has examined neo-Indigenous identity movements in different places in the Americas, from Peru to Canada. Early scholarship has tended to be highly critical of such movements, seeing them as a kind of invented traditions, parasitic on authentic forms of indigeneity.[1]

More recently, scholars like Haley (2009) and Sturm (2010, 2002) have worked to move beyond the "authenticity" debate about whether neo-Indians can be considered legitimately Indigenous. Instead, they strive to understand how neo-Indigenous movements and communities interact with the political

---

[1] Kuper 2003; Friedlander 1975; de la Peña Martínez 2002, 2012; Galinier and Molinié 2013.

claims of Indigenous communities with longer histories and more obvious claims to Indigenous rights, and how they operate between logics of globalization, nationalism, and multiculturalism, and how they position themselves in relation to ideologies of race.

This chapter aims to understand the political context of Nahuatl use by Mexican Americans, by asking what political project or projects they see themselves as part of. And by inquiring how they relate to Indigenous political movements, to Nahua communities in Mexico, to Indigenous communities in the United States, and to the two nation-states, separated not only by the Great River, but also by iron fences.

Nahuatl and the Mexicayotl Movement in the United States

From the fall of 2014 to spring 2016, I was a fellow at the center for US–Mexican studies in San Diego. Right on the US–Mexican border, San Diego has a strong Mexican diaspora community, including cross-border families, people who work in the United States and live in Mexico, recent arrivals, and Mexican Americans and Chicanos who have been settled for generations, and who often even have family roots in California prior to the state's incorporation into the United States.

While I was at the center for US–Mexican studies, working on my dissertation, I met and interacted with a number of Nahuatl heritage language learners from Southern California and the US Southwest. I began interacting with them online through some of the Facebook groups for sharing knowledge about the Nahuatl language and Mexican Indigenous history.

Most of the learners I interacted with were, in different ways, tied to what I henceforth will refer to as the Mexicayotl movement, a loose movement of people in Mexico and the Mexican diaspora in the United States, who self-identify as Indigenous, Native American, people.[2] In Nahuatl, *mexicayōtl* means something like "Mexica-ness"; the term was used by the Mexica tribe who founded Tenochtitlán to refer to their own ethnic identity. Here it is meant to signal a relation to Mexica culture and identity that can be fuzzy and abstract and not necessarily a concrete claim of "being Mexica." Mexicayotl as it is practiced in the United States today sprang from the earlier paradigm

---

[2] Here it is important to distinguish the *Mexicayotl movement* from the *Mexica movement*. Following the advice of Kurly Tlapoyawa, I use the term *Mexicayotl movement* as an umbrella for the many different Mexica-identity groups and networks that spring out of the Mexicanidad tradition, whereas the Mexica movement is a specific organization within the broader Mexicayotl movement.

of *Mexicanidad* which emerged in Mexico in the 1940s. Activists in the Mexicayotl movement cultivate their Indigenous identity by affiliating themselves in different ways with the culture of the Mexica people, which they study and practice. Not all Mexicayotl practitioners self-identify as "Mexica"; in fact, many identify with ethnic groups Indigenous to the specific territory in Mexico from which they hail. Nevertheless, even those who identify personally as something other than Mexica will tend to use the symbols and practices associated with the Mexica, such as *Danza Azteca*, Nahuatl ritual terminology, and others. In this way, we may consider the Mexicayotl umbrella to include all the organizations that look to the Mexica tradition for inspiration in their cultural practice. The choice of the Mexica culture as a key heritage culture is of course largely motivated by the central role of precisely the Mexica tribe and its symbols in Mexican national mythology, and by the ideology of *Mestizaje*, which has promoted Mexica culture as a source of Indigenous culture common for all Mexican citizens. Paradoxically, in this way the Mexicayotl movement is identifiable as a form of Mexican nationalism, even though it is practiced mostly in the Mexican diaspora in the United States (but also in different ways in Mexico and El Salvador). The national allegiance of the movement is not to the current nation state of Mexico, which its members typically consider a colonial imposition, but specifically to the Indigenous cultures that preceded the colony and the modern nation.

Many of the Neo-Mexica activists who are prominent members of the Mexica History page on Facebook differ from what might be considered the mainstream Mexicayotl movement, in that they are in fact highly aware and critical of the ties between Mexican nationalism and the Mexica identity movement. They seek to find ways of allying with Indigenous communities in Mexico and in the United States, rather than pursuing the claim that the US Southwest was the patrimony of the Mexica nation. Most of the leading members of the forum are associated with a group called *Yankwik Mexikayotl* ("New Mexicanness"). This group has emerged in an effort to renew the Mexica-movement by shedding the ideological ties to Mexican nationalism and New Age–type ideas, and finding a way to be Indigenous and Mexica, while also acknowledging the complicated layerings of intersecting identities and honoring Indigenous sovereignties and cultural rights. The Mexica History group, in this way, is not fully representative of the broader Mexicayotl movement, but sometimes positions itself in opposition to the mainstream, which it seeks to reform. Most of my interviews and interactions have been with participants who represent this branch of the Mexicayotl movement. Since 2014, I have maintained continuous interaction with several of the members of the group, visiting them in California and New Mexico, discussing scholarship and studies of Indigenous Mexican culture, participating together in conferences. Today I would consider several of them to be colleagues and friends. With Kurly Tlapoyawa, who is a leading member and founder of the *Yankwik Mexikayotl* group, I have coauthored an academic article on the relation between Aztlan and the Nahuatl language (Pharao Hansen and Tlapoyawa 2020), a collaboration that I draw on in the following *Aztlán* section of this chapter.

That many Mexican Americans consider themselves to be Native Americans and Indigenous to the US Southwest may be surprising to Anglo-Americans who are used to thinking of them as "Latinos" or "Hispanics," but it is not a baseless claim. While the ideology that leads to this identification is part of a wider tradition of Mexican indigenist and nationalist thought, it is not only motivated by this ideology. The claim that Indigenous Nahuas are Indigenous to the US Southwest is supported by a long history of ties between Nahua peoples and the US Southwest in the period before the region became part of the United States, and before political borders were established. The claim of many Mexican Americans to being Native American is supported by the ideology of identity that sees being Indigenous as a racial category where membership is based on biological ancestry, and also by the fact that Indigenous ancestry is often reflected in their physical appearance, in their family histories, and in their genomes.

In the 2010 census of the Bureau of Indian Affairs, which counts Native Americans by self-identification rather than tribal citizenship, "Mexican American Indian" was chosen as primary identification by 121,221 persons, which makes this grouping the census's third largest "tribal grouping" in the United States after Cherokee and Navajo (the result only counts those who give a single tribal affiliation—if those who have dual affiliation is counted, then Mexican American Indian is fourth after Cherokee, Navajo, and Choctaw.) This number likely includes both diaspora from Indigenous communities in Mexico, such as Zapotecs and Mixtecs who have vibrant communities in California, for example (Velasco Ortíz 2005), but doubtless many are also Chicanos and Mexican Americans affiliated with the Mexicayotl movement. Similarly, longitudinal studies of census trends have shown that many people switch racial identification between censuses, and switching from Hispanic to Native American categories is common (Liebler and Ortyl 2014; Liebler, Bhaskar, and Porter 2016). Certainly, the majority of the over 10,000 members of the Mexica History group are Chicanos and Mexican Americans who would most likely identify as Native American in the census.

Central to the Mexicayotl movement is the ideological claim that the US Southwest is the place called *Aztlān* by the ancient Mexica, which they

Figure 6.1 Danzantes from the *Calpulli Xiuhcoatl* dancing in a park in Los Angeles. Photo by Oman Cuezalin Rios.

considered to be their mythical homeland. Within the movement there are differing interpretations of the concept of Aztlán: some are geopolitical claims to the legitimate ownership of the region, while others are more spiritual, a metaphor for a feeling of belonging and connectedness with the land (Leal [1989] 2017).

Also central to the movement is the practice of *Danza* or *Danza Azteca*, a tradition of dancing, that is considered by its members to be simultaneously a continuation and a recreation of Indigenous Mexican dances from before Spanish colonization (Aguilar 2009). This dance practice is also tied to ritual practice, and though some dancers known as *concheros* integrate their dance practice in a Catholic ritual context, many others, known as Mexica or Azteca dancers, integrate it into a neo-Aztec ritual practice (Example of neo-Mexica 'danzantes' in Figure 6.1).[3] In addition to dancing and ritual practice, other common elements of the Mexicayotl practice includes adopting Nahuatl-language names, and generally striving to decolonize one's lifestyle by removing cultural and symbolic elements imposed by colonialism and choosing Indigenous alternatives instead. For many Mexicayotl practitioners, Nahuatl has a central role in ritual, in naming, and as a means to decolonize

---

[3] Rostas 2009; Aguilar 2009; Nielsen 2017.

one's worldview (Villareal 2011). For some of the people I met, the Nahuatl language was just one element in an entire lifestyle organized around a Mexica cultural heritage. For others, either studying the Nahuatl language or practicing *Danza* was the central element, through which they connected with their Mexica roots.

Many of the members of the Mexica History group on Facebook affiliate with the so-called *Mexica movement*, an ethnopolitical organization based in Santa Ana, Orange County, California, which is one organization under a wider umbrella of *Mexicayotl* organizations. In contrast to the *Yankwik Mexikayotl* group described above, the Mexica movement and most other Mexicayotl organizations build on the tradition of Mexican indigenist nationalism described in Chapter 3. They have a strong nativist element, and argue that all Mexican Americans are of Indigenous Mexica heritage, a heritage which has been denied to them by the process of colonization. Mexica identity is also the de facto norm in the *Danza Azteca* community, which embodies the bulk of the Mexica-identity movement in the United States. Describing the ideologies of the *Mexicanidad* tradition (the original Mexican version of Mexicayotl), Fernando de la Peña Martínez notes how the ideological bricolage of the Mexica-identity movement includes many nativist and even xenophobic elements (de la Peña Martínez 2002, 101–5). This includes the kind of ideology of "Mexica supremacy" that sees the Mexica of the post-classic period as the most important and most advanced of Mexico's Indigenous groups.

Based on my interactions with Nahuatl learners and speakers in the United States, this chapter shows how Nahuatl also plays a role in a variety of political projects in the United States, and depicts the histories and experiences associated with the language north of the Rio Grande.

Aztlán: A Brief History of Nahuatl and Mexican Nationalism in the US Southwest

"*A puto, timiquiz!*" [Motherfucker![4] You're going to die!].[5] Written in 1598 in Ohkay Owingeh Pueblo (then called San Juán Pueblo by the Spaniards), this

---

[4] Spanish *puto* is and was a homophobic slur, but given the context, I think it makes sense to translate it as a more general insult. It is of course quite interesting that an Acoma person would know Nahuatl and use the language when addressing Spaniards. It is also interesting that the Spanish soldier who was the witness understood and remembered the statement in the original language.

[5] With permission from Kurly Tlapoyawa, this section of this chapter incorporates some material previously published in Pharao Hansen and Tlapoyawa (2020).

statement, which mixes Spanish and Nahuatl into a potent threat, may well represent the first Nahuatl words recorded in writing on what is today US territory. The statement was recorded in a witness testimony in the trial against a group of Acoma people who had attacked a troop of Spaniards under Juan de Oñate. Oñate subsequently committed a massacre of the inhabitants of Acoma Pueblo in retaliation, and sentenced the survivors to mutilation and slavery. The witness describes the words as having been spoken in the "Mexican language" (i.e., Nahuatl) by a sword-wielding Indian who participated in the attack on the group of Spanish soldiers and their Indigenous allies (Craddock and Polt 2014). The presence of Nahuatl and Nahuatl speakers in the US Southwest long predates the first use of English in the region. Archaeological findings of Mesoamerican goods such as cacao and macaw feathers at ancient Pueblo sites suggest that is not far-fetched to propose that perhaps Nahuatl-speaking long-distance traders arrived in the region even earlier, centuries before the Spanish set foot in the Americas (Lekson, Windes, and Fournier 2007; Riley 2005).

The concept of *Aztlán* has its origin in the mythico-historical narratives recorded by Nahuatl speakers in the Spanish colonial period. As with most Mesoamerican origin myths, these narratives present a migration motif in which Nahuatl-speaking ethnic groups shared a common origin in a place that they eventually abandon in search for a place in which to build their own city-state (Smith 1984). In his *Historia de Las Indias de Nueva España*, Dominican friar and chronicler Diego Durán (1537–1588) recounted a story told to him by his Nahua informants in which the Aztec ruler Moteczoma Ilhuicamina (ca. 1398–1469) sent emissaries north to search for Aztlān, which they visited and described as an earthly, magical paradise upon their return (Durán [1581] 1994, 10). This suggests that Nahua people in the 16th century, now nominally Christian, continued to tell each other stories about the land of Aztlān. Durán describes the location of this land as northeast toward *La Florida* (a term that in this period included the northern part of the Mexican Gulf Coast) (Durán [1581] 1994, 10).

We know for certain that when Spanish colonization moved north from the Valley of Mexico and eventually into what is now the US Southwest, Nahuatl speakers accompanied the European colonists and brought their language with them (Jeffres 2023). Since Nahuatl was used as a vehicular language in the communication between Spaniards and natives, for many native groups, Nahuatl became simply another language of colonialism, arriving hand-in-hand with Spaniards and the Spanish language. Speakers of Nahuatl, particularly from the area of the Tlaxcala-Puebla Valley, participated in founding many of the early Spanish settlements in the Southwest, including Santa Fe,

New Mexico, and San Antonio, Texas. Nahuatl-language chronicles from the 17th century refer to the Spanish province of Nuevo Mexico in Nahuatl as *Yancuic Mexihco*, literally "New Mexico" (Schroeder 1991, 120; Levin Rojo 2014), and at their founding both Santa Fe and Albuquerque have neighborhoods called *Analco*, meaning "on the other side of the water" in Nahuatl.

Spanish settlers of New Mexico also seem to have believed that the Aztec homeland was located in the US Southwest. In the 16th century, it was common for colonial authorities to propagate narratives of rich unconquered kingdoms such as Cibola and El Dorado in an effort to raise support for expeditions of conquest (Carson 1998). By placing the origins of the Nahuas beyond the frontier of colonization, the northern territories were tied into the nascent national symbolism of Mexico. The quest for the Aztec homeland became a sort of "manifest destiny" myth in the northward spread of Spanish colonialism.

When Mexico ceded the northern territory to the United States in the 1848 Treaty of Guadalupe Hidalgo, the memory of the lost territories lived on as a phantom pain in Mexican national imagination (Saldaña-Portillo 2016). In this period of the defeated national sentiment, Mexican intellectuals seized on the earlier attempts to tie the Aztlán myths to the lost northern territories (Miner 2014, 48–49). Simultaneously, the fact that linguists believe that the ancestors of the Uto-Aztecan languages of Mexico (including Nahuatl as well as Yaqui/Yoeme, Mayo/Yorem, Raramuri, Warihío, Audam [Tepehuán], Wixárika [Huichol], and Náayeri [Cora]) are likely to have originated in what is now the US Southwest some 5,000 years ago, which also today motivates the narrative of Nahuas and Mexicans returning to their "ancestral territories" when they cross the Rio Grande going north (see Figure 6.2, which reconstructs the possible migration routes taken by ancient Uto-Aztecans as they dispersed southward from the ancient homeland).

When the Chicano movement emerged in the Mexican diaspora in the 1960s, it used the ideas of Aztlán as a name for the previously Mexican territories to reconceptualize the presence of Chicano people in the United States. Drawing on imagery of the indigenist *Mexicanidad* movement of the 1940s and 1950s, the romanticized figure of the Aztec warrior (as seen in Figure 3.0 in Chapter 3) also became a core symbol of their Chicano ethnic identity. In the 1970s, Aztec dance traditions from Mexico arrived in the US Southwest, and allowed dancers dressed in brightly colored Aztec costumes with colorful feathers and rattles on their legs to embody this romantic ideal in dance. *Danza* became a highly visible part of the Mexican nationalist movement (Aguilar 2009). The dance communities formed into hierarchically organized

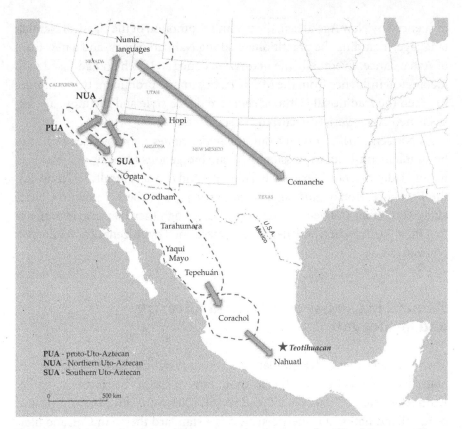

Figure 6.2 Map showing the possible routes taken by the ancient Uto-Aztecans as they dispersed south into Mexico to their current locations.
Map by Christophe Helmke.

calpulli groups, which they see as a continuation of the social structure of Nahuatl cities, which were organized into "neighborhoods" called *calpoltin* [big houses] in Nahuatl (Rostas 2009). Gradually the *conchero* dance tradition became influenced by the *Movimiento Confederado Restaurador de la Cultura de Anahuac* [The Confederate Movement for the Restoration of the Culture of Anahuac] (MCRCA), a Mexican nationalist and indigenist organization founded by Rodolfo Nieva López in the 1950s, with the intention of revitalizing Mexico's imperial Aztec past (Nieva López was closely associated with Juán Luna Cárdenas, mentioned in previous chapters). The MCRCA promoted a Mexica-centric, or even Mexica supremacist, worldview in which Aztec culture was preeminent and responsible for the fluorescence of world civilization (Peña Martínez 2002). The MCRCA had its main influence in urban middle and working-class communities (Friedlander 1975). Its practices mixed Mexican nationalism, neo-Aztec religion (also prominently influenced by New Age ideas), the use and promotion of the classical Nahuatl language, including the practitioners taking Nahuatl names, and a new form of Aztec dance. Eventually the neo-Aztec dance style, which had fused with ideological influence from the MCRCA, became so prominent that a rupture between the traditional Catholic *conchero* dance style and the more aggressively neo-Aztec variety occurred (Rostas 2009).

As Nielsen (2017, 5) points out, today *danzantes* may consider *Danza* to be simultaneously an expression of a pan-Indigenous identity, of a Mexican national identity, of a Mexica tribal identity, and of a specifically Chicano cultural practice. Today *danzantes* often participate in the US powwow circle along with other Indigenous communities, though they may also experience that their participation and identity are questioned by citizens of federally recognized tribes.

Nahuatl in the Genes: Race and Ancestry and Mexicayotl

The ideologies that order the classification of racial categories in the United States have always been conflicted about how to classify Mexicans and other Latin Americans (Cobas, Duany, and Feagin 2009; Rodriguez 2000). This state of racial and national in-between-ness is a standard theme in Chicano literature and also figures prominently in the experiences recounted by many of my Mexicayotl interlocutors. Most Mexicayotl practitioners did not grow up with an Indigenous identity, but have been accustomed to navigating between broad labels like Hispanic and Latino, Mexican, and US national identities and whichever experiences of racial classification their physical appearance has produced in their interactions with others. Many of my interlocutors describe the process leading to seeing oneself as Indigenous as a process of discovery, in which they work to remove layers of distortions and illusions to arrive at a truth about themselves, which had been previously hidden from them. In the quest for finding this truth, they take on the roles of detectives, trying to uncover their ancestry, and finding a language in which to make their ancestry meaningful that is not imposed by structures of colonialism. For many Mexicayotl practitioners, Nahuatl becomes that language: the language that they somehow carry inside, bequeathed to them by their ancestors, waiting to be reactivated.

One way of understanding the Mexicayotl identity project is by thinking with "trans" and "transraciality" in the terms of Brubaker (2016). Comparing the "trans" of "transgender" with the "trans" of "transraciality," Brubaker argues that because racial identities, in the United States, are understood as being determined primarily by ancestry, they are seen as being produced in a domain where individual decisions and subjective experience of identity cannot reasonably alter one's classification. This, according to Brubaker, is part of the reason that the notion of transracial category-switching has been received very differently in public discourse than transgender-switches. Nevertheless, one may consider the movement to escape the classification as "Hispanics" or "Latinos" to achieve recognition as members of the Native American racial category as a case of transraciality, specifically a case of what Brubaker calls the "trans of migration." The identity migrates from one racial category (Hispanic) to another (Native American), but does not challenge the prevailing classification system by placing itself between or beyond existing racial categories. In this migration, the premise posed by Brubaker, that transracial mobility is constrained by the ancestry-based ideology of racial categories, holds true, because ancestry becomes the pivot in the quest for reclassification for many Mexicayotl practitioners. In order to reclassify, they must work to reclassify not only themselves, by performing and embodying their new identity category, but also by reclassifying their ancestry. This is done through all available means, from anecdotal family history, to inferring racial phenotypical traits of one's ancestry from one's own physical appearance, to genealogical research in historical documents and archives, to taking and interpreting commercial DNA tests, to reinterpreting and re-narrating historical narratives about the ethnic origins of specific groups or families that one claims descent from.

Ancestry and Language on Facebook, March 2014

A discussion is unfolding on Facebook, in the "Mexica History" group. The subject is one of the recurring topics in the forum: genes and identity. The group has almost 9,000 members who share information related to the history and culture of the Mexica, or Aztec, peoples, and political memes with slogans such as "we didn't cross the border, the border crossed us" or "not Latino, not Hispanic, not immigrant, but Indigenous peoples of the Americas!" The general purpose of the group is to find ways to integrate Mexica tradition into the daily lives of the group's members, most of whom live in the US Southwest and identify as Indigenous Mexica people, and work to reclaim elements of a Mexica cultural heritage. Although generally US-born, many of the group members have names in Nahuatl, or in the languages of other Indigenous groups they identify with. In the group, the question of genes is raised frequently by members asking for help to interpret the results of genetic tests they have purchased from one of the many companies that provide private genetic testing with promises to provide information about the ethnic and geographic origins of one's ancestors.

The specific topic of discussion this day is the TV show *Decoding Past DNA*, hosted by Harvard Professor Henry Louis Gates, specifically an episode in which actor Jessica Alba receives the result of a genetic test that claims to demonstrate that she has 22.5% "East Asian and Native American" genetic material. In the show, this genetic trace was understood to reflect her Mexican ancestry on her father's side, and scientists traced the DNA markers "back to the Maya civilization." One part of the discussion is the participants trying to wrap their heads around Jessica Alba's weird test results stemming from the way that genetic ancestry testing produces a result by matching genetic markers to markers found in samples from different ethnic groups. "3.7% Maya and 2% Seri, how does that work?" one participant asks. The discussion then quickly turns toward participants sharing their own DNA tests, uploading their certificates with graphs of the breakdown of their genetic haplogroups to the thread. The results discussed are mostly the mtDNA results where a small number of haplogroups and subgroups have been defined by geneticists as originating among pre-colonial Native American populations. "I am also haplogroup A, does that mean we share an ancestor?" one person asks. (In fact, it does, although this ancestor is assumed to have lived more than 40,000 years ago in Asia.) One participant, her name is Xochitl, the Nahuatl word for "flower," points out that a recent bioarchaeological study of the pre-hispanic city of Xaltocan in Central Mexico shows an abrupt shift in the frequency of mtDNA markers, corresponding to an invasion event which is mentioned in many ethnohistorical sources from the area (Mata-Míguez et al. 2012). In this invasion, a group of Nahuatl-speaking Tepanecs invaded the city of Xaltocan, massacring and forcibly relocating the local Otomí-speaking population and repopulating the town with Nahuatl speakers. The study that she read determined that the replacement population had a higher frequency of the A2 haplogroup than the original population, supporting her argument that her possession of the A2 haplogroup bolsters her claim to Nahua/Mexica ancestry. Most people in the Mexica History discussion group share this ideology of identity and language, in which their genes, coupled with diligent study of the past, hold the key to finding out which heritage languages they carry inside.

Americans have long tended to think about race and racial category membership as determined on the basis of the race of one's known ancestors. In

Mexico, being Indigenous is usually defined by cultural and linguistic traits that index a belonging to an Indigenous community, whereas in the United States being officially Indigenous in most instances requires passing a threshold of blood quantum set by the officially recognized tribe with which one seeks affiliation (TallBear 2013; Reardon and TallBear 2012).

In the Mexica History Facebook group, various types of evidence are used to support claims about Indigenous ancestry. As in the discussion about the TV show, the most common type of evidence is genetic in the form of result reports from "ethnic composition" analysis by companies that offer commercial DNA testing. The Mexican National Institute of Genomic Medicine has declared that the average Mexican genome is around 50% Indigenous (Wade et al. 2014), and this declaration is echoed by commercial DNA tests, in which many people in the Mexica History group are told that they have high amounts of "Native American DNA," often more than 50%. For someone who has a physical appearance suggestive of non-European ancestry and who has family ties to a historically Nahuatl-speaking region in Mexico, this declaration may be enough for them to confidently claim to be of Indigenous ancestry and Nahua ethnicity. Many others, however, rely on commercial DNA tests and their "ethnic breakdown" of genetic markers. Group members frequently shared their results and their experiences with different testing companies. In such analyses, specific DNA markers are typologized as being diagnostic for specific ethnic groups, when that particular marker has a high frequency in a test sample with a particular ethnic label. By looking at the totality of markers and their associated ethnic correlations, the test subject's DNA is apportioned into different percentages of ethnic heritage. A DNA test will not usually say "Mexica" or "Aztec," but usually will return something like "Mexican Native" or "South Mexican Indigenous." Then the person receiving the result must try to use other means, such as genealogy, to trace the specific ethnicities represented by their "Native American DNA."

Some Mexicayotl practitioners in the Mexica History group are also avid hobby genealogists, scouring their family trees for links to Indigenous peoples. They typically work with the many online collections of church records, which sometimes reach back to the 16th century, and which often include ethnic and racial categorization, such as the *casta* classifications in Spanish colonial records. Several group members have been able to bolster their sense of Nahua and Mexica heritage by finding ancestors that can link them to Mexica nobility. Sometimes they can even trace their own genealogy to the Aztec ruler Moteczoma, whose daughter married a Spaniard and whose many children and grandchildren spread through Mexico and even into New Mexico.

In the end, DNA and genealogy can only do so much. It may tell us "*what we are*," but to make oneself feel like that, to really be what we are, perhaps one has to embody the identity in some way or other. This seems to be where the Nahuatl language (and *Danza Azteca*) becomes important to many Mexicayotl activists.

Mexicayotl Nahuatl Purism and Educational Practice

Nahuatl is taught and studied in the United States, both formally and informally: in universities and community colleges, in study groups and cultural centers, in at least one Los Angeles charter school, in private homes, and as we will see in the next section, even in prisons (Figure 6.3). In most cases, the Nahuatl being taught and studied is the variety of the early colonial sources, the one often called "classical Nahuatl." This is for several reasons. In academic environments, the colonial variety is a logical choice, because there are so many educational materials that teach it, and its value for reading historical sources and studying Aztec culture is significant. For this reason, in universities, teachers have typically taught Nahuatl as a written language only or primarily, in the way one might also teach Latin or Ancient Greek.

In Mexicayotl circles, however, the choice of "classical Nahuatl" as the language of study is often motivated by a purist ideology that sees the early variety not only as less influenced by Spanish, but also as more sophisticated and closer to the speech of Mexica nobility and priesthood. Mexican Mexicayotl

Figure 6.3 Various promotional materials for Nahuatl courses in Southern California, organized by Mexicayotl groups.
Public domain.

leader Tlacatzin Stivalet told the anthropologist Francisco de la Peña that modern varieties of Nahuatl are degraded and bastardized forms of the classical language, and should be replaced by a reformed version of the classical language (de la Peña Martínez 2002, 171). Similarly, in his online Nahuatl course,[6] activist leader Frank Díaz, who calls his movement Toltecayotl (i.e., Toltec-style) instead of Mexicayotl, first says that no language is pure or superior to others. Nevertheless, the reason for his preference for "Toltec" over "Mexica" is motivated by Carlos Castaneda's New Age writings, which depict the Toltecs as spiritually superior to the subsequent Aztec culture. Then he goes on to argue that the "dialectization" of Nahuatl (as many others, he erroneously considers the modern languages to be derived from the "classical variety") is a loss of refinement caused by the disappearance of an Indigenous political authority that could impose strict grammatical rules on the language. According to him, such a loss of valuable norms should not be respected for the sake of a misguided idea of "diversity." For the same reason, Díaz is against allowing Indigenous students to write theses or academic work in their own languages until they have been taught the "proper" rules of Nahuatl. These are exactly the ideas that were brought to Hueyapan in the 1950s by Juan Luna Cárdenas, one of the founders of the Mexicayotl movement described in Chapter 4. Such ideas contributed significantly to the decline of the Nahuatl language there in the same period, as Cárdenas and his followers told locals that they were speaking the language wrong. Such a purist language ideology, with its associated practice of shaming speakers of Indigenous languages, is clearly oppressive rather than liberatory. Those Mexicayotl practitioners who adhere to these views position themselves as allied with the nationalist mythos and its idealized Aztecs, and hence stand with the state against Indigenous sovereignties.

Within the Mexicayotl movement, these purist ideals are not universal. Groups under the Mexicayotl umbrella are increasingly adopting perspectives that recognize Mexican Nahua people as stewards of ancestral knowledge, and they see their own movement as allied to other Indigenous struggles against national and colonial regimes. These perspectives nurture ideologies of language that recognize living Nahua languages and the knowledge encrusted within it as a direct link to the knowledge of ancient ancestors. In this view, learning to converse in a living Nahuatl variety becomes an emblem of connectedness with the ancestral community. This is similar to how Circe Sturm

---

[6] https://tolteca.atavist.com/gramtica-del-nahuatl-clsico-1 (accessed October 25, 2020, now defunct but archived at https://web.archive.org/web/20210214175150/https://tolteca.atavist.com/gramtica-del-nahuatl-clsico-1).

describes the relation between Cherokee language proficiency and community belonging expressed by many Cherokee elders: "fluency stands for time shared" (Sturm 2002, 121). By this measure, acquiring Nahuatl from a book or by doing university course work may in fact stand for time spent away from the community, and represent a broken continuity with the ancestral tradition.

A major factor in promoting an alliance between the Mexicayotl movement and Indigenous Nahuas has been the IDIEZ project (Sullivan 2011; McDonough 2014). Founded in 2002, the mission of the *Zacatecas Institute for Teaching and Research in Ethnology* (IDIEZ) has been to empower Nahuatl-speaking students to reclaim and revitalize Nahua language and culture, and to invite them into an educational environment where they can become stewards of their own cultural heritage. The project has provided scholarships for Nahuatl-speaking students, which have been partly funded by organizing Nahuatl language classes, taught by the students, primarily for American college students. These classes have been taught both in Mexico as field schools, but also as intensive summer courses in the United States through collaborating institutions including Yale, the University of Texas at Austin, and the University of Utah. This model has had the benefit of empowering Nahuatl students as teachers of the language and cultural authorities, and facilitating their entry into academia. Several of the Nahuatl speakers who have taught through IDIEZ are now pursuing PhDs or are employed at US universities. One former IDIEZ teacher, Victoriano de la Cruz Cruz (who goes by *Tepoxteco*, the name of his town of origin), has positioned himself as a prominent public intellectual in Mexico: he now hosts a popular radio show in Guadalajara and has edited the Nahuatl-language online magazine *Yolitia*, and has translated the novel *Pedro Páramo* into Nahuatl. However, without probably intending to, IDIEZ has also had an immense impact on the way Mexicayotl activists engage with the Nahuatl language. Many activists have studied Nahuatl through IDIEZ, studying at Zacatecas, visiting the community of Chicontepec, Veracruz, with the teachers, and taking intensive summer courses several years in a row. Some have become highly proficient speakers.

One of these is John "Yan" García of Los Angeles. In high school he had already become interested in understanding his roots, which prompted him to read about Mexican history, including historical works about the Nahuatl language. During his second and third years of college, he took the intensive IDIEZ summer course in Zacatecas and was thrilled by what he experienced: "It's difficult for me to overstate how effective their teaching was, and how rare it is to see." John ended up doing his MA thesis as an analysis of the diversity of Nahuatl varieties in the Huasteca region, and became a fluent speaker of the Huastecan variety himself. His desire to contribute to the continued development of Nahuatl has led him to create Nahuatl-language learning apps and videos, and he has published a beginners' textbook (García 2016), and has even collaborated on a translation of Mary Shelley's *Frankenstein* together with Victoriano "Tepoxteco" de la Cruz (García and de la Cruz 2016). He organizes and teaches Nahuatl language classes and conversations in Los Angeles, and this has brought him closer to the Mexicayotl movement. He also participates in the group *Nechikolli Se Ome Tlahtolli* [One-two language gathering], which hosts bimonthly live-streaming interviews with Nahua intellectuals on various topics, and hold the conferences entirely in Nahuatl. In this case, Garcia's fluency in the Nahuatl language has allowed him to function as a participant in political and intellectual discussions within the Nahua community and in this way function as a link of communication between a Nahua public sphere and the Mexicayotl community.

At the East Los Angeles charter school *Semillas del Pueblo*, or *Anahuacalmecac*, learning from Nahuatl speakers is also highly valued. Until his death in 2015, Felix Evodio Cuaxtle of Copalillo, in the Mexican state of Guerrero, was a strong intellectual force in the school's educational approaches. Cuaxtle composed songs in Nahuatl and used them pedagogically as a way for students to become acquainted with Nahuatl as a living language. The school also hires Nahuatl-speaking teachers from Mexico, mostly from Morelos and Guerrero, to work as language instructors. These teachers come back to Mexico with a strong sense of the value of their own language, and the way that it can be used outside of their own community (one teacher was from Hueyapan, and after returning participated in the revitalization project described in Chapter 4). At the same time, their presence in the Anahuacalmecac establishes a direct flow of knowledge from the Nahuatl-speaking communities in Mexico, which lends authenticity to the school's position as carrying out a mission of intellectual decolonization.

The focus on heritage language education as a source of connection to an ancestral community can also be understood as being motivated by the way many Chicanos experience the identity conflict of being "in between" through what Jonathan Rosa (2016) calls the "raciolinguistic ideology of languagelessness." This is the idea that Mexican Americans are not bilingual, but in fact are without a language, because neither of the two languages they speak conform to the standards set by educational authorities. This experience of being denied legitimate ownership of any language may also push Mexicayotl activists toward claiming Nahuatl as their true heritage language. My friend Kurly Tlapoyawa, for example, has told me of his dislike for speaking Spanish, and the feeling of not speaking it well enough, having been chided by *hispanos* who claim to speak a pure and ancient form of Spanish. By claiming Nahuatl as one's heritage language, Spanish and English can both be rejected as imposed, and the ideology of the standard language can be dismissed. In this way, among the Mexicayotl activists, the use of Nahuatl functions as a way to subvert a raciolinguistic order that makes standard languages desirable and prestigious (Rosa and Flores 2017).

Language is not just a medium of communication and meaning-making, it is also an embodied activity. By taking a Nahuatl name, one alters one's identity in a way that also forces one to embody that new identity every time the name is spoken. By using Nahuatl, in speech, even a few words or phrases, one's mouth participates in a chain of transmission from the ancestors. Fluency stands for time shared, but even speaking a single word in a language can be experienced as a way to be in a dialogic relation with those voices who spoke the words before and gave them meaning. This, too, is the power of language: it is what Foucault has called a "technology of the self" (Foucault 1993, 204), a medium through which we can change, and through which we can finally "become who we are" (Franco 2018). Learning a language may offer a degree of control and freedom in a world of strictures.

Nahuatl on the Inside: Chicano Gang Culture

In the US Southwest, Nahuatl and Aztec symbols are also a part of Chicano gang culture, which has at times lead to the stigmatization of their use. During the gang scare of the 1990s, anti-gang units were very attentive to the symbols and imagery of the gangs, which were used to identify gang membership and affiliations. The Nahuatl language came to be one of the signs that they tracked. In prisons, Aztec symbols and the Nahuatl language were periodically prohibited, not only because of the gang connotations, but also because of the risk that it could be used as a form of covert communication among prisoners. The prohibition of course only increased the language's prestige and significance among imprisoned Chicanos. Police officers from the anti-gang units came to see Nahuatl primarily as a kind of secret criminals' cant. The following quote describing a police perspective on Nahuatl is from the Policemag blog, written by the former leader of the LA Sherriff's Department's anti-gang unit, Richard Valdemar:

> The Aztec Culture was a barbarian warrior culture that invaded and conquered the more civilized cultures and peoples of the region. They stole from the Toltec's [sic], Mayans, Zapotecs and many others. Chief Montezuma lived in the capital surrounded by his nobles and served by thousands of slaves. Their dark and bloody religion was at the center of their culture and they practiced human sacrifice. Today, these Aztec myths and fantasies continue to be preached by racist college professors, schools like Academia Del Pueblo in Los Angeles, and by Latino gangs. Mexicans and Mexican Americans who can barely say taco are being taught dialects of the ancient Aztec language Nahuatl. In California prisons both the Mexican Mafia and the rival Nuestra Familia use this Aztec mythology to recruit and train soldiers for their wars. (Richard Valdemar, "Do you speak Nahuatl?," Policemag, 2011)[7]

The antagonism toward Aztecs, Nahuatl, and related cultural practices, as well as the attempt to stigmatize any association with these symbols, is clear.

Several Chicano life experience narratives that I have encountered have pointed toward a significant role of gang culture, and particularly the carceral experience, as catalysts in Mexicayotl identity processes. This is not in itself surprising or new; in Northern Ireland during the "troubles," for example, a successful Irish Gaelic revitalization movement formed among the IRA prisoners at Long Kesh (Chríost 2012). In the context of the Northern Irish prisons described by Chríost, the Irish language became meaningful to prisoners as an aspect of ethnic resistance against British colonial domination. The use of Nahuatl as a part of Mexican American prison culture is less clearly legible as a form of political resistance. In the hyper-racialized context of the US prison, the Nahuatl language takes on new meanings—both for gang members, for the guards, and for those who are trying to stay clear of either of those.

Among the various Mexican gangs of the US Southwest, Aztec identity ideology, including Aztec symbolism and language, was perhaps first adopted by the so-called Mexican Mafia, who in turn got it from the Chicano movement (Rafael 2013). West Coast gang culture is structured on the kind of "hemispheric localism" described by Mendoza-Denton (2008), which orders its stock of symbols in a polarization between "north/Norteño and south/Sureño." Mexica identity and Nahuatl language are mostly practiced by Sureño-affiliated gangs since the south is indexically tied to Mexican-ness.

---

[7] Accssed at: https://www.policemag.com/blogs/gangs/blog/15318023/do-you-speak-nahuatl; https://www.policemag.com/blogs/gangs/blog/15318022/a-nahuatl-dictionary.

I corresponded with two Chicano men who are imprisoned serving life sentences in California's Pelican Bay and Corcoran State Prisons. They had both worked extensively to promote the use of the Nahuatl language inside the prison system. In 2007 one of them attempted to sue the state for violating prisoners' human rights by prohibiting the use of Nahuatl and the possession of Nahuatl language materials. As a "validated" member of the Mexican Mafia, he had been prohibited from possessing any literature or images related to Indigenous Mexico. He filed a formal lawsuit alleging that his basic rights were violated by denying him a right to a cultural identity. The state in turn maintained its right to limit prisoners' rights to accessing materials deemed to pose a danger for security and the case was dismissed. The other man, who was less litigious in his approach, described to me how he had copied by hand an entire dictionary of the Nahuatl language (the one written by Frances Karttunen) and kept it hidden in his cell. Both described their work to me as heritage cultivation, and described how the acquisition of knowledge and cultural codes had helped them cope—though of course I cannot know if this is the only thing they used the language for. The possession of knowledge and materials about the Nahuatl language, in this way, constitutes both a source of identity and a source of social capital within the microcosm of the prison. As dictated by the laws of supply and demand, the effect of the prison systems' attempts to limit prisoners' access to the language was simply to increase its value to them.

Also in the Mexica History Facebook group, some members have carceral experiences of Nahuatl, and made the following comments when I inquired about whether anyone in the group knew if Nahuatl was still prohibited in US prisons:

"Michigan prisons banned it and sent brothers to the hole and higher levels for having these documents... not gang lit. But codices, lessons, and trying to educate other brothers to a higher purpose."

"The only "bad" is that Nahuatl is used for code talk. For most I think it's safe to say that that's not why Nahuatl is learned because the majority of the prison population is not in the SHU, so there's no reason for code talk. Just like a lot of you, it all starts off with young Chicanos growing up in the Varrio. Mexica calendars hanging in our room, little statues of popo and ixtac or cuauhtemoc flags. Then some take the gang route and end up in jail and prison where they learn discipline and are at times given books and encouraged to read about mexica culture and who we are and where we came from and to be proud of that, which most of us already are. So a lot of people continue to study and mind their own business and do their time while other guys start messing with prison politics and it goes on from there. Basically it all starts from good which is learning and being encouraged to learn about our culture or Mexica culture I should say. In my opinion I don't think it's bad at all but everybody's different."

"In California, it's used and not banned, they do twist words and meaning, so guards won't know what they are saying, and they do use it to do gang activities and run hits (green lights). And officers in facilities also try to learn it and they just can't."

Apart from avoiding surveillance and signifying gang identities, the Nahuatl language can also have other uses in prison. By phone, I interviewed another Chicano man whom I met in the Mexica History Facebook group, and whom I only knew by his online handle, the name of an Aztec deity. He had been incarcerated in Arizona and told me that there the use of Nahuatl was tolerated as part of religious practices, although he also acknowledged that gang members sometimes used the language as a code for avoiding being overheard by guards, or to speak around the guards to give the appearance of being up to something. In that way, Nahuatl may be used in power struggles between guards and prison inmates, and as a source of symbolic capital. He contrasted this instrumental usage of Nahuatl with its use as a medium of self-cultivation and self-discipline, that he described as characterizing a more authentic neo-Mexica practice. He stated that when he had arrived in prison he was a young man bent on joining the gangs to prove his worth.

"When I first arrived in prison, I was pretty wild. I wanted to be fighting all the time, and I was trying to get into the big gang stuff. I had one gentleman sit me down and tell me "relax, calm down, or you'll get in trouble." He was kind of an older guy, who knew. He loaned me the analytical dictionary [of Nahuatl], and told me to study it. "Find your roots. You need to know who your ancestors are and how they acted. They weren't doing that kinda shit." The people who take up these books in prison are critical thinkers. They are the ones who know about self-discipline, and that is what they teach. "Look this is what our ancestors were teaching about discipline and this is what you need to do; Rise with the sun, keep your path clear, treat people with respect." Studying it took my mind further from gang related activities. I was reading poetry by Nezahualcoyotl about how to carry yourself, about how a father should speak to a son, or his daughter, how a son should treat his mother, how to act with rectitude, and restraint and discipline. In a way, it saved me from going down a destructive path." (Testimony of Chicano man who started studying Nahuatl while imprisoned in Arizona)

Another Nahuatl activist whose knowledge of Nahuatl and Native American identity enabled him to evade inclusion in gang-related activities while incarcerated is Chris Cuauhtli. He was born in Mexico, but his parents brought him and his siblings to the United States in the late 1980s—unfortunately both parents perished in the desert, leaving him and his brothers orphans. They were adopted, though not legally, by a Mormon family in Northern California. The Mormon faith is often particularly invested in the idea of tracing one's ancestors back through biblical times. The adoptive parents missed no opportunity to let him and his brothers know that they were heirs of the Aztecs, who in turn descended from the Lamanites described in the Book of Mormon. Their foster family disintegrated through divorce, and Chris and his siblings ended up in tough circumstances in east Sacramento, where he was sucked into the local gang environment. He ended up spending years in juvenile detention centers, and later in state prisons. In the hyper-racialized environment of the prison, his identity as a Native American, and his knowledge of Nahuatl, which he had begun studying already as a young teenager, took on crucial importance, as he was able to convert this knowledge into cultural capital in prison. Many other imprisoned Chicanos were interested in learning Nahuatl, and Chris, whose physical appearance suggests Indigenous ancestry, and was born in an Indigenous region in Mexico, and who knew the language, had both the knowledge and authenticity to become a respected and sought-out teacher of the language on the inside. I met Chris through the Mexica History forum, where I was impressed with his knowledge of the Nahuan varieties of Jalisco. These varieties are no longer spoken and have only been scantily documented. His birth family was from a historically Nahuatl-speaking area in Jalisco, and he wanted to reclaim that heritage through his studies. Chris had collected all the existing sources about the Nahuatl of Jalisco, and was elaborating a dictionary based on these materials. He was even able to speak the language with an impressive degree of fluency. I interviewed him in Sacramento, where he told me his story. He described how, by focusing on studying and on being a keeper of this valuable knowledge, he had managed to maintain his own integrity while he was incarcerated, and how the community of Aztec *Danza* and Indigenous spirituality helped him reform once he was finally free.

The use of the Nahuatl language in prisons is motivated by the hyper-racialized environment that forces inmates to understand blood and ancestry as the source of community and heritage. But it also seems that imprisoned Chicanos use Nahuatl not only, or primarily, as a tool for criminal activities, but also as a source of identity, community, and even rehabilitation—finding positive role models among their ancestors and, by emulating them, recreating the best of the past in an uncertain present.

Politics of Nahuatl in the Mexicayotl Movement

There is a political tension inherent in Mexicayotl practitioners' claim to being Native American. Just as they denounce colonial hegemony as the process that has caused them to become estranged from their own heritage, they are themselves vulnerable to accusations of aiding colonialism by appropriating Indigenous cultural elements and severing Indigenous identity-creation from community membership.

In settler–colonial contexts, acts of "playing Indian," in which settlers don Indigenous costumes, or entire identities, and perform stereotypical representations of "the Indian" have been described in many forms (e.g., Green 1988; Deloria 1998). They may take the form of sports mascots, as a part of events in the scouting movement, as actors in Western cinema, as vendors of New Age spiritual services or merchandise, or simply as a part of cultivating a more interesting persona (e.g., the Canadian conservationist and author Grey Owl, or the American actor "Iron Eyes" Cody). One way of understanding these acts of "playing Indian" is as a kind of fetishism, where the "Native American" is reduced to stand for a single magical or romantic idea, such as connectedness with nature, access to spiritual powers, pride and resistance, authenticity of being, or original ownership rights to land and territory.

It is not straightforward to distinguish in a principled way between the practice of "playing Indian" and the identity project of the Mexicayotl movement. Mexicayotl aesthetics often draw on Mexican national romanticist stereotypes of "Aztec warriors," and their ritual and dance practices often combine re-enaction of elements extracted from ethnohistorical sources about the Aztecs with elements inspired by Plains rituals, such as Plains-style drumming and singing, sweat lodges, and even occasionally expressions in the Lakota language. When noticed, such bricolage points conspicuously to the fact that Mexicayotl practices have a shallow history, and have not emerged from a deep and continuous community tradition. In the Mexica History Facebook group, members often discuss the authenticity of specific elements of Mexicayotl practice, whether they are documented in historical sources, or can be traced to specific Mexicayotl elders, or whether they should be considered foreign or appropriated elements that should be avoided. The members are acutely aware of the risks of being accused of appropriation, and actively seek to avoid or preempt them. In the end, whether one would consider Mexicayotl practices appropriative largely comes down to whether one accepts their identity claim as valid or not. Mexicayotl groups often participate in Indigenous events and organizations, such as powwows where many

Indigenous nations come together to dance, and they gain some recognition and acceptance from other Indigenous groups in this way.

The complicated relations between ancestry, heritage, and indigeneity are not unique to the Mexicayotl movement. In the United States, there are a great many Indigenous groups that are not officially recognized. Some of these unrecognized tribes are organized by people who have only found their Indigenous identities as adults, and who have undergone a kind of racial conversion similar to that of many Mexicayotl activists. Circe Sturm has written about the many unofficial Cherokee tribes and bands whose status as Indigenous is often questioned or outright rejected by recognized Indigenous groups. Enrollment as a citizen in the Cherokee Nation depends exactly on being able to document descent from one of the individuals whose names appear in the earliest official tribal records such as the Dawes Roll. Those people who are confident that they have Cherokee ancestry, but cannot document it to the satisfaction of the tribe, may opt to organize themselves in one of the unrecognized tribes and practice their identities in ways that are similar to Mexicayotl practitioners (Sturm 2010, 63–88).

Similar processes have been described in California, where Chicanos adopt not only Mexica but also Chumash identities (Haley and Wilcoxon 1997, 2005). In Canada, a controversial movement of people self-identify as Métis, and seek to support their claim by demonstrating mixed European-Indigenous ancestry, even if they have no community ties with the Métis nation (Andersen 2014). In Puerto Rico, where the mainstream history has long held that all Indigenous peoples were wiped out by the onslaught of early colonization, today there is a strong movement reclaiming Taíno Indigenous identities, who also support their claims with genealogy, genetics, and family histories (Haslip-Viera 2006) and language reclamation (Feliciano-Santos 2017, 2021). In Peru, an Indigenous identity movement uses the Inca Empire and its associated Quechua language and culture, similarly to how the Mexicayotl/Mexicanidad movement uses Aztec/Mexica (Galinier and Molinié 2013).

The emergence of these Indigenous identity-reclamation movements across the Americas has come at a time when Indigenous political movements stand strong and are able to advance claims on the nation-states with a stronger force than they have for a century. This raises the question of the political relation between projects of identity-reclamation and preexisting and traditionally recognized Indigenous groups and political movements. Where do Mexicayotl and other identity-reclamation movements stand in relation to the wider Indigenous political movement?

"Natives Against Aztlán"

In October 2014, a feud broke out on Facebook between the anonymous operators of a page called "Natives Against Aztlán," and those of another called "Natives Against Divided Natives." The former page, "Natives Against Aztlán" (NAA) advanced a pointed critique of the practices and ideas of the Mexicayotl movement. This page, written anonymously, spoke through the positionality of tribal members of federally recognized US tribes. The page's authors accused Mexica-practitioners of "hobbyism" and appropriation of Indigenous cultural elements that they were not entitled to because they had no community ties to recognized Indigenous communities. They used salty ridicule to criticize the "Aztlanista" movement. They parodied Mexica dancers' colorful costumes, disparaged their inability to speak their heritage languages, parodied their lack of traditional elders, and their need to access their traditions through books. But they also advanced a strong political critique: they denounced the aspect of Mexicayotl ideology that sees the US Southwest as "Aztlán," the mythical homeland of the Mexica people and their descendants. They argued that even though many Mexicans do have Indigenous ancestors, the concept of Aztlán disrespects and undermines the land claims of federally recognized tribes. By claiming as a homeland a territory that is already claimed by others, it poses a threat to the sovereignty of Indigenous Nations of the US Southwest. By extension, when Mexicayotl activists claim to be Indigenous to the US Southwest, they are encroaching on the lands of other Indigenous people.

The critique was responded to by another Facebook page called "Natives Against Divided Natives." Also anonymous, this page spoke from a positionality of Mexicayotl activists and defended against NAA's accusations using a discourse of pan-ethnic unity among Native Americans against settler-colonialism and white supremacy. It asserted that Mexicans and Mexican Americans are Native by blood and ancestry, grounding the claim to Indigenous identity in the discourse of blood quantum, and it accused the former page of causing divisions within the native community and thereby aiding the colonizers and the perpetuating dynamics of white supremacy.

The claim to an Indigenous status outside the established system of tribal recognition is bound to put the Mexicayotl movement at odds with tribal sovereignty activists. Especially the Aztlán ideology, which asserts a claim of ownership of Southwest Tribal lands, is problematic when it comes to producing alliances or even working relations between the Mexicayotl movement and other Indigenous people (Saldaña-Portillo 2016; Gutierrez Nájera and Maldonado 2017). Lately, however, major Chicano organizations such as MeChA have dropped Aztlán from their ideological repertoire—precisely to avoid these problems (Hidalgo 2019). Kurly Tlapoyawa and other Mexicayotl activists in the *Yankwik Mexikayotl* group are not keen on letting go of Aztlán as a central idea of Chicano-ness, but they are quick to emphasize that for them Aztlán is a state of mind, and not a claim to territorial ownership (similar to the way it is conceptualized by Fernando Leal ([1989] 2017).

Mexicayotl activists also have many points in common with other indigenous political activists, and many also have friendships, family ties, cultural ties, and organizational ties to Native American communities on both sides of the border, maintained for example by participation in the US powwow circle, or the Indigenous art production circle. The conflicts that arise may also be a generative kind of friction in Anna Tsing's sense (Tsing 2005), that is a necessary part of the process through which exclusionary nativist ideas are challenged on both sides and solidarities are created.

The anthropological literature on globalization has seen political movements organized around indigeneity as an aspect of the globalization of identities, and have described different kinds of resulting friction. The Comaroffs described a rampant commodification of ethnicity and indigeneity (Comaroff and Comaroff 2009), and Kuper (2003) warned of a return toward a regime of rights based on essentialized identities. Undoubtedly, both would find some of their predictions fulfilled in the Mexicayotl movement. Jonathan Friedman's early work on globalization and identity argued that the globalization of elite identities would create a backlash of indigenization of identities among the less mobile lower classes. Friedman contrasted the indigenization of the identities of marginalized minorities with the reactionary nationalisms of lower-class members of the dominant group (Friedman 2000, 652). He predicted that this backlash would result in a nativist majority politics of the kind that we have witnessed move into political ascendancy over the past years. He considered minority indigenization of identity to be, essentially, a political move meant to enable minority groups to advance claims to territory and political rights against a state that was a natural ally of the majority. Haley (2009) in turn argued that, in a context of a multicultural state where Indigenous minorities had access to certain protections guaranteed by the state, indigenization of identity could equally well take the form of an alliance between the indigenizing movement and the state and state nationalism—for example, by positioning indigeneity as opposed to immigration. In reference specifically to the Mexicayotl movement, Haley argued that in moral terms little was won by simply reversing the role of "immigrant" and "indigene," so that Anglos and Hispanos came to be seen as illegitimate illegal invaders who could, once so labeled, be denied political rights (Haley 2009, 176).

It is true that some groups under the Mexicayotl umbrella, for example the Mexica Movement, spend a lot of time organizing to counteract aspects of white Anglo-American hegemony. They organize counter protests when anti-immigrant or white supremacist organizations organize events, and they mount campaigns against proposed legislation with racist implications. But they also act in solidarity with immigrants: protesting against the mistreatment of detainees by ICE (the US Immigration and Customs Enforcement), organizing translation services and material help to refugees and asylum seekers, and so on. As Haley suggests, it is true that when justifying acts of solidarity with Latin American immigrants, Mexicayotl activists will often argue that those immigrants are, like themselves, Indigenous and therefore cannot legitimately be denied freedom of movement between Indigenous territories or civic rights on "their own land." Haley is understandably put off by the nativist implications of Mexicayotl discourse, but by equating these rhetorical strategies with the white Anglo-nativism entrenched in the political system of the state against which they are reacting, we risk missing that the implications of the two are very different. Mexicayotl activists calling Anglos invaders do not expect Anglos to suddenly realize that they are themselves immigrants and self-deport to Europe so as to stay consistent with their own ideology. Rather, they use it as a way of turning the racial logics entrenched in a settler-colonial society on itself. It demonstrates that the dominant rhetoric of "illegals" and "immigrants" is itself invented and questionable, and indeed reversible. Perhaps such a strategy is better understood as what Alim calls "the political project of transracialization" (Alim 2016). He defines this as a strategic deployment of racial categories and discourses in ways that subvert existing racial orders by drawing their contingent and political nature into focus. By transgressing against an established racial categorization scheme and deploying this transgression rhetorically, Mexicayotl transraciality may contribute to unsettling the belief in racial categories and hierarchies as natural and immutable. Nevertheless, the risk is that it does the exact opposite, and instead further extends the American ancestry-based understanding of race and community to contexts where it has not previously existed.

Additionally, as I have shown, there are also other strands of action within the Mexicayotl identity-reclamation movement, strands that are not primarily about claiming territorial and political rights. Some Mexicayotl activists focus on spirituality and personal development, others on genealogy and family histories, others on cultivating sustainable relations with the land through Indigenous concepts of land stewardship, or on decolonizing scholarship on Mexican Indigenous people and making it available to a general public. Reducing the Mexicayotl movement to a single exclusionary nativist position erases all of these forms of political and cultural action, in which individual existential stances and life decisions of activists and organizers add up to a complex movement, united mainly by its emblematic symbols.

Another way of understanding the politics of Mexicayotl, then, would be exactly by understanding the organization of its symbols. Norma Mendoza-Denton (2008) developed a concept of "hemispheric localism" to describe an organizing principle (or totalizing ideology) in the way that youths in California's Chicano gang culture semiotically construct identities. She noted that the idiom of oppositions between local Norteño and Sureño gangs metaphorically projected local conflicts at the neighborhood level onto a global scale. This projection created a universe of sign alignments, where all signs were recruited to align with either north or south. The youths then made use of these alignments when expressing and interpreting affiliation. The hemispheric localism of the Sureños and Norteños contrast a Global South, indexically tied, opposite economic conditions (poverty/wealth), languages (Spanish/English), national origins (Latin America/US), phenotypes (brown/white), neighborhood, and so on. Haley's proposed indigene/immigrant opposition, which he sees as the political principle behind Mexicayotl discourse of indigeneity, is also one of the elements in the Norteño/Sureño polarity described by Mendoza-Denton, with immigrant status being coded as "south." But for Mendoza-Denton the oppositions come from the bottom up; they are experiences from the everyday life of youths that are projected onto international politics. Politics come to be understood through the everyday meanings that emerge from social life, not the other way around.

In the same way, the Mexicayotl semiotic universe can be understood as a totalizing ideology based on a similar set of recursive projections; they just project their hemispheric alignments differently: onto a West/East or Americas/Europe axis. The Western Hemisphere stands for the Americas, the Indigenous, the resistance to colonial oppression, the brown-skinned, black-haired phenotype, and spirituality centered in communion with ancestors and the land and community-based political organization. The Eastern Hemisphere stands for Europe, colonizing oppression, white phenotypes, a spirituality and politics based on hierarchic relations, and an economy based on capitalist exploitation. Additionally, the Indigenous West stands for a metacultural principle valuing tradition, authenticity, and rootedness, whereas the entire Eastern Hemisphere represents vacuous, unrooted modernity. These processes of mapping from one domain or scale to another is what Irvine and Gal call "fractal recursivity," the process that causes differentiation between two groups by projecting an opposition that is "salient at some level of relationship, onto some other level" (Irvine and Gal 2000, 38).

Mendoza-Denton notes that the concept of the Indigenous does not fit within the north/south hemispheric organization—it is in a way perhaps "too far south" to be on the Sureño map. But the map may change. Rotating the hemispheric axis 90 degrees, the Mexicayotl movement makes the organization fit a model contrasting indigeneity with settler colonialism. It is perhaps revealing that Mexicayotl activists typically talk about their becoming Indigenous as an act of "claiming," and they talk about ethnic affiliations in the same way that Mendoza-Denton's young interlocutors talk about neighborhoods and gangs. They will say, for example, "I don't personally claim Mexica, because my ancestors are from Michoacán, so I am Purhépecha," or "I feel comfortable claiming Mexica, since this is the culture I grew up in" (by a person who has grown up in the Mexicayotl movement).

A narrow focus on the geopolitics of identity and indigeneity risks losing sight of the way the wider political movement and its struggles for rights are anchored in the ground of individual lives where life choices, such as becoming Indigenous, may become a political choice only after they have been made. We may observe that Mexicayotl activists are (among other things) carrying out a nativist political program in response to Anglo dominance, but the reason they are doing this may be located in the realm of lived experiences and strategies for making those experiences meaningful, rather than in a political program. It may be that individual quests to find a way to define oneself in terms that are outside the established census boxes grow into a political movement aiming to achieve that same semiotic sovereignty as a collective.

In order to better become able to see Indigenous futures, Yásnaya Aguilar Gil (2020a, 2018) challenges us to imagine an Indigenous world without states and their borders. There are already several officially "trans-border" Indigenous nations who do not need to work hard to imagine such a world, because they are already living in it—the Haudenosaunee or Mohawk, with reservations straddling and continuously defying the US–Canadian border (Simpson 2014), and the Kumeyaay, Pai, Cocopah, O'odham, Yaqui, Apache, and Kickapoo nations, with territory severed by the tightening US–Mexican border (Leza 2019), as well as the many Mexican Indigenous migrant communities in the United States (Gutierrez Nájera and Maldonado 2017). Mexicayotl activists are joining them in a collective imagining of a world that can be otherwise, and in which they can be otherwise, and they use the Nahuatl language as a tool in assisting this imagination. This process of collective imagining is not without friction, and not without the risk of repeating mistakes of the past.

In the previous chapters, I have been arguing for the potential of Nahuatl in a political strategy of striving toward semiotic sovereignty. I have described Nahuatl as a language with which Indigenous groups can shut themselves off and become opaque to members of majority society. But throughout its history, Nahuatl has also been a trans-language: a language used to bridge divides, to transgress boundaries, transform socialities. Throughout its existence, the Nahuatl language has participated in networks of hybridization, first with other Mesoamerican languages, then with Spanish, and now with English. Indeed, without all these influences and without having been used as a vehicular language in communication between dozens of tribes, nations, and ethnic groups, the language would not be what it is today. Language not only encloses worlds and cognitive territories, it also discloses them to those who make the effort of acquiring them.

The River and the Wall

I met Chris Cuauhtli and his wife and little daughter in Sacramento just before the 2016 presidential election. He was working as a tattoo artist, using his extensive knowledge of Aztec symbols in his designs. About a year later, his life took another wild turn. He contacted the police when he became the victim of a crime, but he was detained by Sacramento police who turned him over to immigration enforcement, and was scheduled for deportation. In this period, ICE was intensifying their search for undocumented immigrants with prior convictions, and he had an outstanding deportation order against him. His friends fought to help, raising money for legal representation, and his adoptive family sought to legalize the adoption retrospectively, but it didn't work, and soon he found himself in Tijuana, having to start over without connections, and far from his family. Chris now lives as one of the many deportees in Tijuana who arrived in the United States as young children, but never achieved a documented legal status. He continues his studies of the Jalisco variety of Nahuatl, and is now in touch with Mexican linguists who work with that variety, and he sometimes gives talks and language courses in Tijuana. In 2022 he published a learner's manual for the extinct Jalisco variety of Nahua, titled *Ma Tiłatucan Mexicano* (Cuauhtli 2022). His story was included as one of the narratives of deportees collected by the University of California–Davis project, *Humanizando la deportación*.[8] In 2021, the project (the Playas de Tijuana Mural Project at UC Davis, with Lizbeth de la Cruz) created a mural on the border fence at Playas de Tijuana, with portraits of some of the people who had told their narratives of deportation. Chris was one of the people depicted, and along with the faces of others whose lives were uprooted in the same way his was, his portrait is now on the very wall that separates him from his daughter (Figure 6.4).

---

[8] Cuauhtli, Chris w. Mary Kate Vernau, "*And Still I Dream/Y aún sueño*," Humanizando la Deportación, Narrative number #164, http://humanizandoladeportacion.ucdavis.edu/en/2019/05/06/164-and-still-i-dream/?.

Figure 6.4 Chris Cuauhtli standing in front of his portrait on the Mexican side of the border fence at Playas de Tijuana.
Photo by Lizbeth de la Cruz Santana.

Imagining a world without borders is made easier by the fact that we can tell stories about Nahua peoples who moved freely into the US Southwest before the arrival of the Spanish, and about their remote ancestors who left the same region and migrated south to Mesoamerica. The dream of a world without borders is shared both by those thousands of Mexican Nahua people who have migrated for work, and who now can only see their families through video conference, and by those who, like Chris, have ended up south of the border with no easy way back. The Nahuatl language helps them envision a world where the Great River and the big fence no longer hinder their dreams and aspirations.

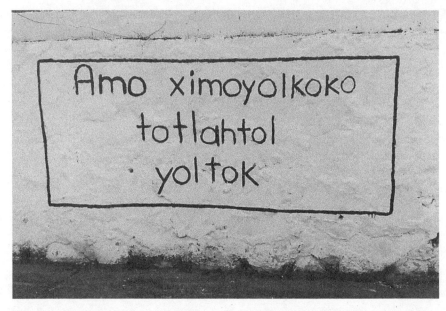

Figure 7.0 *Don't be sad-hearted, our language is alive*; mural slogan by *Acción Poética Náhuatl* carried out by Carlos Octavio Sandoval and a group of students from the Intercultural University and schoolchildren from Tlaquilpa in 2016.
Photo by Carlos Octavio Sandoval.

7
Conclusions
The Current State of Nahuatl

OK TLANEXTIA MASEWALSITLALI	**STILL THE STAR OF THE MASEWALES SHINES**
ipan inin tlalnantli kanin onitlakat	in this motherland where I was born
kanin onikittak pawetsiwa in tonaltsintle	where I saw rise the sacred sun
miak tlalnamikilistle onka ipan ixtlawak	memories extend across the plains
iwan kemeh xochimeh kochi tetlampa mehtzintle	and sleep like flowers 'neath the sacred moon
opanokeh xiwimeh kemeh ehekame	the years passed over us like storms,
iwan tekaxtilkopkeh kemeh se tlalolintle	and earthquake-like turned people into Spaniards
okinehkeh kipoloskeh nochi teokalmeh	who wished to topple temples, adobe huts,
nochi masewalkalmeh nochi tlen tlakaitsmolintle	and erase all that anew makes humans sprout
wel miak otekitiwalokeh masewaltih	the humble *masewales* worked intensely there
ihkwak okichihkeh xoxoktih iwan xalohtih	when they made jars and earthenware
ihkion ipan kakaxtih iwan in teokaltih	like that, on plates and in the churches
kemen okisenkawayah ika miak tlapaloltih	as they completed it with their well-wishes
owalla yaoyotl pampa inon kaxtiltlakameh	wars did come, it was the Spaniards' fault
wan keh sente tlakatl omotewihkeh mexikah	like a single person, the Mexikah fought
tlaxikohkeh nekate ipan ixtlawameh	they suffered and endured upon the plains,
ihkwakon wan satepan Hidalgo okintokak inchan	later, they led Hidalgo to their homes
axan mosiniah tekaxtilkopkeh kihitowah	now those who have turned Spaniards boast:
nelle nochi okipolokoh, nelle nochi otlamik	it all has been destroyed now, all is lost
ipan inin tlalnantli ye akmo tlen mokawa	in this motherland nothing now is left
iwan anmo melawak mexikah ok nochi manik	it is untrue that the Mexikah live here yet
pampa tekitl okichihkeh totatsitsiwan	thanks to burdens that our ancestors bore
iwan totlahtol keh tsotsonalle ok patlani	and because our language still like music soars
iwan tlen otiksalohkeh okachto ok mochiwa	and because our first lessons are practiced still
pampa inon ok tlanextia in tomasewalsitlali	therefore yet our star of *masewales* shines

—Miguel Barrios Espinosa
from *Tlapaliskixochitl*, 1949

Nahuatl Nations. Magnus Pharao Hansen, Oxford University Press. © Oxford University Press 2024.
DOI: 10.1093/oso/9780197746158.003.0008

Histories come to us through language, and they are shaped by the perspective of the storyteller who tells them and by the interests of the audience to which they are told. Miguel Barrios Espinosa, whose poem "*Ok Tlanextia Masewalsitlalin*" tells a history of Nahua survival and resistance, was a schoolteacher in Hueyapan, Morelos, in the 1940s. He was influenced by the American anthropologist and historian Robert Barlow, who also paid for the publication of his poems. Already then, during Mexico's early indigenista period, Barlow realized that Indigenous languages needed institutional support to thrive, and he encouraged Barrios to write in his own language. Barrios's handwritten letters to Barlow are all in Nahuatl, and they evidence a profound devotion to his US benefactor. Published after he had moved to Mexico City, his poems never really reached his hometown, where he is mostly remembered with disapproval as a teacher turned bohemian. The paradox of Barrios's authorship is that his entire work is permeated by a sense of pride and love for his language and his community of origin, yet only by leaving his community did he achieve the possibility of expressing this pride, but for an audience of mostly outsiders. This is a paradox haunting many Indigenous authors. Paja Faudree (Faudree 2013, 236–39) described how this means that Indigenous authors are often accused of being inauthentic, their careers cultivated by economic incentives from the government but disconnected from their communities. Perhaps all outside support for Indigenous language renewal carries this risk of drawing speakers out of their communities, making them clients of whichever institutions support their work. Faudree also shows how this risk can be mitigated when activities of language renewal take place in settings that are integrated in the communal life of those who speak it. This same paradox of intervention has run through all the settings and contexts described in the preceding chapters: whenever some external power intervenes in support of the vitality of an organic process such as language or communal life, it also risks denying that process the chance to achieve a vitality that is sustainable by its own efforts. Political interventions are ambiguous, serving the purposes of the state and the national community, but also creating new spaces where Indigenous communities may sow their seeds, and hope that something useful grows.

I have proposed the concept of semiotic sovereignty to describe how the active use of Indigenous languages and semiotic resources in Indigenous communal life contributes to communities' ability to maintain communal cohesion and political autonomy. I intend this concept to enable educators, activists, linguists, and politicians to approach interventions in support of Indigenous language vitalities from a new angle, asking: How will this intervention support the development of semiotic sovereignty for the community? I believe that more often than not, the interventions most likely to support semiotic sovereignty will be ones that do not necessarily aim at producing new speakers or elaborate learning technologies or educational materials for a language, but rather those that remove the obstacles that are keeping communities from doing this themselves. In her widely disseminated discourse on Indigenous language endangerment at the United Nations for its celebration of the year of Indigenous languages, Yásnaya Aguilar insisted forcefully that Indigenous languages are not "dying," they are being killed by states (Almudena Barragán 2019). The first part of the solution, then, must be to stop whichever processes are effectuating the murder. Only afterward, once the murder has been stopped, will it make sense to administer life support.

Over the course of this book, we have followed Nahuatl through time from the beginning of colonization in the 16th century, through struggles of independence and revolution, and on to the digital and marketized world order of the present day. And we have followed it through space, from the *altepetl* community of Hueyapan on the slopes of Mount Popocatepetl, through the highland region of Zongolica, into the mediatized national public sphere of Mexico, and beyond, across the rivers and border fences, into the United States. It has taken us through the social and political lives of families, educational organizations and institutions, through *altepetl* town-communities, ethnic networks, to the imagined community of the Mexican nation-state.

Nevertheless, even so, the perspective is narrow, and necessarily misses much. By choosing to focus on the role of language, I have disregarded many other practices and fields of action where semiotic sovereignty can potentially be produced: foodways and subsistence, activism and practices in favor of environmental and territorial integrity, craft production, and sociopolitical and religious networks such as the cargo system. I have chosen to focus on language to illustrate the generative and *re*-generative potential of separate semiotic systems and discursive spheres for the development of sovereign politics, but not to suggest that it is the only or even the primary semiotic system through which Indigenous communities fortify their sovereignties. By focusing on Nahuatl, and the paradox inherent in the way it has been adopted by Mexican nationalism, I have kept many other, and perhaps stronger, examples out of view: salient cases for the role of semiotic sovereignty in the service of political autonomy could have been the Zapatista *caracoles* with their independent and collective education system (Mora 2017; Baronnet, Mora Bayo, and Stahler-Sholk 2011), or the autonomous municipality of Cherán in Michoacán (Aragón Andrade 2019); or the many places where Indigenous communities, including Mixes (*ayuuk jay*), Otomíes (*hñähñú/yühü*), Huicholes (*wixáritari*), and Yaquis (*yoeme*), struggle to enforce legitimate ownership rights to their designs and artwork in the face of market exploitation. All across Mexico, there are struggles that suggest the importance of semiotic sovereignty as an important aspect of Indigenous sovereignties. But even more importantly, by focusing on the semiotic aspect of sovereignty, I have not dedicated as much effort as I would like to represent other aspects: such as the ongoing resistance against the physical destruction of Indigenous communities and their lifeways, and of the material conditions for their survival. These struggles are precisely the ones that must be resolved favorably, before the threat against linguistic vitalities can be said to have been mitigated.

This is not to say that semiotic politics are superficial or merely symbolic. Rather, I have tried to demonstrate how the semiotic aspects of community politics are not separate from a community's relations with the material conditions of communal life, but integral to them. As Urban (1996) argues, we cannot make sense of the sensible material world, except through semiotic mediation. It is precisely when language is reduced to an emblem of identity, and the intimate connection between meaning and matter is severed, that semiotic sovereignty comes under threat.

By describing how Indigenous language use is embedded and integrated in community life, and in the lives of individuals, I have posed a distinction between identity-based communities, such as the "imagined community" of the Mexican nation to whom Nahuatl can be a generic emblem of a shared identity and claimed national territory, and *experience-based communities*, such as Indigenous *altepetl* communities that are united by shared experiences of a specific corner of the material world, mediated by specific varieties of Nahuatl and other locally relevant semiotic means of meaning-making.

Communities and Language: Theorizing the Dynamics of Revitalization

The account of the Nahua glottopolitics advanced in the preceding chapters has proposed that the process of the contraction of Nahuatl has not been uniform, but is mediated by politics, advancing slower where Indigenous communities see themselves as more politically distinct. A community's maintenance of a separate political identity also supports their maintenance of a separate language, just as the maintenance of a separate language increases the ability for a community to maintain a sense of political separateness from the nation-state. Throughout the *longue durée* of Mexican history, it has been the case that face-to-face communities that were linguistically distinct from the imagined community of the nation have been more likely also to resist political domination, either through open rebellion or through silent defection. It has also been the case that the more resistant a community has proven to outside attempts at domination, the more likely they have been to maintain their Indigenous languages.

This poses a paradox for the standard sociolinguistic explanation of language endangerment: the more benevolent the nation-state is and the more rewards it offers to speakers of minority languages who reorient their attention away from their local communities and toward the national community, the more likely they are to abandon their Indigenous language. In contrast, when the state is at its most oppressive, marginalizing Indigenous people and depriving them of access to resources outside of the community, the more vital will be their languages. Standard sociolinguistic models, such as Terborg's ecology of pressures, posit that systematic socioeconomic marginalization of speakers of minority languages creates a negative incentive to language shift, in effect pushing Indigenous people away from their language. In contrast, one may consider whether the major threat to Indigenous languages is the benefactor state, which lures people away from their languages with offers of a better life within the mainstream public. Speakers do not choose to abandon their languages, but simply choose to pursue better lives outside of the sphere of existence where the language is meaningful. This argument is borne out by the ethnographic data that shows how in Hueyapan and in Zongolica, individual choices of maintaining or abandoning the language are directly motivated by the access it provides to desirable life projects (Pharao Hansen 2016).

The main argument here, however, is that language maintenance is not simply the sum of individual language choices. Within a framework where a subaltern language exists inside the sphere of dominance of a hegemonic one, individual life choices do add up to language endangerment. But the reverse is not the case: languages do not sustain themselves through the accumulation of conscious choices of their individual speakers. Long-term language vitality requires the support of a public, which in turn imprints its lifeworld, and language, onto the existence of those who interpret their lives in relation to the forms of life it offers.

Here we may return to the concept of "function" and the claim that "language survival requires the language to have a function," that Kenan Malik has attributed to Miguel León-Portilla.[1] If, as Malik, we were to adopt what Silverstein called "denotational ideology" and understand the function of a language to be purely denotational communication, then small languages would prima facie be less "functional" than larger ones. Larger languages allow intelligible communication with a broader community of interlocutors. Linguistic anthropology has done much to expose the "denotational ideology" as precisely that, an ideology, and to demonstrate that the potential functions of language are both much more complex and much more variable than this ideology suggests. No linguistic anthropologist would be surprised at this book's claim that among the functions of language is that of exercising power, and of producing politics. But the claim here goes a little further than that, suggesting that the political function of language, as providing the semiotic infrastucture for a circumscribed sense of "we-ness," is fundamental for language vitality. A highly significant finding which also supports this argument is that of Olko et al. (2022), who demonstrated that language vitality was also correlated with higher levels of social well-being in the community. The present work would motivate the question whether language use is the cause of higher well-being, or whether it is rather social well-being stemming from a positive intersubjective stance within the community that provides the foundation on which language vitality can be grounded.

The theoretical argument of this book claims a significant relation between language maintenance and the intensity of the political solidarity of the community of speakers. This relation stems from the recognition that language serves several functions within a community. One such function is as a semiotic vehicle through which the qualia of everyday life, the sensible world, are turned into meaningful experience that is intersubjectively communicable. Another function is as a shared but exclusive semiotic code that enables the production of a dialogue that both produces and implies a sense of we-ness that includes those who speak the language and excludes those who do not. These two functions integrate to produce a community of experience, where the exclusive code indexes a shared, intersubjective lifeworld. This argument

---

[1] In his essay "Let Them Die," in which he argues that language death is a natural consequence when a language is no longer useful to its speakers, Kenan Malik attributes the statement that "in order to survive, a language must have a function" to León-Portilla (http://www.kenanmalik.com/essays/die.html). I have not been able to verify that León-Portilla made the statement. Malik's idea of "function" is based on a purely denotational ideology of language and is limited to the function of establishing communication between people—it follows that people are better served by speaking languages with more speakers. Whether or not León-Portilla made the statement or not, in other work he clearly shows that he recognizes many other important functions, other than denotational communication, that small Indigenous languages serve for their speakers (e.g., here: http://www.juridicas.unam.mx/publica/librev/rev/derhum/cont/51/pr/pr35.pdf, "*las lenguas indígenas en el tercer milenio*"). The view he describes in this work is basically the one represented by Hale et al. (1992), which I would consider the standard view in contemporary descriptive linguistics.

is supported by the existence of localocentric linguistic purism, which takes the specificity of the local ways of speaking and the way it indexes the local landscape of geographical, spatial, social, and moral relations as the backdrop when defining what is pure and authentic. From the community of experience, a political community, a public, may emerge, when the dialogue takes on the character of communicative action, through which the community seeks to define a collective path forward. This can be seen, for example, when a community decides to reclaim their language and the lifeworld it indexes through overt activism, or when it decides to use the same language revitalization activism to pursue political interests by emphasizing its indigeneity in the national public.

From this theoretical position emerges a political argument that can be applied to critique and analyze social phenomena located at the intersection of language and community politics. This argument is supported by the ethnographic data that elucidates the complex articulations between the language policy of the Mexican nation, the localocentric language revitalization projects of Indigenous communities, and the ongoing negotiations of sovereignty and domination between them. Because of the close relation between linguistic and political vitality, projects of linguistic revitalization may be conducive to strengthening local political identity. Conversely, the argument implies that unless revitalization projects integrate a political component and carry out some political function for the would-be speech community, they are unlikely to succeed. When I apply these arguments to the state-sponsored language revitalization projects currently carried out by INALI across Mexico, it motivates a significant skepticism. In fact, I am forced to conclude that state-sponsored language revitalization is likely to undermine the vitality of Indigenous languages for three distinct reasons:

1. State control of language renewal is likely to induce Indigenous communities to increasingly orient themselves away from the localocentric public and take on a nation-centric stance, lobbying for resources and support. Additionally, because Spanish is the vehicular language used in engagements with the state, this reorientation contributes further to making the Indigenous language obsolete as a language of a political community.
2. Second, because state-driven revitalization efforts are highly centralized, with linguistic authority being constituted outside of the communities themselves, it amounts to an expropriation of the Indigenous resources by the state, removing ownership of the languages from the local political community.

3. Because state-driven revitalization efforts seem to be largely used by the state to divert attention from urgent problems of realpolitik, it is never adequately supported by the institutional infrastructure, and does not receive sufficient economic resources to be able to handle the tasks that could potentially improve linguistic vitality. The critical arguments by scholars who have interrogated the consequences of multiculturalist policies implemented within the frameworks of neoliberal policy (e.g., Hale, Povinelli, Murray Li) also hold for the field of government-sponsored language revitalization.

However, a second argument tempers the skeptical conclusion of the first: when the discourse of national public sphere assigns a positive value to Indigenous languages, this provides the Indigenous communities with a new currency that can be used in its negotiations with the state, and which may serve to advance localocentric agendas, and to bolster local public spheres. Additionally, by constructing new infrastructure for the production and circulation of local knowledge, such as local community-driven revitalization projects or intercultural educational institutions, the state also creates fissures within its own totalizing infrastructure of knowledge and discourse, which can be used by Indigenous communities in the pursuit of their own purposes. These are the sociopolitical and semiotic dynamics that underlie the concept that I have called "semiotic sovereignty."

The State of the Nation: Indigenous Mexico Now

Maintenance of the semiotic resources of a community is as significant for its political empowerment and long-term political survival as the politics that involve its tangible resources. Nonetheless, it must be acknowledged that by brute necessity the struggle for short-term physical survival holds the priority in many Indigenous communities. Therefore scholars and communities alike must be wary of allowing the state to use its support of cultural rights to divert attention from the more problematic aspects of its politics against Indigenous communities. It is clear that while the Mexican state enjoys emphasizing its liberal record on cultural rights as a major achievement, it is simultaneously pursuing an authoritarian policy in other aspects of its engagement with Indigenous communities, and in doing so, is routinely violating fundamental human rights.

When I was in the field in 2013–2014, the issue of Indigenous language revitalization was not what dominated the media landscape. The war on drugs took on a new phase in the first months of Enrique Peña Nieto's presidency as the media reported that across the state of Michoacán local militias, so-called *autodefensas*, were taking up arms against the cartels—also in Nahual-speaking towns such as Ostula on the Pacific coast (Gledhill 2014). In Indigenous communities in the states of Guerrero and Michoacán, many of them Nahuatl-speaking, *policias comunitarias*, armed community police forces working within the *usos y costumbres* legislation, patrolled their communities to keep out strangers, and to curb the extortion and kidnappings that organized criminal organizations inflicted on communities. These issues, which directly impacted the national security situation and which made the state look increasingly incompetent and incapable of providing the most basic security for its citizens, were what dominated discussions in the national public sphere. When Peña Nieto finally acted, it was the *autodefensas* he cracked down on, exactly as it seemed that they would be able to push back the cartels.

Simultaneously with this development, across the country Indigenous communities were protesting against the state. Yaquis in the state of Sonora closed a major highway in an attempt to get the government to respect their right to water from the Yaqui River. In San Luis Potosí, Huichol communities were protesting the granting of mining contracts to Canadian mining companies on areas of previously protected wilderness that were traditionally sacred to them. In southern Veracruz, marines invaded the Nahua community of Tatahuicapan when they shut off the water supply to the city of Coatzacoalcos, as the city refused to pay for the water that was being supplied to them from the community's springs.[2] And in Morelos, Puebla, and Tlaxcala, dozens of communities, many of them Nahua, protested against the construction of natural gas pipelines through community land that had been expropriated for tiny reimbursements.[3] National media were silent about all of this, except in some cases when the sudden disappearance or imprisonment of a local leader of the protesters caused brief outrage. Moreover, in all of these cases the government strategy was the same: no negotiations, no concessions; instead, crushing the protests by brute force. In Morelos, the pipelines were scheduled to pass through the community of Amilcingo, a community where Nahuatl was spoken until some 50 years ago, and where many still identify as Indigenous Nahuas. In Morelos, the hope of a more amiable engagement with community activists from the new leftist government was crushed as the first

---

[2] Information from interviews with people of Tatahuicapan in March 2013. See also this article: https://agua.org.mx/biblioteca/maestros-dejan-sin-agua-a-coatzacoalcos-2/

[3] Field notes from interviews with activists in Amilcingo, March 2013. Also: http://www.proceso.com.mx/374048/anuncian-caravana-de-pueblos-contra-el-gasoducto-morelos.

months of Andrés Manuel López Obrador's presidency (and Cuauhtemoc Blanco's governorship of the state) saw the assassination of Samir Flores from Amilcingo, who had been leading protests against the expropriation of his community's lands. Assassinations of Indigenous activists speaking out against state-sponsored megaprojects remain an appallingly frequent occurrence.

The dismaying situation of rampant violence and insecurity also characterizes Mexican education politics. Two weeks after I left the Mexico in September 2014, the news reported that 43 students of the Raul Isidro Burgos rural teachers' college in the town of Ayotzinapa had disappeared after being attacked by police on the way to a protest. All of these students were training to become teachers, and the teachers' college had a reputation for encouraging its students' radical politics. Many of the missing students came from Nahuatl-speaking communities in central Guerrero. It soon became clear that police, acting in collusion with cartels and under direct orders of the mayor of the vity of Iguala, had attacked the students, killing three of them, and kidnapped 43 who didn't manage to escape—and they have been disappeared since then, widely presumed dead. The event of course sparked national as well as international outrage and protests. Moreover, it completely falsified to the public both the government's claims to have curbed the drug-related violence (the mayor of Iguala turned out to be part of a cartel) and its denial of police and military involvement in organized crime.[4] Nearly 10 years later, it is clear that several state institutions played criminal parts in the disappearances. In 2022, the administration of President López Obrador (AMLO) arrested the former attorney general Murillo Karám on charges of having obstructed the course of justice in the investigation of the events (he was accused of having produced a version of events that exculpated the state with information extracted by torture called the *verdad histórica* [historic truth]). If it needed further demonstration, the events also showed with all possible clarity that in the Mexico of today it is an extremely dangerous business to engage in radical politics. In Hueyapan and at the UVI, I had witnessed that individual teachers, driven by passion for their work and for social change, were the ones opening and exploiting spaces of possibility within the institutional and political structure. After Ayotzinapa, Mexico had 43 fewer of such teachers, and probably countless others who were deterred from trying to become one.

---

[4] Navarro, L. H. (2015). Ayotzinapa: el dolor y la esperanza. *El Cotidiano, 189*, 7. See also a detailed description of the events at: http://www.proceso.com.mx/415839/iguala-la-noche-del-horror-minuto-a-minuto.

In the years since 2016, when the first version of what eventually became this book was finished, the importance of Indigenous issues in Mexican national politics has not diminished. With the election of López Obrador in 2018, a new chapter in the history of relations between the Mexican nation and Indigenous communities began. Many Indigenous groups celebrated his victory, which was widely perceived as a victory for the Mexican working class broadly defined, over an established political elite of crony capitalists.

In the weeks and months after his inauguration, AMLO visited many Indigenous communities and participated in a political ceremony that had not been performed by any of his presidential predecessors—a ritual called *entrega del bastón de mando* [offering the staff of leadership] (Alonso Gutiérrez 2019). In these rituals, Indigenous representatives, dressed in local ethnic garb, greeted the similarly dressed president, and handed him a staff symbolizing the legitimate rulership of their community and the nation (Ortega Sánchez 2020). In some Indigenous communities, particularly in Oaxaca, such ceremonies have traditionally been used following the election of local authorities. Now the ceremony was transmitted on Mexican national TV. Like so many other engagements between the Mexican nation and Indigenous communities, the ceremony was fraught and ambiguous: Did it symbolize the president's intention to be a leader for all Mexicans, also the Indigenous ones, his respect of the self-determination of Indigenous communities and their traditional ways, or was it a ritual in which Indigenous communities swore fealty and allegiance to the nation and its leader, preempting any subsequent attempts to disavow his legitimacy? Under AMLO, the Indigenous politics of the Mexican state continues to be characterized by this kind of double-voiced communication, and already his presidency has been marked by the inherent contradictions of this kind of politics.

For the Mexican left, and for Indigenous communities affected by it, a mayor point of disaffection with AMLO's presidency has been the plan for the *Tren Maya* [The Maya Train]: a planned train route from Cancún through the Calakmul biosphere to Chiapas, with the aim of drawing some of the tourists from Yucatán's beaches toward a more cultural form of tourism, as they pass through the historical heartland of various Maya peoples. Environmentalist critics maintain that far from contributing to the protection of the national park, the train and the kind of tourism it seeks to develop will be devastating for the biodiversity of the area. Indigenous critics further argue that the project has been developed without legitimate consultation with the Indigenous communities that are claimed to be likely to benefit from tourism. Indigenous activists have largely seen the project as another example of the state ignoring the territorial and political rights of

Indigenous communities as soon as prestigious megaprojects are on the line. Mexican law (and international conventions) stipulates that Indigenous communities have a right to prior consultation before their territories are affected by such projects, and some consultation meetings were arranged by the state. Critics argue, however, that these were mock consultations, in which only community members who stand to gain from or are otherwise favorably disposed from the outset were heard. The process leading to the *Tren Maya* has been used as a demonstration that such consultation processes are essentially dishonest, and fail to adequately respect Indigenous political rights (Casanova Casañas 2021). Simultaneously, AMLO closed the CDI (Comisión de Desarrollo de Pueblis Indígena) and instead created INPI (Instituto Nacional de Pueblos Indígenas) to take care of Indigenous issues. He also proposed closing INALI, which perhaps was seen as a stepchild created by previous PRI and PAN governments, putting the responsibility for language policy also under INPI. This, however, was met with widespread disapproval, and a clear sign of lowering the political priority of Indigenous language, just as the UN Decade of Indigenous Languages commenced. Predictably, reports are now that INALI is being deprioritized economically, being incorporated into INPI. Instead, López Obrador's prestige project for Indigenous peoples is the opening of an Indigenous University in Milpa Alta, a Nahua community in the southern part of Mexico City, which was scheduled to open in the fall of 2023. It is of course not at all clear what the effects of these policies will be for Indigenous communities, but in spite of a relentless critique of his politics by right-wing pundits and radical activists, López Obrador also remains highly popular among many Indigenous intellectuals, many of whom see him as a president attuned to the needs of rural and Indigenous communities.

What is clear, however, is a growing tendency of Indigenous communities to seek autonomy through the *sistemas normativos internos* ([internal normative systems], what was previously called *usos y costumbres* [practices and customs]), opting out of party politics altogether. One of the first towns to do this was the Purhépecha community of Cherán, which opted to adopt a local government based on *sistemas normativos internos* in 2011, during a conflict with illegal loggers who were considered to be in cahoots with leadership of the political parties (Aragón Andrade 2019). Instead, since then, Cherán has governed itself with a council that is elected directly in public assemblies. The success of Cherán has inspired many more towns to opt out of electoral party politics—in Michoacán, in Oaxaca, in Chiapas, and, as we saw in Chapter 4, also in Hueyapan, Morelos. This growing desire in Indigenous communities to govern themselves without participating in the electoral politics of the state can be seen as a result of a deep-seated frustration with the inability of the Mexican state to secure the basic safety, basic rights, and basic resources of Indigenous citizens, but it is also in many cases a repudiation of a class of local political elites who have been seen as operating for their own gain, against the local common good, and in collaboration with criminal organizations and state-level political networks.

Like Cherán, many Indigenous communities and rural towns in Mexico find themselves under siege by powerful actors and organizations, not only criminal organizations and political organizations with business alliances, but also foreign extractivist corporations seeking to secure lucrative contracts and concessions, and permits for extraction and construction. For the past decade, every year dozens of environmentalist activists, many of them Indigenous, have been killed or disappeared, as they worked to hinder business interests, legal and illegal, from usurping land rights and degrading natural resources. This threat, which is undermining the very foundation of Indigenous communal life, the relation between people and territory, is a crisis of Indigenous sovereignties that is much more acute, and which has much higher stakes, than current threats to semiotic sovereignty. Nevertheless, the argument that I put forth here is that semiotic sovereignty and the communal cohesion that it represents may be a significant element in building the political foundations to enable Indigenous communities to protect their territorial sovereignty in broad solidarity, instead of letting individual activists take the vulnerable positions at the vanguard of what are truly collective struggles. In addition to the contradictions and paradoxes that surge when the state supports Indigenous language activism, it is reasonable to ask what the state's goodwill in the protection of Indigenous languages even means, as long as it cannot guarantee the life and safety of those who defend Indigenous lands. If, instead of supporting Indigenous languages, the state could guarantee the integrity of Indigenous territories and the personal safety of those who defend them, it seems that communities themselves would be better able to maintain the vitalities of their languages.

Scales and Publics: Experienced and Imagined Communities

Beyond the question of language vitality, I have examined the political relations between Indigenous communities and the nation-state (Urban and Sherzer 1991), and, in doing so, I have relied on the concept of the "public sphere." The conceptualization of the "public" that I have developed differs in some ways from how this concept has been used before. Typically, as described by Cody (2011), the concept of political publics has been reserved for mass-mediated forms of "stranger-sociality," in which technology supports the creation of "imagined communities" of unprecedented scope. The primary way in which this study adds to previous approaches is by attending to the phenomenological foundations of the public as well as its tangible semiotic infrastructure. No community, imagined or otherwise, can come into existence without somehow making its way into the conceptual systems of its members through experience. In the case of "stranger sociality," this means that the sensible signs that are to be interpreted as indicating the existence of a metaphysical community must be present within the field of experience of individual lives (Urban 1996). The community's indexes must insert themselves into experience in order for the imagined community to integrate itself into the subjective and intersubjective lifeworlds of a group of human beings. In this way, even the most abstract national community is also only viable as long as it is also an "experiential community" of some sort. The mass-mediated public works in this way, by saturating lifeworlds with its own signs: flags, national institutions, public officials, national celebrations, the salute to the flag every Monday morning, parades, tricolors, elections, television shows, and words such as *mexicano, méxico, el país* [the country], *pátria* [the fatherland], *nosotros los mexicanos* [we Mexicans], *la bandera* [the flag], among others. But in spite of the seeming all-pervasiveness of these signs of the nation, they matter little if a group of people is not paying attention to them. Or if they live in a lifeworld where signs of another public are even more pervasive than the signs of the nation. Or if a local public consistently interpret the signs of the nation as representing an oppositional force to that which they identify as members of (as in the case of a counter-public). This is the strength of the local face-to-face public and the counter-public, what allows them to live in spite of being embedded within the scope of a national community.

Publics are not discrete impenetrable bubbles; they intersect and subsume each other at recursive scales. Blommaert's concept of "sociolinguistic scales" (2007) allows us to understand how it is that publics can exist within publics. For Blommaert, scales are a hierarchical or vertical order of semiotic contexts that serve as indexical grounds for the interpretation of signs (Blommaert, Westinen, and Leppänen 2014). Using Silverstein's concept of indexical orders, Blommaert proposes a scalar embeddedness of semiotic communities, so that at the highest level only the most essential or denotational indexes contribute to meaning, whereas semiotic communities at lower scales each add specific local indexes. Blommaert describes the asymmetry in indexical associations in terms of intertextuality, a difference in the number of co-texts associated with a given sign. Another way to think of it would be as an experiential asymmetry. Under this view, experiential communities can be said to exist at different scales, but the one who has limited personal experience with a community associates fewer indexes with the symbols of the community than those who live in it, and consequentially the interpretation becomes "thinner" (in the sense of Geertz 1973). At the higher semiotic scales, indexical networks are thin, but at the lowest scales, they are thickly saturated by the minutiae of everyday experiences, shared between the members of the local place-based community who see and interact with each other directly. There is a continuum of different degrees of "indexical thickness" from the local experiential community to the national imagined community. Social scale then covaries with *experiential intensities*, and therefore different qualities of identity.

Blommaert, however, does not consider the role of locality in producing thicker webs of indexicality, or how these scalar differences may impinge on the formation of communities and identities. This question, however, has been central to the present endeavor, and that is why a phenomenological approach has been necessary. We may understand the relation between a national public and its embedded publics as a constant struggle for attention between publics at different scales, at different levels of abstractness, and at different degrees of distance from the everyday lives of people. The mass-mediated public has the advantage when it comes to commanding the attention of large numbers of strangers in wide swaths of space. But everyday interaction between people who know each other in a local public sphere has the advantage in terms of frequency of exposure (especially if the location is relatively isolated from the macro-public by a semiotic membrane provided by a separate denotational language indexing a distinct local lifeworld, or by sheer physical distance).

Within the context of superdiversity, Blommaert posits the existence of "light communities" (Blommaert and Varis 2015) united, for example, only by the identifying as the same kind of consumer (e.g., the identity of being a "BMW-owner" or an "Apple guy"). The type of consumer who buys the work of Indigenous artists to support "national art" would be this type of consumer, and in such a context the "imagined nation" would be a light community in Blommaert's sense. The Mexican nation's efforts at branding itself reproduces the type of light identities found in consumer culture, and consequently its engagements with Indigenous symbols are necessarily shallow.

Probably a "national community" and other forms of "stranger sociality" will by necessity be "lighter" than communities based on continuous everyday interactions.

In relation to the process of national expropriation of Indigenous signs posited in Chapter 3, one might say that the expropriated signs are never "lost" to the community. This expropriation then would be a victimless crime. But the critique advanced here proceeds from the premise that nationalizing the signs strips them of their local indexes, making them semiotically shallow. They also risk becoming one more index of the nation, contributing to the saturation of Indigenous lifeworlds with national signs. Therefore, the ability of Indigenous peoples to maintain the value of their semiotic resources depends again on their ability to maintain their meaningfulness within the local lifeworld, without shifting the interpretational context to the scale of the nation. The richness of indexical meaning wanes as the signs travel further away from the local context and up through the semiotic scales. This is one of the ways that "imagined communities" are fundamentally different from "experiential communities": they represent different experiential textures and intensities (Kockelman 2022).

Consequently, this book also seeks to motivate anthropologists to attend to the different phenomenological qualities of publics, qualities that depend, among other factors, upon their semiotic infrastructure, and their scale. One may guess that different types of publics, with different phenomenological qualities and different semiotic structures, may significantly correlate with the affective and emotional aspects of publicness. This is a venue for future research.

Moreover, by pointing to the existence of oral publics, it becomes possible to attend to the ways that publics at different scales compete for the attention of individuals, each public seeking to saturate local and individual lifeworlds with their indexes. I believe such a perspective can contribute significantly to the concept of "superdiversity" by not only acknowledging the shallowness, superficiality, and delocalized nature of identity processes in superdiverse environments, but also attending to the existential and experiential worlds in which superdiverse publics coexist and co-articulate. If the observable superdiversity of signs is understood as indexes of competing publics, and as signposts that people use to navigate between those publics, then we may arrive at new ways of interpreting the superdiverse environment of a global world. And we may discover new ways of understanding gradient identities and community memberships when we see them as arranged along a spectrum of experiential intensities, rather than as a binary inside/outside distinction.

Semiotic Sovereignties

The idea of "semiotic sovereignty" that I have developed is first and foremost meant as a call for scholars working with the semiotic resources of small communities (especially scholars who are themselves outsiders to the publics they study), to be mindful of the political stakes of such work, which may be much greater than we can easily imagine. At this point, non-Indigenous scholars working with Indigenous communities cannot be ignorant of how "research" has at many times been experienced by those communities as deeply exploitative and allied with oppressive colonial forces (after all, Tuhiwai Smith's "decolonizing methodologies" is now in its third edition). But even as we try to avoid this, and we seek to work decolonially and in engagement with Indigenous communities and nations, there is a risk that this engagement becomes so light as to be a mere metaphor, or that it becomes extractive in spite of our efforts to the contrary. I hope that by focusing on sovereignty and the relation between semiotic resources broadly construed and the experience of communal life, we may establish a rule of thumb that makes it easier to steer clear of such dangers. We may ask ourselves, how does my engagement with Indigenous semiotic resources affect the semiotic sovereignty of the community? How does it contribute to the community's ability to maintain control of their own semiotic resources within their own public sphere? If the effect is negative, then regardless of whether we see our work as decolonial and empowering, it may in fact be the opposite.

However, I have also shown that we have to be extremely attentive to political scales, and recursively embedded publics, and the way semiotic resources flows between them. What aids the semiotic sovereignty of the Mexican nation-state and consolidates its control of Indigenous semiotic resources may be based on expropriating resources from Indigenous communities. And even the formulation and promotion of an Indigenous ethnic identity tied to a specific language may undermine the sovereignty of local communities whose publics are tied not to a general ethnolinguistic affiliation, but to a specific variety of Nahuatl. This challenges us to always be specific about which public it is that we are engaging, at what scale, and at what intensity of experiential engagement.

Another important effect of scale that we can take from the ethnographic contexts here is that politics and political action operate at several different scales at the same time. This means that there is not necessarily an inherent contradiction between Indigenous communities critiquing the state and its practices, or opting out of national party politics, while at the same time participating in its institutions to further their local agendas, or even celebrating the national community and national identity, as they demand full, and meaningful, inclusion.

Secondarily, I hope that the notion of semiotic sovereignty may be of use in theories and analyses of nationalism. While most theories of nationalism have attended to the relation between the national community and its language, it has not been explained in terms that are sociologically or linguistically adequate. Explanations have ranged from the magical thinking of the early romantics, which attributes almost spiritual powers to language, to the prosaic material analysis that would have the national language be simply the language of whichever powerful elite can impose its language on others. These do not account well for situations where the language seen as central to the nation's stock of symbols is not the language that is most widely spoken (e.g., Nahuatl in Mexico, Irish in Ireland), nor for the ways in which language users may experience a language as an affective force uniting them with a community that uses it. Semiotic sovereignty could be understood as an essential property of nationalism, through which the nation simultaneously exerts a functional exclusion of those who do not have access to its language, and a compelling emotional inclusion of those who do.

Nahuatl Futurity

There is no reason to think that Nahuas lack the scientific expertise to guide their own linguistic future and maintain their semiotic sovereignty. Nahua scholars and intellectuals are working on this in many different contexts. Nahua poets and writers produce literary works in Nahuatl for the consumption of Nahua publics—Martín Tonalmeyotl, Mardonio Carballo, Victoriano de la Cruz Cruz, Crispin Martínez Rosas, Irma Estela Martínez, and Ethel Xochitiotzin Pérez are all prominent members of a new generation of Nahua writers and intellectuals. Simultaneously, Nahua linguists and educators in the academy work determinedly on devising useful approaches to strengthening Nahuatl in the communities where it is spoken. Refugio Nava Nava at the University of Tlaxcala is studying how to improve bilingual education (Nava Nava 2017, 2013), Abelardo de la Cruz Cruz and Ofelia Cruz Morales are working with language maintenance and strengthening in their own communities of Chicontepec, Veracruz (Melton-Villanueva, Cruz, and Morales 2022), Humberto Iglesias Tepec is writing a dictionary of his own Nahuatl variety of Atliacac, Guerrero; Rafael Nava Vite as director of the Intercultural University of Veracruz continues the work of creating monolingual Nahuatl higher education;[5] Malaquías Sánchez of Tlaquilpa coordinates the Tequila

---

[5] Nava Vite, Santes Gómez, and Mirenda Landa 2022; Figueroa Saavedra, Lorenzo, and Vite 2022.

campus promoting the use of the language there; Guillermo Garrido Cruz is now fomenting similar programs at the Intercultural University of Puebla; and many Nahuas are working in many ways to ensure that the Nahuatl language is integrated in the process as Nahua communities move toward the future. Linguist Lucero Flores Nájera at the National Autonomous University of Mexico studies Nahuatl syntax and morphology but also works on language reclamation and the use of children's group-learning for Nahuatl language acquisition; she emphasizes the role of creating spaces for children to play and speak using the language:

> *Nikihtos in tehwan (tonanwan, totahwan, tokokoltsitsiwan, totiohwan, wanoksekin) de welika tikpiah se weyi tekitl para timotlapwiskeh wan tikititiliskeh in mexikano inpiltontsitsin, wan nihki matikkawakan in yehwan mamotlapwikan ika mexikano ihtek in koneololistli ipampa ihkón sehsen pipiltontsin yes aka akin kinchihchiwa wan kinititia in mexikano wan in mexikayotl.* [I will say that we (our mothers, our fathers, our grandparents, our uncles and others) really have a great task, that we may tell and show *Mexicano* to the children, but we must also let them speak together using Mexicano in child-groups because that way it will be the children themselves who create and teach the Mexicano language and the culture]. (Flores Nájera 2023, 11–12)

Ancient Nahuas did not live in the belief that the world they inhabited, including their ways of life and their communities, would remain as they were, unchanged forever. They saw themselves as living in the fifth epoch of creation, illuminated by the Fifth Sun, which had begun when two boys sacrificed themselves by self-immolation, becoming the current sun and moon, and the Gods then sacrificed their blood to put the spheres in motion. The world lit by this Fifth Sun would in turn end, in a cataclysm of earthquakes, and be substituted by another, as yet unknown, epoch. Revolution and cataclysmic change have always been integral in Nahua conceptions of the world, and understood as a force that may lead to new, and perhaps better, futures. The force of change and motion, called *olin* in Nahuatl, was so central to Nahua conceptions of time and history, that it gave its name to one of the 13 day signs in the Nahua calendar, and to the Fifth Sun called *Nahui Olin* "4 motion." Nahuas know that we live in a time of change.

In November 2022, I visited Tequila again for the first time since the pandemic. I was there to visit Gabriela Citlahua, with whom I had been collaborating on a new research project in which we studied how Nahua people in different communities communicate about their local landscape, and how they use landscape features when they describe location and spatial relations.

Since I had seen her last, Gabriela, her partner Ángel, and their little daughter had moved up on a west-facing slope northwest of the Tequila town center. We walked up there by the winding muddy paths, Gabriela carrying the little one on her back, wrapped in her *rebozo*. The baby's eyes were open all the way, quietly observing her environment as trees, leaves, flowers, sky, and mountain flowed past her at the rhythm of her mother's gait.

From up there on the hill, where the family built their little wooden house, there is a perfect view down toward the town to the south, and north toward Orizaba and the extinct volcano that Nahuas call *Istaktepetl* "White Mountain," or *Sitlaltepetl* "star mountain," but which appears as *Pico de Orizaba* on the maps. I stood there, taking in the breathtaking panorama for a while, before entering the house. Because of the move, and because of becoming a mother, Gabriela had put the little school *Nikan Tipowih* on pause, but the teaching materials in Nahuatl were all there in her house—ready for neighborhood children to come and play and learn.

Gabriela and I spoke Spanish together as we worked, discussing a chapter we were writing about placenames and landscape rituals in Tequila. But when she attended to her daughter in her cot, she switched to Nahuatl, the little one grabbing at her fingers, or playing with a ball of wool. The little one didn't answer yet, but her full attention was on her mother's voice, speaking to her caringly. This little girl, with her eyes glinting, full of curiosity for the world around her, represents the future of the Nahuatl language. Her name is *Olin*.

Figure 7.1 View of Tequila (own)
View of Tequila from Gabriela and Ángel's home

Works Cited

Agha, Asif. 2007. *Language and Social Relations*. Cambridge: Cambridge University Press.
Aguilar, Mario E. 2009. *The Rituals of Kindness: The Influence of the Danza Azteca Tradition of Central Mexico on Chicano-Mexcoehuani Identity and Sacred Space*. Doctoral dissertation, Claremont Graduate University.
Aguilar Gil, Yásnaya Elena. 2013. "La diversidad lingüística y la comunalidad." *Cuadernos del Sur* 34: 71–81.
Aguilar Gil, Yásnaya Elena. 2018. *Un nosotrxs sin estado: Una nota sobre lectura y colonialismo*. México, D.F.: ONA Ediciones.
Aguilar Gil, Yásnaya Elena. 2020a. *Ää: Manifiestos sobre la diversidad lingüística*. Mexico City: Almadía Ediciones.
Aguilar Gil, Yásnaya Elena. 2020b. "The Map and the Territory: National Borders Have Colonized Our Imagination." *The Baffler* 53. https://thebaffler.com/latest/the-map-and-the-territory-aguilar-gil.
Aguilar Gil, Yásnaya Elena. 2023. "El beisbol y las lenguas indígenas de México. Këyät." *El País México*, February 27, 2023. https://elpais.com/mexico/opinion/2023-02-27/el-beisbol-y-las-lenguas-indigenas-de-mexico-keyat.html.
Aguirre Beltrán, Gonzalo. 1967. *Regiones de refugio*. México, D.F.: Instituto Indigenista Interamericano.
Alim, H. Samy. 2016. "Who's Afraid of the Transracial Subject?: Raciolinguistics and the Political Project of Transracialization." In *Raciolinguistics: How Language Shapes Our Ideas about Race*, edited by H. Samy Alim, John R. Rickford, and Arnetha F. Ball, 33–50. New York: Oxford University Press. https://academic.oup.com/book/8148/chapter-abstract/153636513?redirectedFrom=fulltext.
Almudena Barragán, Gaspar. 2019. "Yásnaya Aguilar: 'Las lenguas indígenas no se mueren, las mata el Estado mexicano.'" *El País* 3: 5.
Andersen, Chris. 2014. *Métis: Race, Recognition, and the Struggle for Indigenous Peoplehood*. Vancouver, BC: UBC Press.
Anderson, Benedict. 1983. *Imagined Communities: Reflections on the Origin and Spread of Nationalism*. London: Verso.
Andrews, J. Richard. 1975. *Introduction to Classical Nahuatl*. Austin: University of Texas Press.
Andrews, J. Richard. 2003. *Introduction to Classical Nahuatl*. Revised. Norman: University of Oklahoma Press.
Ansotegui, Elena. 2020. "Tren Maya o barbarie: Comunidades indígenas en el contexto de la globalización." In *Pensamiento social danés sobre América Latina: Colección Antologías del Pensamiento Social Latinoamericano y Caribeño*, edited by A. M. Edjesgaard Jeppesen, E. G. Palomares Rodríguez, and G. Wink, 113–31. Buenos Aires: CLACSO.
Appadurai, Arjun. 1996. *Modernity at Large: Cultural Dimensions of Globalization*. Minneapolis: University of Minnesota Press.
Aragón Andrade, O. 2019. *El derecho en insurrección: Hacia una antropología jurídica militante desde la experiencia de Cherán, México*. México, D.F.: Universidad Nacional Autónoma de México.
Arias, Patricia, and Lucía Bazán. 1979. *Demandas y conflicto: El poder político en un pueblo de Morelos*. México, D.F.: Centro de Investigaciones Superiores del Instituto Nacional de Antropología e Historia: Editorial Nueva Imagen.

Arías Sandí, Marcelino, and Miriam Hernández Reyna. 2010. "Interculturalismo y hermenéutica: De la tradición como pasado a la actualidad de la tradición." *Cuicuilco* 17 (48): 69–85.

Asad, Talal. 1986. "The Concept of Cultural Translation in British Social Anthropology." In *Writing Culture: The Poetics and Politics of Ethnography*, edited by James Clifford and George E. Marcus, 141–64. Berkeley: University of California Press.

Ávila Romero, Agustín, and León Enrique Ávila Romero. 2014. "El asalto a la interculturalidad: Las universidades interculturales de México." *Argumentos* 27 (76): 37–54.

Báez, Gabriela Pérez, Chris Rogers, and Jorge Emilio Rosés Labrada. 2016. *Language Documentation and Revitalization in Latin American Contexts*. Berlin: Walter de Gruyter.

Báez-Jorge, Félix. 2002. "Los indios, los nacos, los otros . . . (apuntes sobre el prejuicio racial y la discriminación en México." *La Palabra y el Hombre* 121: 21–40.

Bakhtin, M. M. 1981. *The Dialogic Imagination: Four Essays by MM Bakhtin*. Edited by M. Holquist. Austin: University of Texas Press.

Baronnet, Bruno, Mariana Mora Bayo, and Richard Stahler-Sholk. 2011. *Luchas "muy otras": Zapatismo y autonomía en las comunidades indígenas de Chiapas*. México, D.F.: UAM.

Barrett, Rusty. 2008. "Linguistic Differentiation and Mayan Language Revitalization in Guatemala." *Journal of Sociolinguistics* 12 (3): 275–305.

Behrman, Jere R., Susan W. Parker, and Petra E. Todd. 2011. "Do Conditional Cash Transfers for Schooling Generate Lasting Benefits?: A Five-Year Followup of PROGRESA/Oportunidades." *Journal of Human Resources* 46 (1): 93–122. https://doi.org/10.3368/jhr.46.1.93.

Benton, Joseph P. 1999. "How the Summer Institute of Linguistics Has Developed Orthographies for Indigenous Languages in Mexico." Summer Institute of Linguistics. http://www.sil.org/americas/mexico/ilv/L001i-SILOrth.pdf.

Berdan, Frances. 2008. "Concepts of Ethnicity and Class in Aztec-Period Mexico." In *Ethnic Identity in Nahua Mesoamerica: The View from Archaeology, Art History, Ethnohistory, and Contemporary Ethnography*, edited by Frances F. Berdan, John Chance, Alan R. Sandstrom, Barbara Stark, James Taggart and Emily Umberger, 105–32. Salt Lake City: University of Utah Press.

Bernal-Lorenzo, Daisy, and Miguel Figueroa Saavedra. 2019a. "A New Postgraduate Program in Intercultural-Studies: The Masters Program in Nahua Indigenous Culture and Language at the University of Veracruz, Mexico." *Revista Educación* 43 (2): 494–507. https://doi.org/10.15517/revedu.v43i2.32934.

Bernal-Lorenzo, Daisy, and Miguel Figueroa Saavedra. 2019b. "Concepciones de un currículum intercultural: el caso de la Maestriah ipan Totlahtol iwan Tonemilis." *EntreTextos* 11: 33.

Biehl, João. 2005. *Vita: Life in a Zone of Social Abandonment*. Berkeley: University of California Press.

Bierhorst, John. 2009. *Ballads of the Lords of New Spain*. Austin: University of Texas Press.

Blommaert, Jan. 2007. "Sociolinguistic Scales." *Intercultural Pragmatics* 4 (1): 1–19.

Blommaert, Jan. 2013. "Citizenship, Language, and Superdiversity: Towards Complexity." *Journal of Language, Identity & Education* 12 (3): 193–96.

Blommaert, Jan, and Piia Varis. 2015. "Enoughness, Accent and Light Communities: Essays on Contemporary Identities." *Tilburg Papers in Cultural Studies* 139: 3–58.

Blommaert, Jan, Elina Westinen, and Sirpa Leppänen. 2014. "Further Notes on Sociolinguistic Scales." *Tilburg Papers in Social Studies* 89: 1–11.

Boas, Franz. 1917. "El Dialecto Mexicano de Pochutla, Oaxaca." *International Journal of American Linguistics* 1 (1): 9–44.

Boitel, Quentin. 2021a. "'Anyone Who Speaks Just a Little Bit of Náhuat Knows She's Only Babbling . . .': Metapragmatic Discourses on Proficiency in the Náhuat Language Revitalization (El Salvador)." In *Metalinguistic Communities: Case Studies of Agency, Ideology, and Symbolic Uses of Language*, edited by Netta Avineri and Jesse Harasta, 51–71.

Palgrave Studies in Minority Languages and Communities. Cham: Springer International. https://doi.org/10.1007/978-3-030-76900-0_3.

Boitel, Quentin. 2021b. "Le Náhuat fleurit, mais pas ici à Santo Domingo: Une sociolinguistique politique de la revitalisation de la langue Náhuat (El Salvador, Amérique Centrale)." Thèse de doctorat, Université Paris Cité. https://www.theses.fr/2021UNIP7093.

Boitel, Quentin. 2022a. "Discourses of Endangerment and Appropriations of the 'Indigenous': What Indigeneity Means in Non-Indigenous Spaces." In *The Routledge Handbook of Language and the Global South/s,* edited by Sinfree Makoni, Anna Kaiper-Marquez, Lorato Mokwena, 121–33. London: Routledge.

Boitel, Quentin. 2022b. "Revitalisation linguistique, colonialisme et rapports sociaux de race. Contribution à partir du cas de la revitalisation du náhuat au Salvador." *Langage et société* 177 (3): 83–109. https://doi.org/10.3917/ls.177.0076.

Bourdieu, Pierre. 1979. *La Distinction: Critique sociale du jugement.* Paris: Minuit.

Bourdieu, Pierre. 1986. *Distinction. A Social Critique of the Judgment of Taste.* Translated by Richard Nice. London: Routledge.

Brading, David A. 1991. *The First America: The Spanish Monarchy Creole Patriots and the Liberal State, 1492–1867.* Cambridge: Cambridge University Press.

Brewster, Keith. 2003. *Militarism, Ethnicity, and Politics in the Sierra Norte de Puebla, 1917–1930.* Tucson: University of Arizona Press.

Brubaker, Rogers. 2016. *Trans: Gender and Race in an Age of Unsettled Identities.* Princeton, NJ: Princeton University Press.

Brylak, Agnieszka, Julia Madajczak, Justyna Olko, and John Sullivan. 2020. *Loans in Colonial and Modern Nahuatl: A Contextual Dictionary.* Berlin: Walter de Gruyter.

Bucholtz, Mary. 2003. "Sociolinguistic Nostalgia and the Authentication of Identity." *Journal of Sociolinguistics* 7 (3): 398–416.

Burkhart, Louise. 1987. *The Slippery Earth: Nahua-Christian Moral Dialogue in Sixteenth-Century Mexico.* Tucson: University of Arizona Press.

Caballero, Gabriela. 2011. "Behind the Mexican Mountains: Recent Developments and New Directions in Research on Uto-Aztecan Languages." *Language and Linguistics Compass* 5 (7): 485–504.

Campbell, Lyle. 1985. *The Pipil Language of El Salvador.* Berlin: Mouton Publishers.

Campbell, R. Joe. 1976. "Underlying/Nw/in Hueyapan Nahuatl." *International Journal of American Linguistics* 42 (1): 46–50.

Campbell, R. Joe, and Frances E. Karttunen. 1989. *Foundation Course in Nahuatl Grammar.* Institute of Latin American Studies, The University of Texas at Austin.

Campos, Isaac. 2012. *Home Grown: Marijuana and the Origins of Mexico's War on Drugs.* Charlotte: University of North Carolina Press.

Canger, Una. 1988. "Nahuatl Dialectology: A Survey and Some Suggestions." *International Journal of American Linguistics* 54 (1): 28–72.

Canger, Una. 2011a. "El nauatl urbano de Tlatelolco/Tenochtitlan, resultado de convergencia entre dialectos, con un esbozo brevísimo de la historia de los dialectos." *Estudios de Cultura Nahuatl* 42: 243–58.

Canger, Una. 2011b. "The Origin of Orthographic hu for /w/ in Nahuatl." *Ancient Mesoamerica* 22 (1): 27–35.

Canger, Una, and Anne Jensen. 2007. Grammatical Borrowing in Nahuatl. In *Empirical Approaches to Language Typology,* edited by Yaron Matras and Jeanette Sakel, 38: 403–18. Berlin: DeGruyter.

Carochi, Horacio. 2001. *Grammar of the Mexican Language with an Explanation of Its Adverbs.* Edited and translated by James Lockhart. Stanford, CA: Stanford University Press.

Carson, P. 1998. *Across the Northern Frontier: Spanish Explorations in Colorado.* Boulder: University of Colorado Press.

Casanova Casañas, Laura. 2021. "Megaproyectos y conflictos ecoterritoriales: El caso del Tren Maya." *Relaciones internacionales: Revista académica cuatrimestral de publicación electrónica* 46: 139–59.

Cayuqueo, Pedro. 2018. *Porfiada y rebelde es la memoria: Crónicas mapuche*. Barcelona: Editorial Catalonia.

Chambers, J. K., and Peter Trudgill. 1998. *Dialectology*. Cambridge: Cambridge University Press.

Chance, J. K., and W. B. Taylor. 1985. "Cofradías and Cargos: An Historical Perspective on the Mesoamerican Civil-Religious Hierarchy." *American Ethnologist* 12 (1): 1–26.

Chevalier, Jacques M., and Daniel Buckles. 1995. *A Land without Gods: Power and Destruction in the Mexican Tropics*. London: Zed Books.

Chríost, Diarmait Mac Giolla. 2012. "Jailtacht: The Irish Language and the Conflict in Northern Ireland." In *Languages and the Military: Alliances, Occupation and Peace Building*, edited by Hilary Footitt and Michael Kelly, 148–74. Palgrave Studies in Languages at War. London: Palgrave Macmillan UK. https://doi.org/10.1057/9781137033086_11.

Cifuentes, Bárbara. 1996. "Algunas dificultades para la periodización: Ejemplificadas en las obras de Francisco Clavijero y Crisóstomo Náxera." *Estudios de Lingüística Aplicada* 1 (23/24): 37–46. https://doi.org/10.22201/enallt.01852647p.1996.23.294.

Cifuentes, Barbara. 2002. *Lenguas para un pasado, huellas de una nación: Los estudios sobre lenguas indígenas de México en el siglo XIX*. México City: Plaza y Valdés.

Clavijero, Francisco Javier. 1844. *Historia antigua de México y de su conquista: Sacada de los mejores historiadores españoles y de los manuscritos y pinturas antiguas de los indios*. Mexico: Imprenta de Lara.

Cobas, José A., Jorge Duany, and Joe R. Feagin. 2009. *How the United States Racializes Latinos: White Hegemony and Its Consequences*. Boulder, CO: Paradigm Press.

Cody, Francis. 2011. "Publics and Politics." *Annual Review of Anthropology* 40: 37–52.

Collins, James. 1998. "Our Ideologies and Theirs." *Language Ideologies: Practice and Theory* 16: 256.

Comaroff, John L., and Jean Comaroff. 2009. *Ethnicity, Inc.* Chicago: University of Chicago Press.

Coon, Adam W. 2014. "Ixtlamatiliztli/Knowledge with the Face: Intellectual Migrations and Colonial Displacements in Natalio Hernández's Xochikoskatl." In *The Oxford Handbook of Indigenous American Literature*, edited by James H. Cox and Daniel Heath Justice. 215–33. Oxford: Oxford University Press. https://doi.org/10.1093/oxfordhb/9780199914036.013.007.

Coon, Adam W. 2015. "*Iajki Estados Onidos / She Went to the U.S.*: Nahua Identities in Migration within Contemporary Nahua Literature, 1985–2014." PhD dissertation, University of Texas, Austin.

Coon, Adam W. 2019. "Living Languages as the Acoustic Ecologies within the Contemporary Literatures of Anahuac." *LASA Forum* 50 (1): 25–29.

Coulthard, Glenn Sean. 2014. *Red Skin, White Masks: Rejecting the Colonial Politics of Recognition*. Minneapolis: Minnesota University Press.

Craddock, J. R., and J. R. Polt. 2014. *The Trial of the Indians of Acoma 1598–1599*. Berkeley: University of California Press. https://escholarship.org/uc/item/14v3j7sj.

Crapanzano, Vincent. 1986. "Hermes' Dilemma: The Masking of Subversion in Ethnographic Description." In *Writing Culture: The Poetics and Politics of Ethnography*, edited by James Clifford and George E. Marcus, 51–76. Berkeley: University of California Press. https://doi.org/10.1525/9780520946286-005.

Cuauhtli, Chris. 2022. *Ma Tiłahtucan Mexicano: Let's Speak Mexicano*. Self-published.

Davis, Jenny L. 2017a. "Resisting Rhetorics of Language Endangerment: Reclamation through Indigenous Language Survivance." In *Language Documentation and Description*, edited by Wesley Y. Leonard and Haley Korne, 14: 37–58. London: EL Publishing.

Davis, Jenny L. 2017b. *Talking Indian: Identity and Language Revitalization in the Chickasaw Renaissance*. Tucson: University of Arizona Press.

Dawson, Alexander. 1998. "From Models for the Nation to Model Citizens: Indigenismo and the 'Revindication' of the Mexican Indian, 1920–40." *Journal of Latin American Studies* 30 (2): 279–308.

Dawson, Alexander. 2004. *Indian and Nation in Revolutionary Mexico*. Tucson: University of Arizona Press.

de Korne, Haley, and Wesley Y. Leonard. 2017. "Reclaiming Languages: Contesting and Decolonising 'Language Endangerment' from the Ground Up." In *Language Documentation and Description*, edited by Wesley Y. Leonard and Haley de Korne, 14: 5–14. London: EL Publishing.

de la Peña, Guillermo. 2006. "A New Mexican Nationalism? Indigenous Rights, Constitutional Reform and the Conflicting Meanings of Multiculturalism." *Nations and Nationalism* 12 (2): 279–302.

de Reuse, Willem. 2010. "Mariano Rojas and His 'Manual de la lengua nahuatl' (1927)." In *Análisislingüístico: Enfoques sincrónico, diacrónico e interdisciplinario*, edited by Rosa María Ortiz Ciscomani, 225–46. Hermosillo: Universidad de Sonora.

Debenport, Erin. 2015. *Fixing the Books: Secrecy, Literacy, and Perfectibility in Indigenous New Mexico*. Santa Fe: School for Advanced Research Press.

Deloria, Philip J. 1998. *Playing Indian*. New Haven, CT: Yale University Press.

Díaz Gómez, Floriberto. 2001. "Comunidad y Comunalidad." *La Jornada Semanal* 314: 12.

Díaz Gómez, Floriberto, Sofía Robles Hernández, and Rafael Cardoso Jiménez. 2007. *Ayuujktsënää'yën-Ayuujkwënmää'ny-Ayuujk Mëkäjtën*. Vol. 14. Mexico City: UNAM.

Díaz González, Gualberto. 2016. "Construyendo acción colectiva en la sierra de Zongolica, 1974–2010." In *Resistencia y protesta social en el sureste de México*, edited by Martín Gerardo Aguilar Sánchez, 115–31. Mexico City: Universidad Autónoma Metropolitana-Azcapotzalco/RED Mexicana de los Estudios de los Movimientos Sociales/COLOFÓN/CONACyT.

Díaz González, Gualberto. 2019. "Conflicto social, acción colectiva y represión en la sierra de Zongolica, Veracruz: El movimiento social de Tehuipango, 1966–1980." Xalapa, Veracruz: Universidad Veracruzana. Instituto de Investigaciones Histórico-Sociales. Región Xalapa.

Díaz Robles, Tajëëw Beatriz. 2020. "Dinámicas comunitarias de la identidad textil: #MiBlusadeTlahui." *Revista de la Universidad de México*, no. 1: 53–59.

Dietz, Günther. 2009. "Intercultural Universities in Mexico: Empowering Indigenous Peoples or Mainstreaming Multiculturalism?" *Intercultural Education* 20 (1): 1–4.

Dietz, Günther. 2012. "Diversity Regimes beyond Multiculturalism? A Reflexive Ethnography of Intercultural Higher Education in Veracruz, Mexico." *Latin American and Caribbean Ethnic Studies* 7: 173–200.

Dietz, Günther, and Laura Selene Mateos Cortés. 2011. "Multiculturalism and Intercultural Education Facing the Anthropology of Education." In *A Companion to the Anthropology of Education*, edited by B. A. U. Levinson and M. Pollock, 495–516. Oxford: Wiley-Blackwell.

Dimas Huacuz, Bertha. 2006a. "¿Interculturalidad de papel? Apuntes sobre la idea de universidad indígena." *Educación Superior: Cifras y Hechos* 5 (27–28): 36–41.

Dimas Huacuz, Bertha. 2006b. "Indigenismo de estado: El paradigma mexicano actual." Llacta! http://www.llacta.org/notic/2006/not1031c.htm.

Doyle, Aidan. 2015. *A History of the Irish Language: From the Norman Invasion to Independence*. Oxford: Oxford University Press.

Duchêne, Alexandre, and Monica Heller. 2009. *Language in Late Capitalism: Pride and Profit*. London: Routledge.

Durán, Diego. [1581] 1994. *The History of the Indies of New Spain*. Translated by Doris Heyden. Norman: University of Oklahoma Press.

Duranti, Alessandro. 1994. *From Grammar to Politics: Linguistic Anthropology in a Western Samoan Village*. Berkeley: University of California Press.

Works Cited

Duranti, Alessandro. 2010. "Husserl, Intersubjectivity and Anthropology." *Anthropological Theory* 10 (1–2): 16–35.

Errington, Joseph. 2003. "Getting Language Rights: The Rhetorics of Language Endangerment and Loss." *American Anthropologist* 105 (4): 723–32.

Errington, Joseph. 2008. *Linguistics in a Colonial World: A Story of Language, Meaning and Power*. Malden, MA: Blackwell.

Faudree, Paja. 2013. *Singing for the Dead: The Politics of Indigenous Revival in Mexico*. Durham, NC: Duke University Press.

Faudree, Paja. 2014. "The Annual Day of the Dead Song Contest: Musical-Linguistic Ideology and Practice, Piratability, and the Challenge of Scale." *Journal of the Royal Anthropological Institute* 20: 293–314.

Faudree, Paja. 2015a. "Singing for the Dead, on and off Line: Diversity, Migration, and Scale in Mexican Muertos Music." *Language & Communication* 44: 31–43.

Faudree, Paja. 2015b. "Why X Doesn't Always Mark the Spot: Contested Authenticity in Mexican Indigenous Language Politics." *Semiotica* 203: 179–201.

Faudree, Paja, and Becky Schulthies. 2015. "Introduction: 'Diversity Talk' and Its Others." *Language & Communication* 44: 1–6.

Feliciano-Santos, Sherina. 2017. "How Do You Speak Taino? Indigenous Activism and Linguistic Practices in Puerto Rico." *Journal of Linguistic Anthropology* 27 (1): 4–21.

Feliciano-Santos, Sherina. 2021. *A Contested Caribbean Indigeneity: Language, Social Practice, and Identity within Puerto Rican Taíno Activism*. New Brunswick: Rutgers University Press.

Figueroa Saavedra, Miguel. 2021. La motivación para el aprendizaje de segundas lenguas minorizadas: El caso del estudio de la lengua náhuatl por universitarios hispanohablantes. *Diálogos sobre educación. Temas actuales en investigación educativa* 12 (23): 1–28.

Figueroa Saavedra, Miguel, Daisy Bernal Lorenzo, and Rafael Nava Vite. 2022. "In tlahkuilolyotl ken se nawatlahtolchikawalistli ipan weyitlamachtiloyan: De tlachiwalistli tlen moneki axkan mochiwa." *CPU-e, Revista de Investigación Educativa*, no. 35 (July): 91–120. https://doi.org/10.25009/cpue.v0i35.2823.

Figueroa Saavedra, Miguel, and José Álvaro Hernández Martínez. 2014. Efectos de la señalización multilingüe en la activación lingüística de la lengua náhuatl en la Universidad Veracruzana. *Calidoscópio* 12(2): 131–142.

Fishman, Joshua A. 1991. "Reversing Language Shift: Theoretical and Empirical Foundations of Assistance to Threatened Languages." Clevedon: Multilingual Matters.

Fishman, Joshua A. 2000. *Can Threatened Languages Be Saved?* Clevedon: Multilingual Matters.

Flores Farfán, José Antonio. 1995. *Cuatreros somos y toindioma hablamos: Contactos y conflictos entre el náhuatl y el español en el sur de México*. México, D.F.: CIESAS.

Flores Farfán, José Antonio. 2011. "Keeping the Fire Alive: A Decade of Language Revitalization in Mexico." *International Journal of the Sociology of Language* 212: 189–209.

Flores Farfán, José Antonio. 2013. "La variedad misionera del Náhuatl en el vocabulario en lengua castellana y mexicana y mexicana y castellana de Fray Alonso de Molina (1555–1571)." *Estudios de Cultura Náhuatl* 45 (4): 233–66.

Flores Nájera, Lucero. 2023. "In koneololistli kan ok yoltokeh in chiwaltlakayotl wan in Tomexikano: El grupo de pares de niños como un espacio para la conservación de la cultura y lengua Náhuatl/Mexicano." *Ichan Tecolotl: La Casa Del Tecolote*. February 21, 2023. https://ichan.ciesas.edu.mx/27837-2/.

Foucault, Michel. 1977. *Discipline and Punish: The Birth of the Prison*. Translated by Alan Sheridan. New York: Vintage.

Foucault, Michel. 1993. "About the Beginning of the Hermeneutics of the Self: Two Lectures at Dartmouth." *Political Theory* 21 (2): 198–227.

Franco, Paul. 2018. "Becoming Who You Are: Nietzsche on Self-Creation." *Journal of Nietzsche Studies* 49 (1): 52–77. https://doi.org/10.5325/jnietstud.49.1.0052.

Fraser, Nancy. 1990. "Rethinking the Public Sphere: A Contribution to the Critique of Actually Existing Democracy." *Social Text* 2 (5/26): 56–80.
French, Brigittine. 2010. *Maya Ethnolinguistic Identity: Violence, Cultural Rights, and Modernity in Highland Guatemala.* Tucson: University of Arizona Press.
Friedlander, Judith. 1975. *Being Indian in Hueyapan.* New York: St. Martin's Press.
Friedlander, Judith. 2006. *Being Indian in Hueyapan: A Revised and Updated Edition.* New York: Palgrave MacMillan.
Friedman, Jonathan. 1993. "Will the Real Hawaiian Please Stand?" *Bijdragen tot de taal-, land- en volkenkunde/Journal of the Humanities and Social Sciences of Southeast Asia* 149, no. 4: 737–67.
Friedman, Jonathan. 2000. "Globalization, Class and Culture in Global Systems." *Journal of World-Systems Research* 6 (3): 636–56.
Gal, Susan. 1989. "Language and Political Economy." *Annual Review of Anthropology* 18: 345–67.
Gal, Susanm and Kathryn Woolard. 1995. "Constructing Languages and Publics." *Pragmatics* 5 (2): 129–282.
Gal, Susan, and Kathryn Woolard. 2001. "Languages and Publics: The Making of Authority." Manchester: St. Jerome Publishing.
Galinier, Jacques, and Antoinette Molinié. 2013. *The Neo-Indians: A Religion for the Third Millennium.* Boulder: University Press of Colorado.
Gamio, Manuel. (1916) 2010. *Forjando Patria: Pro-Nacionalismo.* Edited and translated by Fernando Armstrong Fumero. Boulder: University Press of Colorado.
García, Yan. 2016. *Learn Nahuatl: Language of the Aztecs and Modern Nahuas.* California: CreateSpace Independent Publishing Platform.
García, Yan, and Victoriano de la Cruz. 2016. *Ixtlamatiquetl Frankenstein.* California: CreateSpace Independent Publishing Platform.
Garibay K., Angél María. 1937. *La poesía lírica azteca: Esbozo de síntesis crítica.* Mexico: Abside.
Garibay K., Angél María. 1953. *Historia de la literatura Nahuatl.* Mexico City: Editorial Porrua.
Gasparello, Giovanna, Violeta R. Núñez Rodríguez, and Giovanna Gasparello, eds. 2021. *Pueblos y territorios frente al Tren Maya: Escenarios sociales, económicos y culturales.* Primera edición. Oaxaca: Centro Intradisciplinar para la Investigación de la Recreación.
Geertz, Clifford. 1973. *The Interpretation of Cultures: Selected Essays.* Basic Books.
Gellner, Ernest. 1983. *Nations and Nationalism.* Ithaca, NY: Cornell University Press.
Gillingham, P. 2011. *Cuauhtémoc's Bones: Forging National Identity in Modern Mexico.* Santa Fe: University of New Mexico Press.
Gledhill, John. 2014. "Indigenous Autonomy, Delinquent States, and the Limits of Resistance." *History and Anthropology* 25 (4): 507–529.
Gould, Jeffrey L., and Aldo A. Lauria-Santiago. 2008. *To Rise in Darkness: Revolution, Repression, and Memory in El Salvador, 1920–1932.* Durham, NC: Duke University Press.
Graham, Laura. 1995. *Performing Dreams: Discourses of Immortality among the Xavante of Central Brazil.* Austin: University of Texas Press.
Gramsci, Antonio. 1971. *Selections from Prison Notebooks.* Translated by Geoffrey Nowell Smith and Quintin Hoare. New York: International Publishers.
Green, Rayna. 1988. "The Tribe Called Wannabee: Playing Indian in America and Europe." *Folklore* 99 (1): 30–55.
Greenhill, Simon J., Hannah J. Haynie, Robert M. Ross, Angela M. Chira, Johann-Mattis List, Lyle Campbell, and Carlos A. Botero. 2023. "A Recent Northern Origin for the Uto-Aztecan Family." *Language* 99 (1): 81–107.

Grosfoguel, Ramón. 2016. "From 'Economic Extractivism' to 'Epistemical Extractivism' and 'Ontological Extractivism': A Destructive Way to Know, Be and Behave in the World." *Tabula Rasa* 24: 123–43.

Grosfoguel, Ramón. 2019. "Epistemic Extractivism: A Dialogue with Alberto Acosta, Leanne Betasamosake Simpson, and Silvia Rivera Cusicanqui." In *Knowledges Born in the Struggle*, edited by Boaventura de Sousa Santos and Maria Paula Meneses, 203–18. New York: Routledge.

Guevara-Martínez, Rolando. 2021. "Latin American Thinking in Communication and Advances in Communication Rights." In *The Handbook of Communication Rights, Law, and Ethics: Seeking Universality, Equality, Freedom and Dignity*, edited by Loreto Corredoira, Ignacio Bel Mallén, Rodrigo Cetina Presuel, 241–52. New Jersey: John Wiley & Sons. https://doi.org/10.1002/9781119719564.ch20.

Gumperz, John J. 1968. "The Speech Community." In *International Encyclopedia of the Social Sciences*, edited by D. L. Sills, 381–86. New York: Macmillan.

Gumperz, John J. 1962. "Types of Linguistic Communities." *Anthropological Linguistics* 4 (1): 28–40.

Gustafson, Bret. 2009. *New Languages of the State: Indigenous Resurgence and the Politics of Knowledge in Bolivia*. Durham, NC: Duke University Press.

Gustafson, Bret. 2017. "Oppressed No More? Indigenous Language Regimentation in Plurinational Bolivia." *International Journal of the Sociology of Language* 246: 31–57.

Gustafson, Bret, Félix Julca Guerrero, and Ajb'ee Jiménez. 2016. "Policy and Politics of Language Revitalization: Latin America and the Caribbean." In *Indigenous Language Revitalization in the Americas*, edited by Serafin L. Coronel-Molina and Teresa McCarty, 47–66. London: Routledge.

Gutiérrez Chong, Natividad. 1999. *Nationalist Myths and Ethnic Identities: Indigenous Intellectuals and the Mexican State*. Lincoln: University of Nebraska Press.

Gutiérrez Chong, Natividad. 2010. "Los Pueblos indígenas en los nacionalismos de independencia y liberación: El colonialismo interno revisitado." In *Independencia y revolución: contribuciones en torno a su conmemoración*, edited by María Luisa Rodríguez-Sala, 117–51. Mexico: UNAM. https://ru.iis.sociales.unam.mx/handle/IIS/4020.

Gutierrez Nájera, Lourdes, and Korinta Maldonado. 2017. "Transnational Settler Colonial Formations and Global Capital: A Consideration of Indigenous Mexican Migrants." *American Quarterly* 69 (4): 809–21. https://doi.org/10.1353/aq.2017.0067.

Haake, Claudia. 2007. *The State, Removal and Indigenous Peoples in the United States and Mexico, 1620–2000*. London: Routledge.

Habermas, Jürgen. 1962. *Strukturwandel der Öffentlichkeit*. Neuwied: Luchterhand.

Habermas, Jürgen. 1989. *The Structural Transformation of the Public Sphere: An Inquiry into a Category of Bourgeois Society*. Boston: MIT Press.

Hale, Charles R. 1997. "Cultural Politics of Identity in Latin America." *Annual Review of Anthropology* 26 (1): 567–90.

Hale, Charles R. 2004. "Rethinking Indigenous Politics in the Era of the 'Indio Permitido.'" In *Nacla Report on the Americas. Report on Race* 38 (2): 16–21.

Hale, Charles R. 2005. "Neoliberal Multiculturalism: The Remaking of Cultural Rights and Racial Dominance in Central America." *PoLAR* 28: 10.

Hale, Kenneth, Michael Krauss, Lucille Watahomigie, Akira Yamamoto, Colette Craig, Jeanne Laverne, and Nora England. 1992. "Endangered Languages." *Language* 68 (1): 1–43.

Haley, Brian D. 2009. "Immigration and Indigenization in the Mexican Diaspora in the Southwestern United States." In *Imagining Globalization*, edited by H. H. Leung, M. Hendley, R. W. Compton, and B. D. Haley, 165–84. New York: Palgrave Macmillan. https://doi.org/10.1057/978023010.

Haley, Brian D., and Larry R. Wilcoxon. 1997. "Anthropology and the Making of Chumash Tradition." *Current Anthropology* 38 (5): 761–94. https://doi.org/10.1086/204667.

Haley, Brian D., and Larry R. Wilcoxon. 2005. "How Spaniards Became Chumash and Other Tales of Ethnogenesis." *American Anthropologist* 107 (3): 432–45. https://doi.org/10.1525/aa.2005.107.3.432.

Hanks, William F. 1992. "The Indexical Ground of Deictic Reference." In *Rethinking Context: Language as an Interactive Phenomenon*, edited by A. Duranti and C. Goodwin, 43–76. Cambridge: Cambridge University Press.

Hanks, William F. 1996. *Language and Communicative Practices*. Boulder: Westview Press.

Hartch, Todd. 2006. *Missionaries of the State: The Summer Institute of Linguistics, State Formation, and Indigenous Mexico, 1935–1985*. Tuscaloosa: University Alabama Press.

Harvey, David J. 1996. *Nature and the Geography of Difference*. Malden, MA: Blackwell.

Harvey, David J. 2000. *Spaces of Hope*. Berkeley: University of California Press.

Haskett, Robert. 1991. *Indigenous Rulers: An Ethnohistory of Town Government in Colonial Cuernavaca*. Santa Fe: University of New Mexico Press.

Hasler Hangert, Andrés. 1996. "El Náhuatl de Tehuacán-Zongolica." Mexico City: CIESAS.

Haslip-Viera, Gabriel. 2006. "The Politics of Taíno Revivalism: The Insignificance of Amerindian MtDNA in the Population History of Puerto Ricans. A Comment on Recent Research." *Centro Journal* 18 (1): 260–75.

Haugen, Einar. 1966. "Dialect, Language, Nation." *American Anthropologist* 68 (4): 922–35.

Heath, Shirley Brice. 1972. *Telling Tongues: Language Policy in Mexico, Colony to Nation*. New York: Teachers College Press.

Heller, Monica. 2010. "The Commodification of Language." *Annual Review of Anthropology* 39: 101–14.

Hernández de León-Portilla, Ascensión. 1988. *Tepuztlahcuilolli, impresos en náhuatl: Historia y bibliografía*. Mexico City: UNAM.

Hernández Hernández, Natalio, and Zósimo Hernández Ramírez. 2010. "Amatlanahuatili Tlahtoli tlen Mexicameh Nechicolistli Sentlanahuatiloyan: Constitución Política de los Estados Unidos Mexicanos." Mexico City: Senado de la República, LXI legislatura.

Hernández Orellan, Severiano. 2011. "El Centro Coordinador Indigenista de la Sierra Nahuatl de Zongolica: Recapitulacion, reflexiones y opiniones criticas." MA thesis, Universidad Veracruzana, Facultad de Antropologia.

Hernández Reyna, Miriam. 2013. "Interculturalismo: Entre la memoria y la historia." In *Repensar la Conquista: Reflexión epistemológica de un momento fundador*, edited by Guy Rozat, 105–21. Xalapa: Universidad Veracruzana.

Hernández Reyna, Miriam, and Juan A. Castillo Cocom. 2021. "'Ser o no ser indígena': Oscilaciones identitarias dentro de la interculturalidad de Estado en México." *The Journal of Latin American and Caribbean Anthropology* 26 (1): 147–71.

Hidalgo, Jacqueline. 2019. "Beyond Aztlán: Latina/o/x Students Let Go of Their Mythic Homeland." *Contending Modernities (Blog): University of Notre Dame/Keough School of Global Affairs)*. https://contendingmodernities.nd.edu/global-currents/beyond-aztlan/.

Hidalgo, Margarita. 2006. *Mexican Indigenous Languages at the Dawn of the Twenty-First Century*. Berlin: Walter de Gruyter.

Hill, Jane H. 2009. *The Everyday Language of White Racism*. New York: John Wiley & Sons.

Hill, Jane H. 2019. "How Mesoamerican Are the Nahua Languages?" In *Migrations in Late Mesoamerica*, edited by C. S. Beekman, 43–65. Gainesville: University Press of Florida.

Hill, Jane H., and Kenneth C. Hill. 1978. "Honorific Usage in Modern Nahuatl: The Expression of Social Distance and Respect in the Nahuatl of the Malinche Volcano Area." *Language* 54 (1): 123–55. https://doi.org/10.2307/413001.

Hill, Jane, and Kenneth C. Hill. 1986. *Speaking Mexicano: Dynamics of Syncretic Language in Central Mexico*. Tucson: University of Arizona Press.

Hill, Jane H., and William L. Merrill. 2017. "Uto-Aztecan Maize Agriculture: A Linguistic Puzzle from Southern California." *Anthropological Linguistics* 59 (1): 1–23.

Works Cited

Hindley, Jane. 1999. "Indigenous Mobilization, Development, and Democratization in Guerrero: The Nahua People vs. the Tetelcingo Dam." In *Subnational Politics and Democratization in Mexico*, edited by Wayne A. Cornelius, Todd A. Eisenstadt, and Jane Hindley, 207–38. San Diego: Center for US-Mexican Studies, UCSD.

Hobsbawm, Eric J., and Terence Ranger. 1983. *The Invention of Tradition*. Cambridge: Cambridge University Press.

Horcasitas, Fernando. 1969. "Proclama en náhuatl de don Carlos María de Bustamante a los indígenas mexicanos." *Estudios de cultura Náhuatl* 8: 271–78.

Horcasitas, Fernando, and Luz Jimenez. 1968. *De Porfirio Díaz a Zapata: Memoria náhuatl*. México, D.F.: UNAM.

Horn, Rebecca. 2014. "Indigenous Identities in Mesoamerica after the Spanish Conquest." In *Native Diasporas: Indigenous Identities and Settler Colonialism in the Americas*, edited by Gregory D. Smithers, 31–78. Lincoln: University of Nebraska Press.

Hu-deHart, Evelyn. 2016. *Yaqui Resistance and Survival: The Struggle for Land and Autonomy, 1821–1910*. Revised. Madison: University of Wisconsin Press.

Hylland Eriksen, Thomas. 1993. *Ethnicity and Nationalism: Anthropological Perspectives*. London: Pluto Press.

INALI. 2012. *México: Lenguas indígenas nacionales en riesgo de desaparición*. México, D.F.: INALI.

INALI. 2020. "Lingüistas y especialistas coinciden en la importancia de normalizar la escritura de la lengua náhuatl." 2020. https://www.inali.gob.mx/detalle/2020-10-19-19-53-07.

INEGI. 2005. "Perfil sociodemográfica de la populación hablante de náhuatl." In *XII Censo General de Población y Vivienda 2000*. Aguascalientes, Mex: INEGI. https://www.inegi.org.mx/contenidos/productos/prod_serv/contenidos/espanol/bvinegi/productos/historicos/76/702825498085/702825498085_2.pdf.

Ireland, Government of. 2010. 20-Year Strategy for the Irish Language 2010–2030. Dublin: Government of Ireland. https://assets.gov.ie/88781/087bbace-b392-4671-b51a-149720d3f6ff.pdf.

Irvine, Judith T., and Susan Gal. 2000. "Language Ideology and Linguistic Differentiation." In *Regimes of Language*, edited by Paul Kroskrity, 35–83. Santa Fe, NM: SAR Press.

Jacobsen, Casper. 2018. *Tourism and Indigenous Heritage in Latin America: As Observed through Mexico's Magical Village Cuetzalan*. London: Routledge.

Jeffres, Travis. 2023. *The Forgotten Diaspora: Mesoamerican Migrations and the Making of the U.S.-Mexico Borderlands*. Lincoln: University of Nebraska Press.

Jensen, Anne. 2008. "Hispanisation in Colonial Nahuatl?" In *Hispanisation: The Impact of Spanish on the Lexicon and Grammar of the Indigenous Languages of Austronesia and the Americas*, edited by Thomas Stolz, Dik Bakker, and Rosa Salas Palomo, 3–26. Hague: De Gruyter Mouton.

Johansson, Patrick. 2002. "'Cuecuechcuicatl, 'canto travieso': Un antecedente ritual prehispánico del albur mexicano." *Literatura Mexicana* 13: 7–48.

Johnson, Benjamin. 2018. *Pueblos within Pueblos: Tlaxilacalli Communities in Acolhuacan, Mexico, ca. 1272–1692*. Boulder: University Press of Colorado.

Karttunen, Frances. 1983. *An Analytical Dictionary of Nahuatl*. Austin: University of Texas Press.

Karttunen, Frances. 1994. "The Linguistic Career of Doña Lúz Jiménez." *Estudios de Cultura Náhuatl* 30: 267–74. https://nahuatl.historicas.unam.mx/index.php/ecn/article/view/9215.

Karttunen, Frances. 1996. "Between Worlds: Interpreters, Guides, and Survivors." In *Frontiers: A Journal of Women Studies* 17: 31. https://doi.org/10.2307/3346871.

Karttunen, Frances, and James Lockhart. 1976. *Nahuatl in the Middle Years: Language Contact Phenomena in Texts of the Colonial Period*. Berkeley and Los Angeles: University of California Press.

Works Cited

Kaur, Ravinder. 2020. *Brand New Nation: Capitalist Dreams and Nationalist Designs in Twenty-First-Century India*. Stanford, CA: Stanford University Press.

Keen, Benjamin. 1971. *The Aztec Image in Western Thought*. New Brunswick, NJ: Rutgers University Press.

Kleinert, C. V., and C. Stallaert. 2015. "La formación de intérpretes de lenguas indígenas para la justicia en México: Sociología de las ausencias y agencia decolonial." *Sendebar* 26: 235–54.

Knight, Alan. 1986. *The Mexican Revolution*, Vol 1: *Porfirians, Liberals and Peasants*. Cambridge: Cambridge University Press.

Kockelman, Paul. 2010. *Language, Culture, and Mind: Natural Constructions and Social Kinds*. Cambridge: Cambridge University Press.

Kockelman, Paul. 2022. *The Anthropology of Intensity: Language, Culture, and Environment*. Cambridge: Cambridge University Press.

Kroeber, A. L. 1919. "On the Principle of Order in Civilization as Exemplified by Changes of Fashion." *American Anthropologist* 21 (3): 235–63.

Kroeber, A. L. 1963. *Style and Civilizations*. Berkeley: University of California Press.

Kropotkin, Peter. (1903) 2021. *Mutual Aid: A Factor of Evolution*. Montreal, Quebec: Black Rose Books.

Kroskrity, Paul V. 2009. "Language Renewal as Sites of Language Ideological Struggle: The Need for 'Ideological Clarification.'" In *Indigenous Language Revitalization: Encouragement, Guidance & Lessons Learned*, edited by J. Reyhner and L. Lockard, 71–83. Flagstaff: Northern Arizona University.

Kroskrity, Paul V., and Barbra A. Meek. 2017. *Engaging Native American Publics: Linguistic Anthropology in a Collaborative Key*. New York: Routledge.

Kuper, Adam. 1988. *The Invention of Primitive Society: Transformations of an Illusion*. London: Routledge.

Kuper, Adam. 2003. "The Return of the Native." *Current Anthropology* 44 (3): 389–402.

Kymlicka, Will. 1995. *Multicultural Citizenship: A Liberal Theory of Minority Rights*. Oxford: Oxford University Press.

Labov, William. 1972. *Sociolinguistic Patterns*. Philadelphia: University of Pennsylvania Press.

Landerl, Karin. 2005. "Reading Acquisition in Different Orthographies: Evidence from Direct Comparisons." In *Handbook of Orthography and Literacy*, edited by M. Joshi and P. G. Aaron, 513–30. Hove: Erlbaum.

Launey, Michel. 1986. "Catégories et opérations dans la grammaire nahuatl." Thèse d'état, Université de Paris IV. https://www.vjf.cnrs.fr/celia/FichExt/Etudes/Launey/tm.htm.

Leal, Luís. [1989] 2017. *In Search of Aztlan*. Edited by Rudolfo Anaya, Francisco A. Lomelí, and Enrique R. Lamadrid. Albuquerque: University of New Mexico Press.

Leavitt, John. 2015. *Words and Worlds: Ethnography and Theories of Translatoin*. Edited by William F. Hanks and Carlo Severi. Chicago: Chicago University Press.

Lee, Jongsoo, and Galen Brokaw. 2014. *Texcoco: Prehispanic and Colonial Perspectives*. Boulder: University Press of Colorado.

Lehmann, D. 2013. "Intercultural Universities in Mexico: Identity and Inclusion." *Journal of Latin American Studies* 45 (4): 779–811.

Lekson, S. H., T. C. Windes, and P. Fournier. 2007. "The Changing Faces of Chetro Ketl." In *The Architecture of Chaco Canyon, New Mexico*, edited by Stephen H. Lekson, 155–78. Salt Lake City: University of Utah Press.

Leonard, Wesley Y. 2018. "Reflections on (de)Colonialism in Language Documentation. In *Language Documentation & Conservation Special Publication No. 15 Reflections on Language Documentation 20 Years after Himmelmann 1998*, edited by Bradley McDonnell, Andrea L. Berez-Kroeker, and Gary Holton, 55–65. http://nflrc.hawaii.edu/ldc/ http://hdl.handle.net/10125/24808.

León-Portilla, M., and A. Mayer. 2010. *Los indígenas en la Independencia y en la Revolución Mexicana*. México, D.F.: Universidad Nacional Autónoma de México–Instituto de Investigaciones Históricas.
León-Portilla, Miguel. 1978. *Los Manifiestos en Nahuatl de Emiliano Zapata*. 1a. ed. Instituto de Investigaciones Históricas. Serie Monografías de Cultura Nahuatl: 20. Mexico City: Universidad Autónoma de México.
León-Portilla, Miguel. 2003. *Maximiliano de Habsburgo; Ordenanzas de tema indígena en castellano y náhuatl*. Querétaro: Instituto de Estudios Constitucionales de Querétaro.
Levin Rojo, Danna A. 2014. *Return to Aztlan: Indians, Spaniards, and the Invention of Nuevo México*. Norman: University of Oklahoma Press.
Lewis, Oscar. 1951. *Life in a Mexican Village: Tepoztlán Restudied*. Champaign, IL: University of Illinois Press.
Leza, Christina. 2019. *Divided Peoples: Policy, Activism, and Indigenous Identities on the US-Mexico Border*. Tucson: University of Arizona Press.
Liebler, C. A., R. Bhaskar, and S. R. Porter. 2016. "Joining, Leaving, and Staying in the American Indian/Alaska Native Race Category between 2000 and 2010." *Demography* 53 (2): 507–40.
Liebler, C. A., and T. Ortyl. 2014. "More than One Million New American Indians in 2000: Who Are They?" *Demography* 51 (3): 1101–30.
Llanes Ortiz, Genner de jesús. 2008. "Interculturalización fallida: Desarrollismo, neoindigenismo y universidad intercultural en Yucatán, México." *Trace. Travaux et Recherches dans les Amériques du Centre* 53: 49–63.
Llanes Ortiz, Genner de jesús. 2010. "Indigenous Universities and the Construction of Interculturality: The Case of the Peasant and Indigenous University Network in Yucatan, Mexico." Doctoral thesis, University of Sussex.
Lockhart, James. 1991. *Nahuas and Spaniards: Postconquest Central Mexican History and Philology*. Stanford and Los Angeles: Stanford University Press and UCLA Latin American Center Publications.
Lockhart, James. 1992. *The Nahuas after the Conquest: A Social and Cultural History of the Indians of Central Mexico, Sixteenth through Eighteenth Centuries*. Stanford, CA: Stanford University Press.
Lomnitz, Claudio. 1992. *Exits from the Labyrinth: Culture and Ideology in the Mexican National Space*. Berkeley: University of California Press.
Lomnitz, Claudio. 2001. *Deep Mexico, Silent Mexico: An Anthropology of Nationalism*. St. Paul: University of Minnesota Press.
Loncon Antileo, Elisa. 2020. "La Coexistencia entre Chilenos y Mapuche: Chile, estado plurinacional e intercultural." *ARQ (Santiago)* 106 (December): 150–52. https://doi.org/10.4067/S0717-69962020000300150.
Loncón Antileo, Elisa, and Ana Carolina Hecht. 2011. *Educación intercultural bilingüe en América Latina y el Caribe: Balances, desafíos y perspectivas*. Santiago de Chile: Fundacion Equitas.
Mallon, Florencia E. 1994. "Reflections on the Ruins: Everyday Forms of State Formation in Nineteenth-Century Mexico." In *Everyday Forms of State Formation Revolution and the Negotiation of Rule in Modern Mexico*, edited by Gilbert Joseph and Daniel Nugent, 69–106. Durham, NC: Duke University Press. https://doi.org/10.1515/9780822396666-006.
Mallon, Florencia E. 1995. *Peasant and Nation: The Making of Postcolonial Mexico and Peru*. Berkeley: University of California Press.
Mannheim, Bruce. 2015. "All Translation Is Radical Translation." In *Translating Worlds: The Epistemological Space of Translation*, edited by William F. Hanks and Carlo Severi, 199–221. Chicago: University of Chicago Press.
Manning, Paul. 2010. "The Semiotics of Brand." *Annual Review of Anthropology* 39: 33–49.

Marcus, George E. 1995. "Ethnography in/of the World System: The Emergence of Multi-Sited Ethnography." *Annual Review of Anthropology* 24 (1): 95–117. https://doi.org/10.1146/annurev.an.24.100195.000523.
Martínez Canales, Luís Alejandro. 2010. "Tlen Yawi Ne Wehka: Cultura trabajo y conciencia de los migrantes Nahuas de la sierra de Zongolica." PhD thesis, UNAM.
Martínez Luna, Jaime. 2003. "Autonomía y Autodeterminación. Pasado y Futuro de y Para Nuestros Pueblos." In *La Comunalidad: Modo de vida en los pueblos indios. Tomo I*, edited by Juán José Rendón Monzón, 78–84. México, D.F.: CONACULTA.
Martínez Luna, Jaime. 2009. *Eso que llaman comunalidad*. Colección Diálogos. Pueblos originarios de Oaxaca; Serie: Veredas. Oaxaca, México: Culturas Populares, CONACULTA/Secretaría de Cultura, Gobierno de Oaxaca/Fundación Alfredo Harp Helú Oaxaca, AC.
Mata-Míguez, J., L. Overholtzer, E. Rodríguez-Alegría, B. M. Kemp, and D. A. Bolnick. 2012. "The Genetic Impact of Aztec Imperialism: Ancient Mitochondrial DNA Evidence from Xaltocan, Mexico." *American Journal of Physical Anthropology* 149 (4): 504–16.
Mateos Cortés, Laura Selene. 2017. "Indigenous Youth Graduating from Intercultural Universities: Capability Building through Intercultural Higher Education in Veracruz, Mexico." *Journal of Intercultural Studies* 38 (2): 155–69.
Matthew, Laura E., and Michel Oudijk. 2007. *Indian Conquistadors: Indigenous Allies in the Conquest of Mesoamerica*. Norman: University of Oklahoma Press.
McDonough, Kelly. 2014. *The Learned Ones: Nahua Intellectuals in Postconquest Mexico*. Tucson: University of Arizona Press.
Medrano, Ethelia Ruiz. 2011. *Mexico's Indigenous Communities: Their Lands and Histories, 1500–2010*. Boulder, CO: University Press of Colorado.
Meek, Barbra A. 2012. *We Are Our Language: An Ethnography of Language Revitalization in a Northern Athabaskan Community*. Tucson: University of Arizona Press.
Melton-Villanueva, Miriam. 2016. *The Aztecs at Independence: Nahua Culture Makers in Central Mexico, 1799–1832*. Tucson: University of Arizona Press.
Melton-Villanueva, Miriam, Abelardo de la Cruz, and Ofelia Cruz Morales. 2022. "Práctica autóctona para revitalizar la lengua Náhuatl en comunidades bilingües de México." *Lenguas Radicales* 1 (3): 31–46. https://doi.org/10.56791/lr.v1i3.20.
Mendoza-Denton, Norma. 2008. *Homegirls: Language and Cultural Practice among Latina Youth Gangs*. New York: John Wiley & Sons.
Mentz, Brígida von. 2008. *Cuauhnáhuac 1450–1675, su historia indígena y documentos en "mexicano": Cambio y continuidad de una cultura nahua*. Mexico City: Miguel Ángel Porrúa.
Messing, Jacqueline. 2002. "Fractal Recursivity in Ideologies of Language, Identity and Modernity in Tlaxcala, Mexico." *Proceedings of the Tenth Annual Symposium about Language and Society. Austin: Texas Linguistic Forum* 45: 95–105.
Messing, Jacqueline. 2007a. "Ideologies of Public and Private Uses of Language in Tlaxcala, Mexico." *International Journal of the Sociology of Language* 187–88: 211–27.
Messing, Jacqueline. 2007b. "Multiple Ideologies and Competing Discourses: Language Shift in Tlaxcala, Mexico." *Language in Society* 36 (04): 555–77.
Messing, Jacqueline. 2013. "I Didn't Know You Knew Mexicano!" In *Indigenous Youth and Multilingualism: Language Identity, Ideology, and Practice in Dynamic Cultural Worlds*, edited by Leisy Wyman, Teresa McCarty, and Sheila Nichols, 111–27. New York: Routledge.
Miller, Marilyn Grace. 2004. *Rise and Fall of the Cosmic Race: The Cult of Mestizaje in Latin America*. Austin, TX: University of Texas Press.
Milroy, James, and Lesley Milroy. 1999. *Authority in Language: Investigating Standard English*. London: Routledge.
Miner, Dylan. 2014. *Creating Aztlán: Chicano Art, Indigenous Sovereignty, and Lowriding across Turtle Island*. Tucson: University of Arizona Press.

Mitchell, Timothy. 1999. "Society, Economy and the State Effect." In *State/Culture: State-Formation after the Cultural Turn*, edited by George Steinmetz, 76–98. Ithaca, NY: Cornell University Press.

Moore, Robert E. 2003. "From Genericide to Viral Marketing: On 'Brand.'" *Language & Communication* 23 (3): 331–57.

Mora, Mariana. 2017. *Kuxlejal Politics: Indigenous Autonomy, Race, and Decolonizing Research in Zapatista Communities*. Austin: University of Texas Press.

Morales Carbajal, Claudia, and Carlos Alberto Casas Mendoza. 2020. "Ritual y construcción histórica de una comunidad utópica: Xochitalis en La Sierra de Zongolica." *Revista de El Colegio de San Luis* 10 (21): 5–29.

Moreno, Julio. 2003. *Yankee Don't Go Home: Mexican Nationalism, American Business Culture, and the Shaping of Modern Mexico, 1920–1950*. Chapel Hill: University of North Carolina Press.

Morris, Mark. 2007. "Language in Service of the State: The Nahuatl Counterinsurgency Broadsides of 1810." *Hispanic American Historical Review* 87 (3): 433–70.

Moynihan, Kathryn. 2018. "How Navajo Nation v. Urban Outfitters Illustrates the Failure of Intellectual Property Law to Protect Native American Cultural Property Notes." *Rutgers Race & the Law Review* 19 (1): 51–73.

Muehlmann, Shaylih. 2008. "'Spread Your Ass Cheeks': And Other Things That Should Not Be Said in Indigenous Languages." *American Ethnologist* 35 (1): 34–48.

Muehlmann, Shaylih. 2012. "Von Humboldt's Parrot and the Countdown of Last Speakers in the Colorado Delta." *Language & Communication* 32 (2): 160–68.

Muehlmann, Shaylih. 2014. "The Speech Community and Beyond: Language and the Nature of the Social Aggregate." In *The Cambridge Handbook of Linguistic Anthropology*, edited by P. Kockelman Nick Enfield and J. Sidnell, 577–98. Cambridge: Cambridge University Press.

Murray Li, Tania. 2000. "Articulating Indigenous Identity in Indonesia: Resource Politics and the Tribal Slot." *Comparative Studies in Society and History* 42 (1): 149–79.

Nahmad Sitton, Salomon. 2008. "Mexico: Anthropology and the Nation State." In *A Companion to Latin American Anthropology*, edited by Deborah Poole, 128–50. Malden, MA: Blackwell.

Nairn, Tom. 2003. *The Break-up of Britain: Crisis and Neo-Nationalism*. 3rd ed. Altona, VIC: Common Ground.

Nakassis, C. V. 2012. "Brand, Citationality, Performativity." *American Anthropologist* 114 (4): 624–38.

Nava Nava, Refugio. 2013. "Malintzin Itlahtol." *Totlahtol Series*. Warsaw: Faculty of "Artes Liberales," University of Warsaw & Instituto de Docencia e Investigación Etnológica de Zacatecas.

Nava Nava, Refugio. 2017. "La socialización infantil bilingüe en San Isidro Buensuceso, Tlaxcala, México." *Revista Española de Antropología Americana* 46 (0): 29–47. https://doi.org/10.5209/REAA.58286.

Nava Vite, Rafael, Juana Santes Gómez, and María Isabel Mirenda Landa. 2022. "Fortalecimiento del náhuatl en la Casa del Niño Indígena de Atlahuilco, Veracruz, México: Una experiencia de investigación vinculada." *UVserva* 14 (October): 192–211. https://doi.org/10.25009/uvs.vi14.2850.

Nava Vite, Rafael. 1996. *La Huasteca—Uextekapan: los pueblos nahuas en su lucha por la tierra*. Mexico: SEP, Dirección General de Culturas Populares.

Navarrete Linares, Federico. 2016. *México racista: Una denuncia*. Primera edición. México, D.F.: Grijalbo.

Nevins, M. Eleanor. 2013. *Lessons from Fort Apache: Beyond Language Endangerment and Maintenance*. New York: John Wiley & Sons.

Nielsen, Kristina F. 2017. "Composing Histories: The Transmission and Creation of Historicity, Music and Dance in the Los Angeles Danza Community." Doctoral dissertation: UCLA.

Nutini H. G. and B. Bell. 1980. *Ritual Kinship: The Structure and Historical Development of the Compadrazgo System in rural Tlaxcala*. Vol. 1. Princeton, NJ: Princeton University Press.

Ochs, Elinor, and Lisa Capps. 2001. *Living Narrative: Creating Lives in Everyday Storytelling*. Boston: Harvard University Press.

OECD. 2020. *OECD Tourism Trends and Policies 2020*. OECD. https://doi.org/10.1787/6b47b985-en.

Olko, Justyna, Robert Borges, and John Sullivan. 2018. "Convergence as the Driving Force of Typological Change in Nahuatl." *STUF-Language Typology and Universals* 71 (3): 467–507.

Olko, J., A. Galbarczyk, J. Maryniak, K. Krzych-Miłkowska, H. I. Tepec, E. de la Cruz, E. Dexter-Sobkowiak, and G. Jasienska. 2023. "The Spiral of Disadvantage: Ethnolinguistic Discrimination, Acculturative Stress and Health in Nahua Indigenous Communities in Mexico." *American Journal of Biological Anthropology* 181 (3): 364–78. https://doi.org/10.1002/ajpa.24745.

Olko, Justyna, and K. Lubiewska, J. Maryniak, G. Haimovich, E. de la Cruz, B. Cuahutle Bautista, E. Dexter-Sobkowiak, and H. Iglesias Tepec. 2022. "The Positive Relationship between Indigenous Language Use and Community-Based Well-Being in Four Nahua Ethnic Groups in Mexico." *Cultural Diversity and Ethnic Minority Psychology* 28(1), 132–43.

O'Rourke, Bernardette. 2011. "Whose Language Is It? Struggles for Language Ownership in an Irish Language Classroom." *Journal of Language, Identity & Education* 10 (5): 327–45. https://doi.org/10.1080/15348458.2011.614545.

Özkirimli, Umut. 2010. *Theories of Nationalism: A Critical Introduction*. Basingstoke: Palgrave Macmillan.

Pareyón, Gabriel. 2021. *Resonancias del abismo como nación: Aproximaciones transdisciplinarias a la filosofía de la música y la musicología en México*. Facultad de Música, UNAM. http://www.repositorio.fam.unam.mx/handle/123456789/114.

Patrick, P. L. 2008. "The Speech Community." In *The Handbook of Language Variation and Change*, edited by J. K. Chambers, P. Trudgill, and N. Schilling-Estes, 573–97. Oxford: Blackwell.

Payàs, Gertrudis. 2004. "Translation in Historiography: The Garibay/León-Portilla Complex and the Making of a Pre-Hispanic Past." *Meta: Journal Des Traducteurs / Meta: Translators' Journal* 49 (3): 544–61.

Peña Martínez, Francisco de la. 2002. *Los hijos del sexto sol: Un estudio etnopsicoanalítico del movimiento de la mexicanidad*. México, D.F.: Instituto Nacional de Antropología e Historia.

Peña Martínez, Francisco de la. 2012. "Profecías de la mexicanidad: Entre el milenarismo nacionalista y la new age." *Cuicuilco* 19 (55): 127–43.

Peperstraete, Sylvie, and Gabriel Kenrick Kruell. 2014. "Determining the Authorship of the Crónica Mexicayotl: Two Hypotheses." *The Americas* 71 (2): 315–38. https://doi.org/10.1353/tam.2014.0139.

Perales Franco, Cristina, and Tristan McCowan. 2020. "Rewiring Higher Education for the Sustainable Development Goals: The Case of the Intercultural University of Veracruz, Mexico." *Higher Education* 81: 69–88.

Perley, Bernard C. 2011. *Defying Maliseet Language Death: Emergent Vitalities of Language, Culture and Identity in Eastern Canada*. Lincoln: University of Nebraska Press.

Pharao Hansen, Magnus. 2008. "Huitzilopochtlis Anden Genkomst i Hueyapan [The Second Coming of Huitzilopochtli in Hueyapan]." In *De Mange Veje Til Mesoamerika: Hyldestskrift Til Una Canger*, edited by Jesper Nielsen and Mettelise Fritz Hansen. Copenhagen: Department of Native American Languages and Cultures, 131–47. Institute for Cross-disciplinary and Regional Studies, University of Copenhagen.

Pharao Hansen, Magnus. 2014. "The East-West Split in Nahuan Dialectology: Reviewing the Evidence and Consolidating the Grouping." In *Annual Meeting of the Friends of Uto-Aztecan*. Tepic, Nayarit, Mexico. https://www.researchgate.net/publication/272507445_The_E

ast-West_split_in_Nahuan_Dialectology_Reviewing_the_Evidence_and_Consolidating_the_Grouping.

Pharao Hansen, Magnus. 2016. "The Difference Language Makes: The Life-History of Nahuatl in Two Mexican Families." *Journal of Linguistic Anthropology* 26 (1): 81–97.

Pharao Hansen, Magnus. 2018. "Becoming Autonomous: Indigeneity, Scale and Schismogenesis in Multicultural Mexico." *PoLAR: Political and Legal Anthropology Review* 41 (S1): 133–47.

Pharao Hansen, Magnus. 2024. "Words in Revolution: How the Nahuas Disappeared from the State of Morelos and from the Historiography of the Mexican Revolution." In *Nahuatl Studies, Past and Present*, edited by Galen Brokaw and Pablo García Loaeza, 115–32. Boulder: University of Colorado Press.

Pharao Hansen, Magnus, and Kurly Tlapoyawa. 2020. "Aztlán and Mexican Transnationalism: Language, Nation, and History." In *Handbook of the Changing World Language Map*, edited by Stanley D. Brunn and Roland Kehrein, 667–84. Cham: Springer International. https://doi.org/10.1007/978-3-030-02438-3_68.

Poole, Stafford. 1995. *Our Lady of Guadalupe: The Origins and Sources of a Mexican National Symbol, 1531–1797*. University of Arizona Press.

Postero, Nancy G. 2005. "Indigenous Responses to Neoliberalism." *PoLAR: Political and Legal Anthropology Review* 28 (1): 73–92.

Postero, Nancy G. 2007. *Now We Are Citizens: Indigenous Politics in Postmulticultural Bolivia*. Palo Alto, CA: Stanford University Press.

Postero, Nancy G. 2017. *The Indigenous State: Race, Politics and Performance in Plurinational Bolivia*. Los Angeles: University of California Press.

Povinelli, Elizabeth. 2001. "Radical Worlds: The Anthropology of Incommensurability and Inconceivability." *The Annual Review of Anthropology* 30: 319–34.

Povinelli, Elizabeth. 2002. *The Cunning of Recognition: Indigenous Alterities and the Making of Australian Multiculturalism*. Durham, NC: Duke University Press.

Povinelli, Elizabeth. 2012. "The Will to Be Otherwise/The Effort of Endurance." *South Atlantic Quarterly* 111 (3): 453–75.

Povinelli, Elizabeth. 2016. *Geontologies: A Requiem to Late Liberalism*. Durham, NC: North Carolina: Duke University Press.

Rábasa, José. 2011. *Tell Me the Story of How I Conquered You: Elsewheres and Ethnosuicide in the Colonial Mesoamerican World*. Austin: University of Texa Press.

Rafael, Tony. 2013. *The Mexican Mafia*. New York: Encounter Books.

Rappaport, Joanne. 2005. *Intercultural Utopias: Public Intellectuals, Cultural Experimentation, and Ethnic Pluralism in Colombia*. Durham, NC: Duke University Press.

Reardon, Jenny, and Kim TallBear. 2012. "'Your DNA Is Our History': Genomics, Anthropology, and the Construction of Whiteness as Property." *Current Anthropology* 53 (S5): 233–45.

Rebolledo, Nicanor. 2021. "Educación intercultural: Reflexiones sobre dos décadas de Interculturalismo en México RevistAleph." *RevistAleph* 36: 36–52.

Redfield, Robert. 1930. *Tepoztlan, a Mexican Village: A Study of Folk Life*. Chicago: University of Chicago Press.

Reina, Leticia. 1980. *Las rebeliones campesinas en México, 1819–1906*. México, D.F.: Siglo Veintiuno.

Rendón Monzón, Juan José. 2003. *La comunalidad: Modo de vida en los pueblos indios, tomo I*. Oaxaca: Consejo Nacional para la Cultura y las Artes.

Reyes Garcia, Luis. 1976. *Der Ring aus Tlalocan: Mythen und Gebete, Lieder und Eretihlungen der Heutigen Nahua in Veracrue und Puebla*. Berlin: Mexiko.

Richardson, J., and A. L. Kroeber. 1940. *Three Centuries of Women's Dress Fashions, a Quantitative Analysis*. Berkeley: University of California Press.

Riley, C. L. 2005. *Becoming Aztlan: Mesoamerican Influence in the Greater Southwest, AD*. Salt Lake City: Utah University Press.

Rios, Gerardo. 2017. *Por la Patria Chica: Indigenous Rebellion and Revolution in the Oriente Central de México, Tlaxcala and Puebla, 1853–1927*. Doctoral dissertation, University of California, San Diego.

Rivera Cusicanqui, Silvia. 2012. "Ch'ixinakax Utxiwa: A Reflection on the Practices and Discourses of Decolonization." *South Atlantic Quarterly* 111 (1): 95–109.

Rivera Moreno, Donna. 1991. *Xochiapulco: una gloria olvidada*. Puebla: Gobierno del Estado de Puebla.

Rodriguez, Clara E. 2000. *Changing Race: Latinos, the Census, and the History of Ethnicity in the United States*. New York: New York University Press.

Rodríguez, Juán Luís. 2021. *Language and Revolutionary Magic in the Orinoco Delta*. London and New York: Bloomsbury Academic.

Rojas, Mariano Jacobo. 1927. *Manual de la lengua Nahuatl: Método práctico para hablar, leer y escribir la lengua Mexicana*. México, D.F.: José Donaciano Rojas.

Romero, Sergio. 2012. "'They Don't Speak Our Language Right': Language Standardization, Power and Migration among the Q'eqchi' Maya." *Journal of Linguistic Anthropology* 22 (2): 21–41.

Romero, Sergio. 2015. *Language and Ethnicity among the K'ichee' Maya*. Salt Lake City: University of Utah Press.

Rosa, Jonathan D. 2016. "Standardization, Racialization, Languagelessness: Raciolinguistic Ideologies across Communicative Contexts." *Journal of Linguistic Anthropology* 26 (2): 162–83.

Rosa, Jonathan, and Nelson Flores. 2017. "Unsettling Race and Language: Toward a Raciolinguistic Perspective." *Language in Society* 46 (5): 621–47. https://doi.org/10.1017/S0047404517000562.

Rosado-Zaidi, Samuel. 2021. "The 'Mayan' Train: Mexico's Latest Industrial Expansion Renewed / El Tren Maya: la renovación de la última frontera industrial de México," January. Humanities Commons. https://hcommons.org/deposits/item/hc:33835/.

Rostas, Susanna. 2009. *Carrying the Word: The Concheros Dance in Mexico City*. Austin: University of Texas Press.

Rugeley, Terry. 2009. *Rebellion Now and Forever*. Stanford, CA: Stanford University Press.

Ruíz Medrano, Ethelia. 2011. *Mexico's Indigenous Communities: Their Lands and Histories, 1500–2010*. Translated by Russ Davidson. Boulder, CO: University of Colorado Press.

Saldaña-Portillo, María Josefina. 2016. *Indian Given: Racial Geographies across Mexico and the United States*. Durham, NC: Duke University Press.

Sandoval Arenas, Carlos Octavio. 2017. "Displacement and Revitalization of the Nahuatl Language in the High Mountains of Veracruz, Mexico." *Arts & Humanities in Higher Education* 16 (1): 66–81. https://doi.org/10.1177/1474022216628390.

Sandstrom, Alan. 1991. *Corn Is Our Blood: Culture and Ethnic Identity in a Contemporary Aztec Indian Village*. Norman: University of Oklahoma Press.

Sapir, Edward. 1949. "The Grammarian and His Language." In *Selected Writings in Language, Culture and Personality*, edited by David G. Mandelbaum, 150–60. Los Angeles: University of California Press.

Sartorello, S. C. 2009. "Una perspectiva crítica sobre interculturalidad y educación intercultural bilingüe: El caso de la Unión de Maestros de la Nueva Educación para México (UNEM) y educadores independientes en Chiapas." *Revista Latinoamericana de Educación Inclusiva* 3 (2): 77–90.

Schmelkes, Sylvia. 2009. "Intercultural Universities in Mexico: Progress and Difficulties." *Intercultural Education* 20 (1): 5–17.

Schroeder, Susan. 1991. *Chimalpahin and the Kingdoms of Chalco*. Tucson: University of Arizona Press.

Schroeder, Susan. 1997. "Introduction." In *Codex Chimalpahin*, edited by Artuhur J. O. Anderson and Susan Schroeder, 3–18. Norman: University of Oklahoma Press.

Schroeder, Susan, and Anderson, Arthur J. O., eds. 1997. *Codex Chimalpahin: Society and Politics in Mexico Tenochtitlan, Tlateloloco, Texcoco, Culhuacan, and Other Nahua Altepetl in Central Mexico: The Nahuatl and Spanish Annals and Accounts.* Norman: University of Oklahoma Press.

Schryer, Frans J. 1990. *Ethnicity and Class Conflict in Rural Mexico.* Princeton, NJ: Princeton University Press.

Schryer, Frans Jozef. 1987. "Class Conflict and the Corporate Peasant Community: Disputes over Land in Nahuatl Villages." *Journal of Anthropological Research* 43 (2): 99–120. https://doi.org/10.1086/jar.43.2.3630220.

Schütz, Alfred. 1967. *The Phenomenology of the Social World.* Evanston, IL: Northwestern University Press.

Seymour, Philip H. K., Mikko Aro, Jane M. Erskine, and collaboration with COST Action A8 Network. 2003. "Foundation Literacy Acquisition in European Orthographies." *British Journal of Psychology* 94 (2): 143–74. https://doi.org/10.1348/000712603321661859.

Shaul, David Leedom. 2014. *A Prehistory of Western North America: The Impact of Uto-Aztecan Languages.* Albuquerque: University of New Mexico Press.

Shulist, Sarah. 2018. *Transforming Indigeneity: Urbanization and Language Revitalization in the Brazilian Amazon.* Toronto: University of Toronto Press.

Silverstein, Michael. 1976. "Shifters, Linguistic Categories, and Cultural Description." In *Meaning in Anthropology*, edited by Keith Basso and Henry A. Selby. Albuquerque: University of New Mexico Press.

Silverstein, Michael. 1981. *The Limits of Awareness.* Austin, TX: Southwestern Educational Laboratory.

Silverstein, Michael. 1992. "The Uses and Utility of Ideology: Some Reflections." *Pragmatics* 2 (3): 311–23.

Silverstein, Michael. 1993. "Metapragmatic Discourse and Metapragmatic Function." In *Reflexive Language: Reported Speech and Metapragmatics*, edited by John A. Lucy, 33–59. Cambridge: Cambridge University Press.

Silverstein, Michael. 1998. "Contemporary Transformations of Local Linguistic Communities." *Annual Review of Anthropology* 27: 401–26.

Silverstein, Michael. 2003. "Translation, Transduction, Transformation: Skating 'Glossando' on Thin Semiotic Ice." In *Translating Cultures: Perspectives on Translation and Anthropology*, edited by Paula G. Rubel and Abraham Rosman, 75–109. Oxford: Berg.

Silverstein, Michael. 2014. "The Race from Place: Dialect Eradication Vs. The Linguistic "Authenticity" of "Terroir." In *Indexing Authenticity: Sociolinguistic Perspectives*, edited by Véronique Lacoste, Jakob R.E. Leimgruber, and Thiemo Breyer, 159–88. Hague: Mouton DeGruyter.

Silverstein, Michael. 2018. "Monoglot 'Standard' in America: Standardization and Metaphors of Linguistic Hegemony." In *The Matrix of Language*, edited by Don Brenneis, 284–306. London: Routledge.

Simpson, Audra. 2014. *Mohawk Interruptus: Political Life across the Borders of Settler States.* Durham, NC: Duke University Press.

Simpson, Leanne Betasamosake. 2017. *As We Have Always Done: Indigenous Freedom through Radical Resistance.* Minneapolis: University of Minnesota Press.

Simpson, Leanne Betasamosake, and Naomi Klein. 2017. "Dancing the World into Being: A Conversation with Idle No More's Simpson." *Tabula Rasa* 26: 51–70.

Smith, Benjamin T. 2021. *The Dope: The Real History of the Mexican Drug Trade.* New York: W. W. Norton.

Smith, Michael E. 1984. "The Aztlan Migrations of the Nahuatl Chronicles: Myth or History?" *Ethnohistory* 31 (3): 153–86.

Sotelo Inclán, J. (1943) 1970. *Raíz y razón de Zapata.* México, D.F.: Comisión Federal de Electricidad.

Stephen, Lynn. 1999. "Declaration: Never Again a Mexico without Us." *Cultural Survival Quarterly* 23 (1): 39–40.

Stolz, Thomas. 2018. "On Classifiers and Their Absence in Classical and Colonial Nahuatl." *STUF-Language Typology and Universals* 71 (3): 339–96.

Sturm, Circe. 2002. *Blood Politics: Race, Culture, and Identity in the Cherokee Nation of Oklahoma*. Berkeley and Los Angeles: University of California Press.

Sturm, Circe. 2010. *Becoming Indian: The Struggle over Cherokee Identity in the Twenty-First Century*. Santa Fe, NM: SAR Press.

Sullivan, John. 2011. "The IDIEZ Project: A Model for Indigenous Language Revitalization in Higher Education." *Collaborative Anthropologies* 4 (1): 139–54.

Suslak, Daniel F. 2003. "The Story of ö: Orthography and Cultural Politics in the Mixe Highlands." *Pragmatics* 13 (4): 551–63.

Swinehart, Karl, and Kathryn Graber. 2012. "Tongue-Tied Territories: Languages and Publics in Stateless Nations." *Language & Communication* 32: 95–97.

Taggart, James M. 2008. "Nahuat Ethnicity in a Time of Agrarian Conflict." In *Ethnic Identity in Nahua Mesoamerica: The View from Archaeology, Art History, Ethnohistory, and Contemporary Ethnography*, edited by F. Berdan, J. Chance, A.R. Sandstrom, B. Stark, J. Taggart, and E. Umberger, 183–204. Salt Lake City: University of Utah Press.

Taggart, James M. 2010. *Remembering Victoria: A Tragic Nahuat Love Story*. Austin, TX: University of Texas Press.

Taggart, James M. 2020. *The Rain Gods' Rebellion: The Cultural Basis of a Nahua Insurgency*. Boulder, CO: University Press of Colorado.

TallBear, Kim. 2013. *Native American DNA: Tribal Belonging and the False Promise of Genetic Science*. Minneapolis: University of Minnesota Press.

Taller de Tradición Oral, C.E.P.E.C. 1994. *Tejuan tikintenkakiliayaj in toueyitatajuan— Les oíamos contar a nuestros abuelos: Etnohistoria de San Miguel Tzinacapan*. México, D.F.: Instituto Nacional de Antropología e Historia.

Tanck de Estrada, Dorothy. 1989. "Castellanización, política y escuelas de indios en el arzobispado de México a mediados del siglo XVIII." *Historia Mexicana* 38 (4): 701–41.

Tanu, Danau, and Laura Dales. 2015. "Language in Fieldwork: Making Visible the Ethnographic Impact of the Researcher's Linguistic Fluency." *The Australian Journal of Anthropology* 27 (3): 353–69.

Taylor, Charles. 1994. *Multiculturalism*. Princeton, NJ: Princeton University Press.

Terborg, Roland, and Laura G. Landa. 2013. "The Ecology of Pressures: Towards a Tool to Analyze the Complex Process of Language Shift and Maintenance." In *Complexity Perspectives on Language, Communication and Society*, edited by Àngels Massip-Bonet and Albert Bastardas-Boada, 219–39. Berlin: Springer.

Tone-Pah-Hote, Jenny. 2019. *Crafting an Indigenous Nation: Kiowa Expressive Culture in the Progressive Era*. Chapel Hill: University of North Carolina Press.

Townsend, Camilla. 2009. *Here in This Year: Seventeenth-Century Nahuatl Annals of the Tlaxcala-Puebla Valley*. Stanford, CA: Stanford University Press.

Townsend, Camilla. 2016. *Annals of Native America: How the Nahuas of Colonial Mexico Kept Their History Alive*. Oxford: Oxford University Press.

Townsend, Camilla. 2019. *Fifth Sun: A New History of the Aztecs*. Oxford: Oxford University Press.

Tsing, Anna. 2005. *Friction: An Ethnography of Global Connection*. Princeton, NJ: Princeton University Press.

Tuck, Eve, and K. Wayne Yang. 2012. "Decolonization Is Not a Metaphor." *Decolonization: Indigeneity, Education & Society* 1 (1): 1–40.

Turner, Dale. 2020. "On the Politics of Indigenous Translation: Listening to Indigenous Peoples in and on Their Own Terms." In *Routledge Handbook of Critical Indigenous Studies*, edited by Brendan Hokowhitu, Aileen Moreton-Robinson, Linda Tuhiwai-Smith, Chris Andersen, Steve Larkin, 175–88. London: Routledge.

Tzul, Gladys. 2018. "Rebuilding Communal Life." *NACLA Report on the Americas* 50 (4): 404–7. https://doi.org/10.1080/10714839.2018.1550986.

Tzul, Gladys, Ana Silvia Monzón, Guillermo Toriello, Edelberto Torres Rivas, Matilde González-Izás, Claudia Dary, Alfredo Guerra Borges, et al. 2019. "Sistemas de gobierno comunal indígena: La organización de la reproducción de la vida." In *Antología del pensamiento crítico Guatemalteco contemporáneo*, edited by Ana Silvia Monzón, 71–82. Bunos Aires: CLACSO. https://doi.org/10.2307/j.ctvtxw2km.7.

Urban, Greg. 1996. *Metaphysical Community: The Interplay of the Senses and the Intellect*. Austin: University of Texas Press.

Urban, Greg. 2001. *Metaculture: How Culture Moves through the World*. Minneapolis: University of Minnesota Press.

Urban, Greg, and Joel Sherzer. 1991. *Nation-States and Indians in Latin America*. Austin: University of Texas Press.

Uribe, Verónica Moreno. 2021. "Interdependencia, cuidados y resistencia: Nikan Tipowih y la reproducción de la vida en Zongolica, Veracruz." *Ecología Política* 61: 103–6.

Urla, Jacqueline. 1995. "Outlaw Language: Creating Alternative Public Spheres in Basque Free Radio." *Pragmatics. Quarterly Publication of the International Pragmatics Association (IPrA)* 5(2): 245–261.

Valentine, Lisa Philips. 1995. *Making It Their Own: Severn Ojibwe Communicative Practices*. Toronto: University of Toronto Press.

Valiñas Coalla, Leopoldo. 2010. "Historia lingüística: migraciones y asentamientos. Relaciones entre pueblos y lenguas." In *Historia sociolingüística de México*, edited by Rebeca Barriga and Pedro Martín Butragueño, 97–160. México, D.F.: COLMEX.

Van Der Aa, J., and J. M. E. Blommaert. 2014. "Michael Silverstein in Conversation: Translatability and the Uses of Standardisation." In *Tilburg Papers in Culture Studies*, vol. 91. Tilburg: University of Tilburg.

Van Young, Eric. 2001. *The Other Rebellion: Popular Violence, Ideology, and the Mexican Struggle for Independence, 1810–1821*. Stanford, CA: Stanford University Press.

Van Zantwijk, Rudolf. 1960. *Los indígenas de Milpa Alta: Herederos de los Aztecas*. Amsterdam: Royal Tropical Institute.

Velasco Ortíz, Laura. 2005. *Mixtec Transnational Identity*. Tucson: University of Arizona Press.

Vertovec, S. 2007. "Super-Diversity and Its Implications." *Ethnic and Racial Studies* 30 (6): 1024–54.

Villareal, Belén. 2011. "El náhuatl en Los Ángeles: El papel de la lengua indígena en la creación de la identidad chicana." *Mester* 40 (1): 81–100.

Vizenor, Gerald Robert. 1999. *Manifest Manners: Narratives on Postindian Survivance*. Lincoln: University of Nebraska Press.

Volcic, Zala, and Mark Andrejevic. 2011. "Nation Branding in the Era of Commercial Nationalism." *International Journal of Communication* 5: 598–618.

Volcic, Zala, and Mark Andrejevic, eds. 2015. *Commercial Nationalism: Selling the Nation and Nationalizing the Sell*. London: Palgrave Macmillan.

Wade, Peter, Carlos López Beltrán, Eduardo Restrepo, and Ricardo Ventura Santos. 2014. *Mestizo Genomics: Race Mixture, Nation, and Science in Latin America*. Durham, NC: Duke University Press.

Warner, Michael. 2002. "Publics and Counterpublics." *Public Culture* 14 (1): 49–90.

Warren, Kay B. 1998. *Indigenous Movements and Their Critics: Pan-Maya Activism in Guatemala*. Princeton, NJ: Princeton University Press.

Weafer, Ciarán. 2016. "Elite Origin of the Irish Language Revival Is Hindering Learning." *Wide Orbits: Ideas Issues and Culture*. https://wideorbits.com/life/opinion-elite-origin-of-the-irish-language-revival-is-hindering-learning/.

Webster, Anthony K. 2010. "On Intimate Grammars with Examples from Navajo English, Navlish, and Navajo." *Journal of Anthropological Research* 66 (2): 187–208.
Webster, Anthony K. 2016. *Intimate Grammars: An Ethnography of Navajo Poetry*. Tucson: University of Arizona Press.
Whittaker, Gordon. 2021. *Deciphering Aztec Hieroglyphs: A Guide to Nahuatl Writing*. Oakland: University of California Press.
Whorf, Benjamin Lee. 1946. "The Milpa Alta Dialect of Aztec: With Notes on the Classical and the Tepoztlán Dialects." In *Linguistic Structures of Native America*, edited by C. Osgood and H. Hoijer, 367–97. New York: Viking Fund.
Wittgenstein, Ludwig. 2010. *Philosophical Investigations*. New York: John Wiley & Sons.
Womack, John. 1968. *Zapata and the Mexican Revolution*. New York: Vintage Books.
Wood, Stephanie. 2012. *Transcending Conquest: Nahua Views of Spanish Colonial Mexico*. Norman: University of Oklahoma Press.
Woodbury, Anthony. 1993. "A Defense of the Proposition, "When a Language Dies, a Culture Dies." In *SALSA 1 (Texas Linguistic Forum 33)*, edited by Robin Queen and Rusty Barrett, 102–30. Austin: University of Texas Department of Linguistics.
Woolard, Kathryn A. 1998. "Introduction: Language Ideology as a Field of Inquiry." In *Language Ideologies: Practice and Theory*, edited by Bambi Schieffelin, Kathryn A. Woolard, and Paul V. Kroskrity, 1–50. Oxford: Oxford University Press.
Wright Carr, David Charles. 2007. "La Política lingüística en la Nueva España." *Acta Universitaria* 17 (3): 5–19. https://doi.org/10.15174/au.2007.156.
Wroblewski, Michael. 2021. *Remaking Kichwa: Language and Indigenous Pluralism in Amazonian Ecuador*. London: Bloomsbury.

With warm thanks to those who have supplied illustrations:

Alicia Smith (Image 6.0 & cover art)
Alex Maya (Image 4.5 & 4.6)
Christophe Helmke (Map 6.2)
Diego Mendoza (Map 1.2)
Carlos Octavio Sandoval Arenas (Image 7.0)
Joe Roe (Map 4.2 & Map 5.1)
Lizbeth de la Cruz Santana (Image 6.4)
Oman Cuezalin Ríos (Image 6.1)
William Cameron Townsend Archives of SIL International (Images 2.2 & 2.3)
Calendarios Landín/MUCAL – Museo del Calendario (Image 3.0)

Index

For the benefit of digital users, indexed terms that span two pages (e.g., 52–53) may, on occasion, appear on only one of those pages.

Figures are indicated by italic *f* following the page number.

A2 haplogroup, 234
Abad, Alejandro, 173
Academia Veracruzana de Lenguas Indígenas (AVELI), 124–25
acts of transduction, 49–50
Africans, 71–72, 136–37
Aguilar Gil, Yásnaya Elena, 24–25, 26, 33, 182–83, 251, 258–59
Aguirre Beltrán, Goonzalo, 190–91, 193, 194–95
altepetl, 9–10, 28–29, 31–33, 43, 45–46, 69, 70–71, 72, 75–76, 84, 85, 191–93, 211, 218, 259, 260
  and community, 18, 21–22, 24–25, 28, 31–32
  definition of, 9
  and orthography, 57–59
  as political community, 28–29, 85
  and public sphere, 30–31
  and sovereignty, 43
Alurista, 222–23
Alvarado Tezozomoc, Hernando, 69, 70–71, 74–75
American Phonetic Alphabet (APA), 53–54, 56n.2
Americans, 234–35
Analco, 229–30
Analytical Dictionary of Nahuatl (Karttunen), 59–60, 243
Anderson, Benedict, 1, 26–27, 31–32, 42–43
Andrews, J. Richard, 59–62
Anenecuilco, 97
angle of listening, 130
Anglo-Americans, 226
Antonio Flores, José, 14–15
Anzaldúa, Gloria, 39n.17
Apache, 40–41, 42–43, 251
Arenas, Domingo, 100

Arte de la lengua mexicana (1645), 53
Arte mexicana (1595), 53
Arte para aprender la lengua mexicana (1547), 53
Atlihuayan, 99
Axayacatl, 69, 70–71
Ayaquica, Fortino, 99
Aymara, 36
Ayuuk (Mixe), 24–25, 29
Aztecs, 69, 110*f*, 183–84, 244, 245–46
  and *Aztlán*, 222–23
  and cultural heritage, 131
  and Mexico, 196–97
  and Mexihco-Tenochtitlan, 7–8
  and Nahuatl, 1, 241
  and nationalism, 17, 236–37

bachillerato, 174, 195–96
Bakhtin, Mikhail, 8–9, 122–23, 130
Balsas River, 113
Baranda, Francisco, 132–33
Barbados Declaration, 29
Barlow, Robert, 56–57, 242
barrier of contextualization, 33
barrier of translation, 33
barrios (neighborhoods), 128–29, 161–64, 174
Barrios, Gabriel, 100, 101
Barrios Espinoza, Miguel, 56–57, 258
Battle of Puebla, 92, 95–96
Benito Juárez International Airport, 119, 121*f*
Blanco, Cuauhtemoc, 265–66
Blommaert, Jan, 270–72
Boas, Franz, 53–54
Bolivia, 34–35, 36–37
"The Border" (Anzaldúa), 222–23
Bourdieu, Pierre, 135–36
bourgeois public sphere, 69–70, 111, 217
Bustamante, Carlos Maria, 82–83

Index

cabecera, 153–54, 156, 157, 159, 160–62
cabildo, 85–86, 160–61
calpulli, 230–32
Calpulli Xiuhcoatl, 227f
Campbell, R. Joe, 59–12
Cancino, Francesco, 138, 139
Canger, Una, 10, 60–61, 72–74
Cantares Mexicanos, 132–33
Carballo, Mardonio, 129, 274–75
Cárdenas, Juán Luna, 159, 162–64, 230–32, 236–37
Cárdenas, Lázaro, 103–11
cargo system, 85–86, 259–60
Carochi, Horacio, 53, 59–60
Carrancistas, 96, 100
Carranza, Venustiano, 96, 100
casta, 71–72, 80, 84, 235
Caste War, 20–21
Cázares, Agustín, 99
census data, 97–99, 251
Central America, 7–8, 28–29
Central Mexican Nahuatl, 74–75, 86–87
Centro Coordenador Indigenista (CCI), 193–95
chairo, 145–46
Charles V (Spain), 74–75
Cherán, 259–60, 268–69
Chicanos, 222, 224, 226, 239–40, 242–43, 244, 246
Chickasaw, 40–41
Chicontepec (Veracruz), 110f, 238, 274–75
Chimalnahuatlajtole, 152–53, 178–79
Chimalpahin, 57–59, 58f, 69
Citlahua, Gabriela, 128–29, 212, 215, 216–17, 275–76
classical Nahuatl, 11–12, 59–60, 132, 183–84, 230–32, 236–37
classical tradition, 132
Clavijero, Francisco Javier, 80–81
code of power, 14–15, 86–87
code of solidarity, 14–15, 86–87, 168
coevalness, 28–29, 158
cofradías, 85, 86–87
Colegio de Santa Cruz de Tlatelolco, 70–71
colonial administration, 69–70
colonial *cabildo*, 85–86
colonialism, 2, 22, 200–1, 222–23, 227–28, 229–30, 232, 245, 247
    settler, 23, 250–51
colonial language, 44–45, 59–60
colonial Nahuatl, 55, 59, 68, 74–75, 79–80, 87

colonial orthographies, 61, 126–27
colonial period, 7–8, 52–53, 56, 60–61, 69–75, 77–78, 79–80, 111–12, 115–16, 162, 190–91, 222, 229
    and Indigenous community, 165
colonial texts, 76–77, 79, 80–81, 132, 235, 236
Comisión para el Desarrollo de los Pueblos Indígenas (CDI), 176–79, 200, 202–3
communalect, 9–10, 182–83
communality, 9–10, 24, 29–31, 69–70, 91, 104
communal politics, 25, 263
compadrazgo, 85–86
Concejo indígena, 153–54
concheros, 227–28, 230–32
Consejo Nacional para la Prevencion de la Discriminación (CONAPRED), 143–45
constituencies, 32, 129–30
    and Hueyapan, 166
    and Indigenous populations, 103, 104, 107–9, 110–11
    and Nahua population, 87, 90–91
    and Nahuatl, 88–89
Constitution of Mexico, 4, 84, 123–25, 126
constructionist (view of nationalism), 18
contemporary writers, 57–59
Cortés, Hernán, 52–53, 71–72, 82–83, 102, 142n.20
Coulthard, Glen Sean, 20
covert publics, 86, 90–91
COVID-19, 62f, 128–29
criollos, 71, 80–81, 93
Cristina, Doña, 197–99
Crónica Mexicayotl, 69n.1
de la Cruz, Juana Inés, 80–81
de la Cruz, Lizbeth, 252
de la Cruz Cruz, Abelardo, 274–75
de la Cruz Cruz, Victoriano "Tepoxteco," 224, 238–39, 274–75
Cruz Morales, Ofelia, 274–75
Cruzoob Maya, 20–21
Cuahuixtlahuac, 188n.1
Cuauhtemoc, 70–71, 102, 109–10, 118f, 265–66
Cuauhtli, Chris, 244, 252
Cuaxtle, Felix Evodio "Tata," 239
Cuernavaca, 45–46, 165, 178–79, 183–84, 185f
cultural politics, 4–5, 28n.11, 38–39, 142–43, 145–46, 166–67, 183–84, 200
    Aztec, 105–6, 131, 163–64, 230–32, 236–37, 241

consumer, 140–42, 271–72
culture, 1–2, 80, 90, 103, 115–16, 125, 133, 139, 148, 156, 163–64, 168, 169, 189, 195–96, 212–14, 224–26
  gang, 240, 241, 250
  Mexican, 132, 139–40, 213–14, 224–26, 233–34, 242–43, 250–51, 275
  national, 22, 136, 204
  and nation-building, 20–21
  prison, 241
  and state, 162–63
Cusicanqui, Silvia Rivera, 22, 39

Dakin, Karen, 191n.3
Danza Azteca, 224–25, 227–28, 230–32, 236, 244
danzantes, 227–28, 232
Davis, Jenny L., 40–41
decolonization, 39, 56–57, 201–2, 218, 239, 249, 273
Democratic Revolutionary Party (PRD), 167
denotation
  denotational code, 27
  denotational communication, 245
  denotational ideology, 261–62
  denotational indexes, 270–71
  denotational language, 271
  denotational meaning, 11–12, 49–50
Dia de la Cruz, 196
dialect, 4–5, 6–7, 10, 25–26, 54–55, 124–25
Díaz, Frank, 236–37
Dìaz Gomez, Floriberto, 24, 29–30
Díaz, Porfirio, 89, 101–2
Dietz, Günther, 203, 206–7
diglossia, 74–75, 79
Dimas Huacuz, Martha, 201–2
Dirty War, 112–13
double-voiced communication, 122–23, 130, 267
Durango, 5–6, 55

earthquake (Tlalolintle, 2017), 155–56
Ebrard, Marcelo, 1–3, 4
education, 2, 82–83, 93, 183–84, 218, 259–60
  bilingual, 36, 200, 274–75
  elementary school, 160–61, 195–96
  higher, 39–40, 167, 195–96, 214, 218, 274–75
  indigenista, 194–95
  Indigenous, 62–64, 104, 109n.15, 173, 193–94, 203–4, 206–7

intercultural, 45–46, 189, 194–95, 201–2, 204–5, 212, 214–15
ejido, 103–4
emergent vitalities, 43
encomiendas, 71
Escuelita Nikan Tipowih, 212
Estela Martínez, Irma, 274–75
ethnic affiliations, 69
ethnic composition, 235
ethnic demography, 97–99
ethnic divisions, 26
ethnic groups, 18–19, 27, 91, 110–11, 158, 182, 203, 214–15, 259
  and allegiance, 72
  and *altepetl*-communities, 18
  and authority, 126
  and DNA, 235
ethnic hierarchy, 71–72
ethnic identity, 6, 79–80, 95–96, 162–63, 168–69, 170–71, 224–25, 230–32, 273
ethnic symbols, 136–37, 158–59
ethnography, 44–46, 47–49, 51, 162–63, 188–89, 197–99, 203
experiential intensities, 43, 270–71, 272

Facebook, 129–30, 223
  and Gabriela Citlahua, 216–17
  and Hueyapan, 168–69
  and memes, 143
  and Mexica History group, 225–26, 228, 233–34, 235, 242, 243, 245–46
  and Nahuatl language groups, 120–22, 224
  and "Natives Against Aztlán," 247
  and "Natives Against Divided Natives," 247
  and *Yolotl*, 143–45
Faudree, Paja, 10, 44, 51–52, 57–59, 131, 258
First Aztec Congress, 56–57, 109–10
Florentine Codex, 53, 59–60, 70–71
Flores Farfán, José Antonio, 14–15
Flores Nájera, Lucero, 274–75
Flores, Samir, 265–66
folklorization, 169, 183–84
"forced identity" 158–59, 162–63, 181
foreignizing, 50
form feeling, 16–17
Foucault, Michel, 190, 240
Fox, Vicente, 202–3
Franciscan order, 53, 57–59, 70–71
Francisco, Juan, 92–93

Francisco Lucas, Juan, 95–96
French Intervention, 28–29, 88–89, 92, 95–96
fresa, 141–42, 145–46
Friedlander, Judith, 105–6, 157, 158–59, 162–64, 169, 182
function (of language), 24, 33–34, 40–41, 67, 122–23, 126, 152, 175–76, 182–83, 218, 238–39, 261–63

Gaeltacht, 35
Galicia Chimalpopoca, Faustino, 88–89
Gálvez, Xochitl, 202–3
Gamio, Manuel, 104, 131
Garcia Canclini, Nestor, 203
García, John "Yan," 238–39
Garcia Landa, Laura, 181
García, Luís Reyes, 60–61, 124n.1
Garrido Cruz, Guillermo, 274–75
Gates, Henry Louis, 234
General Commission for Intercultural and Bilingual Education (CGEIB), 200, 202–3
Ley General de Derechos Lingüísticos de los Pueblos Indígenas (General Law of Linguistic Rights, 2003), 34–35, 123, 128–29, 200
General Direction of Indigenous Education (DGEI), 173
Global North, 38–39
glottopolitical regime (glottopolitics), 43, 51–52, 260–61
Gramsci, Antonio, 91–92
Greek, 30, 80–81, 109–10, 236
Gross Domestic Product (GDP) of Mexico, 137–38
Guerrero, 55, 115–16, 120–22, 124–25, 129–30, 143, 264–65, 266, 274–75
  and Dirty War, 113
  and indigenist nationalism, 102
  and phoneme systems, 61
  and Spanish, 14–15
  and Zapatistas, 99–100
Guerrero Nahuatl, 5–6, 14–15, 120–22
Guillermina, Maya Rendón, 170–71, 173, 176–78, 179, 184–85

hacienda, 82–83, 87–88, 92, 96–97, 101, 103–4
haplogroup A, 234
Haro Sánchez, Ana-Bertha, 165, 166
Hasler, Andrés, 56–57, 67

Health Secretary of Puebla State, 61, 62*f*
Hecho en México, 137–38
"hemispheric localism," 241, 250
Herder, Johann Gottfried, 25–26
heritage, 138, 168–69, 212, 223, 224–25, 235, 242, 244–45, 246
  Aztec, 132
  cultural, 15–16, 20–21, 131, 137–38, 140–41, 171–72, 179–80, 223, 227–28, 238
  Indigenous, 137, 169, 222
  languages, 223, 224, 234, 239–40, 247
  Mexica, 228, 233–34, 235
  Mexican national, 1, 2–3, 105–6, 139–40, 146, 147
  Mixe, 138–39
  tourism, 137–38
Hernandez, Jorge, 165
Hernández, Natalio, 62–64, 124–25
Hernández Orellán, Severiano, 194–95
Hidalgo, 5–6, 113, 193–94
hierarchy, 39
  casta, 71–72
  class, 139–40
  ethnic, 71–72
  language, 74–75
Hill, Jane, 14–15, 86–87, 142–45
Hill, Kenneth, 14–15, 86–87
Historia Antigua de Mexico (1844), 80–81
Hobsbwam, Eric, 26–27, 42–43
Hueyapan, 11*f*, 12, 17, 41–42, 44, 164–65, 168–69, 172, 183
  and culture, 183–84
  and Miguel Barrios Espinosa, 56–57
  and municipal independence, 159
  Nahuatl, 67, 152–54, 163–64, 168, 169, 173, 175, 178–80, 183–84, 185, 236–37, 261
  and Tetela, 160–62, 163–64, 165–66, 168, 181
Huēyātoyātzintli, 220*f*, 222
huipil, 138–39, 183–84
Huitzilan de Serdán, 114–15
Huitzilopochtli, 163–64
Humanizando la deportación, 252

identity, 15, 27, 38–39, 226, 240, 271–72
  and *altepetl*, 28–29, 69
  and Chicanos, 239–40, 244
  Chickasaw, 40–41
  class, 9, 170–71
  local, 78–79, 156, 169, 171–72, 180, 191

Iglesias Tepec, Humberto, 274–75
Immigration and Customs Enforcement (ICE), 248–49, 252
import substitution, 140–41
indexical ground, 18, 135–36, 270–72
indexical relations, 49–50
indexical thickness, 270–71
indigeneity, 9, 38–39, 115–16, 163–64, 165–67, 169, 223, 246, 248, 250–51, 262–63
indigenista (indigenismo), 101–3, 104, 110–11, 115–16, 131, 159, 194–95, 200, 258
indigenization, 169, 248
Indigenous identity
  definition of, 158–59
  and Hueyapan, 157, 169
  and Indigenous intellectuals, 102
  and language revitalization, 148
  and Mexicans, 247
  and Mexicayotl, 224–25, 232, 245, 248
  and Nahuatl, 244
  and nationalism, 115–16
  and neo-Indigenous identity movements, 223
  and pan-Indigenous identity, 232
Indigenous politics, 5, 21–22, 23, 24–25, 86, 90, 122–23, 134–35, 158–59, 267
Indigenous rebellions, 90–91, 96–97
Indigenous University in Milpa Alta, 267–68
indio, 71–72, 75–76, 80, 82–83, 140–43, 145–46, 162–63, 165, 166
indio permitido, 22–23
Institute of Statistics and Geography (INEGI), 190–91
Institutional Revolutionary Party (PRI), 103, 110–11, 161–62, 267–68
Instituto Lingüistico de Verano (ILV), 62–64
Instituto Nacional de Lenguas Indígenas (INALI), 4, 5–6, 7, 123–25, 126–30, 183–84, 263, 267–68
Instituto Nacional Indigenista (INI), 162–63
Instituto Nacional de Pueblos Indígenas (INPI), 267–68
Instituto Tecnológico de la Siera de Zongolica, 195–96
interculturality, 189–90, 200–6, 208–9
intercultural universities, 43, 201–2
Intercultural University of Michoacán, 201–2
Intercultural University of Puebla, 274–75
Intercultural University of Veracruz, 128–29, 188–91, 193–96, 197, 200, 202–5, 206–15, 216–17, 218–19, 266, 274–75

internal colonialism, 22
International Phonetic Alphabet (IPA), 53–55
intimate grammar, 16–17
Ireland, 34–36, 37, 241, 274
Irish Gaelic, 241

Jacobsen, Casper, 137–38
Jesuits, 53, 59–60, 80–81
Johansson, Patrick, 132–33
Juárez, Benito, 88–89

Karttunen, Frances, 59–62, 76–77, 102, 242
Kaur, Ravinder, 136–37
Kroeber, Alfred, L., 135–36

La Filosofia Náhuatl estudiada en sus fuentes, 131
land reclamation, 114–15
language reclamation, 4–5, 38–39, 40–41, 45–46, 168, 180, 218, 274–75
language revitalization, 15–16, 28–29, 34–35, 122–23, 178–79
  as activism, 38–39, 262–63
  and anthropology, 12–14
  and decolonization, 39
  and fashion, 135–36
  Indigenous, 25, 38–39, 263, 264–65
  in Mexico, 16, 21–22, 263
  and minority policies, 41–42
  and Nahuatl, 40–41, 134–36, 212, 218
  and politics, 22–23, 37–38
  practices of, 39, 146–47
  projects, 14–15, 16–17, 25, 34, 39–41
  state-sponsored, 37, 39–41, 263, 264
  value of, 40
Laso de la Vega, Luís, 80–81
Latin America, 166–67, 195–96, 200, 250
Latin Americans, 232, 248–49
Latin, 70–71, 74–75, 79–81, 109–10, 236
Latinos, 226, 232–34, 241
Launey, Michel, 59–61
Lavana, Isabel "Chavelo," 151
Lavana, Modesta, 129–30
Lee Whorf, Benjamin, 53–54
León-Portilla, Miguel, 131, 261–62
Ley General de Derechos Lingüísticos de los Pueblos Indígenas, 4
life projects, 39–40, 201–2, 261
light communities, 271–72
lingua franca, 49

linguistic anthropology, 11, 12–14, 15, 16–17, 30–31, 32, 40–41, 140, 261–62
linguistic authority, 16, 35, 263
linguistic diversity, 4, 9–10, 37–38, 51, 127–28, 182–84, 190–91, 205, 206–7
linguistic pluralism, 203
linguistic revitalization, 21–22, 28–29, 37, 178–79, 263
linguistic revival, 134–35, 157
linguistic rights, 7, 123, 126, 129, 146–47
linguistic signs, 11–12, 77
linguistic sovereignty, 21–22
linguistic varieties, 6–7, 16–17, 18, 34–35, 85
linguistic vitality, 40–41, 259–60, 264
literacy, 2, 51–52, 56–57, 62–64, 75–76, 79, 87
Llanes Ortíz, Genner, 201–2
Lockhart, James, 76–80
Lomnitz, Claudio, 45–46, 102, 103, 140–42
López Obrador, Andrés Manuel (AMLO), 145–46, 266, 267–68
Lucas, Manual, 92–93
Luz Jímenez, Doña, 69

Maestriah Ipan Totlahtol Iwan Tonemilis, 195–96, 208, 214
Malinche, 14–15
"The Malinche of the Constitution," 82–83, 87
malinchista, 141–42
Mallon, Florencia, 68, 92–93
Marant, Isabel, 138–39
Martínez Canales, Luis Alejandro, 193
Martínez Luna, Jaime, 24, 29–30, 31–32
Martínez Rosas, Crispin, 274–75
Maya, 22–23, 71–72, 120, 137–38, 201–2, 234, 241, 267–68
Maya, Alex, 170–72, 173–74, 179–80
Maya, Ildefonso, 62–64
mayordomías, 85
McDonough, Kelly, 88–89
memes, 4–5, 143–45, 233–34
Méndez Huaxcuatitla, Martín (Rú Martín), 106, 108f
Mendoza-Denton, Norma, 241, 250–51
Mesoamerica, 28, 31–32, 69, 71–72, 190–91, 253–54
Messing, Jacqueline, 14–15
mestizaje, 20–21, 225–26
mestizo, 9, 87, 95–96, 97–99, 107, 114–15, 145, 147, 157, 160–61
metalinguistics, 11–12, 16, 51–52

metapragmatics, 15
Mexica, 226, 230–32, 236–37, 247, 248–49, 250–51
  and Aztecs, 3–4, 246
  culture, 224–25, 227–28, 233–34, 242–43
  and *danzantes*, 227–28, 232
  identity, 225–26, 228, 241, 242–43
  and Mexica History Facebook group, 234–35, 242, 243, 244, 245–46
  and Mexicayotl, 224n.2, 226–27
  supremacy, 228
  tribe, 70–71
Mexica-identity movement, 224n.2, 225–26, 228, 232, 241
Mexican Americans, 45–46, 223, 224, 226, 228, 239–40, 241, 247
Mexicanidad
Mexican independence, 81, 82–84, 85, 90–91, 94, 115–16, 123
Mexican national anthem, 183–84
Mexican nationalism, 5, 90, 140–41, 228–29, 230–32
  contemporary, 5, 140–41
  development of, 1, 92–93, 140–41
  and Hernando Alvarado, 69
  and Lázaro Cárdenas, 71–72
  and Mexican language policy, 24
  and Mexicayotl movement, 224–26
  as state project, 20–21
mexicano, 7–9, 14–15, 80–81, 269–70, 275
Mexican Revolution, 28–29, 43, 69–70, 96–97, 103, 154–56, 168
Mexicayotl, 8n.4, 232, 237–38, 247–48
  and activists, 47–48, 225–26, 235, 238, 239–40, 247–51
  and Chicanos, 226
  and *Mexicanidad*, 69, 105–6
  and transraciality, 248–49
Mexicayotl identity, 232–33, 241, 245–46, 249
Mexico
  and independence, 82–83
  and national anthem, 183–84
  and national heritage, 1, 146
  and national space, 123, 140–41
  as nation-state, 7–8, 9, 21–22, 24, 25, 34–35, 87–88, 90–91, 102, 103, 119–20, 122–23, 166, 167, 260, 268–69, 273
  and racism, 143
  and superdiversity, 136
  and United States, 194–95, 229–32

and United States-Mexican border lands, 38–39, 222, 225–26, 251
Mexico City, 3–4, 12, 57–59, 78–79, 102, 155–56, 258, 267–68
Mexihco-Tenochtitlan, 7–8, 69, 70–71, 72–75, 73f, 142n.20, 152, 224–25
Michoacán, 5–6, 55, 106, 124–25, 201–2, 250–51, 259–60, 264–65, 268–69
migration, 140–41, 168, 170–71, 193, 194–95, 229, 230, 232–33
and migrants, 10, 156, 157, 164, 170–71, 190–91, 193, 222
Milpa Alta, 56–57, 78–79, 97–99, 102, 109–10, 132–33, 267–68
missionaries, 4–5, 37, 62–64, 74–75, 104, 106
missionary Nahuatl, 74–75, 79–80
Mock Nahuatl, 143–45
Mock Spanish, 143–45
de Molina, Alonso, 53
monolingual speakers, 36, 152, 195–96
and Indigenous languages, 32–33, 62–64, 127–28
and Nahua people, 97–99
and Nahuatl, 87, 125–26, 207–8, 274–75
and Spanish, 5–6, 32–33, 97–99, 193–94, 207, 208
Montes, Javier, 152–53, 165–66, 172, 174, 176–78
Morales, Evo, 36, 193, 274–75
Morelos, 12, 44, 55, 134–35, 148, 151, 154f, 155–56, 159–60, 166, 167, 258, 265–66, 268–69
and Graco Ramirez, 129–30
and Nahua population, 28, 44–46, 96–97, 109–10, 113
and Nahuatl language, 5–6, 170–71, 173, 183–84, 239
revolution, 82–83
and Tetelcingo, 61, 106
and Zapata revolution, 20–21, 96–100, 101, 103–4
Morelos, Jose Maria, 82–83
MORENA Party, 145–46, 166
Mormon (faith), 244
Book of Mormon, 244
Mount Popocatepetl, 150f, 259
Movimiento Confederado Restaurador de la Cultura de Anahuac (MCRCA), 230–32
Movimiento Estudiantil Chicano De Aztlán (MeChA), 222–23
mtDNA, 234

multicultourism, 137–38
multicultural nationalism, 8n.4
municipal independence, 21–22, 45–46, 148, 153–54, 156, 159, 160–61, 167
Museo Nacional de Arqueología, Historia y Etnografía (National Museum of Archeology, History and Ethnography), 102
mutual aid, 86–87, 104

naco, 140–42, 145–46
Nahua people, 210, 218–19, 222, 229, 234, 235, 237–38, 252–54, 258, 260–61, 275–76
and *altepetl*, 191
and *Aztekah*, 109–10
and colonial Nahua society, 76–77
communities, 132–33, 134, 148, 167, 216–17, 224, 238–39, 265–66, 267–68, 274–75
and *criollos*, 93
culture, 59, 70–71, 131, 147, 195–96
intellectuals, 74–75, 87–89, 91–92, 132, 238–39
and monolingual speakers, 97–99
and Morelos, 28, 44–45, 83, 96–97
and Nahuatl language, 21, 52–53
and pan-Nahua ethno-political project, 9
and political activists, 21–22
and political agency, 90–91
and political sovereignty, 43
Nahuatl manifesto, 100
Nairn, Tom 82–83
National Action Party (PAN), 167, 267–68
national census (1910), 87
national census (2001), 36
national census (2010), 226
national identity, 80–81, 101–2, 131, 232, 273
nationalism, 25, 26–27, 28n.11, 42–43, 59, 68, 69, 70–71, 79–80, 82–83, 92–94, 102–3, 104, 115–16, 142n.20, 182, 223–24, 274
and language, 18–19, 26
state, 20–21, 25, 69–70, 248 (*see also* Mexican nationalism)
national mythology, 2, 80–81, 224–25, 230
national space, 123, 140–41
Native Americans, 226, 247
Nava Nava, Refugio, 274–75
Nava Vite, Rafael, 113, 114–15, 205–8, 274–75
Nechikolli Se Ome Tlahtolli, 238–39

neo-colonial regimes, 38–39
New Spain, 69n.1, 71–76, 77–78, 80
Nezahualcoyotl, 80–81, 109–10, 131, 243

de la O, Genovevo, 99
Oaxaca, 24, 29, 51–52, 127–28, 267, 268–69
de Olmos, Andrés, 53, 60–61
Oportunidades, 167, 171–72
orthography, 42–43, 51–55, 56–64, 67, 83, 105–6, 107, 109–10, 120–22, 175–76
  colonial style, 61, 62f, 126–27
  and Don Rosalio, 17
  Franciscan, 57–59
  historical, 59
  intuitive, 64–66
  Nahuatl, 207–8
Ostula, 264–65
"the otherwise," 41–42, 50, 218–19, 251

Pareyón, Gabriel, 132–33, 147
y Pavón, Jose Maria Morelos, 82–83
peasant rebellions, 91
Pedro Páramo, 238
Peirce, C.S., 11
de la Peña Martínez, Fernando, 228, 230, 236–37
Peña Nieto, Enrique, 129–30, 137, 264–65
phoneme, 52, 54–57, 59–61, 65–66, 67, 83, 175–76
phonetic documentation, 59
phonetic representation, 52, 53–54, 62–64
phonology, 56, 76–77, 143–45
"Plan Espritirual de Aztlán" (Alurista), 222–23
"playing Indian," 245–46
Policemag, 240–41
politics, 250, 264, 267–69, 273
  and Faustino Galicia Chimalpopoca, 88–89
  and Hueyapan, 159, 165
  and *maseualmej*, 114–15
politics of recognition, 18–19
  and Hispanics, 232–33
  and Indigenous communities, 90, 132, 182, 245–46
  and Indigenous languages, 22–23, 146–47, 158–59, 217
  and interculturality, 200–1
  and language, 262–63
  and tribes, 247–48
Porfiriato, 101–2

prescriptivism, 13–14
primordialist (view of nationalism), 18, 25–26
Protestantism, 104, 106
publics, 270–71, 272–73
  and common good, 30–31
  and communicative action, 31–32
  counter, 91–92, 100, 217
  Indigenous, 32, 33, 34, 40, 42–43, 69–70, 85, 90–91, 93, 96–97, 111, 112, 130, 157, 215
  language, 115–16, 209
  local, 83–84, 100, 112, 212
Puebla, 5–6, 128–29, 174, 190
  Highlands, 7–8, 92, 93–94, 95–96, 100, 101, 114–16
  North, 61, 62f
  southern, 154f, 155–56
  and Tlaxcala–Puebla Valley, 229–30
  valley of, 100
pueblos indígenas (Indigenous peoples), 21, 215
Pueblos Mágicos, 137–38
pueblos originarios (aboriginal peoples), 21
purism, 12–17, 147, 262–63

Quetzalcoatl, 183–84

raciolinguistic ideology, 239–40
racism, 38–39, 82–83, 142–43, 166–67
Ramírez, Graco, 129–30, 167, 178–79
Ramírez, Ignacio Fortino, 125, 128–29
recognition (of identity), 18–20, 22–23, 90, 92, 146–47, 158–59, 182, 200–1, 217, 232–33, 245–46, 247–48, 262–63
regions of refuge, 190–91, 193, 197–99
repúblicas de indios (Indian Republics), 71–72, 75–76, 80, 84, 87, 90, 115–16
Reversing Language Shift, 35–36, 37–38
revitalization, 42–43, 77–78
  and community, 182–84, 264
  cultural, 38–39, 155
  and Indigenous communities, 22, 42–43
  politics of, 8n.4
  practices of, 4–5, 39, 40–41
  projects, 40–41, 239
  state-sponsored, 37, 40–41, 263–64 (*see also* language revitalization)
del Rincón, Antonio, 53, 59–60
Rivera, Angélica, 137, 139
Rivera, Diego, 102

Rivera Moreno, Donna, 93–94
Rojas, Mariano Jacobo, 102
Rosa, Jonathan, 239–40

de Sahagún, Bernardino, 53, 70–71
Salazár, Amador, 99
saltillo (phoneme), 55, 56, 59–61
Sánchez, Malaquías, 207–8, 274–75
Sánchez, Refugio, 99
Sánchez Rosales, Adán, 188–89, 210, 213–14
Sandoval Arenas, Carlos Octavio, 205–8, 256*f*
San Luís Potosí, 5–6, 265–66
San Miguel Tzinacapan, 94, 95–96, 100
Sapir, Edward, 16–17, 56–57
scale, 18, 27, 39–40, 180, 217, 250, 272, 273
 social, 16–17, 45–46, 270–71
Seco, Ricardo, 139, 143
Secretaría de Educación Pública (SEP
   Ministry of Public Education), 64–65,
   103, 107, 111, 162–63, 200–1
self-recognition, 20, 23, 25, 158–59, 182,
   189, 218
Semillas del Pueblo, 239
semiotic capital, 148
semiotic code, 262–63
semiotic expropriation, 147
semiotic extractivism, 39–40
semiotic infrastructure, 33–34, 261–62, 269–
   70, 272
semiotic membrane, 33, 34, 125–26, 271
semiotic politics, 260
semiotic process, 130, 135–36
semiotic resources, 41–42
 and community ownership, 39–40, 264
 control over, 42–43
 Indigenous, 43, 147, 258–59, 273
 and Indigenous communities, 20–21, 39–
    40, 42–43, 148
 and sovereignty, 273
 value of, 272
semiotics, 40–41, 122–23, 135–37, 145–46,
   181, 190, 217, 250, 260, 270–71
semiotic sovereignty, 251–52, 273, 274–75
 definition of, 258–59, 264
 and Indigenous communities, 42–43
 and Indigenous languages, 258–59
 and language, 259–60
 and language revitalization, 43
 protection of, 42–43, 260, 269
semiotic theories, 11
"semiotic vehicles," 33–34, 262–63

settler-colonialism, 20, 23, 245, 247, 248–
   49, 250–51
settler languages, 39
settler states, 18–21, 22–23, 24, 182
Sierra Norte de Puebla, 55, 95–96
Silverstein, Michael, 15
Simpson, Audra, 20, 22, 24–25
Simpson, Leanne, 23
Smith, Alicia, 222, 223
Soberanes Pérez, Mario, 165
social action, 2–3, 22–23, 40–41
social capital, 102–3, 242
social change, 76–77, 168, 203–4, 208–9, 266
social cohesion, 29, 167, 180
social critique, 38–39, 143, 148
social media, 128–29, 138–39, 144*f*
social mobility, 84, 194–95
social organization, 85, 171–72, 176
sociolinguistic scales, 16–17, 270–71
students, 35, 47n.18, 176–80, 189, 195–96,
   200, 202–3, 204–10, 211, 212–13, 215,
   216–17, 218, 236–37, 238, 239, 266
 and *bachillerato*, 174
 and *clausura*, 174
 and Luís Reyes García, 60–61
Sullivan, John, 59
Summer Institute of Linguistics (SIL), 62–64
superdiversity, 136, 271–72
survivance, 22
Swadesh, Maurice, 56–57

Taboada, Francesco, 167, 171–72, 176–78
"technology of the self," 240
Televisa, 142–43
Templo Mayor, 3*f*
Tepoxteco de la Cruz, Victoriano, 238–39
Tepoztlán, 28, 99, 102
territory, 23, 30, 41–42, 91, 119–20, 188–89,
   190–91, 215–16, 222, 224–25, 247, 248,
   251, 269
 cognitive, 25
 of Hueyapan, 165, 183
 Indigenous, 245
 national, 26, 260
 United States, 228–29, 230
 and University of Veracruz, 218–19
 and Zongolica, 212
Tetela del Volcàn, 44–45, 83, 152–55,
   153*f*, 156, 157, 159, 160–61, 165, 166,
   168, 171–72
Texas, 72–74, 229–30, 238

Tezcatlipoca, 183–84
three-stage model, 77–78
Tiburcio Sandoval, Rafael, 83
Tlacotepec, 162–63, 178–79
Tlahuitoltepec, 29, 138–39
Tlalokan (Tlalocan), 187–89, 193, 196, 197–99, 210
Tlaltizapán, 99
Tlapoyawa, Kurly, 224n.2, 225–26, 239–40, 247–48
Tlaquilpa, 46–47, 186f, 188–89, 188n.1, 191–93, 196–97, 210–12, 213–14, 256f, 274–75
tlasohkamati, 129–30
Tlatelolca, 70–71
Tlatelolco, 70–71
Tlaxcala, 5–6, 14–15, 65–66, 71–72, 86–87, 100, 229–30, 265–66
Tlaxcalteca, 71–74, 100
Tochimilco, 99, 100
Toltecayotl, 125, 125n.2, 236–37
Tonalmeyotl, Martín, 274–75
Townsend, William Cameron, 104, 106, 107
traditionalists, 42–43, 106, 107, 159–60, 161–63, 168, 203, 218
translation, 83, 89, 120–22, 127f, 128–29, 131, 132–33, 223, 238–39, 248–49
  challenges of, 34
  and Constitution of Mexico, 123–26
  and language development, 35
  practices of, 48–50
  style, 50
transraciality, 232–33, 248–49
Tren Maya, 137–38, 267–68
Trinidad Palma, Miguel, 89
Turner, Dale, 16

United States, 87–88, 173, 194–95, 229–32, 252, 259
  and American linguists, 53–54
  and Cherokee, 226
  and Chicanos, 222–23, 230–32
  and colonization, 20–21
  and Hueyapan, 164–65, 168–69, 171
  and Indigenous communities, 19–20, 24, 224, 225–26, 234–35, 246, 251
  and Indigenous languages, 53–54
  and Mexica identity movement, 228
  and Mexican diaspora, 43, 223, 224–25, 232, 244, 251
  and *Mexicanidad*, 105–6
  and Mexicayotl, 47–48
  and migrants, 10, 193
  and Nahuatl, 45–46, 168, 228, 236, 238
  and Navajo Nation, 139–40, 226
  and racism, 142–43, 232–33
  and residential school systems, 109n.15
  and Rio Grande, 222
  and state nationalism, 20–21
  and Treaty of Guadalupe Hidalgo, 230
  and United States Southwest, 226
United States-Mexican borderlands, 38–39, 45–46, 168–69, 172, 222–23, 224, 225–26, 251
University of Texas at Austin, 238
University of Tlaxcala, 274–75
"Un nosotrx sin Estado" (Aguilar Gil), 182–83
Urban, Greg, 135–36, 260
urban Nahuatl, 72–75
Urban Outfitters, 139–40
usos y costumbres, 167, 248, 268–69

Valiñas, Leopoldo, 9–10
vehicular language, 80, 229–30, 251–52, 263
Veracruz, 61, 92–93, 190, 202–3, 206–7, 238, 265–66, 274–75
  and AVELI, 124–25
  and colonial period, 7–8
  and Indigenous communities, 112
  and Ixhuatlancillo, 78–79
  and Morelos, 82–83
  and Nahua population, 44–45
  and Nahuatl language, 5–6, 80–81
  and Tequila, 44, 128–29
  and Zongolica, 82, 188–89
Villa, Pancho, 96
Villistas, 96, 99–100
Virgin of Guadalupe, 28–29, 80–81
Vocabulario en lengua castellana y mexicana (1571), 53

War on Drugs, 164
Warner, Michael, 217
whitexican, 145–46
Whorf, Benjamin Lee, 53–54
Wittgenstein, Ludwig, 18, 31n.13

Womack, John, 96–100
"Writing Culture," 48–49

Xaltocan, 234
Xochiapulco, 92–94, 95–96
Xochitiotzin Pérez, Ethel, 274–75
Xochitlahtolli, 67
xochitlalilistli, 193, 197–99

Yankwik Mexikayotl, 225–26, 228, 247–48

van Young, Eric, 83–84

Zacatecas Institute for Teaching and Research in Ethnology (IDIEZ), 238–39
Zapata, Emiliano, 96, 99–100
Zapata revolution, 96–97, 99–100, 103–4
Zapatistas, 20–21, 96–97, 99–100, 101, 103–4, 111–12, 200, 259–60
Zócalo, 3–4